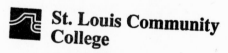

the
Reality Effect

the
Reality Effect

Film Culture
and the
Graphic
Imperative

Joel Black

ROUTLEDGE
NEW YORK & LONDON

for Linda, a fighter

Published in 2002 by
Routledge
29 West 35th Street
New York, NY 10001

Published in Great Britain by
Routledge
11 New Fetter Lane
London EC4P 4EE

Routledge is an imprint of the Taylor & Francis Group.

Printed on acid-free, 250-year-life paper
Manufactured in the United States of America
Design and typography: Jack Donner

10 9 8 7 6 5 4 3 2 1

Library of Congress Cataloging-in-Publication Data

Black, Joel, 1950–
 The reality effect: film culture and the graphic imperative / Joel Black.
 p. cm.
 ISBN 0–415–93720–5 — ISBN 0–415–93721–3 (pbk.)
 1. Realism in motion pictures. I. Title.
PN1995.9.R3 B59 2001
791.43'612—dc21   2001019642

Truth becomes fiction when the fiction's true;

Real becomes not-real where the unreal's real.

—Cao Xueqin, *The Story of the Stone*

Contents

part three   film dreams

Introduction
The Filmed Century

The twentieth century is *on film*. It's the filmed century. You have
to ask yourself if there's anything about us more important than
the fact that we're constantly on film, constantly watching
ourselves. The whole world is on film, all the time. Spy satellites,
microscopic scanners, pictures of the uterus, embryos, sex, war,
assassinations, everything.

—Don DeLillo, *The Names*

Before (and Beyond) Art and Entertainment

Now that the twentieth century is behind us, what does it mean to refer
to it as the filmed century—the first century to be documented, from
start to finish, on film? How significant is it that all sorts of events are
being graphically preserved as never before, that phenomena of all kinds
never previously recorded are now showing up on film, from newly
discovered galaxies at the edge of the universe to PET and CAT scans,
sonograms and mammograms, and confessions by heads of state about
their sex lives? "Like no previous generation," writes James Gleick, "we
see our history in our mind's eye: Neil Armstrong stepping onto the
moon; Lee Harvey Oswald taking a bullet in the gut; the century's
cyclonic hurricanes and mushroom clouds."[1] If "much of what the
world knows about the last 1,000 years it has learned from artists," does
the fact that the twentieth century was the first century not only to be
subjectively and symbolically rendered in one of the traditional representational art forms (literature, sculpture, the graphic arts), but also to
be objectively registered by the ostensibly more accurate audiovisual
media mark a sea change in culture and human history?[2] Have the relatively new recording technologies somehow altered what we take for

reality, so that reality is no longer what it used to be? And if so, how is such a transformation itself to be documented?

If answers to these questions aren't readily available, it's because the twentieth century's definitively filmic nature—entailing a peculiar mix of reality and artifice, high and low culture—has yet to be generally acknowledged. Ironically, the impact of film on culture may have been more widely recognized before the advent of the academic discipline of film studies, and even before the medium's appropriation by the arts and the entertainment industry. For film came into being, after all, in the middle of the recording revolution, midway between photography and phonography. Even before the medium was invented, as Siegfried Kracauer noted, the forerunners of film theory took it "for granted that film would continue along the lines of photography" and "looked forward to what we have come to label newsreels and documentaries—films devoted to the rendering of real-life events." This "insistence on recording,"[3] and the original cinematograph's scientific purpose of documenting movement over time, was rooted in the "most basic theoretical understanding of film realism ... the view that photographic images, unlike paintings or line drawings, are indexical signs: they are causally or existentially connected to their referents."[4] Yet despite this early recognition of cinema as a recording technology, it quickly became clear that the movies' chief—and certainly most lucrative—purpose would be that of entertainment, and that for a movie to be entertaining it must be "different from real life."[5] And so by the middle of the century, despite the continued emphasis of critics such as Kracauer and André Bazin on "the photographic nature of film" and on its ability to reproduce physical reality, cinema's scientific origins were largely forgotten as film increasingly came to be regarded as a representational, illusionist medium for the primary purpose of entertainment and the secondary purpose of art.[6]

The "film-as-art idea" gained wide currency especially in the 1950s, after the breakup of the studio system and the rise of independent film-making.[7] As film studies programs began to take their place in the academic curriculum, movies were treated much as literature and the fine arts had been—as a coded discourse that could be analyzed either sociologically (as a form of cultural production and mass entertainment for the purpose of indoctrination, diversion, or subversion), or else aesthetically (as a formal construct with its own internal laws and organization that made every film a world unto itself). The tendency among film scholars and critics to treat "cinema" primarily as an art form, and even to consider the director a kind of artist or auteur, grew out of an effort to legitimate movies as more than just a popular form of entertainment. Yet this formalist, film-as-art approach tended to downplay, and sometimes even to reject outright the traditional realist conception of motion pictures. Even if, as Noël Carroll claims, contemporary theorists reject "the notion that film is a slice of reality" but "nevertheless agree that in its standard uses, film imparts a *realistic effect* to its viewers," this is no more than "a psychological effect" whereby "film gives the impression of reality narrating itself; film causes an illusion of reality; or film appears natural."[8] Reacting against the strong reality claims of classical theorists, contemporary theorists thus reduce the *"reality* effect" of film to psychologistic *"realistic* effects," ignoring the degree to which film, adopting the recording technologies of the photograph and later the phonograph, shapes and fixes the very notion of reality itself by registering seemingly objective, indexical images of the world-as-it-is.[9]

By shifting the emphasis from content to form, theoretically trained academicians brought a new sophistication to film studies, but they also tended to limit the field's *object* of study to cinema as art and entertainment at a time when visual media were coming to pervade every sector of modern life.[10] For mass culture, by its very nature, "is that content which alters form"—form being increasingly mediated in any case by cinematic technology.[11] As a recording medium, film "gravitate[s] toward the expanses of outer reality—an open-ended, limitless world which bears little resemblance to the finite and ordered cosmos" conventionally depicted by the representational arts.[12] Far from being explainable or even containable by formal analysis, the explosion of content in mass culture has steadily made its way into both mainstream and independent art films, where it has been steadily challenging and altering conventional notions of form and representation. Even as older literary critics such as Harold Bloom lament the "tyranny of the visual"[13]—the decline of literature in a culture increasingly dominated by TV, movies, and the Internet, and the corresponding subordination of the writer's status to that of "content providers,"—the new recording media (and even newer digital media) have forced a fundamental critique of literature and the other representational arts, showing them to be grounded in "the analogue technologies of print culture" and to be dependent on "a depth model of interiority" and on "relations of resemblance between the interior and surface" and ultimately between mind and soul.[14] Over the span of a century, a whole new range of reality effects deployed by the recording media have swiftly supplanted the "neutralized ... hallucination[s]," as Friedrich Kittler calls them, of literature and the representational arts—"the soul, the inner self, the individual: they all were only the effects of an illusion."[15]

The impact of the new generation of postrepresentational reality effects has yet to be gauged—those produced by the twentieth-century recording technology of cinema, which at least continue to engage the eye, ear, and other senses, and those that we can expect to be produced in the twenty-first century by virtual-reality technologies that bypass the aesthetics of sensory perception altogether and feed directly into the brain as the "technologically induced hallucination[s]" of "machinic vision."[16] But we need not anticipate future developments. The eye and other senses are already habitually overstimulated and overwhelmed by the formless explosion of mass cultural "in-formation" filtering down from the new media technologies with their drive toward hyperindexicality into more conventional forms of cinematic and other visual experience. Consider the vastly expanded content made possible by new cinematographic techniques (instant replay, slow motion, time-lapse photography, digitalization) and by the enhanced graphic displays of the new technologies (video media and video games, the Internet, spy satellites, surveillance cameras). And we shouldn't forget those exhibitionistic Web-cam sites (e.g., JenniCam, Web-Dorm.com) that enable anyone to turn their lives into reality TV or EdTV (as in the 1998 movie of that name), so that everyone can peer into the most intimate—but more often the most banal—moments of their lives.

It used to be that only movies were on film; now the whole world is. More than ever, visual technologies seem intent on striving for what Kracauer called "the status of total record." And not only does it seem at the start of the new century that everything is on film or video (although it is unclear, given the unstable nature of videotape and other recording media that began replacing film at the century's end, how long this recorded material will *remain* viewable),[17] but thanks first to video and then the Internet, scenes that were never shown before—from natural disasters and human atrocities to sexual intimacies and ecstasies—are now public spectacles that are instantly shown everywhere.[18]

The fact is that film is *the* medium of modern mass culture. Not only is it consumed by the masses more than any other medium, but in no other commodity does mass culture itself provide the content to the degree it does in film. One need only think of all the product placement in movies, the tie-ins with fast food, soft drinks, and sports cars that are increasingly transforming blockbuster films into nonstop advertisements, and the increasing instances of cross promotion in the wake of media megamergers.[19] So ubiquitous and influential are the movies in film culture that they are no longer just movies, but have expanded into other modes of entertainment such as video games and thrill rides using the latest animatronics and 3-D technology. At Hollywood's Universal City, after a ride that immerses you in the world of blockbuster action-adventure films such as *Jurassic Park* or *Back to the Future*, you can tour one of the nearby studios where tomorrow's movies are currently in production. The visit itself is a back-to-the-future time trip or time loop in which families share fantasies by taking rides based on past movies and previewing movies that may end up as future fantasy rides.

Faced with the impact of movies and visual media on mass culture, some critics have gone from the extreme of treating film exclusively as an elitist art form to the opposite extreme of considering it merely as a form of mass entertainment. Neal Gabler may be right that movies and popular culture have overwhelmed American life, but his 1998 book *Life the Movie* (which is really not about movies but about how American life has assumed the characteristics of the generic motion picture) gives the impression that mainstream movies are the only kind of film affecting viewers.[20] Left unexamined are art and documentary films and their influence on commercial movies. Terry Gilliam's *Twelve Monkeys* (1995), for example, was based on Chris Marker's 1962 experimental film *La Jetée*, while Penny Marshall's 1990 movie *Awakenings*, about Oliver Sacks's experiences with "sleeping sickness" patients, relied heavily on a 1973 documentary made for British television, even duplicating some of the scenes. (One of Sacks's original patients who appears in the documentary was actually filmed in a scene with Robert De Niro for the Hollywood feature, but the scene was ultimately cut—possibly, Sacks speculated, because the producers "thought real patients weren't authentic enough.")[21] Gabler's study of the impact of *fictional* movies on American culture and consciousness to produce a surreal cultural landscape glaringly omits the role of *nonfictional* film in what has been called the "Century of Reality"[22]—not only classic documentaries such as *Nanook of the North* and *Triumph of the Will*, but also memorable newsreel footage of World War II military campaigns and early nuclear-weapons tests, filmed and taped records of the Vietnam and Gulf Wars, and unedited amateur footage such as Abraham Zapruder's home movie of John F. Kennedy's assassination or George Holliday's videotape of Los Angeles police officers beating Rodney King. And with the growing reliance on satellite surveillance and security camera footage, the presence of a human operator behind the camera has become increasingly superfluous. Such graphic, evidentiary instances of cinema verité cannot be reduced to mass entertainment, although they are often quickly appropriated by the commercial media.

When *Time* magazine published a special issue on "The Columbine Tapes" at the end of 1999, the casual reader may well have assumed the tapes in question to be the video record provided by the Colorado high school's security cameras of the massacre eight months earlier. After all, the issue's cover featured a photograph, captioned "The school-cafeteria surveillance video," showing Eric Harris and Dylan Klebold armed with automatic weapons, stalking fellow students. Yet the focus of the special report was the five home videos the assailants had secretly made in the months before their murderous rampage in which they discuss their attack. In the controversial tapes, which parents of two of the slain victims sought to keep from being televised, Harris and Klebold not only referred to the computer game that inspired them ("That fucking shotgun is straight out of Doom"), but also planned their attack on the school as a movie with, in Harris's words, "a lot of foreshadowing and dramatic irony." Klebold envisioned directors "fighting over this story," with Harris suggesting "Tarantino ... Spielberg" as likely possibilities.[23] There could be no clearer illustration of late-twentieth-century film culture than this combination of various recording media—surveillance and home video, computer games and movies—whose involuted interplay produced such a surreal sequence of events. Not only did Harris and Klebold model their rampage on the movies, but they could only imagine their "story" becoming a reality when it became a film in its own right. As the reclusive writer Bill Gray observes in another DeLillo novel, *Mao II*: "Everything around us tends to channel our lives toward some final reality in print or on film."[24]

On the one hand, film is largely responsible for shaping the virtual state of reality that increasingly surrounds us; on the other hand, this same medium is also capable of making us aware of our mass-mediated condition by revealing it to us. Certain movies usually classified as artistic or entertaining fictions actually exploit and explore media-related issues by presenting actual events in unsuspected, illuminating ways. This is the case with many of the films discussed in this study. Rather than focus either on art films or on mainstream movies per se, I want to call attention to cinema's vital affiliations with the nonartistic domains of science and technology (e.g., forensic analysis and police surveillance) as well as with such marginal and manipulative forms of entertainment/indoctrination as advertising, politics, and pornography. I suggest that conceptions of film as solely an artistic or entertainment medium are only part of the story, and certainly not the most significant one. How could they be when it's increasingly the case that what winds up on film is not only the artistic vision of filmmakers, and not even "the movies" themselves, but "the whole world"?

We may take it as a sign of the times that the passage from DeLillo's *The Names* cited at the beginning of this introduction is even more relevant today, when the twentieth century is over, than it was when it appeared in 1982. It's also revealing that the observation "the whole world is on film" is not made in a film or in real life but uttered by a fictional filmmaker in a novel. The fact that a statement about the filmic nature of reality happens to be made in a book rather than in a film at first seems self-contradictory, a postmodern version of the ancient liar's paradox. And yet the statement's novelistic context actually illustrates what it says: we're so caught up in the media of moving images that we're unable to understand what's happening to us *in* these media. The only way to begin to grasp the implications of the insight that "the whole world is on film," and even to articulate that insight, is to turn to the very medium that has largely been superseded by the movies. For it may be up to "books to record," as Kittler writes, "how that which is written in no book came to pass ... Pushed to their margins even obsolete media become sensitive enough to register the signs and clues of a situation."[25] A reliance on literature's outmoded verbal perspective would seem to be all the more urgent at a time when literary works are routinely adapted to the screen (yet another instance of the world becoming film) and when they are themselves increasingly adopting cinematic techniques in the genres of the film and graphic novel. Only by staking out a vantage apart from the primarily visual medium of film can the verbal medium of literary and critical discourse reflect and comment on film as something more than escapist entertainment, or as something other than an art form that presents alternative views of the world.[26] As the fictional filmmaker in DeLillo's novel elliptically declares,

> Film is more than the twentieth-century art. It's another part of the twentieth-century mind. It's the world seen from inside. We've come to a certain point in the history of film. If a thing can be filmed, film is implied in the thing itself. This is where we are.

The Reality Effect

> Virtual reality, O.K. You know what virtual means? O.K., it is like really real. So virtual reality is practically, totally real. But not.
>
> —Jennifer Jason Leigh as Lois Kaiser
> in Robert Altman's *Short Cuts*

Not only is film more than a medium of art or entertainment, then, but it plays a key role in shaping viewers' notions of "reality" itself. As a result, it is often no longer meaningful or even possible to categorize movies into the traditional dichotomy of fictional films and documentaries—or "nonfiction films," as they're now called. More than ever, big-budget fictional entertainments invoke real historical references (*Forrest Gump*, *Titanic*) or even *pre*historic references (*2001: A Space Odyssey*, *Jurassic Park*), or they implicitly claim documentary status for themselves (*Schindler's List, Amistad*). Meanwhile, so-called docudramas freely adulterate historical fact with far-fetched conspiracy theories, as in Oliver Stone's *JFK*. Moreover, while special effects once allowed filmmakers to present glimpses of the unreal world of dreams (*Un chien andalou, The Wizard of Oz, Spellbound*), today's sophisticated effects are increasingly used to produce a heightened illusion of reality itself (crashes, disasters, wars, space travel, etc.)—of truth as visible spectacle, of reality as anything that is filmable, or, borrowing from recent French theorists, what I call the reality effect.[27]

This is not at all to say that movies are becoming more "realistic," more like real life; if anything, they tend to be less credible and plausible than ever.[28] But they are certainly more *graphic*—more physical and explicit—which is an entirely different matter. We need to recognize film as being first and foremost a "literalist medium" whose nature is to make things *explicit*—to reveal or display the world in an evidentiary sense that is beyond the capability of traditional representational or art media.[29] It's becoming a commonplace to hear commentators remark that "literalism has been gathering force," that a "renewed embrace of explicitness has ... spread all over the ur-American realms of merchandising, TV, [and] the mass market,"[30] that "the arts have never been more probing or explicit,"[31] and that "the media are more explicit than they've ever been."[32] Such observations demonstrate a growing awareness of and concern with film's unique status as a recording medium versus a representational one.

As a graphic medium, film doesn't literally make things "real," of course. Documenting actual objects, characters, and events (referential realism), or even making objects, characters, and events *seem* real (perceptual realism), is altogether different from making them explicit.[33] Nevertheless, the visual media are increasingly called upon to provide a record of reality, and some literalists have adopted the extreme view that only what can be filmed exists, or at least can be known with certainty. Thus, in 1999 the Kansas Board of Education decided to remove evolution and the big-bang theory from the state's science curriculum on the grounds that these phenomena have not been directly observed or recorded and thus are open to doubt. Such radical skepticism is rooted in a faith in graphic realism fostered by film culture whereby events must be confirmed by eyewitness testimony or photographic evidence.

Ironically, the visual evidence of evolution required by the Board of Education (which reversed its decision in 2001) was not long in coming: alarmed parents were already beginning to observe the increasingly early onset of puberty in their daughters. Here was what seemed to be graphic evidence of human evolution—a significant change in the biological development of the species, or at least in the rate of its development, that was happening within a single generation. At a loss to account for the earlier occurrence of puberty, researchers have cited biological, environmental, and even psychological factors (obesity, chemical pollution, and the "absent father theory"). The fact that more girls at age eight or even younger are showing secondary sexual characteristics associated with puberty—budding breasts and pubic hair—has understandably concerned parents. They worry that their daughters' precocious sexual development will only make them more susceptible to the ever more graphic, market-driven, and youth-oriented media. Yet some researchers suspect that the media's graphic imagery may not merely opportunistically target early puberty, but may actually trigger it. "Can visual images also have a biological effect?" asks Marcia Herman-Giddens, author of the 1997 study that called widespread attention to the early puberty phenomenon. "Does constant exposure to this sort of thing act as a premature trigger? I certainly think we need to find out." If Herman-Giddens's suspicion of the media's influence on sexual development were to be verified (she repeatedly invokes the Pavlovian image of someone salivating at the sight of slicing open a juicy grapefruit as an "example of how what you see can have a biological effect on your body"),[34] then the mass appeal of Britney Spears may turn out to be the most literal example to date of life imitating art.

The Kansas Board of Education and Britney Spears underscore the two-pronged nature of the reality effect: on one hand, the recording media are called upon to establish the truth of (or to cast doubt on) scientific theories about the world; on the other hand, the recording media are capable of giving reality to fictions and fantasies by producing a vivid, graphic semblance of truthfulness. To be sure, this sort of reality *as* effect is quite a different matter from the effect *of* reality—the sudden and often violent impact of the physical and historical world on the pseudoreality of film and the other media. But one must always consider the more subtle and permanent effect that the graphic media may be exerting upon real life.

The paradox that extreme graphic realism is rarely real is concisely expressed in Heidi Dawidoff's observation that "life isn't itself graphically realistic to our minds. We are always altering (coloring and discoloring) experience by means of memories, fantasies, and feelings." Thus, sex as it is presented in pornography is unrealistic (and in Dawidoff's view, not "sexy") because it "becomes more plainly physical than it ever really is."[35] This paradox pertains to the full range of recorded imagery, from adult movies to children's animation (not to mention pornographic animation of the sort found in Japanese *hentai*—the ultimate example of the reality effect in which the "innocent" medium of children's cartoons is twisted, bent, and warped to depict graphic "adult" sexual behavior).

"Technologically speaking," acknowledges the supervising technical director for the 1999 state-of-the-art computer-animation feature *Toy Story 2*, "the closer you get to trying to do something that's really, accurately human, the farther away it's actually going to be."[36] And we shouldn't forget the genre of horror movies in which this paradox is particularly evident—namely, in the way that all manner of special effects are used to produce the illusion of "realist horror."[37] As movies use special effects to produce increasingly vivid sensations, they actually tend to become less lifelike. Directors of big-budget films find themselves caught in a double bind. Ever more talent and resources are devoted to making artifice seem natural, the nonvisible appear visible, and the realm of the imaginary come across as convincing and credible. In an increasingly artificial and visual world, *nothing must appear to be unreal*, meaning that *nothing must be left unseen*.

Having come into being and come of age during the recording revolution, film now stands to be at once superannuated and supercharged by the digital revolution, much in the way sound recordings have.[38] The transition from the photographic to the digital image—a virtual visual effect and not "a physical inscription of any this-has-been"[39]—is already evident in the movie industry, where the task of filmmaking has shifted significantly from the production (recording) to the postproduction phase (editing, special effects). One only has to compare the number of closing credits at the end of today's feature films with those from twenty years ago to realize the degree to which special effects have come to dominate commercial filmmaking. The displacement of the conventional recording apparatus by computerized digital technologies has, as one commentator has noted,

> further diminish[ed] the traces of photographic, indexical contingency in the final product. Not only can "mistakes" made during shooting be "corrected" and recorded effects be maximized, but on the very level of production live-action images and sounds can be generated independently of any referent in the outside world.[40]

Whereas special effects were formerly reserved for isolated scenes except in the case of full-length animated features, such effects are now routinely used throughout the entire picture. Portions of many films are routinely transferred from film to video for digital editing and color corrections and then back to film, and entire movies are now being shot in digital format or digitally edited years after their original release.[41] This conflation of the recording and representational processes enables filmmakers to introduce special effects more easily, effectively, cheaply, and quickly—immediately after shooting the image, or even *in place of* shooting the image. A growing number of science-fiction and action-adventure films, such as the *Star Wars* series, *Terminator II*, and *Jurassic Park*, don't just use special effects; they *are* special effects.

As the postproduction phase has steadily infiltrated the recording process, the contingency of the audiovisual trace has given way to the wholesale generation of an entire Lucas-world of image and sound effects without worldly referents. The advent of digitalization, morphing, and "Flo-Mo" (the technique popularized in *The Matrix*, which allows filmmakers to shoot scenes at normal speed while slowing down or freezing portions of the surrounding action), has enabled FX artistry to replace "actual" recorded elements in the mise-en-scène. There is now little to keep George Lucas—who used over two thousand digitally generated shots, or 90 percent of the movie, in his 1999 *Star Wars* prequel, *Episode I: The Phantom Menace*—from doing away with actors altogether, and replacing them with animatronic robots and fully digitalized characters. In the Lucasian spectacle of carefully programmed digitalized effects, as little as possible is left to chance, to the contingencies of real life, and to the vagaries *and* verities of the recorded image.

Reality Bites Back: Kernel Truths

As commercial animation, action-adventure, and sci-fi movies leave the medium of recorded film behind in order to devote ever greater shares of their budgets to digitalized special effects, raw footage is coming to play a greater role in low-budget, independent cinema. Instead of using special effects to alter, enhance, or simply dispense with recorded images, noncommercial filmmakers have devised innovative ways of presenting the unedited film record of the real itself, recontextualizing it through a variety of what might be called "general effects."

We may note, for example, how fictional movies have increasingly adopted the long-standing documentary practice of using archival photographs and films. In a number of recent foreign features the narratives are motivated by some piece of unedited footage. The trend can be traced back to Antonioni's 1966 film *Blow-Up*, with its story of a photographer who records a murder in a public park but doesn't realize it until he develops and enlarges the pictures he has happened to shoot. In more recent movies the segment of raw film footage is depicted as being rare and elusive, as in Harvey Keitel's Balkan odyssey in *Ulysses' Gaze* to recover an early documentary film that has been presumed lost. The piece of raw footage may be life-threatening: Ziad Doueiri's 1999 feature *West Beirut* focuses on the perils of two Lebanese boys who try to develop some home-movie footage they have shot with a Super8 camera during the 1975 civil war. In recent Iranian and Chinese cinema, where the roles in fictional stories are often played not by professional actors but by individuals playing themselves, the distinction between fiction and nonfictional cinema has become especially blurred.[42]

The convention of documentary footage within fictional films is more than an instance of modern cinema's self-consciousness and self-reflexivity. The presence of some prized, elusive piece of raw footage in movies functions much like the pea that keeps the princess from falling asleep; in the feature films mentioned above, the documentary footage is a kernel of "truth" around which the cinematic fiction persistently circles.[43] And as in the fairy tale, it is the girl's hyperawareness of the pea hidden beneath all those mattresses that marks her as a true princess, so these cinematic fictions derive a semblance of authenticity from the documentary kernels at their core.[44]

As the story in fictional films may be centered on a kernel of raw film footage that provides a semblance of documentary truth, so documentary filmmakers who are unable to directly record their subject incorporate whatever existing filmed footage is available. Thus they routinely incorporate still photographs to establish the actuality of events that may have taken place before the invention of motion pictures.[45] And as with kernel documentaries in fictional films, the found footage used in documentary films is often incomplete or biased, and requires some form of metadocumentary (or metafiction) to complete or correct it. Indeed, archival images in documentary films frequently serve as a point of departure for quasi-fictional scenes that reenact or reimagine historical events. Thus in his 1999 film *Wisconsin Death Trip*, director James Marsh staged some of the real-life horrors documented in Michael Lesy's 1973 book about the rural farming community of Black River Falls, Wisconsin. In the 1890s, many of the town's mostly immigrant population either went mad or turned violent after being hit with a triple whammy of economic depression, freezing temperatures, and a staggering infant mortality rate caused by diphtheria. Based on Lesy's compilation of vintage photographs of the town's haunted citizens (Diane Arbus–like portraits taken by the town photographer, Charles Van Schaik) and newspaper clippings about the town's murders and suicides (read in the film by Ian Holm), Marsh re-created grainy reenactments of Black River Falls's more sensational crimes. These black-and-white "silent-movie tableaux vivants" are juxtaposed with color sequences of present-day Black River Falls; the effect is less to point up the obvious differences between life in the town in the 1890s and in the 1990s than to suggest the unexpected similarities of the two periods.[46]

Whereas Van Schaik's portraits and late-nineteenth-century newspaper accounts provided the kernel truths in *Wisconsin Death Trip* that

Marsh used to stage his reenactments of actual past crimes, the kernel truths in *The Blair Witch Project*—the mock horror documentary released the same year—were pure fabrication. This surprise, low-budget hit passed itself off as a homemade documentary about witch-craft made by three film students who mysteriously disappeared in the Maryland woods. Actually, the movie was made—rather than found—in the woods, its grainy, jerky footage shot by the actors themselves. The directors, Daniel Myrick and Eduardo Sánchez, who reportedly made the movie for under $60,000, fabricated a Blair Witch mythology that took on a reality of its own, thanks to the numerous Websites that sprang up, ostensibly devoted to investigating and debating the mystery, but ultimately serving to promote the film long before its commercial release. Driven by a combination of clever marketing and fortuitous Internet buzz, *The Blair Witch Project* (or "Sales Pitch Project," as it was dubbed by critics) proved far more profitable than its big-budget, high-tech competitors.

In a year of movies saturated with special effects, *The Blair Witch Project* appeared all the more "special" by rejecting such gimmicks. Yet at least contemporary movies such as *The Phantom Menace* or *The Matrix*, for all their high-tech wizardry, never pretended to be docu-mentary accounts of actual events in the way that *The Blair Witch Project* did. As a result, this most "realistic"-looking of films exceeded all its high-tech competitors in fakery. Even as it appeared to dispense entirely with special effects, the movie was a special effect from start to finish, "wholly created by the production process," in which "grainy equals real, immediate," and "the jerk of a video camera or the crackle of a scratchy vinyl record has come to stand for the truer reality behind the process."[47] In its avowed avoidance of artifice, *The Blair Witch Project* succeeded in turning the general effects associated with the recording/distribution process into a special effect of the sort normally introduced in the representation/production phase. Movies such as the *Star Wars* films, which employ the most advanced FX technology to create realis-tic visions of made-up worlds, are in the end merely products passively watched by the viewer. *The Blair Witch Project* owed its success less to the finished product—the film itself—than to the unpredictable, inter-active promotional *process* leading up to and following its release, a process that involved numberless chance exchanges on the Internet by individuals having no direct connection with the film. "This isn't a movie," critic Stuart Klawans declared, "it's an item of business news, about one of those gazillionaire-producing Internet stocks."[48] The next logical step in this Internet-driven marketing process was soon evident. In what has been called "the most remarkable movie-promotion gimmick ever created for the Web," two pre-release online trailers for

Steven Spielberg's 2001 film *AI* contained subtle clues leading the initiated user into "a nameless puzzle-and-adventure game, with (so far) nameless designers, presented through a vast collection of sites portraying an entire universe of the future." As Charles Herold comments, "The 'A.I.' game would be fascinating even if the movie didn't exist."

Such intense interactivity in real life, triggered by (and feeding back into the promotion of) a fictional film, is a good example of what I call a filmic event, an increasingly prevalent phenomenon in film culture. Paradoxically, the rash of filmic events triggered by the intensifying interaction between the filmic record and real life may be signaling the marginalization of the film product itself. After several millennia of the representational, illusionist arts, the past century and a half of recording arts has produced a public dream world of real virtuality—"the use of factual material to satisfy the need for a fictional world." The movie-mediated twentieth century is turning out to be a brief, transitional stage on the way toward the kind of transpersonal, virtual reality that a fully interactive technology is bound to achieve—"the use of fictional material to simulate a factual world."[49] Signs of this transition were already clearly visible in 1999: besides the AOL–Time Warner merger in that year and the exodus of several prominent movie moguls from Hollywood to Silicon Valley, where they joined Internet entertainment start-ups,[50] for the first time sales of video games surpassed the domestic box-office gross of movies.[51] Often video games are modeled on, or aspire to, the same level of dramatic realism of the movies.[52] Some critics even regard video games as surpassing film as a "mechanism which equips the child to take his fantasies and turn them into reality."[53] Costing far less to produce than commercial films and often bringing in twice the revenue, interactive media will almost certainly continue to outperform noninteractive media (i.e., movies as well as books, paintings, and the other representational arts) in the indefinite future. Media critic Bob Schwabach predicts that interactive video games will force passive movies "into obscurity, a future entertainment category subsidized by taxes and private charity and viewed by a select audience, much like opera and ballet today." Schwabach ridicules attempts to produce interactive movies, and remains dubious about the success of such game-based 2001 films as *Tomb Raider, Final Fantasy: The Spirits Within*, and *Resident Evil*.[54] And even if movies continue to thrive, film won't: 1999 was also the year in which a full-length movie (*The Phantom Menace*) was first exhibited in a digital format, anticipating the time when high-definition digital cameras and projectors will make the bulky, expensive, and fragile medium of film obsolete. And as Darren Aronofsky's 1998 film π inaugurated an era of made-for-Internet movies by becoming the first feature-length movie offered for downloading over the Web, it seems likely that the twentieth century will turn out to be not only the first filmed century, but also the last.

From Cinema Verité to Reality TV

The networks not only remain enthusiastic about the reality genre, but the next iterations are all about one-upping the others.

—Ben Silverman, the William Morris Agency

The media's growing influence in the digital age would seem to support the claims of critics such as Jean Baudrillard and Paul Virilio about the "crisis in the reality principle," and has led a number of commentators to lament the gradual disappearance and ultimate loss of "reality" itself.[55] For some, the problem goes back six thousand years to the earliest media technology, writing, which heralded the separation of signs and things that caused reality to become increasingly symbolic and virtual.[56] Others, such as James Carey, call attention to the fact that reality is increasingly being coopted, "preempted," "defined," and "restricted" by ever more powerful global media conglomerates that debase news and history into mindless diversions.[57] Such critiques of the media and information technology are valid as far as they go, but they overlook several key matters. By calling attention to the media's distortions of reality, they give the impression that there is some independent state of affairs "out there" that can be objectively verified. Yet as philosophers from Vico onward have insisted, human reality is always a construct and has been so since the earliest poets came up with supernatural explanations for natural phenomena. If anything, the recording revolution of the nineteenth and twentieth centuries has worked to stabilize meaning and limit interpretation rather than promote rampant invention and distortion. (Of course, this could all change with the digital revolution now under way, in which fabricated images are capable of simulating indexical records.)

Then there are claims such as Neal Gabler's that entertainment now plays such an overwhelming role in people's lives that reality hardly "seems to count ... After all, when life is a movie, who needs reality?"[58] On the contrary, reality is never more in demand than it is in our global mass-mediated film culture, where it has become, in Carey's words, "a scarce resource." And while reality has never been more in demand, it has also never been more at issue. Reality in liberal, democratic, mass-mediated societies no longer is self-evident, but is constantly contested and up for grabs. It isn't merely that movies compete with reality; rather, movies compete with other movies (and studios with other studios) in rendering an authentic—that is, graphic—view of reality. Thus in 1998, for example, the movies *Deep Impact* and *Armageddon* both took up the hot new post–Cold War scare of an asteroid hitting the earth, while *Saving Private Ryan* and *The Thin Red Line* presented directors Steven Spielberg's and Terrence Malick's strikingly different accounts of American soldiers' experiences of World War II, and *Antz* and *A Bug's Life* offered the DreamWorks and Disney/Pixar studios' competing computer-animated visions of the anthropomorphized world of insects.

Besides the rival views of reality presented by different movies is the competition in our "mixed media culture" between movies and other media, such as TV, video, and the Internet.[59] An entire subgenre of movies has emerged, from *Network* to *Quiz Show*, critiquing the impact of television on daily life. While the protagonist of the 1998 movie *The Truman Show* is the unwitting star of a real-life TV serial and the two 1990s teenagers in *Pleasantville* become the unwilling captives of a 1950s black-and-white television drama, Ed of *EdTV* is only too eager (at least at first) to allow himself to become the star of a real-life soap opera. In each case, the medium of television is presented in all its contrived artificiality—especially in its pretense as reality TV to give viewers a direct glimpse of life. Yet movies critical of television do precisely what they fault television for doing: they present themselves as a transparent lens through which we watch the absurd interaction unfold between the artificial medium of TV and "real life." Film's own status as an artificial (and artificing) medium goes unexamined in these intramedial movies that critique TV as a mediating agency standing between viewers and (one particular view of) reality. Watching these movies about TV, we are led to forget that we are watching a movie, and more precisely a movie fiction. When the protagonists Truman and Ed renounce their fake TV world for real life, no acknowledgment is made that "real life" in these movies is nothing but another media fiction—that of *The Truman Show* and *EdTV* themselves.

Even as these end-of-the-century films critique television as an artificial medium, a case can be made that movies themselves have historically been a fantasy medium and that it is in fact TV that has led the way in presenting the real in all its gritty, graphic immediacy.[60] Whereas cinema verité uses the pretense of documentary to dramatize events or fabricate a story in order to present a thesis or to convey some deeper truth, reality TV documents "actual" events that are intrinsically dramatic, sensational, and voyeuristic (car chases and crashes, man-made and natural disasters, feuding spouses, even surgical operations).[61] The fact that the phrase "reality TV" has largely displaced "cinema verité" is itself revealing: in contrast to the immediacy of television, movies only offer a staged (after)image of reality, reality as an effect. Yet as media researcher Sandra J. Ball-Rokeach asks of infotainment TV, "in what sense is it reality programming? ... These shows desensitize the audience to the fear and the emotions [of actual chases and shoot-outs]. The fictional police dramas are sometimes more 'real' because they give you that context. You get a much more subtle understanding of character instead of just the action."[62] Arguing along similar lines, Lincoln Kaplan points out that fictional police and courtroom dramas on television "are more effective in framing important legal choices than most of what [the real-life cable channel] Court TV broadcasts. In an era when 'reality' TV blurs the line between nonfiction and fiction by recreating events, what people see on [fictional television dramas] gets closer to the truth—especially since the events they stage are often taken from the news."[63] Once again, what is graphic and documentary is not necessarily real or true. The so-called "caught-on-video" footage of reality TV is marked by its own artificial

> vérité aesthetic (shaky camerawork, static and technical glitches, time codes, and other aesthetic techniques that suggest that the footage was not studio-produced) ... [Reality TV's] claim of realism is not achieved by stripping the imagery of all mediation to somehow reveal an unadulterated "reality"—an impossible feat. In fact, it tends to require *more* mediation to assert that these images are real.[64]

Narrative filmmakers might think twice before emulating the dubious realism of reality TV. Still, the fact that a number of filmmakers are striving for television's nonfictional edginess suggests that "reality" still counts for a great deal in the movies, and that film has a deeper commitment to, and connection with, the "real world" than formalist critics suspect.

Nowhere is television's vaunted realism more dubious than in the new genre of "reality shows" flourishing at the turn of the century. Many of these popular American products are not even original, but recycled European imports. The number one U.S. TV program *Who Wants to Be a Millionaire* was a British quiz show that ABC first acquired as a summer series. After its success (and the fiasco of Fox's prime-time, publicity-driven special *Who Wants to Marry a Multi-Millionaire*), three networks vied for the rights to the Dutch program *Big Brother* (another losing proposition, it turned out), in which a group of young people is confined to a house loaded with cameras and microphones that record their every move. The CBS summer-of-2000 blockbuster *Survivor*, in which sixteen contestants were stranded on (and gradually eliminated from) a jungle island near Borneo, was originally a Swedish hit. In that version, one cast member committed suicide after receiving a negative vote. If *Los Angeles Times* television columnist Brian Lowry is right, more deaths can be expected as these ratings-driven shows continue "to push the envelope farther and farther in order to make them interesting"[65]—and, we might add, in order to pursue an elusive reality which must appear ever more violent and graphic.

Not only did reality shows have the potential to be immensely popular with audiences, but they were far cheaper to produce, and therefore far more profitable, than sitcoms and crime dramas. As a partner at one talent agency remarked, "Game shows and reality shows will occupy real estate previously rented to fictional entertainment programs."[66] As of this writing, plans are already in place for a televised worldwide scavenger hunt; an American version of the European show *Jailbreak*, in which a group of contestants compete to be the first to break out of a high-technology prison; and a show in which a group of people live in an environment approximating conditions on Mars. There's even a new all-out space race for the new century: NBC's deal with Russia to broadcast a contest in which the winner is sent into space aboard a Russian rocket was followed up by negotiations between the other major networks and NASA for a show in which twenty contestants train with the space agency for the chance to spend a week aboard the new International Space Station.[67]

While the hegemony of the Hollywood movie industry is threatened by far cheaper independent films and video games, the reign of costly fictional programming on TV has been put in jeopardy by the groundswell of inexpensive "reality shows." Clearly the term is an egregious misnomer. The fact that such shows are unscripted hardly makes them real. The ubiquitous presence of television cameras and film crews, and above all the actors' awareness that they are being filmed, undercuts the pretense of reality that informs the film *The Truman Show* or, for that matter, a TV program such as *Candid Camera*—"shows" in which the subject is genuinely ignorant that he or she is on film and is being seen by millions of knowing viewers. But while shows such as MTV's *The Real World* continued to cling to the pretense of presenting people as they are, the new breed of hyperreality shows has dropped this conceit once and for all. The over-the-top, soap-opera stories contrived by the World Wrestling Federation's Vince McMahon have given up any "pretense that wrestling was real." Far from making the sport seem more legitimate and lifelike, McMahon introduced "a second layer of unreality" by alternating the rounds with a lurid, behind-the-scenes glimpse into his own dysfunctional family. In John Leland's words, "here was something to believe in: the candidly, honestly fake."[68] But McMahon seriously misgauged matters when, instead of the honestly fake, he attempted to bring a new level of realism to the hallowed institution of professional football. The XFL, or Extreme Football League, was expressly created in 2000 for a new generation of viewers who appeared to be steadily losing interest in the increasingly artificial spectacle of NFL games. By placing cameras and microphones everywhere—on the field and off the field, in the players' helmets, and in the locker rooms—the XFL promised a glimpse into the behind-the-scenes reality of the game. Such realism couldn't compete with the over-hyped spectacle of the NFL, and the XFL folded after only one season.

If viewers of the common run of reality shows willfully suspend their disbelief to the point that they can believe the "candidly, honestly fake," what's to stop them from doubting the documented truth? Indeed, while a surprising number of people are disposed to believe photographic "evidence" of UFOs and other fantastic phenomena, others reject filmed evidence of the moon landing or the liberation of the death camps at the end of World War II. Straightforward, undoctored amateur recordings of sensational events, such as the Zapruder film of JFK's assassination or the Holliday video of the Rodney King beating, not only fail to show "what really happened," but actually provoke more controversy than if they hadn't been made and hadn't become part of the public record.[69] Such seemingly accurate but ultimately ambiguous and inconclusive recordings have contributed to the skeptical attitude that many feel toward the documentary media today. Others, meanwhile, are disposed to accept whatever they are shown in the movies, regardless of its veracity or even its authenticity, as long as the special effects are sufficiently spectacular and graphic.

More than ever, film audiences are in need, if not of a new hermeneutics of suspicion, then of a code of cinematic literacy that will allow them to maintain a healthy skepticism in the face of ever more spectacular special effects. An innovative media criticism is called for that can expose the ways that film distorts the world in the process—and under the pretense—of documenting it. Of particular interest in this regard are a line of narrative films from the second half of the century—from Hitchcock's 1958 *Vertigo* to Antonioni's 1966 *Blow-Up* and Neil Jordan's 1992 *The Crying Game*—that thematize the pitfalls of credulity and stress the need to doubt visible evidence in the primarily visual medium of film. "You can't believe everything you see" ran the advertising tag for Brian De Palma's 1984 film *Body Double*, while the ads for his 1998 *Snake Eyes* warned, "Believe everything, except your eyes."[70] It's as if filmmakers increasingly find themselves in the role of sorcerer's apprentices, wielding a medium whose seductive power has become so great, thanks to ever more realistic special effects, that they actually need to remind their supposedly media-savvy audiences to suspend not their disbelief but their belief. Yet it may be too much to expect such warnings to be taken seriously by most viewers growing up in the society of the spectacle of contemporary film culture. From their earliest years they have learned that the visible is the only reality that matters and that the truth is out there—namely, on the airwaves, on whatever channel the most vivid and awesome spectacle can be found.

Mediating Reality: *Wag the Dog* to *War Games*

If Tom Brokaw came, then it would be real.

—A Paducah, Kentucky, resident about reports of radioactive pollution
from the town's uranium-enrichment plant

No doubt the most surreal effect associated with the movies has to do with the revolution in human experience that occurred in the late nineteenth century, at the time cinema was invented. Not only were the recording arts beginning to supersede the traditional representational arts, but the very principle of artistic representation itself was in the process of being overturned. The ancient Platonic-Aristotelian doctrine of mimesis that had reigned for more than two thousand years, and which postulated that art was an imitation of life (either for better or for worse), was reversed almost overnight with the dictum popularized by Oscar Wilde and the decadents that life imitates—and ought to aspire to become—art.

Although Wilde, who died in 1900, was unable to realize the implications of this revolution for the new medium of film, they were soon grasped by other writers. The narrator of Luigi Pirandello's prophetic 1915 novel *The Notebooks of Serafino Gubbio* is a camera operator for an Italian movie company who is already well aware that filmmaking goes beyond the other arts in transforming real life into an illusory image. Gubbio compares his camera to a large "spider that sucks in and absorbs the [actors'] live reality to render it up an evanescent, momentary appearance, the play of mechanical illusion in the eyes of the public."[71] But Gubbio also realizes that filmmaking is fundamentally different from all the other arts in that it entails the reverse, perverse process of investing fantasies and fictions with a reality of their own that is simultaneously exposed as a fiction. "It ought to be understood that the fantastic cannot acquire reality except by means of art, and that the reality which a machine is capable of giving it kills it, for the very reason that it is given by a machine, that is to say by a method which discovers and exposes the fiction, simply by giving it and presenting it as real" (87–88). Even at this early stage in the history of cinema Pirandello recognized that film was a unique artistic operation or *technē* that did not merely provide an imitative or imagined appearance *of* reality, but was capable of presenting all that was imaginary and unreal *as* reality, with the result that the real world itself would seem to be—and possibly even come to be—nothing more than an artificial, cinematic effect.[72]

The notion that reality is an artificial effect produced by and on film is by no means just a Pirandellian paradox limited to avant-garde literary fictions. Released the same year that *The Notebooks of Serafino Gubbio* was published, Griffith's classic epic film *The Birth of a Nation* is a striking example of the reality effect at work in real life. Commentators have typically cited scenes such as that of Lincoln's assassination as examples of Griffith's meticulous attention to detail and his fidelity to authoritative sources in the construction of sets and reconstruction of events. Such "historical facsimiles" are taken as proof of his artistry and of his elevation of film to an art form that astounded viewers with its verisimilitude. Yet it is well known that Griffith's pretensions to historical accuracy are thoroughly undercut by his racist views. His idealized portrayal of the Klan (based on Thomas Dixon's 1905 novel *The Clansman*, subtitled *An Historical Romance of the Ku Klux Klan*) provides a striking instance of the way life models itself on cinematic fiction. Contrary to Griffith's and Dixon's depiction of the Klan as reaching the peak of its power during Reconstruction, the movement was actually on the verge of collapse and was pretty much dormant for the next half century, until the time Dixon wrote his novel and Griffith made his film. Their romanticized fictions of the Klan became so popular that they bear some measure of responsibility for the movement's all-too-real revival in its new, more virulent form. Revived in Georgia in the same year as *The Birth of a Nation*, the Klan used Griffith's film to recruit new members across the country.

This early example of how reality is mediated by artistic fictions in a looping effect (old Klan → *The Birth of a Nation* → new Klan) has been succeeded by numerous others. Griffith's 1916 epic *Intolerance* made Lenin aware of the movies' potential as a "medium for the masses" and spurred the rise of early propagandist Soviet films such as Sergei Eisenstein's 1925 *The Battleship Potemkin*; this film, in turn, influenced future revolutionary leaders including Ho Chi Minh and Frantz Fanon. The 1939 Hollywood film *Ninotchka* has been credited with averting a victory by the Italian Communist Party in 1948 national elections. And the Russian director Sergei Bodrov insisted that his film *Prisoner of the Mountains* played a key role in the departure of Russian troops from the rebel republic of Chechnya in 1996.[73] Although these examples may not demonstrate that movies are able to change the course of history—

certainly their historical impact has not nearly been as dramatic as that of some books, especially works of science and religion—they suggest that commercial films interact with actual events in a variety of subtle but significant ways that too often go unnoticed. Then, of course, there is the profound impact that nonfictional film and news footage have on history, as in TV coverage of civil rights marches and the Vietnam War during the 1960s, and the strange looping effects that regularly take place between television dramas and the news.[74]

In the late twentieth century, it's become increasingly common to find examples of movies that uncannily anticipate actual events. Besides the "wag the dog" phenomenon—named after the 1998 film that many credited with exposing President Clinton's stratagem, and even with giving him the idea in the first place, of ordering overseas military strikes to distract public attention from the mounting scandals in his personal life—one could cite such earlier instances as *The China Syndrome*, dealing with a mishap at a nuclear power plant and released just days before the actual Three Mile Island disaster in 1979; *Pripyat*, Nikolaus Geyrhalter's 1999 documentary about the ravaged area near the Chernobyl nuclear power plant, whose New York opening happened to coincide with the worst nuclear accident in Japan's history; *Deal of the Century,* a satire about the international arms trade that anticipated the Iran-contra scandal of the '80s; *Wall Street*, which was made just prior to, and released just after, the 1987 stock market crash; *The Silence of the Lambs,* with its terrifying portrayal of Hannibal Lecter, which appeared shortly before the world learned about the real-life cannibalistic serial killer Jeffrey Dahmer; and David Cronenberg's 1996 film *Crash*, which heralded the death the following year of Princess Diana with its fateful conjunction of celebrity, the media, sex, violence, and large black automobiles. Then there is the 1999 film *The Matrix*, in which two warriors in black trench coats are shown blowing away everyone in sight—a scene that eerily coincided with the contemporaneous rampage of two members of the "Trench Coat Mafia" at Columbine High School.

Whether the Manson "family's" grisly murder of the pregnant actress Sharon Tate and four others in 1969 was triggered by the release the previous year of *Rosemary's Baby*, a film about satanic gestation directed by Tate's husband, Roman Polanski, the murder clearly influenced Polanski's choice and treatment of his next film. In *Macbeth* (1970) he shifted the dramatic focus "from Macbeth and Lady Macbeth to Macduff—to the horrible murder of Macduff's family and, particularly, to the fiercely imagined intensity of Macduff's experience as he learns of those murders so far away."[75] (Like Macduff, Polanski was abroad in England when his wife was killed back home.)

The uncanny interplay between the movies and reality is particularly acute in the case of Sidney Lumet's 1975 film *Dog Day Afternoon*. The movie was based on an actual 1972 bank robbery in Brooklyn, which was in turn inspired by Francis Ford Coppola's *The Godfather*. Lumet's decision to cast Al Pacino as the robber John Wojtowicz seems almost inevitable, since Wojtowicz happened to look a lot like Pacino, who appeared in *The Godfather*, which Wojtowicz had seen the same day he committed the crime. After serving a twenty-year sentence for his deed, Wojtowicz went on to play himself in a film that explores the interrelations between the real robbery and the two movies. French filmmaker Pierre Huyghe's 2000 film *The Third Memory* uses a simulation of the Brooklyn branch of Chase Manhattan Bank to reenact the crime. Now in his fifties, Wojtowicz appears simultaneously as actor, commentator, and director, not to mention the actual robber he was nearly thirty years earlier.[76]

These examples are related to, but not quite the same as, those instances of copycat violence involving the movies that have become all too familiar: John Hinckley Jr.'s assassination attempt on President Reagan after seeing *Taxi Driver*, the 1995 North Hollywood bank heist modeled on the thriller *Heat*, the numerous murder sprees attributed to *Natural Born Killers* and *Scream*, the school shootings that followed *The Basketball Diaries*, and the two sensational murders in Britain blamed on *Child's Play 3*, not to mention all the copycat incidents triggered by live TV coverage of violent news stories. Conservative critics delight in citing such examples of life imitating art, which seem to put the blame squarely on Hollywood rather than on the gun industry. In contrast to acts of violence deliberately modeled on the movies, however, the crises and disasters mentioned earlier are fortuitous events that were surrealistically anticipated—and not directly precipitated—by feature films. In the age of "instant preplay" it's become common to see movies about sensational events (wars, storms, epidemics, assassinations) before they take place. There's a fair chance that the next feature film you see may turn out to be a preview of an actual event—a newsreel of some real news story—that has yet to occur. And although there may be no discernible cause-and-effect relation between today's fictional film and tomorrow's real event, the latter, when it occurs, will somehow seem less real (contingent and spontaneous) and more like an effect (contrived and "special").

As if aware of this uncanny relation between movies and reality and of their own role as sorcerer's apprentices who unwittingly anticipate actual events in their movies, filmmakers occasionally present scenarios that seem intended to avoid or avert catastrophes, whether natural (asteroids colliding with the earth) or man-made (computers running amok and triggering all-out nuclear war). By presenting apocalyptic narratives in the fictional form of movies or thrill rides, special-effects technicians play on people's fears, to be sure, but they may also be playing (or banking) on the notion that by presenting these doomsday scenarios in a fictional form, they are *preventing* them from happening. After all, if life doesn't *really* imitate art, then by making movies about all the calamities you can think of, at least they won't take place, right? As Ray Bradbury said of science-fiction writing, "we do this not to predict the future but to prevent it."[77] What might be termed the "*War Games* effect," after the 1983 film of that name, is in fact a strategy of deterrence, a means of using ritualistic, aesthetic acts of simulation to ward off all-too-real scenarios of seemingly imminent global catastrophe.

The Graphic Imperative

Film is the way we see our world, Charles.... So much is happening, and it needs to be recorded.

—J. G. Ballard, *Cocaine Nights*

As cinematic fictions increasingly seem to approximate, anticipate, and even to precipitate actual events, efforts by the documentary media to produce a reliable record of real life have been greeted with growing skepticism. The most lasting legacy of the overhyped spectacle of the O.J. Simpson criminal trial of 1995, in which the jurors were led to doubt seemingly irrefutable DNA evidence, is turning out to have less to do with the expected issues of race relations or domestic violence than with the circus atmosphere created by the presence of TV cameras inside and outside the courtroom, which turned the trial into a national spectacle. Who can forget the tragicomic figure of Judge Ito—determined to be impartial and above the fray, intent on using the trial as a means to uncover the truth, and yet unable to resist the dazzle of the media, and starstruck by his new celebrity status in this real-life episode of *LA Law*? Following the sensational Simpson and Menendez brothers murder trials, the quiet removal or at least retrenchment of television cameras from many courtrooms[78]—a move that echoed the prior injunction of the networks' efforts to broadcast live executions of prisoners[79]—was prompted not only by an awareness of the "uncertain affective power of any documentary medium,"[80] but by a determination to impose some limits on the century's compulsion to put everything on film.

The issue of whether to permit cameras in courtrooms, execution chambers, or, most recently, in the homes of suspects whose arrests are recorded by "news media ride-alongs" for broadcast on reality TV programs, pales beside the perils that some have seen in introducing computers as a standard fixture in the classroom.[81] The Internet's "uncertain affective power," especially when it puts the world at children's fingertips, has raised the stakes in the already heated debate about the dangers posed by graphic depictions of sex and violence in the movies and other visual media. ("Now I bet Clinton's sorry he put computers in the classroom," quipped Jay Leno when the 1998 Starr Report's account of the lurid details of President Clinton's sexual relationship with a White House intern was posted on the Internet.) Less an information than entertainment superhighway, the Internet has become an extension of Hollywood and is routinely denounced for irresponsible programming whenever an episode of schoolyard violence occurs.[82] Yet despite all the talk of ratings systems, V-chips, and even outright censorship, scenes of sex and violence in the mass media show no sign of abating. We are confronted with an escalating spiral of graphic images, fueled on one hand by a public appetite, especially among the young, for such scenes, and on the other hand by the eagerness of producers and media giants to cater to, cash in on, and even create that demand. Rarely is it suggested that the sex-and-violence spiral is a logical and even inevitable tendency in the development of the cinematic and televisual media, that "sex and violence became natural partners" from the moment that "they became graphically visible."[83] The type of content that the media shows at a given time and place may be determined less from on high by political decisions and by ethical and moral considerations than by the nature of the recording media themselves—their ability to provide graphic reproductions of sensational subjects to mass audiences of anonymous consumers.

It's worth recalling that for most of Western history, the arts were not valued for their graphic depiction of reality. "Realism" was not an aesthetic criterion: the artistic image was not ordinarily confused with real life (the occasional story of Zeuxis's grapes or of Pygmalion's Galatea were exceptions that proved the rule), largely because the medium of the representation (stone, paint, or print) was noticeably different from the material being of the represented object. As for the subjects depicted by the arts, these did not typically include activities that were considered indecent or unseemly. Representations of excessive violence or explicit sexuality were generally barred from public exhibition, although actual scenes of violence might readily be encountered at gladiatorial games and state executions, and pornographic imagery could be examined by all those who could gain admission into private collections and "secret museums."

All this changed in the twentieth century with the rise of the recording media. Technological innovations in photojournalism and scientific photography made possible a graphic hyperrealism that has frequently been exploited in the arts. Film was not only capable of reproducing reality to an unprecedented degree, but also had an inherent ability to enhance reality by turning any scene into a larger-than-life spectacle. And with recent technological innovations and fewer restrictions on content, film seems increasingly bent on showing everything. "If the smut of fifty or even twenty years ago looks tame by comparison with today's," wrote Walter Kendrick in 1987,

> the reason may have nothing to do with pornography itself. Every mode of representation had become explicit in the same years, in every nonsexual realm; it has become possible to photograph the earth from outer space, a fetus in the womb, and Vietnamese children in the process of dying.[84]

Kendrick's observation about the increasingly explicit nature of representation has become all the more pertinent—and perplexing—with the subsequent explosion of images on the Internet. Since digital images need not be indexically linked to actual referents, it's all but impossible to distinguish real from virtual images on computer screens. This presents an especially daunting task for prosecutors in child pornography cases, since the 1996 Child Pornography Protection Act was declared unconstitutional by the Ninth Circuit Court of Appeals in 1999. Reasoning that "Congress has no compelling interest in regulating sexually explicit materials that do not contain visual images of actual children," the Court of Appeals required prosecutors to prove that pornographic pictures are photographs of *real* children rather than computerized images. The U.S. Supreme Court has agreed to review the decision, which has been assailed by prosecutors and critics who argue the near impossibility of proving beyond a reasonable doubt that a minor depicted in a picture is a real minor. Since, in one commentator's words, few people can now "tell the difference between a 'real' picture of an actual child and a computer image of a cyber-child," and since virtual pornography often can't be distinguished from real pornography, many believe the two should be treated the same.[85] For all its practical good sense, such an argument effectively ensures the very condition that it assumes and fears is already the case—the obliteration, once and for all, of any distinction between real and virtual imagery. Once the two kinds of imagery are treated as being identical, how long can the realms of reality and virtuality themselves be expected to remain distinguishable?

Amid the promiscuous circulation and widespread availability of formerly restricted imagery, it's easy to forget that until the recording revolution of the twentieth century—itself made possible by the scientific and industrial revolutions of the seventeenth and nineteenth centuries—the impulse to "show everything" was by no means considered ethically acceptable or aesthetically desirable in Western art. In the theater and the performing arts, gruesome and horrific subjects traditionally took place offstage. In ancient tragedy, two kinds of events were removed from view: along with key moments of violence (Oedipus's murder of his father and his own blinding), sexual events such as Oedipus's incestuous relations with his mother/wife could not be presented onstage. The staged action was typically limited to the peripheral action of the drama, the fore- and postplay leading up to and following the key moments of sex and violence, which always occurred offstage.[86]

For the most part, the history of Western drama has continued to show remarkable reserve and decorum. On the relatively rare occasions in the history of drama when sex and violence are shown onstage, they tend to be portrayed in a nonrealistic manner—either comically, in the case of sex, or as stylized, sensational, or over-the-top spectacle, as in Jacobean tragedy and Artaud's theater of cruelty.[87] Although drama may have originated in fertility and sacrificial rites—ceremonial celebrations of sex and violence—it's not normally an occasion for public executions or peep shows.[88] Over time, the convention arose that drama would not directly portray the two most dramatic experiences in human existence: graphic sex and murderous violence. These two scenes depicting the origin and end of human life in the most dramatic form possible were supremely private, taboo moments that could not bear public scrutiny and so had to be presented in some indirect manner. As a result, the most dramatic moments in the theater tend to be those in which the extraordinary or the private threaten to break through into ordinary, public life but don't, or do break through but not onstage.

The restraint demonstrated by ancient poets, playwrights, and performers, first in sublimating in a fictional form acts of violence traditionally practiced in ritual sacrifices and public executions, and then in displacing such scenes of violence offstage, where they would not be directly witnessed, had enormous consequences for human development. By adopting these conventions, the arts succeeded in differentiating themselves from real life in its most charged, violent moments. In order to become an art form, tragedy—and ultimately drama and literature in general—had to develop an array of ritual conventions and mediating devices (the chorus, the narrator, the flashback, the frame story) as a way of distancing spectators from violent acts and catastrophic events, thereby giving audiences the degree of detachment necessary for imaginative engagement. Presentation had to become re-presentation. Eventually, when the discipline of aesthetics was formulated in the European Enlightenment, sensation (the root meaning of the word *aesthetics*) was shown as leading to contemplation, or what came to be known as aesthetic experience.

How did this process of attenuation and detachment come about? It couldn't have happened all at once, but must have evolved over a long period of prehistory. Art is not natural: it entails an extended process of sublimation and socialization, an evolved technique of mimesis whereby reenactment becomes representation, and sensation becomes contemplation. Today, however, we seem to be living through the culmination of this process. For in this neoaesthetic age, when experience is mediated to an unprecedented degree by technology and the mass media, it's all too easy for people to become an-aesthetized, cut off from a sense of the real. And the more desensitized people become, the more sensational are the effects needed to shock them out of (or perhaps only to sustain their belief in) a substitute world of virtual or postreality.

It's not surprising, then, that contemporary filmmakers and other artists so often seem tempted to return to art's primitive, ritual origins—to "regress" from a sublimated aesthetic of ideas and contemplation to an aesthetic of cruelty and sensation. While recent drama has been "more about showing,"[89] films in the "post-literate cinematic age" are more concerned with spectacle than script, to many a critic's dismay.[90] Not only has the graphic medium of film made it possible to show peak experiences of sex and violence as never before, but it has created a demand for such spectacles. Scenes of sex or violence that are merely depicted or described in literature and the representational arts must be enacted in the literal, visible world recorded on film; they *must actually take place so that they can be seen.* Even when the sexual fantasies of fictional characters are portrayed in films, they must be acted out and performed by real actors as if they actually happened; otherwise they cannot be recorded and shown to viewers, who then must learn of those fantasies the old-fashioned, literary way—through the less vivid, verbal means of dialogue or voice-over narration. In the film's fictional narrative the fantasies of characters are just as imaginary as they are in real life, but in the film's actual production those fantasies are just as visible—and therefore just as real—as anything else in the mise-en-scène.

One consequence of the emergence of the recording media in the twentieth century, then, is that primal scenes of sexual passion and sacrificial violence that had taken eons for Western civilization to sublimate in its cultural productions and artistic representations have suddenly returned with a vengeance. Once again such scenes have become widely visible and are routinely featured in theater and performance art as well as in the movies, in videos, and on the Internet. Largely forgotten is the classical ideal of the arts as a means of distancing audiences from volatile, emotionally charged scenes and of enabling audiences to put such scenes in perspective and to reflect on them at their leisure. For some time now the arts have sought to bring "reality" *closer* to us, to rub our faces in its simulated image. Far from offering an escape from reality, movies have tended to present audiences with a heightened experience of the real, whether in the thrill ride of disaster films such as *Titanic* or *Twister* or in the clinical close-ups of pornography. In either case, the documentary impulse reigns supreme.

As always, we need to bear in mind that this increasingly graphic depiction of reality does not necessarily entail greater realism—quite the contrary. The story lines in *Titanic, Twister,* or most pornography, for that matter, are hokey at best, and all their realistic details are nothing but staged effects, as we ought to have learned from that classic parable of the cinema, *The Wizard of Oz.* Comparing pornography to Westerns or horror films, James Atlas notes that pornography is

> different in one major respect: it prefers reality to realism. On the one hand, we think, These people are actually doing these things, while, on the other hand, we realize that the things they're doing are staged in a highly contrived, highly choreographed way. There are formulaic, ritualized stages within each film.[91]

Following the feminist analyses of Linda Williams and Judith Butler, Atlas writes that pornographic "films never seem phonier than at the moment of truth"[92]—namely, at the peak experience of orgasm, which, far from being natural and spontaneous, must be elaborately staged to provide maximum visibility and ocular proof of male climax. (The absence of visible evidence in the case of female orgasm renders its authenticity uncertain from the viewer's perspective.[93]) In short, despite its documentary pretense and its supposedly graphic realism, "pornography is exciting only because it *isn't* anything like real life."[94]

As erroneous as it is to regard the tendency toward increased visibility in the recording arts as a move toward greater realism, it would be just as misleading to dismiss the graphic tendency in the media as a regression toward primitivism. If anything, the graphic impulse is leading forward toward a kind of "techno-primitivism" or "crash aesthetic."[95] Once again we need to bear in mind that the documentary impulse in film is derived from the sciences with their supposedly progressive, enlightened endeavor to "know" nature.[96] Like the scientists they originally were, cinematographers have much in common with pornographers, documenting previously invisible and even unimaginable scenes by placing the observer—and quite literally the camera—in places they have never been. Indeed, the "invention of pornography" at the time of the scientific revolution was the first stage in the modern technoepistemological program of *scientia sexualis*.[97] Amid the outcry that is routinely made against film and the other arts as pornographic media, it's often overlooked that the arts are ultimately engaged in the same heuristic endeavor as the sciences, and that the documentary media in particular have pride of place in the scientific arsenal of truth technologies. Graphic depictions of sex and violence in contemporary film, and cinema's preoccupation with scenes of bodily ecstasy and suffering, all arise out of a quasi-scientific, documentary impulse that has come to pervade even the most nonrealistic fictional entertainments, and that attempts to disclose some elusive truth concealed behind a hypermediated world of special effects. Is the ecstatic moment of *jouissance* real, or is it just being faked? And as in the case of World Wrestling Foundation fans, do we prefer "the candidly, honestly fake" to the complex and often disturbingly real?

In recent years, the media have played an increasingly controversial role in covering sensational events, from JFK's assassination to the O.J. Simpson murder trial, and even in creating them, as was to a certain extent the case in Princess Diana's death. Now that cameras have been banned from execution chambers and many courtrooms, the broadcast media (film, TV, the Internet) have become the last—and also the most graphic—domain in which both fictional and actual violence can be displayed as public spectacle. This became fully evident in 1998 when Dr. Jack Kevorkian made a videotape of himself administering lethal drugs to a man with Lou Gehrig's disease and then sent the tape to *60 Minutes*, where it was seen by an estimated twenty-two million people. Kevorkian's brazen use of the media to confront the world with the reality of euthanasia is a striking instance of a filmic event—in this case, the scandalous eruption of private ritual into the realm of public spectacle, where its "reality" is visible for all to see. "But did we really need to watch it on TV?" was all *Newsweek* could say in reporting Kevorkian's deed.[98] Such a query misses the point: in today's society of the spectacle, the televised appearance of Kevorkian's tape was inevitable regardless of our "needs."

Clearly there's more going on in contemporary film culture than just going to the movies. As cinema has become increasingly graphic, the world has become increasingly filmic—recorded, registered, and increasingly recognizable only as a series of mediated events. The first part of this study explores the phenomenon of the graphic turn in film culture, beginning in chapter 1 with a discussion of the burgeoning business of the pornographic media and its relation to "mainstream" film. The disjunction in the film industry between commercial and X-rated movies reflects the cultural disjunction between "reality" and fantasy, between social exigencies and individual desires. At the end of the twentieth century, the barrier separating porn and mainstream film, such as that separating the private and the public, has proven highly permeable: while very few Americans had even seen a pornographic movie thirty years ago, the average household now watches six porn videos a year.[99] Yet even with the mass production and marketing of formerly private, individual fantasies (the fantasy effect as the flip side of the reality effect), the barrier between the private and public remains intact if not inviolable. Fantasy and reality remain separate, if not incommensurable, realms, although this could change with the further erosion of the boundary between real and virtual pornography.

One wonders: was this Freud's great "sin" as a scientific investigator—to have begun to bridge the two worlds of fantasy and reality by revealing their interactions? Aren't we presently living out the legacy of that initial breach in the barrier between conscious existence and the unconscious? Shouldn't Freud be credited with elevating pornography to the status of a science and with scripting—at the very moment that cinematic technology was coming into its own—the primal mise-en-scène as the first pornographic film? These questions and the extent to which psychoanalysis in particular, and science in general, can be considered (porno)graphic enterprises are examined in chapter 2. Chapter 3 demonstrates the power of the moving image to mediate desire through the specific cinematic technique of the body double. I suggest that the use of this rudimentary "special effect" is by no means limited to movie production and the creation of cinematic illusion, but affects virtually every aspect of cultural—and even biological—life.

Having sketched the general outlines of film culture in Part 1, I focus in Part 2 on filmic events themselves. By demonstrating the interplay between several recent movie fictions and seemingly unrelated real-life events, I hope to suggest some of the consequences of cinema's accelerating convergence with the world. Chapter 4 identifies the Zapruder film of JFK's assassination as a cinematic ur-text and takes up the issue of real versus filmed violence. Specifically, I examine the link between the social problem of serial violence and the geopolitical phenomenon of surveillance technologies, and I ask whether such technologies ultimately serve to deter violence or to incite it. In chapter 5 I study the relation between violence and storytelling as revealed in several films that feature characters who generate fictions (or try to) within the fictional world of the film, usually with disastrous results. The concluding chapter in this section consists of three case studies, each involving the peculiar relation between a recent fictional movie and a contemporaneous nonfictional event. The movies pertaining to the first two case studies—Adrian Lyne's *Lolita* and David Cronenberg's

Crash—were controversial works adapted from novels dealing respectively with the taboo themes of pedophilia and the eroticism of car crashes, and were only released in the United States after a year-long delay. I suggest that the threat posed by these films was their unveiling of uncomfortable cultural truths that happened to be confirmed by two sensational events: the deaths of two contemporary princesses, the six-year-old beauty queen JonBenét Ramsey and Diana, Princess of Wales. The third case study focuses on a film about a fictional subject and a videotape of an actual event: the 1997 movie *Wag the Dog* and President Clinton's 1998 grand jury testimony about his relationship with Monica Lewinsky. The controversy in this instance did not involve a movie's delayed release or "censorship"; on the contrary, it resulted from the videotape's precipitous and unedited worldwide release. In all three examples, a commercial film functions unintentionally, and seemingly coincidentally, as a commentary on a sensational news story that is already in the process of being transformed under intense media coverage from a real filmed event into a hyperreal filmic event.

Such spectral phenomena are barely distinguishable from dreams, and the study's third and last section addresses this blurriest of boundaries. Here it is less a matter of reiterating arguments about mass-mediated images infiltrating the individual's inner dreamworld than of noting a few of the more striking ways in which movies and their cultural network have come to function as a public dreamscape. Movies are no longer the place where our dreams come true, but the place where we discover what our dreams are. As envisioned by writers such as Delmore Schwartz and filmmakers such as Wim Wenders, it's as if our dreams themselves have been (pre)recorded and are being played back for us, and for everyone else, while we are awake. Or, as I suggest in the afterword, it is as though we were viewing our worldly existence as if for the first time, and seeing it as it really is, from the hyperreal perspective of the beyond. Such correspondences and confusions between art and life, waking and dreaming, living and seeing, are only to be expected in the midst of a revolution in graphic communication out of which a full-blown film culture has already emerged and a postfilm culture is in the process of emerging.

part one

film
culture

Pornographic Science

Missing Scenes: Coover's *Casablanca*

The unconscious is that chapter of my history which is marked by a blank ... : it is the censored chapter.

—Jacques Lacan

Sexuality in literature is a language in which what is not said is more important than what is.

—Italo Calvino

The fact that everything seems to end up, sooner or later, in the graphic medium of film doesn't mean that movies show "everything," let alone that what they show is "real." Even by today's relatively permissive standards, the Motion Picture Association of America's rating system determines which commercial pictures can be shown to whom, based on the type of content they depict. In order to avoid the dreaded NC-17 rating, commercial filmmakers cannot present actual sex acts, and even simulated sex scenes must be carefully edited. Nevertheless, such scenes are far more graphic today than they were before the 1960s, when they were virtually nonexistent. Clearly the trend is toward greater explicitness.

Take the great love scene in *Casablanca*. While her husband, Victor Laszlo, is at an underground meeting of resistance fighters, Ilsa returns to Rick's apartment above the Café Américain to plead with her former lover to give her the letters of transit that would allow her to leave the Nazi-controlled territory with her husband. When the embittered Rick fails to be moved by Ilsa's entreaties and by her reference to their affair in Paris on the eve of the war ("I wouldn't bring up Paris if I were you. It's poor salesmanship"), she draws a gun on him in desperation. Rick calls her bluff ("Go ahead and shoot. You'll be doing me a favor"); Ilsa drops the gun and surrenders to his embrace, saying, "The day you left Paris … if you knew how much I missed you. If you knew how much I loved you … how much I still love you." Discreetly, the scene fades out to show the airport beacon across from the café, its light beam sweeping the city. We next see the camera fade in on Rick, who is watching the beacon—at once a beckoning symbol of escape and a premonition of loss—from his balcony. Turning to Ilsa, who is sitting on a sofa, he asks, "And then …?," urging her to continue the story she has apparently been telling him about her relationship with Victor and about her failure to show up at the train station and to flee Paris with him when the Germans occupied the city.

Schooled in the cinematic conventions that governed Hollywood movie production in the 1940s, most viewers have no trouble grasping that the fade-out to the beacon after the lovers' embrace signals an unseen scene of lovemaking.[1] But what if director Michael Curtiz had followed a set of conventions from a later era—say, the 1980s or '90s? Or what if today's viewers interpreted the film according to the conventions of an age of R, NC-17, and X ratings, filling in the discreet gap after the fade-out? This is exactly what Robert Coover did in his 1987 collection of cinematically inspired short fictions entitled *A Night at the Movies*. In the volume's concluding piece, entitled "You Must Remember This," Coover depicts an imaginary scenario of the intimate details of Rick and Ilsa's rekindled love affair during their night together in the Moroccan city. After transcribing Ilsa's nighttime visit as it is presented in the film, the story continues to describe the scene between the fade-out and the fade-in in a twenty-page pornographic description of orgiastic lovemaking, punctuated by Ilsa's comment "It was the best fokk I effer haff."[2]

Coover's story brilliantly illustrates Peter Lehman's observation that "hardcore pornography is devoted to virtually nothing but the fade of the classical cinema; it is a form which shows in explicit detail what was unthinkable under the Hays Code, and still is forbidden in Hollywood cinema."[3] Readers of "You Must Remember This" are jolted into an awareness of what the classic Hollywood movie doesn't, and indeed can't, show. Given the prevailing conventions of the time, sexual intimacy cannot be graphically depicted without appearing obscene. It may be, as the film's signature song "As Time Goes By" affirms, that the "fundamental things apply," but it is only through the organized forgetting and repression of those fundamental things that a film such as *Casablanca* achieves an enduring reputation as an artistic, rather than pornographic, classic. In entitling his piece "You Must Remember This," Coover would perversely have his readers "remember" those fundamental things that good taste and aesthetic decorum customarily cause them to "forget." By reworking the film's tactful presentation of the rekindled love affair enacted by Bogart and Bergman as an explicit sexual encounter, Coover uses the nonvisual medium of literature to overthrow well-established cinematic conventions and to mix and adulterate genres that have been kept rigorously separate. In short, he transforms this classic film into a porn flick.

Despite the disingenuous remark that opens *A Night at the Movies*—"Ladies and Gentlemen May safely visit this Theatre as no Offensive Films are ever Shown Here"—Coover's pornographic piece seems calculated to offend traditionalist film buffs who bemoan the tendency toward explicitness. Michael Medved, one of the most vocal of such critics, has blasted the Hollywood film industry of the 1980s and '90s, claiming that

> few observers would suggest that the *overall* quality of motion pictures has improved since the removal of the [Hays] Production Code [in 1966]. Considering all of the films of the '80s and '90s, for instance, and comparing them to the Hollywood product of the '30s and '40s, it is difficult to imagine that anyone could claim that the increased latitude for filmmakers has brought about a more distinguished body of work.[4]

In fact, one can easily imagine any number of today's directors disputing this claim and taking Martin Amis's view that if "cinema is just mass entertainment, then Medved is an eloquent awakener. If cinema is art, then Medved is just a noisy philistine."[5] But many of those same directors might well find themselves agreeing with Medved's claim in the case of recognized masterworks, agreeing that the original *Casablanca* would be infinitely preferable to a steamy modern remake. Such major filmmakers as Steven Spielberg and Martin Scorsese have lobbied for the protection of classic films from studios that seek to sell the rights for commercial purposes. Their concern stems from the fact that while the consecrated status of movies such as *Casablanca* and *Gone with the Wind* has so far deterred even the most ambitious filmmakers from doing a remake, that may be about to change. Literary sequels of *Casablanca* and *Gone with the Wind* have already appeared; the *GWTW* sequel has been filmed, and Warner Bros., which produced *Casablanca*, has the option of turning Michael Walsh's sequel, *As Time Goes By*, into a feature film or a miniseries. One special effects company, Virtual Celebrity, which acquired the "digital rights" to a number of deceased film actors, even considered making a prequel to *Casablanca* starring a digitally resuscitated Marlene Dietrich. ("I always said it would have been great to see Dietrich win her first Academy Award," said the company's owner, Jeff Lotman.[6]) Even as the *GWTW* sequel was in production, Steven Spielberg warned that "we're only a couple of years away from being able to remake *Gone With the Wind* with other actors as Rhett and Scarlett. The icons of the 1930s, '40s, '50s and '60s are the pop culture of the 21st century, and I don't think that's right."[7]

The canonization of *Casablanca* in American cinema, and the threat posed by a modern cinematic remake to that film's artistic integrity and cultural authority, makes Coover's pornographic treatment of the film's love scene seem all the more scandalous, even in its literary guise. (Spielberg's anxiety about the possibility of someone remaking *Gone with the Wind* "with other actors as Rhett and Scarlett" would be all the greater had he considered the prospect of a hard-core remake of *Casablanca* featuring digital facsimiles of Bogey and Bergman.) The scene of Rick and Ilsa's orgy is bound to strike *Casablanca* devotees as having no place in the film and as being nothing but Coover's own fantasy—mediated, to be sure, by the literary and cinematic pornographic products of his time, nearly half a century after the original film was made.

Consider, however, the response to *Casablanca* of a non-American critic who is not awed by the movie, and who judges it to be, "by any strict critical standards, ... a very mediocre film," especially when compared to a "masterpiece" such as *Stagecoach*. For Umberto Eco, the secret of *Casablanca*'s undeserved success is its archetypal allusiveness: it "brings with it, like a trail of perfume, other situations that the viewer brings to bear on it quite readily, taking them without realizing it from films that only appeared later."[8] So while the *Casablanca* enthusiast may deplore Coover's revision for anachronistically introducing clichés from pornographic books and films of the 1980s, Eco makes a similar case against *Casablanca* as a film that invites modern viewers to read in cinematic clichés from a later era. The clichés Eco refers to are softcore, romantic references that attach themselves to *Casablanca* "like a trail of perfume"; Coover has simply substituted hard-core, pornographic clichés "from films that only appeared later." And those familiar softcore clichés are every bit as much fantasies as Coover's sexually explicit clichés. In fact, Coover's pornographic clichés are arguably more authentic than the romantic conventions customarily associated with the film because they are explicit rather than allusive. In any case, Coover can't be faulted for introducing extraneous elements into what Eco describes as a fundamentally allusive film. All Coover has done is to alter—to subvert rather than pervert—the expected allusions.

While mainstream film critics may be appalled by Coover's hard-core literary revision of *Casablanca*'s love scene, especially since it anticipates a sexually explicit cinematic remake, literary critics have generally been impressed by what they consider Coover's "spoof." Edmund White praised Coover for having "made literary art out of a total immersion in the movies" and for "enlarging his literary technique by forcing it to assimilate cinematic conventions and to approximate filmic style" in a work that is "vivacious," "entertaining," and "one hundred percent American."[9] The *New York Times* credited Coover for inverting the conventions of Hollywood films, thereby "mak[ing] us question our most fundamental social and cultural preoccupations."[10] And the *Chicago Tribune*'s reviewer found Coover's "wickedly inventive and sacrilegious sendup" of *Casablanca* to be easily the best of the pieces in *A Night at the Movies*.[11] Far from censuring Coover for producing a travesty of a great film, these reviewers praised him for unmasking the inauthenticity of Hollywood's icons. Do these reviews represent a positive critical response to verbal, literary pornography as opposed to a negative critical response to visual, cinematic pornography? Or do they represent the New York– and Chicago-based literary establishment's revenge on Hollywood for turning great novels into tawdry movies? Hadn't Coover succeeded, after all, in reversing the usual process whereby "a scene that is sexy in [a] novel becomes pornographic by transposition to the screen"?[12] Movies based on literary texts are generally not intended to be parodies; nevertheless, the above critics all read Coover's piece as a literary parody of a cinematic work. And it is as a parody, rather than as pornography, that his piece is praised.[13]

One wonders what these critics would say about videos such as *Satin and Lace II, Hollywood Undercover, Penthouse* magazine's 1993 production that features "look-alike pets" imitating famous actresses in soft-core versions of bedroom scenes from classic Hollywood films— Marilyn Monroe in *Bus Stop*, Liz Taylor in *Cat on a Hot Tin Roof*, Marlene Dietrich in *The Blue Angel*. The same critics who approved of Coover's literary parody of *Casablanca* are likely to dismiss the *Penthouse* video's re-creations of Hollywood bedroom scenes on the grounds that they are primarily (if not exclusively) pornographic, and only secondarily (if at all) parodic—parody in hard-core films usually being limited to a tasteless play on the titles of popular commercial movies. But then what would these same critics say about the 1977 *Casablanca* spoof *Disco Dolls in Hot Skin*, a 3-D porn film currently being revived on college campuses? Odds are they would rave about it as parody and as a cult classic—that is, if they deigned to write about it at all. In contrast, *Penthouse*, with its commercial fetishizing of the female body, makes an easy target for highbrow and politically correct critics; its lascivious re-creations of classic cinematic scenes provide yet another occasion to express critical superiority and disdain.

Is there a double standard here, a tacit critical rating code that gives a thumbs-up to parody and a thumbs-down to pornography, or that is more likely to justify verbal rather than visual pornography *as* parody? Readers of literature certainly aren't less inhibited or repressed than viewers of film, but most critics seem to be more comfortable with verbal rather than visual depictions of sexually graphic scenes; it's easier to rationalize (as parody, for example) what you don't have to visualize. Also, literature is different from film in that it has a long—one might almost say distinguished—pornographic tradition: readers are accustomed to the idea of "forbidden" classics, from *Justine* to *Lolita*, and literary masterworks have even been criticized for being too tame. "Why can't they make a *War and Peace* with fucking in it?," the artist R. B. Kitaj has complained, presumably referring to the novel rather than the film.[14] And although a few filmmakers, such as Bernardo Bertolucci in *Last Tango in Paris* and Stanley Kubrick in *Eyes Wide Shut*, have attempted to realize Boris Adrian's dream in Terry Southern's 1970 novel *Blue Movie* of making a big-budget sex film starring Hollywood actors, the gap between commercial and adult film has proven virtually impenetrable.[15] In the nonvisual medium of literature, pornography—and pornographic revisions of nonpornographic works—are now a good deal more acceptable than they are in the visual medium of film. Visual images are simply more potent, seductive, and "in your face" than verbal constructions—especially in the case of sexual representations.

One factor that may keep readers from appreciating Coover's revision is that its verbal description of Rick and Ilsa's lovemaking is so graphic that it could conceivably create an indelible *visual* impression in the reader's mind, making it impossible to ever have an "innocent" viewing of the film again. The issue here is that Coover's text not only is a parody of *Casablanca*, but also can be read as an actual script for an X-rated version of the film. It would be one thing if Coover had offered a behind-the-scenes peek at the real-life relationships of the actors and other personnel involved in the making of *Casablanca*, as a number of cinéastes have done; instead, he explores the hidden sex life of the film's *characters*, which is the stuff of fantasy.[16] Again, Coover would have given no grounds for offense if he had simply found artistic inspiration in the film and used it as an intertext for the creation of an "original" work of art, as Woody Allen did in *Play It Again, Sam*.[17] Instead, he inserted his own pornographic intertext into *Casablanca* itself, infecting it like a virus and undercutting its effect as an artistic work that mediates some profound meaning or that embodies some transcendent truth. Viewers who have been emotionally moved by the movie's love scene may feel unable to enjoy the film again after reading Coover's gross depiction of sexual intimacy.

Maybe such disillusionment is inevitable fifty years after the movie was made, and maybe it's not such a bad thing. As much as Coover subverts *Casablanca*'s ideal of romantic love, he also exposes the sexual reality of Rick and Ilsa's relationship, which the film industry was not prepared to show and movie audiences were presumably not prepared to see. Coover's piece makes us realize that this movie's romantic power, which accounts for much of its greatness as a cinematic icon, is achieved through a total blackout of this sexual reality.[18] Now that movies no longer need to hide visible evidence of sexuality, and even do whatever they can to reveal it, it's no wonder that so few great love stories in the tradition of *Casablanca* come out of Hollywood anymore.[19]

Pornography clearly belongs to an altogether different order of experience than that of romance. It is materialist and reductionist; as Steven Marcus observes, it is concerned with physiology, not psychology.[20] The truth that it obsessively seeks out is nontranscendent, immanent knowledge about (and in) the body. Ernest Becker has warned against attempts "to get metaphysical answers out of the body that the body—as a material thing—cannot possibly give." But while he argues that it is a mistake "to answer the transcendent mystery of creation by experiences in one, partial, physical product of that creation"—namely, the body—as a psychoanalytic philosopher, he would surely not recommend repression or exclusion of the body as a way to approach or represent that mystery.[21] And while pornotopias may be far removed from psychology and from what Marcus calls "external or social reality," they cannot be written off as pure fantasy.[22] For by screening out the world of social intercourse, pornography reveals a raw, hard-edged world of sexual intercourse, a hyperreal display of bodies that is glossed over in the daily exchanges of everyday life. Both the pornographic and the nonpornographic orders, it seems, have their respective blind spots—realms of experience that each is unable to represent and from which each averts its gaze.

The mutual exclusivity of the pornographic and the nonpornographic orders of representation, of the obscene and the on-scene, is more obvious in the primarily visual medium of film than in the verbal medium of literature. Whatever anatomical or physiological gain there might be in a hard-core remake of a cinematic classic (we see many more "love" scenes, and much more *in* the love scenes, than we do in the original) can hardly make up for the loss of the artistic and psychological effects conveyed through dialogue, narrative complexity, and emotional depth, not to mention the nuances of the actors' performances themselves. Given Marcus's characterization of pornography as an escapist mode of representation that flouts social and historical reality, nothing would seem to be more preposterous than the idea of a pornographic remake of *Casablanca*. This is a film, after all, in which the principal characters are torn between a private world of erotic love and a public world of historical events, and in which personal desires are ultimately sacrificed to a greater, public cause. There would seem to be no place here for the hyperreal pornotopia of hard-core film. *Casablanca* poses a formidable challenge to the aspiring pornographer.

How, then, does Coover rise to the occasion? Instead of producing a pornographic adaptation that presents itself as a travesty of the original film, he offers a literary interpolation of a particular scene that is *missing* from the film. It is as if Coover happened upon a trove of forgotten outtakes of *Casablanca* among which he "discovered" the missing love scene, much as the photographer in Antonioni's *Blow-Up* discovers a missing murder scene.[23] An even closer cinematic parallel is Preston Sturges's *Miracle of Morgan's Creek*; as Slavoj Žižek has observed, this movie "is organized around a hole, a central absence (what happened during the night when Betty Hutton went to the farewell party for the soldiers?)." In Žižek's view, the film's "dénouement (the birth of sextuplets) clearly suggests a group orgy ('gang bang') with six men who were her companions that fateful night." What Žižek calls the "eclipse during the fateful night (from the moment Betty Hutton hits her head on the heavy lights, till the time early next morning when she wakes up in the car on her way back to her home town)" invites comparison with the ellipsis following the scene in Heinrich von Kleist's 1808 story "Die Marquise von O——," in which the marquise swoons in the count's arms during the attack on her palace.[24] As the story progresses, the reader and, eventually, the pregnant marquise are provided with information that enables them to fill in the canceled scene: the count's rape of the unconscious woman.

Actually, the typographic figure that conceals the marquise's rape is not an ellipsis but a dash, a *Gedankenstrich*, or a "thought stricken" from the record. The cinematic equivalent of the literary figure of the dash would seem to be the fade-out—as, indeed, it is Eric Rohmer's 1976 adaptation of Kleist's story.[25] In its physical sexuality, the love scene in *Casablanca* is as unrepresentable as the rape scene in "The Marquise von O——." But while the dash—which Dorrit Cohn has called the the "most pregnant graphic sign in German literature"[26]—is able to signify the marquise's rape in Kleist's story (not to mention her own surname, "von O——"), even if only by striking it from the text, the fade-out in *Casablanca* is a nonsign that conceals the love scene without signifying it. A more precise equivalent of the literary (actually, the visual) figure of the dash in *Casablanca* is a verbal sign in the film that reveals as well as conceals the missing love scene—namely, as the title of Coover's piece suggests, the banal demonstrative in the line "You must remember *this*."

By pointing up the full ambiguity of the word *this*, and by suggesting its relation to the vague notion of "fundamental things" in the song "As Time Goes By," Coover calls attention to the missing love scene's problematic relation to the visible film.[27]

The subliminal (or desublimated) sex scenes in *Casablanca* and "The Marquise von O——" invite consideration as adult reenactments of the original act of repression: the child's "forgetting" of the primal scene of its parents' lovemaking. As theorized by Freud (who was probably familiar with Kleist's story), this early experience instills castration anxiety in the (male) child based on fantasies of identification with and possession of the mother.[28] In cases where a "normal" resolution of the Oedipal complex does not occur (involving renunciation of the mother and identification with the father), the threat of castration continues to haunt the child in later life, albeit in a repressed form. The analyst's task is to make the patient aware of the missing traumatic scene in his past so that it can be incorporated as part of the patient's conscious experience.[29] But as the analyst helps the patient to reconstruct the primal scene—saying words to the effect of "You must remember this"—the patient is bound to wonder whether he or she actually witnessed such a scene. Freud himself failed to resolve this issue and wavered between considering the primal scene as an actual event or as a fantasy; ultimately, he treated it as a *primal* fantasy of indeterminate ontological status. Whatever it was, it was a "fundamental thing."[30]

For Kleist's marquise, the problem is technically not to remember a primal scene (parental lovemaking) but to recall what Freud called a "seduction" scene—the episode of her rape. Although she realizes that she has been molested, she is unable to accept the fact that her assailant was the noble count (she had agreed to marry him before she learned what he had done). "'Go away! go away! go away!'" she tells him after he reveals himself to be the culprit. "I was prepared to meet a vicious man, but not—not a devil!"[31] The marquise becomes reconciled to the count only when, after a year of irreproachable behavior, he again appears to her as the angel he first seemed when he saved her from his own marauding troops, who were themselves about to rape her. In the final lines of the story, the marquise acknowledges to her husband that "she would not have seen a devil in him" when he revealed himself to be the father of her child "if she had not seen an angel in him at their first meeting"—that is, just before she fainted in his arms and he took advantage of her.[32]

Much as the marquise refuses to accept the reality of the rape scene and the duplicity of the man whom she believed to be her savior, Coover's more staid readers will resist his explicit, but quite plausible, scenario of what took place in Rick's apartment after the fade-out in

Casablanca. Viewers accustomed to intimate, softly lit scenes of romantic tenderness in films of the 1940s are bound to reject Coover's hardcore depiction of eager lovers coupling and recoupling under glaring lights. Yet the movie's disavowal of the sexual reality of the lovers' relationship evades the fundamental questions raised by Coover's revision: what is the relation between the romantic, patriotic scenario portrayed in the film and the pornographic scene described in the text? Which is more real and which is more of a fantasy? Which is history and which is hysteria?

Within *Casablanca,* the missing love (or sex) scene is an unrepresented and, indeed, unrepresentable event. A hard-core remake can be expected to focus on this scene, and in doing so, to turn the original film's erotic-political, romantic-patriotic theme into a pornotopian fantasy. Coover's remake doesn't exactly do this; instead, it presents a pornographic portrayal of the love scene as an *alternative* reality to— and even a *truer* reality than—the "external or social reality" shown in the film. The uncanny quality of Coover's takeoff stems from the fact that his "love" scene cannot simply be dismissed as a pornotopian fantasy or critically neutralized as parody; it may be incommensurable with the world of the original film (which is itself, of course, an artistic fiction), but it is also inseparable from that world, and it is even more objectively "real" than that world in the sense that anatomy and physiology deal with more tangible and tactile phenomena than psychology or political science. If Coover's pornographic parody ruins the experience of seeing *Casablanca* for some viewers, it's because that experience was itself a fantasy. The point of Coover's rewrite is precisely *not* to see *Casablanca* the same way again, but to remember its missing scene, just as one will no longer be able to hear the song "As Time Goes By" without registering its destabilizing double entendres, whether or not they were intended as such. After reading Coover's text, viewers of the film *should* no longer be sure whether an explicit scene of orgiastic sex actually takes place in the film or not.

It's absurd to credit or blame Coover for this uncertainty. His (per)version of *Casablanca* is neither an innocent parody nor prurient pornography, but a seriously playful investigation of the relation between fantasy and reality that points up pornography's borderline condition as a fantasy of the real. Coover explores the curious phenomenon we occasionally experience when, with or without the director's prompting, we imagine we "see" incidents in films (especially allusive films such as *Casablanca*) that are not there,[33] or fail to notice shots that *are* there.[34] Such illusions are not merely a matter of special effects; they are rather a "general effect" produced by the combination of the cinematic apparatus itself (the "flicker" effect) and the perceptual, psychological and psychoanalytic operations (the persistence of vision, the *fort/da* game) that enable the viewer/infant to "see" images/objects even in their absence.[35]

In his 1991 novel *Flicker*, described as "a secret history of the movies," Theodore Roszak uncovers a Manichaean conflict in film technology, which he traces back to the medium's origins. The narrator, Jonathan Gates, is a film scholar writing a thesis on the work of an underground German director named Max Castle. During his research, Gates discovers that many of the eerie effects in Castle's films are the result of certain subliminal techniques known as *das Unenthüllte*, "the unconcealed," which make it possible to manipulate the reactions of movie audiences without their knowledge. In association with "the Orphans," a Manichaean religious sect in Germany that infiltrated the Hollywood film industry in the 1920s, Castle exploited the basic cinematic phenomenon of the "flicker"—the alternating play of light and darkness that creates the illusion of the continuously moving image in film projection.

> The man drew upon an ancient tradition, the art of light and shadow used to teach the war of the two gods. The flicker *was* that war. Twenty-four times a second, as the frames of the film raced by—click, click, click—it pounded its way insidiously through the bedazzled eye into the unguarded depths of the mind.
>
> Light against Dark. Flesh against Spirit. The Good God, the Evil God locked in combat. Watching movies was a way of being surreptitiously catechized.[36]

Castle, Gates learns, had succeeded in transforming the "light against dark" mechanism of film into a subliminal drama of "flesh against spirit" by incorporating a subtext of hidden sexual scenes into his movies. "It's a pity you had to spend your career hiding things," Gates tells Castle, whom he unexpectedly meets toward the end of the novel. "Don't you wish you might've simply said what you had to say, shown what you had to show?" To which Castle exclaims, "Never! The art of it all is in the hiding. Don't you know by now? One works always under the surface. That's the only way you get inside their minds: when they don't see you coming" (569).

We could regard the real-life author Coover as revealing the reality effect—in this case, the dark, sexual subtext—in the luminous romantic screenplays of classic films that the fictional director Castle takes such pains to conceal. Indeed, in his younger days, before he incorporated subliminal pornographic images into his own films, Castle worked as a technical assistant with his fellow Orphans on other directors' films. If the Orphans succeeded in leaving their dark subliminal traces (as Gates discovers they did) in such an innocuous shot as the staircase scene in the Shirley Temple movie *The Littlest Rebel*, we can easily imagine them introducing a subliminal sequence of pornographic images into the exemplary Manichaean shot in *Casablanca* of the beam from the airport beacon sweeping across the darkness. As far as we know, of course, *Casablanca* was never doctored by Castle or anyone else. No subliminal pornographic scenes were incorporated into the film. Yet Coover's version of the famous love scene gives the impression that he happened to discover a sexual subtext in the film that its producers had either suppressed or repressed, or in any case left unexpressed.

The uncertain relations between pornographic and nonpornographic discourse, and between fantasy and reality, become especially perplexing at the end of "You Must Remember This." Unlike the "world of plenty" of conventional pornography, in which, according to Marcus, "all men are infinitely rich in substance" and "are limitlessly endowed with that universal fluid currency which can be spent without loss," Rick and Ilsa are shown to be quite spent.[37] Coover shows them coming back to reality—something conventional pornography, with its denial of postcoital existence, cannot show. The party's over, and as Rick says, "We gotta get back into the goddamn world somehow." He'd like, if not to forget this final fling with Ilsa, at least to put it behind them. Determining that "we gotta think ahead," he suggests that Ilsa pull herself together and tell him "that story you've been wanting to tell ... A good story, that may do it—anything that *moves!*" Repeatedly Rick insists that Ilsa get on with the nonsexual narrative that will release them from the hyperreal pornotopia in which they've cut themselves off from the world. Needless to say, the narrative that enables them to do this is the film *Casablanca*, or rather its resumption after their sexual break. The final line in Coover's piece is Rick's urgent prompt, "And then ... ? Ilsa ... ? And *then*?" (187), which are, of course, the first words we hear Bogart say in the film after the elided love scene. The point at which the unseen pornographic world described in Coover's fiction dissolves back into the visible world of the film finds the lovers making up stories designed to cover up their sexual tracks and to prepare them for their "real-world" sociopolitical dealings with Victor Laszlo, Captain Renault, Major Strasser, and everyone else with whom they'll have to come to terms by telling the appropriate tales. (Part of the legend surrounding the making of *Casablanca* is that substantial portions of the script were written on the spot while the film was in progress.) Once the lovers inscribe or narrate themselves back into the film's story line, their night together will seem unreal—"like a dream come true," Ilsa says (186). As for Coover's readers, whenever they hear the cue "You must remember this," they will be reminded of that *other* world, the hyperreal/pornotopian scene that resists being integrated into the world of the filmic story.

Coover's act of retelling the story of *Casablanca* from the other side—describing in pornographic detail a scene that may be imagined as having been cut from, concealed in, or alluded to by the film—requires him to suppress, but not altogether eliminate, the material in the film's familiar, nonpornographic version. The well-known thematic conflict in the film between "love and glory," erotics and politics, self-gratification and sacrifice, masks a far deeper conflict at the structural level that cannot be brought to light. This conflict takes the form of a primal antagonism between the on-scene and the obscene, between the representable romantic order and the unrepresentable pornographic order. At once mutually exclusive and thoroughly interdependent, the romantic and pornographic modes must find a way to accommodate their respective blind spots; each world must find a way of interacting with its counterpart, which cannot be represented alongside it.

At some point in the romanticized world of the movie, the lovers (and, by extension, the viewers) are confronted with the conundrum implicit in the line "You must remember this": how to recollect a repressed, quasi-hypnotic memory of an intense sexual experience—first the memory of the affair in Paris, then the memory of the night in Casablanca. Conversely, at some point in the sexual frenzy portrayed by Coover the lovers must deal with the conundrum implicit in Rick's query "And *then*?": how are the reunited lovers going to make the transition from their private pornotopia back to the public domain?[38] For all its hyperrealism, porn is a graphic rather than real experience. The ultimate or absolute reality that the porn junkie believes he or she has entered is "in fact" a realm of the senses, but more accurately, it is a tyranny of the visual where sight reigns over all the other senses including that of touch. Should one happen to become addicted to the secret pleasures of this purely graphic, media-driven world, the question becomes how to get back to the alternating struggle and ennui of mundane existence, or even to recognize the possibility—let alone the necessity—*of* getting back. Rick and Ilsa cannot occupy both worlds at the same time, and Coover's reader is left wondering which world they inhabit, which world is "real." Unable to represent both worlds in the same work, the 1940s Hollywood moviemaker and the 1980s literary pornographer complement one another, each expressing what must remain missing in the other's text.

Intrusive Scenes: Scorsese's Marriage Manual

Another scene from a film, this time an explicit scene that *is* seen by the viewer:

The down-and-out New York City cabby Travis Bickle (played by Robert De Niro) in Martin Scorsese's *Taxi Driver* succeeds in getting a fashionable woman named Betsy (Cybill Shepherd) to agree to go out with him on a date. Travis takes Betsy to see a movie, but the only movies he ever goes to are the porn flicks on Forty-second Street. Betsy can't believe Travis intends to take her to see a "dirty movie," but Travis assures her that "this is a movie that a lot of couples come to.... All kinds of couples go here." They enter the theater in the middle of *Swedish Marriage Manual*, a hard-core film that passes itself off as a scientific documentary about the latest research in the field of adult sexuality. In the segment of this film-within-the-film, a narrator recites terms in Swedish while various bits of laboratory footage are shown: microscopic shots of an egg and sperm cells, and an obscure X-ray glimpse of genitals during intercourse above the subtitle "Phallus." After these "scientific" images, the camera cuts to a scene of an all-out orgy, while the narrator absurdly continues to announce (as indicated by the English subtitles) that "before the Masters and Johnson studies in America, Swedish research had laid the groundwork." It's at this point that Betsy abruptly gets up and exits the theater, followed by a bewildered Travis. Outside, she bluntly tells him that "taking me to see a picture like that is about as romantic as saying 'Let's fuck.'" Clearly at a loss for words, Travis mumbles an apology and offers to take her to other movies. But Betsy has had enough and hails a cab, leaving Travis behind with a group of prostitutes under the bright marquee.

It's noteworthy that Betsy leaves the theater only when the orgy scene appears on the screen. The sight of naked bodies lolling around on a bed is too much for her, but she doesn't seem at all fazed by the technical photography or by the X-ray close-up of the enlarged male organ probing the vaginal cavity. This shot isn't disturbing, first because it's initially unrecognizable, and second because it's presented as part of the dubious scientific pretext of *Swedish Marriage Manual*. We expect X-ray pictures to yield knowledge about invisible regions of the body. Similarly, we expect an educational documentary about human reproduction to present X-ray images and microcinematography of ovulation, fertilization, and gestation—everything *but* the act of penetration, which, as in the classic Hollywood movie, exists as a kind of missing scene. In short, *we expect science to stop short of where porn begins*.

In fact, nothing could be further from the truth. As Evelyn Fox Keller has argued, scientific observation is intrinsically intrusive, and nowhere is this more evident than in its investigations into "the mysteries of embryogenesis—of reproduction and development."[39] Modern techniques in genetic research, writes Keller, "have revolutionized the study of embryology. They have made it possible—in ways that would have been utterly unimaginable to the great embryologists of even the recent past—directly to observe the generation of life, as it were, *in flagrante delicto*."[40] Pornography is scientific observation taken to the extreme: photographs of coitus—especially those that enhance the reality effect through close-up or enlarged shots that reveal internal activity invisible to the naked eye—record what is in effect the earliest phase of embryological development.

While *Taxi Driver* calls attention to the distinction between an "art film" such as itself and an "adult film" such as *Swedish Marriage Manual*, the latter film promotes the notion of a barrier between science and pornography, which it immediately proceeds to transgress. Juxtaposed with microscopic footage of sperm and egg cells, the X-ray shot of male and female genitals during coitus at first seems to provide an illuminating glimpse of a natural process that otherwise can't be seen. In this unusual, clinical image, penis and vagina are unfamiliar entities; one doesn't at first know what they are. They aren't real but virtual objects, like the homunculi that seventeenth-century investigators imagined they saw when they looked at human sperm cells under microscopes. Those early microscopes—as well as their modern counterparts—often "made visible the invisible rather than the subvisible."[41] In contrast to the X-ray shot in *Swedish Marriage Manual*, there can be no mistaking the X-rated reality of those writhing bodies on the bed. The film's scientific pretext gives way before its actual pornographic subject. No microscopes, X-ray machines, or other ocular prostheses are needed to make the orgy scene larger or clearer. The image is all too visible; it is "in your face."

Betsy leaves the theater at the precise instant that she is forced to recognize the images before her as pornography. She leaves at the moment that she can no longer relate these images to the film's pseudo-scientific code, even if the voice-over narration assures her that "Swedish research" is in the forefront of scientific studies of sexuality. In fact, she has been viewing pornography all the time, even when—especially when—she thought she was "seeing science." According to conventional definitions of pornography (e.g., "the representation, without aesthetic or sociological justification, of sexual acts *with an intrusive vividness*"), the X-ray shot of genitals during intercourse is the most glaringly graphic scene in the film.[42] Yet this shot isn't recognized as pornography, either by Betsy or by viewers of *Taxi Driver*, because of the "sociological justification" it receives by being presented in the guise of science. Baudrillard may be right that the "sham vision" of pornography "reveal[s] the inexorable, microscopic truth of sex," but the use of technological special effects to produce the "real" pornographic image gives it a distorted, virtual, *unheimlich* appearance that may prevent it from being identifiable as such.[43] If missing love scenes such as the fade-out in *Casablanca* are a matter of repression, intrusive sexual scenes such as the X-ray shot in *Swedish Marriage Manual* are a matter of (mis)recognition. Betsy is able to sit through the in-your-face close-up of the phallus, which she can't immediately identify, while she is unable to endure the recognizable medium shot of the orgy.

In Betsy's misrecognition of the close-up image of the copulating genitals in *Swedish Marriage Manual*, viewers of *Taxi Driver* are themselves able to "recognize," as Linda Williams puts it, "how thoroughly scientism and prurience interpenetrate"—that is to say, how completely the scientific truth quest and pornographic fantasy converge.[44] Scorsese's decision to use shots from *Swedish Marriage Manual* in *Taxi Driver* is noteworthy because this particular pornographic film exemplifies those very "clinical documentary qualities" that the genre of visual pornography "has consistently maintained ... at the expense of other forms of realism or artistry that might actually be more arousing."[45] But Betsy's misrecognition of the image of the phallus in *Swedish Marriage Manual* is more than just a matter of her being momentarily duped by the pornographer's ploy of disguising titillating or offensive hard-core sex scenes as clinical documentary information. She doesn't so much tolerate the phallic image as she seems to take a genuine interest in it. This interest stems from its *pre*symbolic status, which prevents her from recognizing it as *anything*—either as penis or as phallus. In Lacanian lingo, both the character Betsy *in Taxi Driver*, who watches *Swedish Marriage Manual*, and the viewer *of Taxi Driver*, who watches Betsy watching the porn film, are not immediately able to recognize the paternal phallus as a symbolic image because they are confronted with a psychotic, hallucinatory glimpse of the "real," the absent/invisible maternal phallus, the penis re-incorporated in the mother's body. For Betsy, the shot of the X-rayed penis corresponds to the visual hallucination of the psychotic, who has not merely repressed the primal scene and the traumatic threat of castration it poses, but who has altogether refused or "foreclosed" this experience.[46] Only the signifiers provided by the voice-over narration (the "Phallus" subtitle that accompanies the unfamiliar image) and the shockingly familiar orgy scene eventually enable Betsy to situate the incomprehensible "real" in a symbolic, scientific context, where it becomes recognizable as pornography. For in this supposedly most realistic of genres, things are not what they appear. The penis in pornography is never just a penis; rather, this "always-big"

organ represents—or is fetishized—as the phallus, "a mythic, symbolic
... fetishistic image" that "signifies the process of transformation
whereby something invisible becomes visible in the fetish."[47] The
pornographic is not reality itself, but a fantasy of the real at the verge of
symbolization, in its very submission/resistance to representation. As
such, the pornographic is what all the sciences as symbolizing/revela-
tory activities simultaneously present and disavow.

While some feminist film theorists have called for an end to the
phallocentric order, which is most visibly exposed in conventional
pornography, other feminists have envisioned an alternative form of
hard-core in which

> the woman's gaze at pornographic films, "disgusted and fascinated,"
> doesn't have to search for and find a phallus behind every penis....
> It may still be possible for women, in spite of their criticism, to take a
> utopian view of pornotopia. This may come to pass if they are able to
> recognise that utopian plenitude is not to be found in a phallocentric
> generalisation, but rather in the details of a quivering world of objects;
> and if, with their gaze, they manage to create, out of the shadow world,
> bodies of flesh and blood.[48]

In *Taxi Driver*, Betsy may experience a glimpse of such a presymbolic
pornotopia in the X-ray shot of the copulating genitals in *Swedish
Marriage Manual*. The scientific strangeness of this "quivering world of
objects" is able to hold her interest until, with the cut to the orgy shot,
she is repulsed by her recognition of one quivering object in particular
as the banal penis/familiar phallus.

The contradictory impulses of the scientific will to knowledge are
themselves made visible in *Taxi Driver*'s quasi-psychotic glimpse of the
real in its film-within-a-film segment. On the one hand, high-tech
gimmickry discloses an uncanny, unrecognizable image of the "thing
itself," the invaginated penis, the penis reincorporated in the mother's
body; on the other hand, the combination of male-voiced narrator and
written subtitle, both signifying the phallus, circumscribe the real and
incorporate it within the symbolic order of language and the law. As
the primal signifier that supposedly designates sexual identity and
difference, that signifies female orgasm, and that originates the entire
symbolic-scientific order, the phallus itself can appear only as a
psychotic object that is real but unrecognizable or as a pornographic
object that is recognizable but not real.

If the viewer's experience of the missing scene in *Casablanca* approx-
imates the neurotic's defensive repression of a traumatic sexual event,
the in-your-face scene in *Taxi Driver* takes the viewer to the brink of

psychosis. An extensive analysis of *Taxi Driver* would show how Travis Bickle's slide into dementia after being rejected by Betsy, and his eventual bloody outburst at the end of the film, illustrate the psychotic's failure (or refusal) to symbolize castration and to submit to paternal law as a way of allaying primal fear. A traumatized victim of the Vietnam War, Bickle no longer recognizes any law, and lives his fear as the real. His habitual viewings of pornographic movies are a primitive form of social science: a pathetic, rudimentary, and borderline psychotic—*but also acutely accurate, hyperanalytical, and overly objective*—way of learning about people and how they interact. In his solitary moviegoing, his obsessive quest to purify New York City of its "filth," his Oedipal assassination attempt against the paternal politician to whom Betsy is devoted, and his violent raid on the Mafia-run tenement (when the camera tracks him, with his head shaven, entering the building and jerkily working his bloody way up the stairs, much as the Swedish sexologists' camera tracked the penis in its travail), we see Bickle in the self-contradictory condition of the scientist/pornographer, seeking empirical knowledge that cannot be reconciled with abstract law, and ultimately achieving apotheosis as the phallic embodiment of his own (t)ruthless will.

Freezing the Scene: Pynchon's Prehistory of Film

They'd had to confront the terror of the irrational, this everlasting slit in the divinity of whole numbers. Subdivide the continuous motion of a point. No common measure this side of madness.

—Don DeLillo, *Ratner's Star*

Film has the dubious distinction of being the pornographic medium par excellence. But the fact that it is, in Stanley Cavell's words, "inherently pornographic"[49] owes less to the widespread use it has eventually acquired as a representational medium in the arts and entertainment than to its original use in the sciences, where, as a recording medium, it provided essential documentation in medicine and other fields.[50] "As a scientific tool," writes James Monaco,

> cinematography has had great significance, not only because it allows us to analyze a large range of time phenomena, but also as an objective record of reality. The sciences of anthropology, ethnography, psychology, sociology, natural studies, zoology—even botany—have been revolutionized by the invention of cinematography.[51]

It's worth noting that the first publicly exhibited film, the Lumière brothers' 1895 documentary of workers leaving a factory, was screened in the same year that the German physicist Wilhelm Roentgen discovered X rays.[52] The discovery of invisible radiation that made it possible to view the body's interior with X-ray vision was only the latest demonstration, following the invention of the telescope and the microscope, that there were many more potentially visible phenomena in the world than what could be discerned by the naked eye, and that those hidden realms would be made visible only with the help of new instruments designed to extend the senses.

It is not simply film's documentary capabilities that make it such an ideal medium both in pornography and the sciences, but the fact that, in Monaco's words, "it allows us to analyze a large range of time phenomena."[53] The basic cinematic principle of ocular fusion, whereby the eye is deceived into perceiving an illusion of continuous movement out of a sequence of static images (or digital video's extension of this principle to produce the illusion of movement out of sequences of bytes and pixels), is a simple reversal of film's grandest illusion of all: its fulfillment of the scientific impulse to arrest natural movement, to freeze it as still life or dead nature (*nature morte*) so that it can be exhaustively studied and systematically manipulated.

In her study of hard-core film, Linda Williams "emphasize[s] the specific cinematic nature of [an] emerging *scientia sexualis*," tracing the origin of pornographic films back to the invention of cinema itself (and vice versa). Referring to the photographic motion studies of Eadweard Muybridge, Williams notes that cinema was invented out of a "desire to see and know more of the human body." True, Muybridge was hired in 1873 by former California governor Leland Stanford to record the body movements, not of human beings, but of one of his prize trotting horses. (Stanford wanted to settle a wager about whether all four feet of the horse leave the ground at the same time during a fast trot.) But, as Williams claims, "it is but a short leap from the 'academic question' of body movement mechanics to the 'pornographic answer,' wherein the elusive and prurient 'truth' is located in increasingly more detailed investigations of the bodies of women."[54] Reflecting on the prehistory of film, Williams concludes that the pleasure accompanying cinematic knowledge is not simply a genderless pleasure in the simulation of genderless movement. Her observation that "Muybridge's first audiences came simply to learn the new truths of bodily motion" but "stayed to see more because this new knowledge was also infused with an unsuspected visual pleasure" (39) leads her to consider the proto-pornographic situation of predominantly male audiences deriving knowledge and pleasure from images of female bodies in motion. The general quest for knowledge about the body inevitably took the specific form of subjective masculine fantasies about the objectified female body.[55] In the earliest years of cinematic history, Williams claims, the scientific impulse was already indistinguishable from a voyeuristic, pornographic impulse. "[W]hat began as the scientific impulse to record the 'truth' of the body quickly became a powerful fantasy that drove cinema's first rudimentary achievements of narrative diegesis and mise-en-scène" (41).

While Williams makes a persuasive point in claiming that cinema was born out of a voyeuristic/scientific "desire to see and know more of the human body" (36), her insistence that it was a predominantly male desire to see and know more of the *female* body is somewhat misleading. Perhaps the most striking example of the voyeuristic impulse behind film as a scientific, documentary medium has been its use in tracking and studying the trajectory of that most phallic extension of the *male* body, the rocket. In *Gravity's Rainbow*, Thomas Pynchon's novel about the German rocket industry at the end of World War II, the narrator remarks,

> There has been this strange connection between the German mind and the rapid flashing of successive stills to counterfeit movement, for at least two centuries—since Leibniz, in the process of inventing calculus, used the same approach to break up the trajectories of cannonballs through the air.[56]

This "strange connection" is developed 150 pages later in reference to "the stairstep gables that front so many of these ancient north-German buildings":

> They hold shape, they endure, like monuments to Analysis. Three hundred years ago mathematicians were learning to break the cannonball's rise and fall into stairsteps of range and height, Δ x and Δ y, allowing them to grow smaller and smaller, approaching zero as armies of eternally shrinking midgets galloped upstairs and down again, the patter of their diminishing feet growing finer, smoothing out into continuous sound. This analytic legacy has been handed down intact—it brought the technicians at Peenemünde to peer at the Askania films of Rocket flights, frame by frame, Δ x by Δ y, flightless themselves ... film and calculus, both pornographies of flight. Reminders of impotence and abstraction, the stone Treppengiebel shapes, whole and shattered, appear now over the green plains, and last a while, and go away. (567)

The analytic impulse common to film and rocket technology is here made evident: the impulse to square the circle, to break up the continuous curve of the movement of flight into ever smaller segments, slowing down motion and ultimately freezing it altogether for the purpose of studying, understanding, and exploiting it.[57]

Pynchon's reference to calculus opens up an important historical perspective on the twentieth-century technologies of film and rocketry. Discovered independently in the seventeenth century by Leibniz and Newton, calculus was one of the major achievements of the scientific revolution. This revolution itself was made possible by an optical epistemology whereby knowledge came to be identified with representations inside the mind, like the optical images in the eye or the visual images in a camera.[58] The power dynamics of such an epistemology inform eighteenth-century novels in which the mind of the knowing subject is portrayed as a container of representational knowledge, as an "epistemological prison" cut off from external reality.[59] By the end of the eighteenth century, the entire world was metaphorically conceived as a kind of prison of the sort suggested by Foucault in his analysis of Bentham's panopticon: the knowing subject withdraws to a position of power at the structure's very center from which it is able to survey in a sweeping glance all the concentric tiers of inmates/objects. A similar technology was employed a half century later in 1834 with the Zoetrope, the precursor of the motion picture projector, in which a succession of images is viewed through a series of slots on a rotating circular screen, producing the illusion of continuous movement.

Beyond Williams's insight into the century-old affiliation between film and pornography, the intertwined technologies of film and rocketry are the fruit of a succession of scientific and philosophical insights that date back at least three centuries. The scientific origins of these technologies are traceable to Newton's pioneering work in calculus and optics; their philosophical origins stem from Locke's optical epistemology. From the start, as evidenced by the early photographic motion studies of Muybridge, and even more so by the chronophotography of Étienne-Jules Marey, cinematic technology was a visual calculus, or a calculus of the visible.[60] On one hand, a sufficiently rapid sequence of separate, static images (twenty-four frames per second) could be used to simulate the reality of continuous movement; on the other hand, the reality of continuous movement could be arrested for purposes of analysis and control.[61] In Pynchon's formulation, the laws of motion were discovered by arresting motion through the scientific inventions of "film and calculus, both pornographies of flight" that are commemorated in those architectural "monuments to Analysis," the Nordic *Treppengiebel*.

Beneficiaries of the heritage that linked truth to visibility and knowledge to optics, the German scientists portrayed in *Gravity's Rainbow* studied films of rocket flights the way Swedish sexologists were later to study the physiology of intercourse—reversing the capability of film to transform static images into movement so that motion could be slowed down and ultimately frozen.[62] As the successive technologies of X-ray, infrared, and fiber-optic photography allowed a greater number of invisible bodies and body parts to be seen, film's capacity to slow down (or, in the case of time-lapse photography, to speed up) time enabled viewers to see processes that couldn't be seen under normal conditions. It remains a question, however, whether the analytic act of reducing the moving picture to the static frame, the slowing down and condensation of narrative to the static scene, produces real power and knowledge, or whether such distortion of time and movement results rather in the "impotence and abstraction" suspected by Pynchon—the illusion of power and knowledge, and indeed, their very opposite.

Your Car's Mind

A film of automobile accidents devised as a cinematic version of Nader's *Unsafe at Any Speed*. By chance it was found that slow-motion sequences of this film had a marked sedative effect, reducing blood pressure, respiration and pulse rates. Hypnagogic images were produced freely by patients. The film was also found to have a marked erotic content.

—J. G. Ballard, *The Atrocity Exhibition*

He felt like somebody had taken the lid off life and let him look at the works.

—Sam Spade, in Dashiell Hammett's *The Maltese Falcon*

By slowing down events that are both momentous and momentary, film makes it possible to give scientific sense to otherwise senseless, tragic events. A cinematic record transforms a sudden, violent, or traumatic event into an object of scientific analysis; it gives the investigator a handle on the incomprehensible, a way of rationalizing tragedy. Even when it is not someone else's past trauma that we experience vicariously on film but something that is happening *now*, to ourselves, in real life, the distancing, conceptualizing techniques of cinema abruptly kick in. We may experience moments of extreme danger as a quasi-cinematic spectacle in which time seems to slow down and our whole life seems to pass before our eyes. Under such slow-motion conditions, a meaningful pattern may begin to appear; we may come to understand what was right and what was wrong about our approach to life, what was important and what didn't matter. But is such a mystical experience real or a cinematic convention that we replay in our minds if we're lucky enough to avoid or survive the threat to our existence? It's really only possible to review life with the critical detachment of the viewer of a film when we're no longer in immediate danger or when it's not our own life that's at risk.

In a 1993 Mercedes commercial, a driver is shown swerving to avoid an object on a rainy road at night. He loses control of his car and braces himself in preparation for a head-on collision. Time seems to slow down, as the words "Your life flashes through your mind" appear on the TV screen. A series of luminous images follows: the face of a young woman (presumably the driver's mother years ago), a boy flying a kite, a bride, a father playing with a child, the face of another young woman (presumably the driver's wife). Then, as the car can be heard screeching into a skid, another message appears—"Fortunately it also flashes through your car's mind"—followed by a second series of images, this time close-up shots in such rapid sequence that they are scarcely recognizable: a computer circuit board, a depressed brake pedal and an antilock brake system springing into action, another printed circuit and an air bag deployed, an overexposed shot of a little girl with outstretched arms running toward the camera. In the next scene, the driver is shown shaken but unhurt, taking a deep breath after the car has come to a stop and the danger is past. With ambulance sirens wailing in the distance, someone off camera asks, "Are you all right?" and the dazed driver can be heard saying "Yuh" as a final message appears on the screen: "Mercedes-Benz has more advanced safety systems than any luxury car line."

In this commercial, both man and machine are shown not only reacting to events with their "reflexes," but as thinking beings with a "memory." While the driver's slower reflexes leave him helpless, recalling emotionally charged peak experiences in his past, the car's rapid response system, coupled with its advanced computer memory, enables it to focus with "single-minded" intensity on the present emergency and to perform complex data-processing and multitasking functions in a no-nonsense manner. The driver's memory is portrayed in the commercial as a Lockean series of analog representations or *scenes* that render him passive and powerless; the car's memory, in contrast, is presented as an information-processing *apparatus*, a cybernetic (steering) mechanism. The situation of the driver is analogous to that of the viewer of a film (or the viewer of the TV commercial) who is completely at the mercy of machines (the car and the cinematic/television apparatus; the automotive and the advertising industries). Like Odysseus, who has himself bound to the mast so that he can listen to the Sirens' deadly song while his earplug-equipped crew devotes all its energy and attention to rowing the vessel past the treacherous shore, the driver passively witnesses a succession of soft-focus images while the machinery in his vehicle does all the work.[63] The dependence of man on machine is total; man merely looks on and feels while the machine acts.

The series of memory images that passes through the driver's mind in the commercial is depicted in a wistful haze, as an ephemeral succession of fantasies about to be forever shattered by the violent reality of the collision. In contrast, the second series of images depicts the dazzling display of technology flashing through the car's "mind." This sequence is far faster than the first series, with the individual shots consisting either of extreme close-ups of machinery or of highly magnified glimpses of computer circuits. These images of state-of-the-art technology are barely recognizable, like the X-ray close-up of mechanically copulating genitals in *Swedish Marriage Manual*. They appear as a graphic display of "greased lightning" seen not by the endangered driver but by the target viewer/consumer the commercial is designed to affect/ seduce. This thirty-second spot advertises advanced automotive technology by celebrating the advertising medium of film itself, showing off its own special effects in the act of showcasing the car's safety features, and thereby suggesting the hidden but essential connection between cars and movies as parallel technologies. This is less a case of a filmed commercial being used to sell cars than it is an instance of technology marketing and promoting *itself*.

The commercial is an effective presentation of the safety features of Mercedes-Benz automobiles, but it is also an exercise in bad faith. While it portrays a man in crisis experiencing a slowed-down, soft-core sequence of peak moments of life, it dazzles the viewer with a special-effects glimpse of the hard-and-fast, lifelike images of cybertechnology— an awe-inspiring sight that is clearly where the real action is. In fact, the technology behind cinema, which caused it to be developed in the first place in the motion studies of Muybridge and Marey, entails its ability *to slow and ultimately to stop movement*. By enabling observers to stop and study movement too rapid to be seen by the unaided eye, cinematography eventually made it possible to develop new technologies to make things go even faster—things such as antilock brakes, for example, that stop the speeding car by operating even more swiftly than it does, or things such as air bags, that "life-saving feature of automobiles," as James Gleick describes it, which "were conceived and designed only when it became possible to visualize complex mechanical sagas happening— beginning, middle and end—in one-tenth of a second. The creators of air bags were carrying on in the trail blazed by Muybridge and [high-speed photographer Harold] Edgerton."[64] Before the advanced, ultrafast safety technologies celebrated in the Mercedes commercial (on fast film, no less) could be devised, film had to make time appear to slow down in much the way as it is shown slowing down for the desperate driver.

Through its potential to maximize the visible by slowing down, freezing, and in effect, representing time, film exemplifies the scientific will to knowledge.[65] Not only is the cinematographic technique of slow motion necessary to produce the high-speed technology that surrounds us, but it must be relied on to analyze those technologies when they go spectacularly awry, as in the 1986 explosion of the space shuttle *Challenger*, as well as to shed light on human acts of violence, as in the frame-by-frame scrutiny of the Zapruder movie of JFK's assassination. While study of the cinematic records of these events may offer clues about what happened (was the design of the O-rings the problem? was there one assassin or several?), the effect of such repeated slow-motion replays is to imprint the event on the minds of viewers as a vivid but dreamlike, hallucinatory event that we seem to have lived through despite the fact we weren't present at, or directly involved in, the catastrophe. Ultimately, the event is transformed into a collective, and even global, trauma. It becomes our reality—something that we know and that is often more familiar to us than events we've actually experienced in our own lives.

Later in this study I will consider certain films that present the world not "as it is," or at least not as it is experienced by characters living "in the world," but as a virtual realm viewed from the perspective of the beyond. For now, we may note one such scene that occurs early in David Cronenberg's 1996 film *Crash*. Immediately after the head-on collision in which Helen Remington's husband is killed, James and Helen gaze at each other from their respective vehicles. In the haunting stillness, surrounded by illuminated crystals of shattered glass, the dazed survivors are not yet fully conscious of what has happened, but are transfixed by the otherworldly state in which they find themselves, and by the peculiar stranger intimacy that has enveloped them as a result of their shared, incommunicable, near-death experience. No doubt Bernardo Bertolucci had this scene in mind when he called the film "a religious masterpiece." J. G. Ballard, the author of the novel on which the film was based, expressed admiration for Cronenberg's evocation of the "sacramental aspect" of the car crash, which is "celebrated" by the characters in the film "as a kind of profane Mass"; indeed, Ballard regards "this profane Mass as the greatest mystery of the twentieth century."[66]

By showing technology working to prevent rather than cause a crash, the Mercedes-Benz commercial stops well short of this mystery. The driver in the commercial is merely vouchsafed a melodramatic glimpse of his life passing before his eyes in the instant before his car comes to a screeching halt, leaving him and the car without a scratch. In contrast, the scene in Cronenberg's film explores the quasi-religious, otherworldly experience of the survivors in the moments *after* the crash; their experience is far more intense and "real" than that of the man in the Mercedes, if only because they came so much closer to dying, as evidenced by the presence of Helen's husband's corpse.

Whether movies present the viewer with a documentary glimpse of reality or a visionary glimpse of some virtual reality may ultimately be of less significance than their capacity to remove the viewer to a hypothetical vantage beyond the dichotomies of reality/illusion and life/death. The sign of a memorable cinematic experience is in some ways similar to the feeling one has after surviving a car crash or some other life-threatening ordeal. After the film is over, the world no longer looks the same because you see it differently. For a while, at least, you see the world with the eyes of someone who is not yet—and who almost was no longer—a part of it.

Primal
Scenes

Questioning the Woman

Perhaps because the birth of cinema happened to coincide with the discovery of X rays, one of film's key effects has been to provide viewers with a kind of enhanced, X-ray vision that allows them to feel that they can penetrate the veil of superficial appearances and see the hidden structure of reality itself. A similar effect was produced by psychoanalysis, whose origins are often traced to the same year, 1895, when Freud and Breuer's *Studies on Hysteria* was published. It's true that Freud saw a movie only once in his life and was "no friend to cinema";[1] like that "primary scientific precursor of the cinema," Étienne-Jules Marey, he regarded the new technology of film as a quasi-pornographic medium that was antithetical to his scientific project.[2] Yet it was precisely as a (porno)graphic medium that cinema bore such a striking affinity to the psychoanalytic enterprise. Freud may have spurned the movies, but filmmakers have been irresistibly drawn to his insights—with a good deal more success, one might add, than other artists such as photographers and especially painters.[3] What filmmakers have found particularly intriguing is Freud's idea that the visible, public, present behavior of individuals often screens a hidden, private, past truth—often a trauma or transgression—that can be uncovered only by the perspicacious analyst/detective. As Stephen Heath suggests, the "fascination of so many films with psychoanalysis" is symptomatic of "the powerful social desire to bring ... analysis into sight."[4]

Freud's teacher Jean-Martin Charcot had already employed the photographic techniques of Muybridge's and Marey's motion studies, directing his assistant Albert Londe to keep a visual, protocinematographic record of patients suffering from hysteria. The fact that the subjects of both Muybridge's and Charcot's photographic studies were often girls and women has led Linda Williams to suggest that these studies anticipated key conventions of pornographic film. An even stronger case can be made that a pornographic mise-en-scène came to inform psychoanalysis, which proclaims that "all femininity will be made visible."[5] Although Freud abandoned Charcot's photographic apparatus,[6] his own early studies of hysteria are essentially a series of cinematic "stagings of sexual truth."[7] Not only was the physical placement of the analyst advised by Freud "a perfect definition of the position of the cinema spectator"—"seated behind" the couch, allowing "him to see without being seen"—but the questions put to young female hysterics invariably occasioned, at least according to Freud's interpretation, a sexual, and indeed a pornographic, response.[8]

From a different perspective, Stanley Cavell has also commented on the close connection between psychoanalytic technique and cinematic technology, noting that they "share an origin as responses to the suffering and knowledge of women." Like psychoanalysis, film "is from first to last more interested in the study of individual women than of individual men"; while men usually figure "in crowds and in mutual conflict … it is women that bequeath psychic depth to film's interests." Cavell has specifically called attention to "the melodrama of the unknown woman," a prevalent scenario in mainstream cinema in which the male protagonist interrogates a female character as a way of gaining "access to her knowledge." Although the quest for knowledge in mainstream films is not necessarily centered on the woman's body, as it is in heterosexual hard-core cinema, the main interest often involves a quest for *sexual* knowledge and, as such, is expressive of the same will to know that Williams finds in pornographic film. In Cavell's view, cinema and psychoanalysis belong to a modern masculinist tradition of scientific and philosophical skepticism that torments itself with questions about the unknown woman: "Were her children caused by me?" "Is her satisfaction real and is it caused by me?"[9] and ultimately—the big question put directly to the woman herself—"How is it that you escape doubt?"[10] As a scientific recording technology, cinema readily adopted the standard analytic scenario in which the female subject appears to possess some sort of secret knowledge that eludes the male investigator. The very act of playing doctor or director offers the investigator a means of satisfying his curiosity and allaying his anxiety.

One way to appreciate the force of the gender dynamics in the analytic scene between male analyst and female subject is simply to reverse their roles. What might be called the psychodrama of the unknown man is vividly displayed in *Death and the Maiden*, Roman Polanski's 1994 film adapted from Ariel Dorfman's 1991 play. Dr. Roberto Miranda (Ben

Kingsley) is being held captive and interrogated by Paulina (Sigourney Weaver), a woman who is convinced that during the former fascist regime he took part in the rape and torture of political prisoners, one of whom was herself. Dr. Miranda maintains his innocence to Paulina and her stunned husband, Gerardo, a lawyer who has just been appointed to head the truth commission assigned to investigate past abuses. Under Paulina's repeated threats, the doctor agrees to make a videotaped "confession," which, however, is hardly credible since it consists of details that Paulina has told Gerardo, who virtually dictates them to the doctor.

Only at the end of the film, when Paulina threatens to push Dr. Miranda off a cliff, does he make what seems to be a sincere confession of his role as Paulina's torturer. He explains how he had originally been able to justify his work for the fascists on humanitarian grounds: "No one died, I swear. I saved many lives. And I made it easier on them. That's how it started. That's how I got into it. They needed doctors. My brother was in the secret police, he told me. They needed to make sure nobody died." But his confession then takes a darker turn:

> The others egged me on. "Come on, Doctor, you're not going to refuse free meat, are you?" I couldn't think straight. And inside I could feel I was starting to like it.... They laid the people out, flesh on the table. And the fluorescent light ... You didn't know, it was bright in those rooms. People lying totally helpless. I didn't have to be nice. I didn't have to seduce them.... I realized I didn't even have to take care of them. I had all the power. I could break anyone. I could make them do or say whatever I wanted.... I was lost. I got curious, morbid curiosity. How much can this woman take? What's going to happen to her vagina? Does it dry up when you shock her? Can she have an orgasm afterwards? [...] I fell in love with it. I could hurt you or I could fuck you—and you couldn't tell me not to. You had to thank me. I ... I loved it. I was sorry it ended. I was very sorry it ended.

Dr. Miranda's confession eloquently expresses the pornographic impulse behind scientific inquiry, the quest for knowledge motivated by the pursuit of power. (In Dorfman's play, the doctor adds the words "partly scientific" after "morbid curiosity.")[11] Yet as sincere as this confession appears to be—documenting the doctor's transformation during the "treatment" of his patient from healer to torturer, from a man concerned about the feelings of his patient to a man caught up in the "excitement" of his own morbid sexual and scientific curiosity—it ultimately fails to satisfy Paulina in her quest for vindication and justice. She is unable to experience the gratification from her interrogation of Dr. Miranda that he presumably derived from his "interrogation" of her.

After all, he was seeking sexual and scientific knowledge through torture, while she seeks justice through the pretense of a formal inquest, a far more elusive endeavor. But Paulina is also seeking a kind of knowledge: knowledge of the man who was her former persecutor, knowledge of the man who is now her victim—knowledge, in short, of *man*. If Paulina cannot obtain the satisfaction she seeks, it's because the act of interrogating the doctor puts her in the same inquisitorial position that he once held with respect to her. The questions she puts to him produce only the same pornographic answers that greeted his scientific "queries."

Films without Film

In several ways, Dr. Miranda's confession in Polanski's film differs from his confession in Dorfman's play. In the play, Gerardo makes an audio recording of his wife's account of her torture; he then uses her account to prep the doctor, who persists in claiming that he knows nothing of her ordeal. In the darkened theater Paulina's taped voice is heard modulating imperceptibly into the doctor's taped "confession." Polanski alters the recording apparatus to suit the visual medium of film: although Paulina begins making an audio recording of the doctor, she soon tells her husband, "I want him on videotape." Moreover, whereas only the doctor's single, taped confession is heard in Dorfman's play, two sharply different confessions are presented in Polanski's film—the doctor's videotaped statement, and the subsequent unrecorded admission on the cliff cited above. Like the audiotaped confession in the play, the videotaped confession in the film is legally useless as an admission of guilt because it is so obviously staged. In contrast, the second confession on the cliff—although of even less legal benefit, since it is undocumented—appears genuine and heartfelt. This seemingly sincere confession from her former tormentor is as much as Paulina can hope for. Having obtained it, she walks away, allowing the doctor to live. The ending of the play is a good deal more ambiguous. Thoroughly dissatisfied with Dr. Miranda's recorded statement of his pornoscientific sadism, which he denies after the recorder is turned off, Paulina prepares to shoot him. But the scene abruptly ends, leaving the audience to ponder the doctor's fate.

Both the stage and film versions of *Death and the Maiden* attest to the limitations of the recording media in documenting truth. However, by presenting the climactic cliffside scene of Dr. Miranda's apparently sincere, undocumented confession, which seems to offer Paulina at least a measure of satisfaction, Polanski's film more pointedly suggests that it is the presence of the recording apparatus itself that distorts the truth and renders any confession meaningless.

Even in the early stages of the ordeal, before Paulina attempts to document the doctor's deeds and create a public record of his guilt, her initial suspicions about his identity are confirmed by recorded evidence. The cassette recording of Schubert's "Death and the Maiden" that Paulina finds in the doctor's car seals his guilt in her mind, since this was the piece of music that her persecutor played while raping her. As she forces her bound and gagged prisoner to listen to the tape that she has taken from his car, she asks, "Is this the very cassette, Doctor, or do you buy a new one every year to keep the sound pure?" (22). Like the taped "confession" she will eventually extract from him, however, the presence of the tape in Dr. Miranda's car is not as incriminating as she believes, and would hardly convict him in a court of law. The tape provides decisive evidence of the doctor's guilt only for Paulina—especially in Polanski's film, in which she makes the doctor her prisoner only *after* she searches his car for evidence and finds the cassette. (In Dorfman's play, she attacks the doctor *before* discovering the tape, and the scene of this discovery is not shown as it is in the film.)

At the end of Dorfman's play, as I've said, the audience is left to wonder whether Paulina has shot and killed Dr. Miranda or not. When he appears in the final scene in the concert hall with Paulina and her husband, the stage directions state, "He could be real or he could be an illusion in Paulina's head" (67). Only Paulina sees the doctor; he is not seen by her husband. No such ambiguity is present at the end of the film: Dr. Miranda is clearly alive and is seen by both Paulina and her husband in the concert hall. What remains ambiguous in the film version is the performance of "Death and the Maiden" itself that the three principal characters have come to hear. For once, it is a live performance of the Schubert trio, rather than the taped recording that Paulina played for the doctor at his interrogation and that the doctor presumably played for Paulina during her captivity. The irony, of course, is that, at least in Polanski's version, the "live" performance is as much a recording as the rest of the film. The film audience never hears a live performance, but only a recorded effect. The pretense involved in presenting a recorded piece of music as a live performance is especially evident in a work that explores the reliability of recorded documents as a means of establishing "the real truth." The very reproducibility and repeatability of the recording medium compromises its integrity and undermines its documentary authority. Paulina's question to her nemesis in Dorfman's play takes on a new meaning in Polanski's film: "Is this the very cassette, Doctor, or do you buy a new one every year to keep the sound pure?" Of course, the sound will never be completely pure in a recording as opposed to a live performance. Polanski self-consciously suggests that the only way to get the truth to reveal itself in all its "purity" is to dispense with the recording apparatus altogether.[12]

This is precisely what Freud did when he abandoned the photographic apparatus used by his teacher Charcot in the treatment of hysteria. Instead, he presented his own analyses of patients as documentary studies in their own right—as a kind of "film without film" (to borrow Lev Kuleshov's phrase) that revealed sexual truths that didn't lend themselves to being recorded.[13] The critical question is whether Freud's move toward *representing* his analytic sessions with his patients in his own words, rather than *recording* them photographically, brought him closer to those truths or not. Do his subjective accounts of his case histories show him discovering sexual truths or fabricating them? In place of the photographic apparatus employed by Charcot, with its dubious claim to reproduce reality with total accuracy, Freud developed his own highly idiosyncratic interpretations of his patients' illnesses, based on his deliberate selection and arrangement of their words. Despite his aversion to the movies, Freud proved himself to be extraordinarily adept at framing and staging his own version of virtual—or what he called psychical, as opposed to physical—reality in the first years of the first filmed century.

Infantilizing the Viewer

The analytic session may have begun with the interrogation of woman, but it quickly evolved into a scenario entailing the infantilization of the patient. A key move in analytic (mis)representation and in the quasi-cinematic staging of sexual truth was the location of that truth in the patient's infancy. Reconstructing the infant's view of the world, Freud and his followers distilled the individual's manifold life experiences—and even at times the species' entire existence—into several key traumatic experiences: seduction, voyeurism, and castration.

Freud's strikingly visual characterization of these charged sexual scenes has been commented on by critics such as Jacqueline Rose:

> Describing the child's difficult journey into adult sexual life, he would take as his model little scenarios, or the staging of events, which demonstrated the complexity of an essentially visual space, moments in which perception *founders* (the boy child refuses to believe the anatomical difference that he sees) or in which pleasure in looking tips over into the register of *excess* (witness to a sexual act in which he reads his own destiny [or, we might add, his own origin], the child tries to interrupt by calling attention to his presence). Each time the stress falls on a problem of seeing.[14]

The infant's intensely visual primal fantasies exceed its powers of understanding and eventually come to shape its view of the world. The potent mix of pleasure and terror, voyeurism and violence that the child experiences when its perception "founders" during these early traumatic encounters constitute a kind of subliminal "body memory" that can be triggered in later life by actual chance events or by calculated cinematic cues. Psychoanalytic film theorists such as Christian Metz describe adult moviegoers as being engaged in "*unauthorised* scopophilia" in which they relive their (real or imagined) infantile experience of the primal scene: "For its spectator the film unfolds in that simultaneously very close and definitively inaccessible 'elsewhere' in which the child *sees* the amorous play of the parental couple, who are similarly ignorant of it and leave it alone, a pure onlooker whose participation is inconceivable."[15] In such accounts, the cinematic viewer regresses to a condition of infancy, uncritically reliving the primal scene in all its pleasure and terror.

One of the most vivid literary illustrations of the psychoanalytic view of the infantilized cinematic spectator is Delmore Schwartz's 1937 story "In Dreams Begin Responsibilities." The twenty-one-year-old narrator describes a dream in which he visits a movie theater in 1909 or so. There he watches a silent film that turns out to be a documentary about his parents before he was born, and that shows them on a date at Coney Island. Watching the film with growing unease, he finally loses his cool during the scene in which his father awkwardly proposes to his mother. Rising to his feet, the narrator shouts to his parents' images on the screen not to go through with a marriage that will result in "nothing good ... only remorse, hatred, scandal, and two children whose characters are monstrous" (194). When, in "terrible fear" (195), the narrator makes a second outburst, repeatedly asking aloud what his parents are doing, he is finally dragged by the usher out of the theater "into the cold light" of day, at which point he wakes up on the morning of his twenty-first birthday from what turns out to have been a dream.

Schwartz's story describes a kind of primal scene experience in which an infantilized adult (rather than an actual infant) is traumatized by the cinematic image (rather than the actual sight) of his parents during their courtship (rather than of their actual sexual relations, although had the narrator's dream-film continued, and had the narrator continued to watch, he presumably would have witnessed his own conception). The uncanny situation points up a key aspect of the reality effect: the more the narrator experiences the dream-movie as his own reality, the more infantilized he becomes. Conversely, the more infantilized the narrator becomes as a result of watching the dream-movie, the more overwhelmingly real it seems to him. As the story unfolds, the reader finds the narrator to be increasingly unreliable, and the dream-movie he describes seems less a documentary record about an episode in his parents' life than his own idiosyncratic imagining. The reader wavers between identifying with the infantilized narrator, for whom the movie is all too real, and identifying with the old lady seated next to him, who reminds him that it is "only a movie." Consciously we identify with the old lady's perspective, knowing that when we go to the movies we are not watching our own lives or our own prehistory. Yet while most of the movies we watch in real life have only a very limited relation to our own lives, certain films strike a chord in us as viewers by depicting some aspect of our personal lives or reminding us of long-forgotten experiences in our past. They affect us in the manner of a dream stirred up in our unconscious.

Psychoanalytic film critics tend to generalize this experience for everyone, identifying it as the infantile experience of the primal scene. Such a reading easily becomes reductive and ignores alternative possibilities. Thus, as I suggested at the end of the preceding chapter, instead of infantilizing the viewer so that he or she relives the primal scene, some films transport or elevate viewers to an angelic position from which they can look back upon a range of different events in their own lives, or in the lives of others, from a privileged perspective of knowledge—a kind of superior X-ray vision—rather than from a limited perspective of ignorance. Nevertheless, a number of movies lend themselves to psychoanalytic readings by thematizing the traumatic experience of the infantilized viewer. Referring to Metz's suggestion that "cinema in general retains something of 'the sight of the primal scene,'" critic Peter Baxter has found adult reenactments of infantile voyeurism in such films as Hitchcock's *Psycho* and *The Birds*, and even in Kubrick's *Dr. Strangelove*.[16] Then there are films such as those discussed in the previous chapter in which the intensely "real" experience of the primal scene is presented by means of cinematic conventions and special effects—the fade-out to the airport beacon in *Casablanca*, and the X-ray shot of the phallus in *Taxi Driver*. The "suppression" of the love scene in *Casablanca* corresponds to the repression of the viewer's experience of the primal scene in the unconscious. As an analogue of the repressed primal scene, the missing cinematic scene leads a phantom existence as an imaginary construct beyond the symbolic codes and conventions of the motion picture industry in the 1940s. And like the repressed primal scene, it's always possible for the missing cinematic scene to emerge into consciousness at some later time, when it is filled in with the sexual memories or fantasies of the voyeuristic viewer.

This, I suggested, is what Coover did in his pornographic revision of *Casablanca*. And indeed, when an imaginative author willfully transforms what seems the most innocent of films into the most explicit hard-core by decoding an artificial cinematic convention as pornographic reality, he's essentially following the lead of Freud, who claimed, as a scientific analyst, to be detecting the graphic sexual truths lurking in his patients' dreams. In fact, as we will see, the "discovery" of the primal scene itself was largely an exercise in plotting just such a pornographic film—Freud himself being a pioneering stage manager of graphic cinematic effects and hyperrealistic fantasies in the early twentieth century.[17]

Hard-core Freud

Let me say at once that I reject completely the vulgar, shabby, fundamentally medieval world of Freud, with its crankish quest for sexual symbols (something like searching for Baconian acrostics in Shakespeare's works) and its bitter little embryos spying, from their natural nooks, upon the love life of their parents.

—Vladimir Nabokov, *Speak, Memory*

Virtually all of Freud's case histories are anchored in the crude reality of quasi-pornographic scenes. Indeed, the most dramatic feature of his analyses are his archaeological reconstructions—or, perhaps more accurately, his creative constructions—of these sexual scenes. (The French term *séance* aptly describes the analytic "session" in which such scenes are cinematically staged,[18] and what is dead and buried in the unconscious begins to speak.)[19] It wasn't even necessary for the recovered scenes to be based on the patient's actual experiences; Freud's great insight, we are so often told, was to have identified these scenes *as* fantasies. Yet Freud's enduring influence may well turn out to have more to do with his recognition that there was something unmistakably *real* about the primal pornotopian fantasies he detected. Indeed, it was their reality that gave them the kind of scientific validity he so persistently sought.

The sexual content of the scenes discovered and recovered by Freud earned him the reputation, if not of a pornographer, then of a "pansexualist." Even if we discount the harsh criticism of his archrival Jung that his scientific views were a form of "soulless rationalism reinforced by a narrow materialist outlook" and that his theory of infantile sexuality was an "obscene caricature" that "merely demonstrates the adolescent smuttymindedness of the explainer,"[20] his own wife reportedly admitted "that if I did not realize how seriously my husband takes his treatments, I should think that psychoanalysis is a form of pornography."[21] Yet stories circulated by Freud's supporters about the hostility incurred by psychoanalysis in its early years for its frank approach to sexuality have been somewhat exaggerated.[22] Throughout its history, psychoanalysis has been criticized less for its (re)constructions of sexual scenes than for its claim to have uncovered a fundamental stratum of psychical reality in those (re)constructions. Such a claim was bound to strike many not only as unscientific, but as sheer intellectual arrogance. It was not simply the emphasis on sexuality that turned so many against Freudian theory, but its penchant for offering sexual experiences and fantasies as an authoritative, *scientific* explanation of the entire range of human behavior and cultural practices.

Even before 1895, as described in the *Studies on Hysteria*, Freud encountered cases in which patients traced their illnesses to incidents from their childhood in which they were disturbed or aroused by sounds emanating from their parents' bedrooms. At the time, however, Freud attached no great significance to such scenes, and when he began using the term "primal scenes" (*Urszenen*) it referred less to such episodes than to the child's real or fantasized experiences of sexual abuse by an older person, or "seduction" as he euphemistically called it. The famous case history of Dora—written up in early 1901 but not published until 1905—was centered on two seduction scenes and technically contains no reference to any primal scene. Already in this case, however, Freud's gift as a hard-core scenarist is evident in his construction of pornographic primal scenes. In his analysis of the first of the two scenes, in which Dora reports being kissed at age fourteen by Herr K. in his office and turning away in disgust, Freud (re)constructs a fantasy in which the girl imagines Frau K. performing fellatio on her father. Freud's analysis/Dora's fantasy stages a graphic scene in which Dora assumes the role of a spectator viewing the quasi-parental couple. But the primal scene that figures most significantly in the Dora case history concerns Freud himself in the voyeuristic role of analyst. Today's readers of the case history tend to regard the fantasized scene of incestuous seduction in which Dora (rather than Frau K.) services her father as Freud's own fantasy (rather than Dora's).[23] What Freud's critics all too often ignore is his achievement, as a result of his own voyeuristic imaginings, in recognizing the pervasiveness of graphic sexual fantasies and the psychic *reality* of those fantasies, which have such a powerful effect on the fantasist's daily life—an insight that twentieth-century filmmakers have not failed to exploit.

Despite intimations of the primal scene in his early case histories, Freud was unable for quite some time to identify it, rather than the seduction scene, as the *Urszene* he had been theorizing.[24] Even as late as 1909, in the case history of the Rat Man, Freud ignored evidence of an early primal scene experience: the fact that this patient had slept with his parents as a child and suffered from the particular illness of obsessional neurosis that Freud would come to associate with early experiences of this kind. Yet instead of identifying a memory or fantasy of parental intercourse as the key scene in the Rat Man's case history, Freud seized on this patient's childhood memory of being beaten by his father and his violent fantasy of his father being anally cannibalized by rats. It wasn't until the analysis from 1910 to 1914 of the twenty-five-year-old Russian emigré known as the Wolf Man that Freud elaborated the full significance of children's observations of parental sex. Only then did he designate such experiences as "primal scenes," which he attributed primarily to his male patients suffering from obsessional neurosis, rather than to his female patients suffering from hysteria as a result of actual or fantasized "seduction" experiences in early life.

Freud's analysis of Sergei Pankejev focused on an intense visual image, a childhood dream that this patient recalled of six or seven wolves in a tree. For some reason, this apparently peaceful scene caused Sergei great anxiety. During the four-year analysis, Freud sought to account for his patient's vivid sense of the dream's reality, and to explain his inordinate terror of the wolves, which—both in the text of Sergei's dream and in a painting he did of the dream scene—appeared as cute, docile creatures that were anything but threatening.[25] Pinpointing the dream as having taken place a few days before the patient's fourth birthday, on Christmas day,[26] Freud regarded it as a reminder "of something that must have belonged to an even earlier period" in the child's life (*SE* 17:33). Based on other incidents in the patient's early childhood—particularly his exposure to various tales about wolves, and a "seduction" episode some nine months prior to the dream in which he was sexually stimulated by his precocious older sister—Freud determined that the dream of the wolves, as well as the chain of neurotic symptoms it triggered, all originated in the fact "that the dreamer had been [a] witness of sexual intercourse in [his] early years," supposedly when he was only one and a half. The vivid dream "[retro]activated" the original scene in the four-year-old child "as though it were a recent experience. The effects of the scene were deferred, but meanwhile it had lost none of its freshness in the interval between the ages of one and a half and four years" (*SE* 17:44).

Of particular interest is the sentence in which Freud describes what Sergei supposedly saw as a child of less than two years: when he awoke in his parents' bedchamber, where he had been brought during a bout of malaria, "he witnessed a coitus *a tergo*, three times repeated; he was able to see his mother's genitals as well as his father's organ; and he understood the process as well as its significance." Dorrit Cohn has tellingly described this sentence as a momentary "lapse" on Freud's part from his own role of reporter and interpreter of his patient's words into a "focalized mode" that presents the scene as (if) it was directly experienced "through the eyes (though clearly not through the language) of the observing child." Cohn admits that "read in isolation, this past indicative sentence might be mistaken for an excerpt from a rather bizarre porno-graphic novel," but she adds that "this impression would be instantly dispelled by the framing context, which so explicitly subordinates the focalized perception of the infant to the self-consciously daring hypoth-esis of the psychoanalyst."[27]

The clear opposition that Cohn detects between sentence and context—between Sergei's infantile, pornographic fantasy and Freud's mature, scientific hypothesis—is compromised, however, by the fact that the reader of the case history lacks a clear sense of where the Wolf Man's account of his experience ends and Freud's analysis begins. More-over, the sentence cited by Cohn need not be "read in isolation" to appear pornographic; it is not the only occasion on which Freud "lapses" into the focalized mode. Several times in the case history Freud becomes a narrator *at* the scene rather than a narrator *of* the scene; that is to say, he adopts the pornographic perspective that Cohn attributes to the infant Sergei.[28] How is one to tell on such occasions if Freud is (intentionally or inadvertently) "lapsing" into the infantile perspective of his patient, or if he is putting his own words in his patient's mouth and his own pornoscientific fantasy into his patient's eyes?

Assuming that a primal scene did take place, what exactly did the young Sergei—or the young Sigmund—see? Was it a peaceful or a violent scene that the child witnessed? Freud suggests that Sergei perceived both an act of sadistic brutality *and* an expression of pleasure on his mother's face, but how was this possible? Reading the curious note that Freud added to the Wolf Man's case history in an attempt to resolve this discrepancy, we are again led to wonder whether we are indeed (as Cohn suggested and then denied) in the middle of a "rather bizarre pornographic novel."

> We might perhaps best do justice to this statement of the patient's by supposing that the object of his observation was in the first instance a coitus in the normal position, which cannot fail to produce the impres-sion of being a sadistic act, and that only after this was the position altered, so that he had an opportunity for making other observations and judgements. This hypothesis, however, was not confirmed with cer-tainty, and moreover does not seem to me indispensable. (*SE* 17:45 n)

This note qualifies "Freud's remarkably detailed, not to say voyeuristic, reconstruction" of the coitus *a tergo* that the one-and-a-half-year-old Sergei is supposed to have seen.[29] Elsewhere in the case history, Freud tries to substantiate this reconstruction by reporting that in every case involving a primal scene that he has analyzed, the patient's parents always turned out to have been engaged in coitus *a tergo* (*SE* 17:59). This is "a posture especially favourable for certain observations" (*SE* 17:55); namely, it is this position "which alone offers the spectator a possibility of inspecting the genitals" (*SE* 17:59). On the basis of the Wolf Man's contradictory account of the primal scene, however, Freud found it necessary to construct a second scenario in which Sergei's parents switched positions during intercourse. The new scenario purported to explain Sergei's contradictory perceptions: he first received a general impression of sadistic cruelty from seeing his parents have sex in the "normal," missionary position; then, when they switched to the *a tergo* position, he was able to observe such specific details as his parents' genitals and the blissful expression on his mother's face.

Not surprisingly, Freud's reconstruction of this scene has come in for a good deal of criticism, and for a variety of reasons. Apart from Nabokov's abhorrence of Freud's antierotic "medievalism," and apart from more recent objections to misogynistic and homophobic elements in his normative accounts of sexual development, literalist critics such as Frederick Crews have taken great delight in exposing the implausibility of Freud's interpretation of the Wolf Man's dream:

> The wolves, Freud explained, were the parents; their whiteness meant bedclothes; their stillness meant the opposite, coital motion; their big tails signified, by the same indulgent logic, castration; daylight meant night; and all this could be traced most assuredly to a memory *from age one* of Pankejev's mother and father copulating, doggy style, no fewer than three times in succession while he watched from the crib and soiled himself in horrified protest.[30]

Other critics have questioned the logic of Freud's sexual descriptions, claiming somewhat dubiously that "the a tergo position of the coitus presumed to have been seen is the least favorable to observe the genital organs."[31] For that matter, one might wonder why frontal copulation rather than penetration from behind is more likely, in Freud's words, "to produce the impression of being a sadistic act." Patrick Mahony, among others, has suggested that "the Wolf Man's primal scene a tergo" was in fact "Freud's own fantasy":

> The amount of perceptual acrobatics in Freud's reconstruction is stag- gering, for the observability assigned to the Wolf baby's angle of vision would exceed the ingenious staging of any pornographic film producer. Rather than clarify the real event, the observable data ascribed by Freud give us an insight into his own fantasy life and his sheerly unre-

alistic conception of voyeuristic and exhibitionistic possibilities. His perceptual construction might be suitable for animated pretzels, not human bodies.[32]

Following Mahony, we might assume that Freud's inaccurate or impossible account of the primal scene stemmed from the fact that he was simply a bad pornographer. For Crews, Freud is both a fraudulent scientist whose "folklore of repression" is the "scientific counterpart" of "demonic possession" and a pornographer who "never flagged in his quest to forge precise causal links between vividly reconstructed sexual events from infancy (either witnessed or personally endured) and adult mental disturbance."[33]

One could, of course, excuse Freud's lapses in the eyes of his late-twentieth-century critics as a result of the relatively primitive state of pornography early in the century. The mass-mediated pornography that is so readily available today was unimaginable in Freud's time. Since the 1980s, anyone with a VCR or a computer can study detailed images of copulation that were accessible to Freud only in fantasies and dreams. Video technology and the Internet have created a mass audience of hardcore connoisseurs who are unable to resist ridiculing Freud for his odd reconstructions of infant's-eye views of coitus, and who can marvel with Mahony that it was not until "the belated year of 1977" that the anatomical inaccuracies of these imaginings were first pointed out. Such criticisms disregard the fact that smut and technology have advanced alongside one another: innovations in scientific photography and photojournalism have made possible a graphic hyperrealism that not only has been exploited by pornography, but is precisely what pornography is all about. Science and pornography have achieved maximum visibility by placing the observing subject (the camera) in places where it has never been before, producing scenes that were previously unimaginable. The long-standing relationship between sex and science that began with the "invention of pornography" at the time of the scientific revolution, and continued into the early twentieth century with the rise of the twin technologies of cinema and psychoanalysis (the primitive, grainy sexual fantasies envisioned by Freud in his consulting room) had been taken to an altogether new level by the end of the twentieth century with the availability of cinematic and cybernetic technology.[34]

It hardly seems necessary, let alone wise, for Freud's remaining adherents to defend their besieged hero as a visionary, albeit primitive, pornographer. It was never his intention, after all, either to produce libidinous narratives for popular consumption or to prepare precise scientific studies of the physiology of intercourse. Far from providing pornographic stimulation or scientific documentation of sexual behavior, Freud attempted to reconstruct infantile fantasies that bore only the most tenuous relation to adult conceptions of reality and "truth." He even suggests that the more detailed and (porno)graphic the description given by a patient of a primal scene, the more likely it is that the patient never actually witnessed the scene.

> [If] the intercourse is described with the most minute details, which would be difficult to observe, or if, as happens most frequently, it turns out to have been intercourse from behind, *more ferarum* [in the manner of animals], there can be no remaining doubt that the phantasy is based on an observation of intercourse between animals (such as dogs) and that its motive was the child's unsatisfied scopophilia during puberty.[35]

One should not expect children's experiences of primal scenes, even as recollected by adults, to have the degree of accuracy that comes from direct "observation of intercourse between animals" or, for that matter, from actual exposure to hard-core pornography. According to this reasoning, the "bizarre" and "impossible" elements in Freud's reconstruction of the Wolf Man's primal scene are by no means shortcomings, as Mahony and other critics suggest, but inevitable distortions on the part of the infant observer. Freud's account seems bizarre not because he is a poor scientist or pornographer but because he is attempting to reconstruct the scene as viewed from the perspective of the infant, who misinterprets what it sees. Such distortions make even the most ordinary sexual scene observed by the young child appear strange—both terrifying and arousing—but nonetheless real. In contrast, "adult" magazines and movies must be deliberately outré, and find ever new ways of presenting sexual reality in the most contrived and unrealistic ways if they are to elicit a similar reaction in their jaded consumers.

It's now apparent why Freud's reconstruction of the Wolf Man's primal scene continues to fascinate and influence readers despite the substantial criticism it has inevitably received. By presenting such a bizarre reconstruction—both regarding what Sergei saw and the circumstances that enabled him to see it—Freud succeeded in *making the scene more indelible, even as it seemed more incredible.*[36] Whether the sexual scene supposedly witnessed by Sergei only appeared strange or was strange, its strangeness was precisely what made it so memorable for the Wolf Man, as well as for Freud's readers. The uniqueness and bizarreness of Freud's pornographic reconstruction that make it seem incredible and absurd from a sober, critical, adult perspective are what give the scene its singular power when glimpsed by an infant or envisioned by Freud's ideal reader—an adult willing and able to suspend disbelief.

A visionary who was ahead of his time as well as a man bound to the technology of his age, Freud has yet to be given credit for anticipating by nearly a century many of the conventions used by hard-core film-makers. Even if Freud elaborated his graphic scenarios for the purpose of inducing awareness in the patient rather than for the purpose of arousing the viewer, the reality effects he produced are strikingly similar to those typically staged in hard-core films. Small wonder, then, that Freud's account of the infantile voyeur in the primal scene has been so widely used in critical analyses of viewers' experiences of pornographic as well as nonpornographic, mainstream cinema. The conventions of hard-core film, which are now standard practice in the adult-film industry, (re)construct the primal scene through a series of alternating perspectives already theorized by Freud:[37]

- *Alternating identifications of the viewer.* The infantilized, male viewer of heterosexual pornography assumes a pregendered condition, allowing him to identify with the different actors in the sexual sequence—with a male father figure or a female mother figure. The viewer/voyeur derives pleasure as well as a sense of power from his ambiguous situation, for he is alternately in the scene and outside it, a participant and an eyewitness who enjoys godlike invisibility and omniscience.

- *Alternating positions of the performers.* This affords the spectator a greater variety of views of the hard-core sequence. One rarely finds a sex sequence in feature-length pornographic films in which the performers maintain a single position from start to finish.

- *Alternating shots and camera angles.* Like the various positions of the performers, shots from different angles enhance the viewer's vision by making it possible to see sexual, and specifically genital, activity from unfamiliar and seemingly impossible angles to which the viewer would ordinarily not have access. These unconventional viewpoints require great agility on the part of the actors. As one hard-core performer remarks, "If anybody tries to screw the way people are screwed on camera, they'll rip out every muscle in their back and in their legs. We get into positions that monkeys are envious of, because the camera has to see what we're doing."[38] "To see the world as it has never been seen before" could well be the motto of the scientist and the pornographer alike. It applies as well to Freud's description of what Sergei saw in the primal scene.

- *Alternating full shots and close-ups of the performers.* These provide the viewer with visual information about the overall scene as well as about specific body parts, thereby satisfying the viewer's sexual curiosity. As theorized by Freud, the full shot gives the infantilized/ infantile viewer a violent impression of coitus, while the close-up of the woman's/mother's face conveys a sense of her bliss.

• *Alternating close-ups of actors' faces and genitals.* As if writing a guide for the hard-core filmmaker, Freud "recommends" the *a tergo* position as being "especially favourable for certain observations"—specifically, "inspecting the genitals" and noticing the "expression of enjoyment" (rather than of pain) on the woman's/mother's face. Cutting back and forth between facial and genital images is a frequently used technique in hard-core film; filmmakers have used increasingly innovative camera angles to depict "meat shots"—close-ups of the actors' genitals during intercourse—in order to include the face of at least one of the performers (usually the woman's) in the shot. This particular convention is more than a purely "artistic" effect; it is required by the logic of pornography, in which, as Lisa Katzman has observed, "the drama of a woman's pleasure is written not on her genitals, but her face."[39]

Yet another key convention of pornographic film is anticipated by Freud's reconstruction of the Wolf Man's experience of the primal scene—the "money shot" showing the male performer's ejaculation at the climax of sex scenes. For this "moment of truth" in pornographic films, as James Atlas calls it—which is also the moment when they "never seem phonier" through their contrived demonstration of male potency and pleasure and their programmatic presentation of spontaneity[40]—is also the climactic event in Freud's case history, except for the fact that it is the child spectator rather than the adult performer (the father) who has a sexual discharge. Sergei "interrupted his parents' intercourse" by means of a "method" that is "the same in every case": in a state of sexual excitement, the child defecates or urinates, whereupon it begins to scream. In Sergei's case, Freud determined that the child "passed a stool," which Freud interpreted as an indication of a homoerotic tendency in the patient to assume "a passive attitude" and of an "inclination towards a subsequent identification with women [more] than with men" that indicates acute castration anxiety. In contrast, the little boy who urinates when he encounters his parents making love, and who thus experiences sexual excitement in the genital rather than in the anal zone, was said to resemble "a grown-up man [who] in the same circumstances would feel an erection," and thus was relatively free of castration anxiety.

Not surprisingly, Freud described himself in precisely this latter situation in *The Interpretation of Dreams*: at the age of seven or eight he urinated in his parents' bedroom, an act that prompted his father's portentous comment "The boy will come to nothing" (*SE* 4:216). In reconstructing the Wolf Man's primal scene, Freud is likely to have drawn on his similar experience as a child in his own parents' bedroom. Yet, having come close to displacing and projecting his own primal-scene experience/fantasy onto his patient, Freud ends his analysis by differentiating their respective experiences. While Sergei had defecated in his sexual excitement, Sigmund had urinated; while Sergei had demonstrated a passive, feminine sexual character, Sigmund had displayed active, masculine behavior; while Sergei had not been scolded but nevertheless suffered severe castration anxiety, Sigmund had suffered a humiliating reprimand from his father, which he sublimated into an ambitious, lifelong drive to prove his (self-)mastery.

By the end of the case history, Freud has distinguished the Wolf Man's primal-scene fantasy from his own, and distanced himself from his patient, who is left uncured and unsatisfied with Freud's explanation of his illness. (Indeed, the Wolf Man's long clinical posthistory shows that whatever childhood traumas afflicted him remained unresolved.) Master scenarist that he was, Freud made good use of his most famous patient to reenact and resolve his own personal and professional fantasies/traumas, (re)constructing a pornographic primal scene that not only provided a model for future analysts, but that also anticipated many of the practices and techniques that would be employed by hard-core filmmakers later in the century as new recording technologies became available, and the impulse to film everything grew irresistible.

The Reality of Fantasy

What I wanted to get at is the value difference between pornographic playing-cards when you're a kid, and pornographic playing-cards when you're older. It's that when you're a kid you use the cards as a substitute for a real experience, and when you're older you use real experience as a substitute for the fantasy.

—Jerry in Edward Albee's *The Zoo Story*

Despite the pornographic realism and narrative truth of his reconstruction of the Wolf Man's primal scene, Freud failed to achieve the degree of scientific realism and scientific truth he ultimately sought for his theory of primal fantasies. No independent evidence exists beyond Freud's notes and conjectures that Sergei's dream was either caused by or referred to a prior experience of the primal scene, or indeed that he had ever witnessed this scene.[41] The Wolf Man himself remained unconvinced, especially after Freud showed signs of doubt about his interpretation years after the analysis.[42] "I have always thought that the memory would come," Pankejev said in an interview conducted in the 1970s, "but it never did."[43] Indeed, he thought that "the whole matter is improbable, because children in Russia slept with the nurse in her room and not with the parents in their bedroom. But," he added, "there could indeed have been an exception once, how can I know."[44] What the Wolf Man *did* remember as definitely having taken place was his seduction by his sister less than a year before the dream. "Here we have a recollection. It is not a fiction, not an inference, and not a construct."[45] Twenty years earlier Freud would have identified this seduction as the crucial *Urszene* that traumatized the three-year-old Sergei. At the time of his analysis of the Wolf Man, however, Freud was less interested in a seduction scene in childhood that his patient *could* remember than in an earlier scene from infancy that Sergei *couldn't* recall and that he doubted had ever occurred. As an experience that Ned Lukacher has described as always "'unknown' (*unbekannte*) and 'forgotten' (*vergessene*)," the primal scene could not be remembered by the Wolf Man, but only (re)constructed by the analyst.[46]

However comfortable poststructuralist critics such as Lukacher are in asserting the undecidability of the primal scene, Freud was by no means content with this indeterminacy. In order to validate his theory, and to demonstrate its historical and scientific as well as its narrative truth, he doggedly endeavored to establish the primal scene's objective reality. This is evident in the note he appended to the case history just before publication:

> I should myself be glad to know whether the primal scene in my present patient's case was a phantasy or a real experience; but, taking other similar cases into account, I must admit that the answer to this question is not in fact a matter of very great importance. These scenes of observing parental intercourse, of being seduced in childhood, and of being threatened with castration are unquestionably an inherited endowment, a phylogenetic heritage, but they may just as easily be acquired by personal experience. With my patient, his seduction by his elder sister was an indisputable reality; why should not the same have been true of his observation of his parents' intercourse? (*SE* 17:97)

Freud's offhand way of downplaying the question of whether the Wolf Man's experience of the primal scene "was a phantasy or a real experience"—and even of acknowledging in another appended note that the reality of the scene "is not clear" (*non liquet*)[47]—scarcely conceals his eagerness to prove the scene's real existence.[48] In desperation, he seizes on the Wolf Man's memory of being seduced by his sister at age three, although Freud had long since come to doubt the reports of his female patients that they had been seduced by their fathers.

During the four-year period (1914–18) between the end of his analysis of the Wolf Man and the publication of the case history, Freud struggled to salvage the notion that experiences of the primal scene were based on actual events, however far back in time those events had to be pushed—even beyond the individual's lifetime into the phylogenetic past of the human species.[49] Freud feared that without a kernel of pornographic reality, psychoanalysis could not prove itself a true science. Even when he reluctantly conceded, just prior to publishing his case history, that the primal scene could have been Sergei's fantasy and not an actual witnessed event, Freud clung to the belief that this fantasy was based on some actual scene that Sergei *had* seen, however "innocent" and nonpornographic it may have been—if not his parents *copulating*, then sleeping; if not his *parents* copulating, then animals.

> It was really on a summer's afternoon while the child was suffering from malaria, the parents were both present, dressed in white, when the child woke up from his sleep, but—the scene was innocent. The rest had been added by the inquisitive child's subsequent wish, based on his experiences with the dogs, to witness his parents too in their lovemaking; and the scene which was thus imagined now produced all the effects that we have catalogued, just as though it had been entirely real and not fused together out of two components, the one earlier and indifferent, the other later and profoundly impressive. (*SE* 17:58)

Combining the innocent scene of his parents that he supposedly witnessed in his illness when he was one and a half with his experience some three years later—shortly before his dream of the diminutive, doglike wolves—of the sheepdogs copulating on his father's estate, young Sergei could have "produced all the effects" of having actually witnessed sex between his parents ("as though it had been entirely real"). He could quite simply have constructed his primal scene fantasy by superimposing the image of copulating animals onto his parents. As Freud wrote elsewhere, such infantile scenes are bound to be "the direct opposite of the historical truth."[50]

Unable to establish documentary evidence for Sergei's primal scene, Freud found it necessary to insist on its virtual reality. And so, despite his avowed distaste for the cinema, he resorted to many of the same techniques and effects that filmmakers at the time were experimenting with (persistence of memory, composite images, double exposure) in an effort to produce a vivid and compelling semblance of reality. The only problem, as Pirandello's fictional cameraman Gubbio realized at the very time Freud was struggling with his case history, was that "the reality which a machine is capable of giving [a fantasy] kills it, for the very reason that it is given by a machine, that is to say by a method which discovers and exposes the fiction, simply by giving it and presenting it as real."

De Palma's Wolf Man

Early in Brian De Palma's 1984 film *Body Double*, Jake Scully returns unexpectedly to his girlfriend's home. Quietly he walks through the hall, planning to surprise her. He hears soft laughter and peers into one room after another. The laughter becomes louder as he proceeds down the hallway to the last door, the door to the bedroom. Eagerly he opens the door—only to see his naked girlfriend straddling a lover on the bed.

This is just the beginning of Jake's problems. He also learns he has lost his acting job in which he plays the part of a wolfish, punk-style vampire in a low-budget thriller. Whenever the script calls for him to climb into a coffin, he has the ill luck to become paralyzed because of an acute claustrophobic condition. The cause of his phobia is revealed during an acting workshop: as part of an exercise, he relives the trauma of being trapped behind a refrigerator as a child. When he breaks down during the exercise, he is befriended by one of the participants in the workshop, an aspiring actor named Sam Bouchard, who invites him to a bar. After a few drinks, Jake is telling his new friend how he caught his girlfriend in the act. "Christ, I keep seeing it," he says. "Carol lying there, her face was glowing." But the viewer has seen exactly what Jake saw, and knows that Carol was not lying down, but was astride her lover. For some reason Jake has altered a key detail in the painful—but also arousing—spectacle of his betrayal, revising the scene of his girlfriend's aggressive lovemaking to a comparatively peaceful scene of her "lying there." Was he perhaps confusing the sight of his girlfriend and her lover with *another* scene he witnessed as a child, after walking down a long hall toward the sound of his parents' laughter?

Presumably suffering from a neurosis rooted in a traumatic experience of the primal scene, De Palma's crippled werewolf Jake Scully bears a striking resemblance to Freud's Wolf Man. Like Sergei, Jake is prone to obsessive behavior, and especially to voyeurism. He also experiences moments of paralysis that leave him incapacitated and frozen with terror, and which seem to be the result of early traumatic experiences that have never been resolved. The loss of his job and his renewed experience of the primal scene (stumbling upon his girlfriend with a lover) have aggravated his infantilized condition, and they lead him to commit a number of childish acts such as panty stealing and watching sex films.

And as Sergei presented Freud with a radically revised account of the primal scene in his dream of the wolves in the tree, so Jake gives Sam a distorted account of the scene he witnessed in his girlfriend's apartment, itself a reenactment of his primal-scene experience in childhood.

This experience is reenacted yet again in *Body Double*—several times, in fact—as part of a diabolical scheme in which Sam restages the primal scene for Jake without his knowledge, first in an erotic and then in a brutally sadistic version. Sam invites the now-homeless Jake to house-sit at a friend's home while he goes to Seattle, where, he tells Jake, he's landed a part in a play. That evening, Sam shows Jake the house he is to occupy (John Lautner's Chemosphere house in the Hollywood Hills), perched high upon a tower and commanding a panoramic canyon view. One of the house's features that Sam points out just before he leaves is a telescope mounted at the window through which Jake can survey the residences across the canyon, including one particular glassed-in home. Every night at the same hour, Sam tells him, a glamorous woman can be seen in the second-floor bedroom window performing an erotic dance. Jake takes a peek through the scope and ogles Sam's "favorite neighbor," as he calls her. Apart from Jake's voyeurism and the woman's exhibitionism, the "dance" itself is an exercise in perversion; a striptease in reverse, the woman proceeds to dress herself up in jewels and lingerie.[51] The following evening Jake watches her perform the same dance "like clockwork," as if for his private enjoyment. Later that night, he also witnesses a man, presumably the woman's husband, returning to the darkened house. After taking money from a safe concealed in the bedroom wall, the man brutally wakens and torments his wife. Before long Jake is obsessed with the abused beauty, whose name, he learns, is Gloria Revelle, and he's soon tailing her about town.

He isn't the only one following her. He notices that she's also being pursued by a sinister-looking American Indian who steals Gloria's handbag at a beachfront hotel. Jake pursues the thief but is overcome by his debilitating claustrophobia when he follows the Indian into a dark underpass. After Gloria arrives and leads Jake out of the tunnel into the fresh air, they join for a moment in a dizzying embrace, which ends when Gloria suddenly runs off. That evening, Jake spies on her again from his eyrie; this time, however, instead of the nightly masturbation ritual he witnesses a robbery in progress. The Indian, who has entered Gloria's house before her arrival with a plastic key card he has stolen from her purse in the tunnel, has opened the safe on the second floor with a huge electric drill, which he turns on Gloria when she surprises him. Jake races across the canyon in a desperate attempt to save her, but once again he fails. Breaking into the ground-level living room, he is attacked by Gloria's white dog, which he tries to fight off as the bloody drill bores through the ceiling above him.

It's fitting that Jake's ultimate reexperience of the primal scene is a grotesque, pornographic spectacle of visual violence: a close-up shot of the monstrous drill descending through the ceiling, thunderously splattering the room with the blood of the woman he adores, who is being hideously "screwed" upstairs while he struggles helplessly below with her dog. (Is it a coincidence that this dog happens to bear a striking resemblance to the white wolves in the painting that the Wolf Man made for Freud?) What De Palma's critics were quick to condemn as a scene of gratuitous, misogynist brutality was also, more significantly, a scene of male impotence and paralysis in which Jake failed to rescue the woman he loved. (Sixteen years later, De Palma replayed the scene with reversed gender roles in *Mission to Mars*, when an astronaut helplessly watches her husband violently end his life during a spacewalk.[52]) In *Body Double* the scene of Gloria's death is an ingenious re-creation from an adult perspective of Freud's account of the (male) infant as passive observer, fantasizing his parents in an act of sadistic sexual penetration. Indeed, the shot from Jake's point of view of the drill poking down through the ceiling enacts the ultimate adolescent fantasy described by Freud—the fantasy "of being in the womb, and even of experiences there"—experiences such as witnessing the bloody intrusion of the paternal phallus, the intrusive scene par excellence.[53] Such primal scenes are bound to appear monstrous, excessive, yet frighteningly real when staged before an adult. Indeed, Jake undergoes the unbearable experience of directly witnessing the eruption of the real (sex as murder, murder as sex) that ordinarily would be screened from view, as Sergei's dream of the wolves in the tree screened his experience of the primal scene.

Both sufferers of obsessional neurosis, the wolf men Sergei and Jake experience bizarre reenactments of an "original," inaccessible scene, which, if it occurred at all, would already have been perceived in a grotesque, distorted form. If Jake had already misrepresented the scene of his girlfriend atop her lover that he had witnessed the previous day, how distorted and exaggerated must his memories and fantasies of his earliest experiences of parental intercourse be? Such infantile scenes, as Freud wrote, are bound to be "the direct opposite of the historical truth." (In fact, as will be seen in the next chapter, Jake's glimpse of Gloria's murder itself turns out to be a misperception that he and the viewer must proceed to analyze, recognize, and revise.) And what about the scene of analysis itself, which supposedly (re)constructs those infantile scenes? Are the analytic and infantile scenes truly distinguishable? Can the analytic scene legitimately claim scientific truth for itself, or is it

of the same order of narrative truth ("the direct opposite of the historical truth") as infantile scenes? Ultimately, it's impossible to tell whose
distortion of reality is greater—Jake's or Sam's, Sergei's or Freud's. Since
Freud's account is the most detailed, the possibilities for misrepresenta-
tion are most evident in his text. As a result, Freud has been unable to
escape his critics' suspicions that his description of the primal scene is
not a genuine clinical reconstruction but a graphic theoretical
construct—his own pornoscientific fantasy of a primal scene qua "big
bang" that he needed in order to hammer home the idea of infantile
sexuality and thereby establish psychoanalysis, once and for all, as a
science.

Body
Parts

The pornographic imagination tends to make one person interchangeable with another and all people interchangeable with things.
—Susan Sontag, "The Pornographic Imagination"

Desire's a funny thing. When you really want something, bits of it
begin to appear in everything you see.
—Laurie Anderson

Multiple Images and Displaced Desire

The movies are often said to have originated with Muybridge's multiplication of the single photographic image in his famous motion studies. In 1878, having used twelve trip-wired cameras to settle Leland
Stanford's bet that all four legs of a horse leave the ground at some
point of its trot, Muybridge turned his attention to galloping horses. He
discovered that their legs also leave the ground, precisely at the point
when their legs meet beneath their body. All those painters who had
depicted horses leaving the ground with outstretched legs had gotten it
wrong.[1] The tide was turning against those artists committed to the
nineteenth-century view that photography could at best be a mere
visual aid to the painter seeking to be true to nature, and who scoffed at
the idea that advances in recording technology had any significant
contribution to make to their representational endeavors. Rather, as
Siegfried Kracauer noted, "scientific camera explorations of the first
decades of the twentieth century were a source of inspiration to artists,
who then began to defy those conventions. It sounds paradoxical that,
of all media, realistic photography should thus have contributed to the
rise of abstract art."[2]

The transition in the 1870s from Muybridge's use of multiple cameras to shoot multiple images of galloping horses to Marey's use of a "photographic gun" to record the "invisible mechanics of the human walk ... on a single photographic plate" was echoed in painting three decades later in the transition from John Singer Sargent's 1908 painting *Cashmere* to Marcel Duchamp's *Nude Descending a Staircase* of 1912.[3] The seven figures in Sargent's scene, set in the Italian Alps, were modeled on a single person, the artist's eleven-year-old niece Reine Ormond. The repetition on the same canvas of the same identically dressed figure in seven different poses creates the impression of a procession of different young women moving from left to right. Duchamp's nude, in contrast, shows a single figure split into the multiple stop-action images of the kind that Marey and other technological innovators had produced. Far from using photography merely as a visual aid in his art, Duchamp was enthralled by the abstract effects revealed by the most realistic photography available at the time—stroboscopic and multiple high-speed exposures.[4]

The multiplication of images made possible by the new photographic and cinematographic technologies gave rise to one particularly curious effect—a general displacement of desire. What makes Sargent's *Cashmere* what Richard Ormond calls "a hymn to the power of female beauty" is its dispersal of Reine's image and its depiction of her variability and multiplicity.[5] Instead of being drawn toward or held by a single figure, as in so many of Sargent's portraits, the spectator's gaze glides across a field of desire, flitting among the seven girls, who are in fact just one. No longer the fixed, delimited subject of a portrait "caught" by the artist, Reine is on her way to becoming the more elusive phenomenon of the motion picture star, a figure in perpetual motion.

The displacement of desire fostered by the emerging medium of cinema is evident not only in filmic paintings such as *Cashmere* but in the early film novel. In Pirandello's *The Notebooks of Serafino Gubbio* of 1915, the great theatrical-actress-turned-film-star Varia Nestoroff inspires the pure love of the artist Giorgio Mirelli, who paints a series of portraits of her—another example of painting aspiring to the multiple images of film. But Giorgio kills himself when the actor Aldo Nuti, who has been courting Giorgio's sister Duccella, falls in love with Nestoroff—in effect, substituting her for Duccella. This chain of displaced desire affects all the characters in the novel who have any connection with the Kosmograph film company: the narrator, the cameraman Gubbio, appears to lack any emotional life of his own until he falls in love with the aspiring starlet Luisetta, who in turn is infatuated with the actor Aldo Nuti, who in turn is smitten with the dramatic Varia Nestoroff, who is involved with the boorish actor Carlo Ferro. At the beginning of the twentieth century it's already clear that the new film culture is hardly a place of stable identity and reciprocated desire. But the effects of the new recording and reproductive technologies—the multiplication of images, fragmentation of identity, and dispersal of desire— were only just beginning to be noticeable. By the end of the century these effects were nowhere more evident than in films themselves.

Split Persons and Body Doubles

More than any other filmmaker except perhaps Hitchcock, Brian De Palma has specialized in producing films in which what the viewer sees on-screen is not what actually takes place. A good example is *Body Double*, the first half of which, as we've seen, is a series of reenactments of the primal scene as experienced by Jake Scully, a postmodern incarnation of Freud's Wolf Man. In the second half of the film, Jake makes a discovery that compels him and the viewer to rethink the primal scene fantasy/trauma that we have witnessed: the woman whose gruesome death-by-drilling Jake sees and fails to prevent is indeed Gloria Revelle, but, we now learn, she was not the woman whose erotic performance first aroused Jake's obsessive interest when he watched her through the telescope.

After a humiliating interrogation by the detective assigned to the case, who accuses him of being a sex pervert and the indirect cause of Gloria's death, Jake returns to his canyon-top home. There no longer being any point in scanning Gloria's house for a glimpse of her, he retires to the bedroom in a drunken stupor and turns on a late-night cable TV show. A porn star named Holly Body (played by Melanie Griffith) is being interviewed, and a clip is shown from her most recent film, *Holly Does Hollywood*. Sporting a holly-leaf tattoo on her buttock as well as a punk-style blond hairdo (much like the wig that Jake had worn early in the film as a vampire in a horror flick), Holly could not look more different from the sultry brunette Gloria (Deborah Shelton). Yet when Jake sees Holly perform the identical dance routine Gloria did each night before her grisly murder (the live private peep show viewed through the telescope now a public recorded performance on TV), he is jolted out of his daze. He buys Holly's video to verify that he is not imagining things (porn film as documentary) and then attempts to meet her by auditioning for a part in her new film.

We next see the infantilized voyeur turned adult-movie actor performing a glitzy sex scene with Holly.[6] During their embrace, Jake flashes back to his passionate kiss with Gloria at the beach and has the uncanny feeling that Holly both is and is not Gloria. Posing as a film producer, he gains Holly's confidence and gets her to admit that she was hired to impersonate Gloria on successive evenings, performing her dance in Gloria's bedroom before Jake's telescopic gaze. The man who hired her was Gloria's husband, Sam Bouchard, who had contrived to make Jake a witness to his wife's murder by the mysterious Indian, who was none other than Sam in disguise. So although Jake's beloved Gloria is indeed dead, her stand-in, Holly Body, is still very much alive. And since it had been Holly's body that Jake had watched through the telescope and that had furnished Jake with his first glimpse of Gloria, the body double Holly was really Gloria's *original*.

De Palma's interest in doubles was already evident in his earlier work. In *Sisters* (1973) Danielle (Margot Kidder) is the psychopathic survivor of a pair of Siamese twins. Her sense of her identity remains tied to her sister, Dominique, who died during the operation that separated their bodies. The doctor who performed the operation loves Danielle, and when she kills a lover in a fit of madness he tries to conceal the deed. When a suspicious newspaperwoman begins her own investigation, the doctor abducts and drugs her so that she can "play" the part of the absent twin, Dominique, in Danielle's psychotic sexual fantasy. By convincing Danielle that her sister is still alive, the doctor hopes to bring about her recovery so that she can reciprocate his love. (It's also possible that the doctor needs to re-create the presence of the other twin in order to become aroused himself.) Insofar as Danielle and the newspaperwoman take turns impersonating the absent twin, we have a striking instance of two actresses playing (at being) a single (non)character.

The usual cinematic convention for representing schizophrenia is role doubling, whereby the same actor plays two different parts or takes on two conflicting identities. Thus Anthony Perkins plays the callow Norman Bates *and* his murderous mother in Hitchcock's *Psycho*, Michael Caine plays the psychiatrist Dr. Elliott *and* the razor-slashing Bobbi in De Palma's 1980 film *Dressed to Kill*, and the character of Sam disguises himself as the murderous Indian in *Body Double*. The inverse technique employed in *Sisters*—or in films such as *That Obscure Object of Desire*, *The Return of Martin Guerre*, or *Despair*—in which a pair of actors portray a single character, would seem to be even better suited to reveal the schizoid nature of everyday reality.[7] From the viewer's perspective, such person doubling disrupts the unity and integrity of the subject, which begins to fall apart. The coherent subject is revealed to be an idealized phantasm, a delusion of the lover whose desire for the beloved is so great that s/he sees one whole person where there are in fact two separate individuals.

The widespread use of the body double in filmmaking is a logical as well as literal development of the person double. Instead of different actors doubling up to play the same role, the bodies (or body parts) of different actors are made to appear as if they belong to a single character. And instead of a deluded or infatuated spectator who perceives distinctly different individuals as a coherent identity, the "spectator perceives the bodies of the actors not as unified totalities but as a kind of vaguely co-ordinated agglomerate of partial objects."[8] In short, the spectator is motivated no longer by desire for the person, but by the drive toward bodies and body parts. This is what happens in pornographic film: when sex becomes "graphically visible" it seems "doomed" to depict "simple drives only ... rather than representations of a richer, more complicated human experience."[9] Thus all the romance in *Casablanca* vanishes the instant that an author such as Coover portrays Rick and Ilsa as oversexed bodies motivated by "simple drives."[10]

When Sam directs Jake's attention to his "favorite neighbor" in *Body Double*, he sets Jake up to become a slave to the drive. Ogling through a telescope to get a better view not of a woman but of a woman's body—and a body, moreover, that isn't even the one it appears to be—Jake experiences sex purely as a visual phenomenon, the way it is experienced in the graphic medium of the movies. The visibility of the body offers no clue about its reality; on the contrary, the revealed body is an ingenious illusion that in this instance is particularly devious and deceptive. Underlying Jake's cinematic fantasy in the Hollywood Hills (a glamorous socialite puts on a show just for him) is a mechanistic stagecraft of body doubling and body partitioning that, far from awakening his desire, has rarely shifted him into overdrive.

Shower Show: *Dressed to Kill* to *Body Double*

De Palma became intrigued by the body-double technique while working on *Dressed to Kill*. The opening sequence features Angie Dickenson in the role of Kate Miller, massaging herself in the shower while gazing longingly at a man shaving before the bathroom mirror, absorbed in his own image and utterly oblivious to her. Like Holly's dance in *Body Double*, Kate's steamy shower fantasy is accompanied by sensuous orchestration. Moreover, both scenes portray solitary women stimulating themselves in the presence of a physically or emotionally distant male—a parallel of the cinematic situation in which exhibitionistic actors perform at both a spatial and temporal remove from their voyeuristic audiences. While the scene of Holly's masturbatory ritual in *Body Double* is shot from the male voyeur's vantage (Jake watching from afar), the shower scene in *Dressed to Kill* incorporates Kate's perspective: close-up, partial shots of her soapy body are intercut with closeups of her face, yearning after the indifferent object of her desire. Then, as her arousal is about to peak, she is suddenly accosted from behind by a stranger in the shower. Desperately Kate struggles to attract the attention of the man shaving, who, impassive as ever, slowly turns toward her without a trace of concern about her attack.

An abrupt cut at this point makes it clear that, unlike the classic scene of Janet Leigh's assault in the shower in Hitchcock's *Psycho*, Kate's "rape" was not real. (Or at least not *yet* real; later in the day she will be both raped and murdered in two separate incidents.)[11] As we see her dutifully submitting to her husband's brutish pounding in a bout of rise-and-shine lovemaking while an insipid DJ announces the next Top 40 selection on the radio, we realize that her shower fantasy was a dream that her boorish husband interrupted. Waking his wife to gratify his morning desire, Kate's husband has cut short her erotic dream about a fantasy lover—or possibly about her husband, whom she can only experience erotically at a distance, in a dream. Thus, Kate's "fantasy" about being raped in the shower is hardly an expression of her own desire, as some of De Palma's critics have charged, but rather the means by which her unconscious registers the violent transition from her delightful erotic dream to a harshly deeroticized reality.[12] Through the rape fantasy, Kate's unconscious transforms the jarring experience of her husband's crude lovemaking into a violent sexual assault by a total stranger, a substitute for her actual husband. Meanwhile, the inaccessible object of her desire—the lover or fantasy husband absorbed in the act of shaving—slowly turns to cast a blank look at her before fading out of the steamy vapors of her consciousness.

The characters Kate Miller in *Dressed to Kill* and Jake Scully in *Body Double* are both dreamers whose erotic fantasies are rudely interrupted by a violent intrusion of reality. As Kate's shower fantasy about her lover is disrupted when her husband awakens her with his brusque lovemaking, Jake's brief idyll with Gloria is cut short by her brutal murder. More significantly, both Jake and Kate are victims of erotic substitution. Jake is seduced not by Gloria, as he believes, but by her body double, Holly, while Kate dreams up a fantasy double of her husband. But Kate is herself a striking example of the special effect of cinematic doubling. For the dripping torso in the shower to which the camera repeatedly cuts from close-ups of Kate's fortyish face isn't that of the actress Angie Dickenson, but belongs to a younger body double. As the character of Kate Miller is played by Dickenson, so the latter's body is played by yet another actress in a standard ploy to engage the (male) viewer's fantasy.

The use of the body double in the opening shower scene would seem to be merely a matter of cinematic expedience. After all, directors commonly substitute other women's bodies for those of the principal actresses in nude scenes, much as stunt men are typically used in place of the principal actors in action films. De Palma's own explanation for using a body double in the shower scene is not because Dickenson's body was unsuitable or because Dickenson was unwilling to be filmed in the nude; rather, it was a matter of practical convenience.

> Why put your principal in a situation in which she's uncomfortable, when she can rest and get ready for the next shot? It saves time, it's more efficient. Why should she sit around and be cold in the shower when she doesn't have to? I never like to put people in situations where I can double them. They have enough to worry about. (*DD* 25)

This explanation is disingenuous not because De Palma had other reasons for using a substitute for Dickenson's body in the shower scene in *Dressed to Kill*, but because the film abounds in doubles: exterior shots of the Metropolitan Museum of Art in New York are intercut with interior shots of the Philadelphia Museum of Art; psychiatrist Dr. Elliott, played by Michael Caine, has a Dr. Jekyll/Mr. Hyde character; and Kate possesses two identities as well as two bodies, that of married wife and single lover, which she clumsily (and fatally) attempts to reconcile. All this doubling suggests that De Palma's use of stand-ins is a matter not of cinematic expedience but of calling attention to the duplicitous nature of cinematic experience, whereby artificial effects are perceived as reality and reality is perceived as an effect.

This suspicion is confirmed four years later in *Body Double*, in which De Palma went even further in exploring the phantasmic basis of the real. The idea for the film occurred to him while selecting Dickenson's body double for the shower scene in *Dressed to Kill*. Clearly he was struck by the absurdity and artificiality of the selection process.

> If I'm hiring a body double, I call a casting agent, and what kind of girls do you think come to audition? They're Pets and Playmates and girls who do sex pictures who have great bodies. The whole process of looking at bodies to find someone to double someone, it's a bizarre experience! They just walk in and say hi, take off their clothes, you look at them, say that's right and that's wrong and thank you very much. I spent a long time just looking at bodies, it was like being in some kind of painting class. (*DD* 24).

The director was looking for the perfect "De Palma body" that he could use to manipulate his movie audience, an audience of unsuspecting voyeurs. So in choosing his ideal body, he was in effect also choosing his voyeuristic audience. From directing a movie—casting characters, manipulating actors and audiences—it was only a step to directing the perfect murder: selecting the ideal bait and the ideal witness. Who were these people? As Susan Dworkin suggests, "it began to shape up that she [the bait] was probably a girl who did sex movies (Holly Body) and he [the witness] was probably a rejected, miserable, lonely guy who was subject to attacks of immobilizing claustrophobia and could easily fall in love with a woman from afar" (*DD* 26). The exhibitionist and the voyeur—this was the ideal erotic relationship that epitomized the aesthetics of the cinema and the aesthetics of murder alike, and which De Palma thought to make the subject of *Body Double*.

As in *Dressed to Kill*, De Palma's use of substitutes in *Body Double* seems purely gratuitous at first; he seems unable to resist using a double, a stand-in, whenever he can. Even the dog in this film is played by two animals—one trained to snarl and one trained to leap (*DD* 55). As in the museum scenes in *Dressed to Kill*, in the scene at the Beverly Hills boutique Bellini's in *Body Double* De Palma uses two sets to portray one location—not because he needs to, but because he wants to. The obsession with doubles is especially obvious in the matter of casting. In creating the character of Holly Body, the adult-film star who doubles as Gloria Revelle in the film, De Palma screen-tested an actual adult-film actress, Annette Haven. Yet instead of using Haven to play the part of Holly, he eventually settled on a "legitimate" actress, Melanie Griffith (*DD* 38–43). Clearly, the "real thing" was not what De Palma wanted—not when he could have someone *else* play the part, and "reality" could be produced by (and exposed as) an effect. And the most efficient way to produce an erotic effect, and to exploit film's powerful appeal as a specular/spectacular medium that not only elicits the spectator's desire but engages the spectator's drive, was to substitute one *body* (or body part) for another at every opportunity.

All the obvious cinematic references in *Body Double* to Hitchcock's *Vertigo* and *Rear Window* on the one hand, and the apparently gratuitous and excessive violence directed against women on the other, have kept critics from appreciating this film's importance and from noting its close connection to De Palma's own *Dressed to Kill* with its innovative use of the body-double technique.[13] It's certainly true that Angie Dickenson's shower sequence in this film, and similar scenes in other De Palma works portraying vulnerable women alone in bathrooms,[14] are indebted to the classic scene in *Psycho*.[15] But it's also important to note how the shower scene in *Dressed to Kill* broke new ground by introducing the element of graphic fantasy in place of fear, and by calling attention to the cinematic effect of the body double—the device that would become the controlling metaphor of *Body Double* four years later. By thematizing this rather banal device as a key narrative element, *Body Double* exposed the basic mechanism not only behind pornography, but behind the reality effect of film and ultimately of film culture as well.

The Erotics of Substitution: *Vertigo* to *Body Double*

Perversion is ... a constant feature of sexual activity
in Hitchcock's films.

—Slavoj Žižek

In films such as *Rear Window*, *Vertigo*, *Psycho*, *Marnie*, and *The Birds*, Hitchcock exploited the movies' intrinsically voyeuristic disposition, their tendency to restrict the audience's viewpoint to that of a troubled, typically male character and to "draw the spectators deeply into his position, making them share his uneasy gaze."[16] De Palma readily admits learning this technique from Hitchcock. "Film is one of the only art forms," he has said, "where you can give the audience the same visual information the character has. It's unique to cinema and it connects the audience directly to the experience."[17] In *Body Double*, De Palma exploits the voyeuristic parallel between male protagonist and masculinized audience to an even greater degree than his predecessor. The movie is offered not merely as a suspense thriller but as an allegory of the cinematic experience itself. It reveals film as the voyeuristic medium par excellence, a medium that engages the spectator's drive and arouses his perverse interest in partial bodies and body parts (as opposed to awakening his desire for the "whole person") through a series of erotic substitutions exemplified by the body-double effect.[18]

Consider De Palma's use in *Body Double* of the basic plot structure of Hitchcock's *Vertigo*—a film De Palma had already "reimagin[ed]"[19] in his 1976 work *Obsession*. In both *Vertigo* and *Body Double*, the audience initially shares the mistaken view of the handicapped male protagonist (the acrophobic Scottie, the claustrophobic Jake) who stands by helplessly as the woman he obsessively loves perishes before his eyes. In *Vertigo*, Scottie (James Stewart) falls for Madeleine (Kim Novak), a woman who he has been led to believe is the wife of his acquaintance Gavin Elster, who asks him to tail her. In fact, she is Elster's mistress, Judy, who helps Elster conceal his murder of the real Madeleine by staging what looks like her suicidal leap from a tower in Scottie's presence. De Palma departs from Hitchcock's scenario in several ways. Structurally, he inverts the story by doubling the number of actual women with whom the male protagonist is involved. In *Vertigo*, Scottie is preoccupied first with the false Madeleine and then with Judy, who appears to be a different character but is in fact the same; in *Body Double* Jake becomes obsessed with Gloria and Holly, two women who appear to be the same character but who are in fact different.[20] Jake's drive is split between two women, while Scottie desires the same woman in two different guises. Yet there *is* a second woman in *Vertigo* besides Judy/the false Madeleine: the *real* Madeleine, who is killed by her husband. It's significant that Scottie never meets the only principal female character who is really herself; indeed, she appears in the film only as she is falling from the tower. In *Body Double*, in contrast, we see quite a bit of the real Gloria Revelle, who is also killed by her husband. In both films, the real wife—the reality principle itself—is sacrificed. However, by greatly enlarging the role of the real wife/victim in his film, De Palma problematizes reality to a far greater degree than Hitchcock, who removes the real Madeleine from the picture in order to focus on Scottie's altogether unreal Madeleine fantasy.

As for the decoy women who impersonate the doomed real wives in each film, they differ in a key respect. The false Madeleine in *Vertigo* is a character double whom Scottie gets to know; he desires her for who (he thinks) she is. In contrast, Holly, the false Gloria in De Palma's film, is a body double whom Jake knows only, at least at first, from a distance as the depersonalized assemblage of body parts displayed in her dance. Yet her depersonalization turns out to be her saving grace: she is genuinely innocent of any knowledge of Sam's plan to murder his wife. She has been led to believe her performance is nothing more than an elaborate practical joke that Sam is playing on a friend.[21] Whereas Holly the body double is a dupe, Judy the character double is very much aware of what is going on. She knows of Elster's murder plot against his wife and is, at least at first, an active accomplice. In her eventual confession to Scottie, she tries to persuade him that she had renounced Elster's plan after meeting Scottie and falling in love with him, and that far from deceiving Scottie at the tower by running up the stairs where he couldn't follow her, she was attempting to stop Elster from carrying out the murder.

Such differences point up the sharply divergent concerns of the two directors. Both films feature a protagonist who is set up to be the unwitting victim of a deception—in the case of *Vertigo*, to cover up a murder as a suicide, and in the case of *Body Double*, to conceal the murderer's identity. Hitchcock portrays the problematic conflict between a woman's *duplicity* and her *ethical integrity*: a man falls in love with a mysterious woman who isn't the person he thought she was—whom he loses, recovers, and then must ultimately renounce when he discovers the truth about her guilty past. De Palma, in contrast, presents the problematic of a woman's literal *doubleness* and its conflict with her *existential unity*: a man becomes obsessed with a mysterious woman who is *not* an individual with a single, self-consistent identity but two separate, *equally real* beings—the body he watches through the telescope and the woman he pursues right up to her death, all the while thinking of her as the image in the scope.

The implications of these divergent approaches are striking. Hitchcock presents a scenario involving an all-or-nothing ethical choice: either Scottie accepts Judy or he rejects her. If only Scottie had managed to overcome his moral scruples and not renounced Madeleine's double Judy, he could still have regained the "Madeleine" he adored. After Scottie refashions Judy in Madeleine's image—the most perverse scene in the film, in which Scottie's scrupulous attention to dress, hairstyle, and gesture actually leads him to the truth—the two women are revealed to be identical, and only Scottie's moral perception, and his judgment of Judy's character based on that perception, serves to distinguish them. De Palma presents a more ambiguous situation emphasizing the erotic double bind: Jake recovers Gloria's double (or original), Holly, but he will never be able to recover his erotic ideal, Gloria, "herself." By arranging for a porn star to impersonate his respectable wife, Sam had cleverly fabricated Jake's inaccessible ideal and made it real. And by impersonating Gloria, the substitute Holly can intermittently ("like clockwork") embody Jake's erotic ideal for him; however, she cannot *be* that ideal in any sustained sense. Even when Jake meets Holly face-to-face in the sex scene they are filming, he fantasizes that he is making love to Gloria, just as he had imagined Holly to be Gloria when he first set eyes on her. As he had watched Holly-as-Gloria through a telescope, he eventually manages to re-possess Gloria-as-Holly before a camera's lens (and during the filming of a porn film, no less), but he can consummate his desire for Gloria only through the mediating figure of Holly's body, which he must imagine as Gloria's. The erotic ideal is not only illusory and elusive, it is composite and artificial—a permanently missing original (re)produced through the interplay of substitute body images.

Body Double lacks the melodramatic poignancy of Hitchcock's *Vertigo* because Jake does not have to make the ethical resolution of renouncing Gloria's substitute, Holly, in the way that Scottie must renounce Madeleine's duplicitous double, Judy. Scottie's anguish truly begins when he discovers Elster's plot and the extent of Judy's involvement in it; in contrast, Jake's perversions, his hang-ups, and even his disabilities quickly disappear once he learns about the plot in which Sam hired Holly to impersonate his wife. Knowledge of the truth frees Jake from his double obsession with Gloria's glamour and Holly's body, and the film's rather tepid concluding section leads us to infer that he is finally able to see Holly as a whole person and to desire her for who she "really" is. But before this tidy resolution, *Body Double* presents a more authentic situation that is even more problematic than that portrayed by Hitchcock: the spectator's seemingly genuine desire for a seemingly whole person is exposed as a deluded obsession with someone else, and ultimately as a perverse drive toward body doubles and body parts. Whereas Scottie, much like Rick in *Casablanca*, experiences the clash between his erotic impulse toward an alluring woman and his ethical need to renounce her, Jake resembles Rick in Coover's "You Must Remember This"—beset by a pornographic phantasmagoria that is the result of his own willful ignorance. Jake shows no moral failure in allowing himself to be seduced by Holly's Salome dance; he simply demonstrates his vulnerability in a culture that routinely manipulates and deceives its citizens through its stock of fairly predictable mass-mediated illusions, special effects, and body doubles.

While film's graphic imagery inevitably elicits a voyeuristic response in viewers, its seductive power relies specifically on the tried-and-true techniques of mediated desire and mistaken identity. Instances of mistaken identity as erotic device abound in De Palma's films: the shower scene in *Dressed to Kill* in which Kate Miller fantasizes about an image of a husband/lover that bears no resemblance to her actual boorish spouse; the telescope scene in *Body Double* in which the "favorite neighbor" whose body Jake ogles from across the canyon is not the respectable socialite she appears to be but a porn star. The erotic circuits deployed in these films are indirect and open, not the simple, closed, unmediated engagements between lover and beloved found in romantic myths of love at first sight. Eroticism frequently entails the intervention of a third party, an intermediary, as Holly's body "fills in" for Gloria's as the object of Jake's voyeuristic gaze, or as in *Sisters* where doctor and patient, lover and beloved, need to re-create the presence of the deceased twin, the absent Other, in order to consummate their "union." Because of the substituted third party, however, and the mistaken identity it entails, that consummation frequently explodes in a paroxysm of violence—a point to which I will return.

Doubling and mistaken identity are hardly innovative techniques introduced by film; rather, they are among the oldest and most familiar theatrical and literary devices. From Plautus to Shakespeare to Dickens to Hitchcock, the device of mistaken identity has served as a (usually comic) means of stimulating characters' desires and titillating audiences. But the reproductive and reproducible technology of film is far better suited than the representational medium of literature to exploit the erotic effects of doubling and substitution. Viewers can be shown exactly what a character sees, although their experience and interpretation of the scene may be considerably different. Mistaken identity can arise in film through a variety of techniques—having the same actor play two or more roles (role doubling), having two or more actors play a single character (person doubling), or substituting one actor's body for another to create a composite being (body doubling). Whereas *Vertigo* relies primarily on role doubling, *Body Double* exploits the technique after which it is named; by making explicit use of this normally subliminal effect, the principle of identity itself is called into question. Not only may the characters in the film not know whom they're seeing, desiring, or even sleeping with, but viewers of the film themselves can never be sure whose body they're seeing.

Hitchcock and De Palma both give the dramatic convention of mistaken identity a specifically cinematic twist by following early misidentification scenes with improbable recognition scenes. Thus in *Vertigo*, Scottie runs into a woman months after Madeleine's death who bears an uncanny resemblance to her; perversely, he re-creates Judy as his dead love only to discover that's who she really is. In *Body Double*, Jake happens to see a film of Holly's dance after Gloria's death and is struck by its resemblance to the dance he glimpsed "Gloria" performing in her bedroom; eventually he learns that the woman he saw through the telescope really was Holly. Yet as similar as these identification scenes may seem, they are actually quite different: Judy really is the Madeleine whom Scottie loved, while Holly is not the Gloria Jake fantasizes about. To paraphrase Yeats, how can he know the dancer from the dance?

Although Jake can never recover Gloria through Holly, Holly was the basis for Jake's obsession with Gloria. Before Jake ever met Gloria or even knew who she was, Holly was the "original" object of his gaze. (And even Holly was only the latest in an extended series of erotic substitutions and voyeuristic reenactments of the primal scene that have obsessed Jake throughout his life.) Had Jake met the glamorous Gloria under different circumstances, without the mediating presence of Holly's body, it is unlikely he would have become obsessed with her to the point of actively pursuing her. As much as Jake may believe he desires Gloria, it's rather the *artificial* nature of the situation in which he first sees Holly-as-Gloria through the telescope—its staged, theatrical mise-en-scène—that enthralls and infantilizes him, stimulates his fascination in body doubles and body parts, and reduces him to a creature of the drive. The unlikely and unreal spectacle of watching a beautiful (and supposedly respectable) woman perform an erotic dance in her home and masturbate in her jewels—something the real Gloria would probably be unlikely to do—is too much for Jake, who finds this decoy Gloria irresistible. On the other hand, had Jake first seen the porn star Holly in one of her widely available films rather than in the persona of Gloria (as well as in the intimate and sumptuous setting of her bedroom), it's unlikely he would have taken more than a passing interest in *her*. Precisely because they are so different from each other, each woman mediates and eroticizes the other in Jake's eyes. Rather than the familiar theatrical technique of mistaken identity, it is the specifically cinematic artifice of the body double (especially in combination with the person double) that produces the erotic effects experienced by the infantilized spectator, the film's protagonist—himself a stand-in for the film's audience of anonymous viewers.

Vamps and Vampires

Big breasts remain [our] cheapest special effect.
> —Jim Wynorski, director of the exploitation film *Chopping Mall*

Jake's erotic ideal, we have seen, is an artificial, composite phantom produced through an elaborately staged process of impersonation. For him Gloria is the personification of Hollywood and, indeed, of the entire film industry: pure impersonation and theatrical illusion. Her loss is the necessary condition for Jake to come to any understanding of how he has been the dupe of his desire and of the hyperreality of Hollywood—of how his supposedly spontaneous responses to his most private fantasies have in fact all been part of a craftily staged, programmatic seduction analogous to the cinematic experience itself.

Ultimately, Jake is cured of his passive voyeurism/claustrophobia by becoming an exhibitionistic performer himself. In *Body Double*'s climactic scene, when Sam is about to bury Jake alive alongside the unconscious Holly, he taunts Jake by assuming the role of a film director who instructs Jake to scream—a response Jake's claustrophobic condition has previously prevented him from doing. At this critical instant, Jake conjures up yet another fantasy in which Ruben, the director of the horror movie in which he was acting, wants to fire him for freezing in a shot in which he plays a vampire lying in a narrow grave. With his job (and actually his life) at stake, Jake resolves to overcome his phobia and to play the scene through. Through an act of sheer willpower somewhat analogous to Scottie's moral will in *Vertigo*, Jake resists Sam and saves himself and Holly from their real grave. Jake's inclination to fantasy—such a debilitating quality up to this point— actually empowers him in this instance to overcome the imminent threat to his life. More darkly, however, De Palma hints at an equation between Sam and Ruben, murderer and film director, both of whom manipulate the hapless victim Jake for their *own* willful purposes.

Body Double may be read, then, as an allegory of a young man's liberation from his debilitating fascination with mass-mediated phantasms, and especially with those doubling effects that have become standard practice in the media's depiction of the eroticized female body. In this respect, the film is a coming-of-age account about a man learning to gain control of the erotic look. Besides objectifying the displayed female body, this look degrades and infantilizes the voyeuristic spectator himself, who becomes enslaved not to the alluring woman he watches and desires but to his automatonlike drive and to his own *looking*. But the film can also be read from the perspective of Holly, who is not only Gloria's double but Jake's. For as the punk vampire starring in Ruben's horror film, Jake sports a blond wig and black leather getup that makes him appear to be a parodic double of the porn star Holly Body. The exhibitionist and the voyeur complement each other perfectly, reinforced as they are in the roles of vamp and vampire with their corresponding specialties of sex and violence. If Jake overcomes his voyeuristic passivity and acquires a degree of autonomy, Holly frees herself to some extent from the exploitative and degrading conditions of the adult-film industry, not to mention Sam's manipulation of her for his own murderous purposes. It's certainly better that Holly does Hollywood rather than that Hollywood does Holly. But it's also the case that, as the dark (or is it the all too brightly lit?) underside of the Hollywood film industry, the adult-movie market is in some ways marked by an honest, realistic view of things that, as Coover demonstrated in the case of *Casablanca*, is ready to expose the romantic illusions and glamorous fictions propagated by the big movie studios for the deceptions they are.

The duplicity of the body-double mechanism is most fully exposed in *Body Double*'s coda. Having overcome his troubling claustrophobia, Jake is back in his starring vampire role. Ruben is filming him as he attacks an attractive girl in a shower—an explicit parody of the shower scenes in Hitchcock's *Psycho* and De Palma's own *Dressed to Kill*. After a take in which Jake suddenly appears from behind the pretty starlet, whose average-sized breasts are discreetly concealed by a towel, Ruben directs him to hold his position while he replaces the starlet with the body double—a rather plain, gum-chewing girl whose only asset is her figure. Ruben positions her into the spot just vacated by the starlet so that he can film the blood from Jake's fangs streaming over her ample bosom. (As the body double steps into place, she asks the accommodating vampire to be careful about touching her breasts, which are tender from her period.) While the bloodletting scene with the body double is being shot, the starlet looks on from offstage, where she is standing next to Holly, Jake's own blond-haired double. The adult-film actress congratulates her horror-film counterpart, telling her that after this picture appears she can expect to have "lots of dates." (No doubt those dates are bound to be disappointed when they discover that the starlet's real body fails to measure up to her body as portrayed in the shower scene.) No one is able to appreciate the deceptiveness of body doubles better than Holly, who played Gloria Revelle's double in the scenario devised by Sam to deceive Jake. Gloria's murder may have been solved and Jake's obsessional neurosis may have been cured by the exposure of the body-double deception—but what about the omnipresent deceptions, the unending cases of mistaken identity and false advertising in the media that regularly go undetected or unheeded by viewers and which routinely entice a mass market of consumers and moviegoers with a charade of erotic substitutions?

Body Double purports to expose this charade for the artificial mechanism it is, suggesting that its manipulative operation must remain unconscious and unrecognized from the voyeuristic viewer's perspective to be effective. By making the role of the body double explicit in the film, De Palma reveals its erotic effect to be less a matter of *mistaken* identity than fundamentally *anathema to the very idea of identity itself*. Impersonation, depersonalization, duplication, substitution—these are the techniques for producing the erotic effect by undermining the conventions of character identity and fragmenting the construct of the "whole person" into body parts, the playthings of the drive. And it is precisely this subversion of cherished assumptions about consistency of character, and even of narrative coherence itself, that makes eroticism—especially in its cinematic form—at once so pleasurable and so threatening, so exquisitely sensual and so horrifically disruptive.

The most systematic explanation of the close connection between eroticism and violence remains Georges Bataille's classic 1957 study *L'Érotisme*. For Bataille, eroticism is chiefly a matter of *dissolution*—not simply in the sense of the "dissolute life" (*la vie dissolue*) customarily associated with unbridled sexuality, but "a partial dissolution of the person" (*la dissolution relative de l'être*) as a defined, delimited, integral identity. "The whole business of eroticism," he maintains, "is to destroy the self-contained character of the participators as they are in their normal lives."[22] Viewed in this way, eroticism inevitably entails a "deliberate loss of self," the violation and dissolution of identity, the violent rupture of the body's limits and eruption of the excess energies in its entrails, the fragmentation of the individual's personality as well as his or her physical body into anonymous body parts.[23]

Bataille's emphasis on dissolution and depersonalization helps to explain why film should be such an ideal medium for producing erotic effects. Recent critics have echoed his insight that dissolution of identity is central to erotic experience. In her analysis of how eroticism functions in film, Laura Mulvey identifies two key cinematic techniques: the interruption and indefinite suspension of narrative in some disconnected, timeless state, and the fragmentation of the body itself into separate and anonymous body parts. Not only does the image of the exhibited woman attract the male gaze and interrupt the narrative's progress through suspension and digression, but it also breaks apart the illusion of spacial distance and depth, and is *itself* fragmented into a series of disconnected body parts: "conventional close-ups of legs (Dietrich, for instance) or a face (Garbo) integrate into the narrative a different mode of eroticism. One part of a fragmented body destroys the Renaissance space, the illusion of depth demanded by the narrative; it gives flatness, the quality of a cutout or icon rather than verisimilitude to the screen."[24] As an early generation of directors such as Griffith and Eisenstein demonstrated the importance of cutting between scenes in film, the generation of De Palma, Lynch, and Cronenberg have dramatized cinema's reliance on cutting between (as well as cutting up) bodies. They deliberately exaggerate film's characteristic technique of segmenting the bodies of actors—and especially actresses—in order to focus on one particular body part (Claire's knee in Rohmer's film of that name, or Katherine's neck in *The English Patient*), or to substitute the body parts of one actress for those of another, as in the breast piece at the end of *Body Double*. This movie makes clear that the much-discussed fantasy or "make-believe" quality of film—especially Hollywood film—is not so much a matter of cosmetics or "make up" as it is of the outright fetishizing and subliminal substitution of actual body parts.

Given its Bataillean concern with eroticism's close relation to violence and its portrayal of the affinity between Holly Body as exhibitionistic porn queen and Jake Scully as both her unwitting voyeuristic dupe and unlikely vampire double, *Body Double* actually has less in common with Hitchcock's movies than with a rash of films that appeared in 1986. Like *Body Double*, movies such as Jonathan Demme's *Something Wild*, Jean-Jacques Beineix's *Betty Blue*, and David Lynch's *Blue Velvet* all follow the same basic fairy-tale plot. As Greg Tate notes specifically in the case of *Blue Velvet* and *Something Wild*, the protagonists in these films are "naive, mild-mannered men" who are sexually "initiated" (although aroused and manipulated would be a more accurate description) "by women who are themselves living in terror of male psychopaths." The inexperienced or duped male protagonist ultimately establishes his manhood and resolves the vicious triangle in which he finds himself trapped by vanquishing the tormentor of the victimizing-victimized woman, avenging and liberating her in the process. Such films conclude with a return to normalcy, a resumption of narrative and social conventions. The aggressive-transgressive female, now freed from her persecutor, is reintegrated into society as a nonthreatening being, whereupon the narrative can draw to a satisfying close. In Tate's words, the "films end with their female leads' transgressive desires repressed back into socially acceptable madonna roles ... True to fairy tale form, rescue from the mouth of the dragon only liberates the ladies so they can be dragged back to the high castle."[25]

Anticipated ten years earlier in *Taxi Driver*, the clearest example of such cinematic fairy tales is *Blue Velvet*. Like Alice in her descent through the rabbit hole, the young protagonist, Jeffrey, is dislodged from his antiseptic small-town life and plunged into a sordid world of ruthless violence after he happens on a walk one day to discover a severed human ear on the ground—a detached body part. Jeffrey's eagerness to unravel this mystery soon leads him into an erotic crisis in which he is torn between two women: his infatuation with Sandy (played by Laura Dern), the blond girl-next-door who happens to be the daughter of the local detective, is threatened by his obsession with an exotic brunette, the nightclub singer Dorothy Vallens (Isabella Rossellini). After the scene in the latter's apartment in which Jake, concealed in a closet, looks on helplessly while Dorothy is savagely violated by Frank Booth (Dennis Hopper), Jeffrey's own desire is compromised and contaminated. As in *Body Double*, where Jake's viewings of Holly's erotic dance lead directly to the spectacle of Gloria's murder, violence constantly accompanies and conditions Jeffrey's voyeurism, from his initial glimpse of the severed ear to his presence at Dorothy's rape. But whereas De Palma employed all the conventional devices (soft blue light, bubbly electronic music, dripping jewelry, and a luxurious bedroom suite) to enhance the voyeuristic scene of Holly's dance before Jake's gaze, Lynch makes Dorothy seem as unappealing as possible to Jeffrey as he looks on from the cramped clothes closet— daubing Rossellini with garish makeup, giving her a hideous wig, locating her in a seedy tenement. The scene's grotesquerie is calculated to undermine Sandy's wholesome innocence in Jeffrey's mind. Henceforth he will be unable to love Sandy without fantasizing about Dorothy. Sandy's pure promise of spiritual, redemptive love will be shadowed by her double, for whom love is inexorably linked to brutality and ugliness.

Scenes of displaced desire proliferate in *Blue Velvet* and ultimately degenerate into violence. In every sexual encounter depicted in this film, "lovers" fantasize not about each other but about someone else: the psychopath Frank conjures up his mother while leering at Dorothy's vulva; Dorothy in turn dreams of her beloved abducted child and, later, of her husband when she seduces Jeffrey; in his turn, Jeffrey makes violent love to Dorothy, imagining her to be Sandy. Such displacement serves to stave off any ultimate communion or consummation and instead shifts the finite sexual act into an indefinite series of deferrals. Under different circumstances, unscripted and undirected substitution might have been an occasion for erotic free play. But when such substitution is a ruse, as in *Vertigo* and *Body Double*, an act of willful deception that conceals murderous violence and that enables its agent to go undetected, or when, as in *Blue Velvet*, such substitution is already the result of violence and only provokes further brutal outbreaks, we no longer have the ostensibly free, arbitrary substitutions of eroticism, but the media manipulation and power (dis)plays of pornography that exploit performers and audience, exhibitionists and voyeurs, alike.

The mid-'80s sadomasochistic fairy tale of "naive, mild-mannered men" who are sexually "initiated by women who are themselves living in terror of male psychopaths" was replayed at the end of the century in Stanley Kubrick's final film, *Eyes Wide Shut*. The premise here is much the same as in *Blue Velvet*: the young doctor William Harford leaves his well-ordered life with his wife, Alice, in their Central Park West apartment in order to seek sexual knowledge and adventure in the private pleasure palaces of New York's power elite. His unauthorized voyeurism at the orgy results in the death of Amanda Curran, a former beauty queen turned hooker whom Bill had once saved from a drug overdose. She returns the favor with interest, accepting the fate Bill has inadvertently brought on himself by sneaking into the secret ceremony. Offering to die in his place, Amanda steps out of her masked anonymity as an interchangeable double for all the other sex slaves at the orgy and becomes Bill's own substitute. Unlike the other versions of this adult fairy tale we have considered, Bill not only fails to rescue the endangered woman, but owes his life to her sacrificial act. And by giving up her life for him, Amanda also becomes Alice's double, since Bill will hardly be able to avoid thinking about her hereafter when making love to his wife. Alice will never be exclusively his wife again, not only because (as he formerly feared) she is fantasizing about someone else, but because he is now haunted by someone else.

Conjugal Adultery and Movie Children

I do not fuck a star. That's a primary rule of mine.... If I did have a real yen for that thing ... then I fuck the stand-in.

—Billy Wilder

The erotics of substitution informs contemporary literature as well as film, especially postmodernist narratives that make use of cinematic conventions. In *Gravity's Rainbow*, Thomas Pynchon repeatedly invokes a key cinematic paradox, exposing film's apparent realism as the result of deceptive artifice—the use of "the rapid flashing of successive stills to counterfeit movement" (407). Even more paradoxical is the phenomenon whereby cinematic artifice itself produces reality. Thus, in response to so-called intelligence reports during the Second World War indicating "that there were indeed in Germany real Africans, Hereros, ex-colonials from South-West Africa, somehow active in the secret-weapons program" (74), a secret Allied counterintelligence unit is formed. Called Operation Black Wing, its task is to enlist the help of German movie director Gerhardt von Göll ("once an intimate and still the equal of Lang, Pabst, Lubitsch" [112]) in fabricating a German propaganda film in England of "documentary" footage attesting to the actual existence of the "Schwarzkommando," a unit of black rocketeers in Germany. This bogus secret operation is said to be in keeping with Eisenhower's wartime propaganda policy: "the 'strategy of truth' idea. Something 'real,' Ike insisted on: a hook on the war's pocked execution-wall to hang the story from" (74). Later we learn that the Schwarzkommando really does exist, though it remains unclear whether it had been the real "hook" upon which von Göll had based his fictional film or whether, in a truly eerie instance of the reality effect, the film has itself somehow created the Schwarzkommando and made it real. There is good reason to suspect, in Friedrich Kittler's words, "that films are more real than reality and that their so-called reproductions are, in reality, productions."26

In another striking conceit, Pynchon extends Walter Benjamin's insight into the inherent reproducibility of film, implying not only that cinematic technology marks the transition from an aesthetics of representation to one of technical reproduction, but that film functions literally as a mediator of "natural," sexual reproduction. We learn that in the years before the war, the rocket engineer Franz Pökler saw a pornographic film in a Berlin theater. That night he returned home and impregnated his wife, Leni, while fantasizing about raping the star of the film, Margherita Erdman. Margherita, in turn, seems to have conceived her daughter Bianca during the actual filming of the sex scene watched by Pökler. Bianca is thus a cinematic twin of Pökler's child, Ilse, who "was conceived because his father saw a movie called *Alpdrucken* one night and got a hard-on" (429).

Such an instance of media-mediated conception is intended to illustrate the unplanned, unpredictable effects of film on its performers as well as on its viewers. But it also reminds us that in the specific case of pornography, two orders of reproduction are involved. For pornographic films are visual reproductions of acts of sexual reproduction: making a pornographic film entails making media copies of the act that produces biological copies of human beings. Moreover, mass-mediated

pornographic reproductions then become the impetus for acts of biological reproduction by those who see them, as happened in the case of
Franz Pökler. We assume that media and biological reproduction are
two separate activities and that each activity is controlled by conscious
agents. But there is good reason to suspect that both these assumptions
are not completely true, if not altogether false. There *does* seem to be a
relation between reproduction in biology and in the media, and both
processes may well follow a logic that is independent of human agency.
Indeed, *Gravity's Rainbow* suggests that the two orders of reproduction
are dialectically related in a manner whereby they mediate and influence
each other.

Stephen Dedalus's modernist observation that paternity may only
be a legal fiction (a sentiment that, despite its cynicism, champions the
artist's imagination over the exigencies of reality, the influence of the
obsessive idée fixe over mere hereditary determinism) receives a postmodernist twist by Pynchon: paternity is now revealed to be a cinematic
fiction and a media function. As a product of the movies, conceived as a
result of her father's pornographic fantasy, Ilse Pökler bears the traces of
her unusual parentage. During the war, she is taken away from Franz on
the orders of his supervisor, Major Weissmann, who allows her to visit
him once a year as a reward for his work on the A4 rocket. In effect,
Franz Pökler experiences the life of his "movie-child" (398) as a very
slow-motion film. His love for his daughter becomes

> something like the persistence of vision, for They have used it to create
> for him the moving image of a daughter, flashing him only these
> summertime frames of her, leaving it to him to build the illusion of a
> single child … what would the time scale matter, a 24th of a second or
> a year (no more, the engineer thought, than in a wind-tunnel, or an
> oscillograph whose turning drum you could speed or slow at will …)?
> (422)

Ultimately, Franz has no way of knowing whether the girl who has
briefly visited him each year for six years ("a daughter a year, each one
about a year older, each time taking up nearly from scratch") is really his
daughter, or even the same person; "the only continuity has been her
name" (422). And if Ilse is a movie child whose life Franz experiences as
a series of frames, what is Franz in Ilse's eyes but a movie parent—a
specter whom the fatherless girl may try to find in her dreams or among
the numberless father doubles in the movies she sees? Indeed, we can
imagine Ilse growing up to become the narrator of Schwartz's "In
Dreams Begin Responsibilities," helplessly watching her parents' lives
unfold, and her own destiny being determined, in every film she sees.

Pynchon anticipates in the verbal medium of literature what De Palma renders visible in the medium of film—namely, the power and persistence of mass-mediated images (including, of course, those of Pynchon and De Palma themselves), and their key role in manipulating the spectator's desire. Specifically, *Gravity's Rainbow* prefigures the insidious, paranoid possibility presented in *Body Double* in which a scene involving substitute love objects (Gloria's and Ilse's doubles) is staged by a demonic artificer (Sam, Weissmann) for an unwitting, solitary viewer (Jake, Franz). But Pynchon goes beyond De Palma in delineating the reproductive results of such mass-mediated eroticism. The dangerous influence of the movies that media critic Henry James Forman already described in his 1933 book *Our Movie Made Children* was even greater than he suspected: not only were the movies shaping children's beliefs and values, but they were involved in the actual process of producing children itself.

For De Palma, Lynch, Kubrick, and Pynchon, sexual desire is not the simple, spontaneous, direct relation between a lover and a beloved it is customarily assumed to be, but a mediated sentiment that easily unravels into perversion and substitution. The dream of romantic love is especially subject to such mediating relations, and in the novels and films under discussion erotic desire is informed and haunted at some level by the machinery of pornography: in *Gravity's Rainbow* Franz Pökler impregnates his wife as a consequence of seeing the rape scene in the movie *Alpdrucken*; the doctor in *Sisters* can seduce his patient only by re-creating the presence of her severed Siamese twin; Jake's desire for Gloria in *Body Double* is triggered by the sight of Holly's erotic dance; Jeffrey fantasizes in *Blue Velvet* about the virginal Sandy while making violent love to the brutalized Dorothy, and no doubt will be fantasizing about Dorothy when he finally consummates his relation with Sandy; Bill will be thinking about the prostitute who died in his place when he gets around to having sex with his wife at the end of *Eyes Wide Shut*. Such instances of substitution are hardly erotic in the sense of free libidinal play, but are better described as pornographic power plays.

And yet the distinction between eroticism and pornography is by no means clear and can't simply be reduced to dichotomies of play/ power or dream/reality. We can only reiterate the idea that pornography is concerned with *visible* sex: the lover is a spectator under the spell of the drive, which aims at bodies rather than persons, objects rather than others, parts rather than wholes. Eroticism is rather a matter of desire directed at another (whole person), who, however, is often only partly visible, if not out of sight, and who may even be an imaginary, composite phantasm derived from multiple individuals and myriad images culled from the media. Humbert Humbert acknowledges as much when he describes his staged love affair with Charlotte Haze in Nabokov's *Lolita*: "The sincerity and artlessness with which she discussed what she called her 'love-life,' from first necking to connubial catch-as-catch-can, were, ethically, in striking contrast with my glib compositions, but technically the two sets were congeneric since both were affected by the same stuff (soap operas, psychoanalysis and cheap novelettes) upon which I drew for my characters and she for her mode of expression."[27] "Ethically," there is a world of difference between Charlotte's "artless" account of her past dalliances and Humbert's "glib compositions"— especially when we consider that Charlotte's confidences about her past are a naive attempt to arouse Humbert's interest, while his made-up account of himself is a ruse to get at her daughter. But Humbert rationalizes that "technically" Charlotte's true confessions are cut from the same cloth as his own inventions, since they both borrow from the media—as if imitating a few stock phrases found in "soap operas, psychoanalysis and cheap novelettes" is the same as lifting entire characters from these popular genres. But while Humbert exposes the mass-mediated artifice behind Charlotte's apparent artlessness and his deliberate fabrications, he fails to recognize that his own erotic obsession with Lolita is no less artificial, no less a composite formation based on barely glimpsed, half-remembered images mediated by literature and the arts. Like Ilse Pökler, Lolita is Humbert's movie child.

Whom is it we finally make love to in film culture? The discrete lover whom we love so discreetly? Or the complex of nondiscrete and indiscreet fantasies we accumulate during our daily contacts with the media in their broad, all-encompassing domain? In their deconstructions of desire, De Palma and Pynchon reveal the beloved as a composite, hypermediated being rather than an individual with a definable identity or stable sexuality. Eroticism conceals what pornography reveals: the doubling of the desired object, its fragmentation into body parts, but also the splitting of the voyeuristic subject who lacks a core-identity and who often cannot perform and must only watch. Amid all the cinematic allusions in *Body Double*, we shouldn't forget Jake Scully's reply to the adult-movie producer who asks why he wants to break into the business: "I like to watch," he says. It's the same line Peter Sellers uses in the movie *Being There* when, as the cipher Chance, he tries to explain that he'd rather watch TV than make love to Shirley MacLaine.

part two

filmic events

Documenting Violence

Serial Violence/Surveillance

In today's film culture, our sense of what is real is determined, conditioned, and mediated as never before by movies and the other recording media. Nowhere has the blurring of fiction and reality occasioned more confusion and controversy than in the media's depiction of violence. Especially in the movies, where such depictions are ever more graphic, the distinction between real and fake violence is becoming ever less clear.

Given their increasingly violent content and the sensory overload of the theatrical presentation itself, the movies undoubtedly contribute to the confusion of real and fake violence in the minds of uncritical, impressionable viewers. But it isn't only—or even primarily—the movies that are responsible for this confusion; their detractors have done much to further obscure the issue. It's become standard practice in American politics for candidates of both parties to blast Hollywood for fomenting real violence through the fictional violence of its movies. Yet this presumed link between entertainment and violence is based on inconclusive and often highly contested social science research that, as critics such as Richard Rhodes point out, has consistently failed to demonstrate a "direct, causal link between exposure to mock violence in the media and subsequent violent behavior."[1] As usual, blaming violence on the media offers politicians a sure way of winning votes as well as a convenient means to avoid confronting the controversial issue of gun control and dealing with the immediate (nonmediated) causes of violence. Pointing out the mimetic fallacy in assuming that watching brutalizing behavior makes viewers brutal themselves rather than feeling brutalized, Rhodes argues that "violence isn't learned from mock violence," but from real-life "personal violent encounters, beginning with the brutalization of children by their parents or their peers." Yet as long as the gun lobby and other special-interest groups have an obvious stake in perpetuating the perception of a causal connection between fake and real violence, such a connection will continue to be made.

Whether the connection will be taken seriously by a population with a seemingly boundless appetite for sensational entertainment is another matter. If British novelist Martin Amis is right that "Americans don't want violence" and "probably don't want art, either," but want "escape from American violence," then it's a peculiar kind of escape that many contemporary movies offer—an escape from real to simulated violence.[2] Even during the debate over media violence following the 1999 Columbine High School massacre in Littleton, Colorado, an Associated Press poll found that only one-third of Americans considered violence the biggest problem with current movies (another third was primarily concerned about ticket prices), while the percentage of viewers who said they would avoid films with violent content fell from 60 percent in the preceding decade to 40 percent.[3] Even if violence in the movies isn't what Americans want, it's not something they particularly seem to mind.

And there's a wide range of simulations from which to choose. At one extreme are purely escapist entertainments in which mayhem is treated either as a joke (as in over-the-top gothic horror films such as Wes Craven's *Scream* and Peter Jackson's raunchy *Dead/Alive*) or as sheer spectacle (as in the meticulously choreographed violence of John Woo's and Ang Lee's action films). Such artificial violence could be mistaken for the real thing only by viewers who are either mentally incompetent or culturally illiterate.[4] At the other extreme are visual recordings of all-too-real acts of violence, as in films about the Holocaust or televised executions. Although such documentaries can hardly be considered simulations, there will always be some viewers who question such filmed evidence and who doubt visual documentation of historical occurrences such as Nazi genocide or the moon landing. As Sara Knox observes, if "fantastic fiction can be mistaken for fact, then certainly documentary media can be taken as other than 'real.'"[5] We can expect more such "mistakes" as documentary footage of actual events continues to be presented in its unretouched, often degraded condition, while events that never happened are made to seem uncannily real through the use of sophisticated digital effects. The example that is often cited is the scene in *Forrest Gump* in which Tom Hanks is shown conferring with Presidents Kennedy and Johnson, although both presidents had been dead for decades when the film was made.

Between the two extremes of absurdly artificial and actual recorded violence lie a number of mixed forms. Filmed violence may achieve the status of art when it evokes the unspeakable terror or horror of taking away a person's life. Artistic depictions of violence are less likely to seem gratuitous and sensational when, as in the case of *In Cold Blood*, they reenact actual incidents and can be considered a form of psychological or social documentary. When the movie *Dead Man Walking* appeared, critic Stuart Klawans had little difficulty deciding that it "came down on the side of art" rather than entertainment: like other "artworks," it expressed the sentiment that "Clint Eastwood's gunslinger says in *Unforgiven*: 'It's a terrible thing to kill a man. You take away everything he's got and everything he's ever going to have.' Whereas, in an entertainment, violent death isn't terrible at all. It's just useful, helping to kick the plot along or keep the audience keyed up till the next dumb thrill."[6] But the assumption of a clear-cut distinction between art and entertainment may not be nearly as evident as Klawans suggests, especially in the case of the genre of "realist horror," in which "violent spectacles [are presented] with an uncanny immediacy right before our eyes, with the immediacy that the camera also allows on our nightly news."[7] At a time when the distinction between news and entertainment has been all but obliterated, the media's presentation of murder—whether as news or art—is always *more* than entertainment; it's a *spectacle* of violence. And such spectacles have an important ritual significance, as we know from the role that human sacrifice, gladiatorial games, and public executions played in the past. They are ways of binding the community together, communal rites in which a certain solidarity, if not wisdom, is imparted.

A very different relation between art and violence is revealed by films such as *Silence of the Lambs* and its sequel *Hannibal*; the refined artist-killer Hannibal Lecter revives the romantic literary perception of the violent criminal as a kind of artist.[8] Other examples of films in this genre are *Assassins*, Todd Haynes's Super8 film made when he was eighteen dealing with the poets Rimbaud and Verlaine, and the 1996 film *The Death Artist*, in which corpses are transformed into sculpture. Also released in 1996, Dario Argento's *The Stendhal Syndrome* features a protagonist who suffers from a psychological condition whereby she becomes possessed by certain works of art. Initially her aesthetic debility leads her to become the victim of violence, but it's not long before she becomes a killer herself.[9] While the 2000 serial-killer hit *The Cell* abounds in allusions to contemporary artists such as Matthew Barney, Damien Hirst, and Nam June Paik, the serial killer in Mary Harron's *American Psycho* subjects the bland, ephemeral pop icons Huey Lewis, Phil Collins, and Whitney Houston to the kind of intensive critical analysis reserved for enduring artistic classics. From audiences' continuing fascination with the motif of the murderer as artist, it's only a step to the science-fiction convention of depicting the murderer himself as a work of "art," as in *Terminator 2*, or to the grotesque cyberpunk violence of Shinya Tsukamoto's *Tetsuo* films.

As artists working in a medium that is so often used to simulate violence, filmmakers occasionally present themselves in a sociopathic guise. While some movies of this sort may simply go for over-the-top black comedy, as in Mark Weidman's *Killer Flick* (1998) or John Waters's *Cecil B. Demented* (2000), the more problematic treatments of filmed violence explore the complicity between the person committing murder and the person recording the murder. In Oliver Stone's *Natural Born Killers* and in the 1992 Belgian movie *Man Bites Dog* (*C'est arrivé près de chez vous*), a news team and film crew are shown working in concert with a killer, not only complicit with his violence but providing an incentive for it. The members of the documentary film crew in *Man Bites Dog* are seduced by their subject, a bigoted but genial serial killer, and eventually join him in one of his murderous orgies. Having dispensed with any moral qualms about their project, the film crew ultimately loses any semblance of objectivity. (As if to underscore the fictional documentarians' identification with their murderous subject, both roles are played by the makers of *Man Bites Dog* themselves.)

Killers in the movies are sometimes portrayed as amateur filmmakers in their own right. In the 1986 movie *Henry: Portrait of a Serial Killer*, director John McNaughton not only collapses the distinction between murderer and moviemaker, but conflates the genres of documentary and narrative film by disavowing any explicit identification of "Henry" as the real-life "recreational murderer" Henry Lee Lucas. As a result, McNaughton's serial killer appears to be as much a fictional creation as one based on fact. But the chief reason that *Henry: Portrait of a Serial Killer* has proven to be so critically problematic is because it presents murder in a way that seems both real and staged. As Annalee Newitz has observed:

> The pseudo-documentary style of the film calls attention to Henry's "normal" act; the grainy photography and cinema verité acting invite audiences to see it as artfully constructed.... What appears to be ordinary in this film turns out to be both realistic and fake at the same time.... One can believe and not believe in these serial killer images at the same time.[10]

Given this degree of undecidability, it's not surprising that critics have differed sharply in their assessments of *Henry*'s "realism."[11]

In one of the most disturbing scenes in the film, Henry and his partner, Otis, watch their slaughter of a suburban family, which they have recorded on a stolen camcorder. Afterward they watch the tape again and again, frame by frame, as if they are filmmakers and film critics, actors and artists themselves. Cynthia Freeland notes that what makes this sequence so troubling, beyond the brutality of its content, is the viewers' discovery that "we are watching this footage alongside the killers." The combination of our identification with the killers in the act of reviewing the video of their deed and the "grainy, tilted ... amateur" appearance of that home video has the effect of "making the murders seem more real."[12] The viewer has the uncanny experience of watching a snuff film—a visual record of a murder filmed (and viewed) by the killer or his accomplices.

As I discuss elsewhere, snuff films lead an elusive, phantom existence that can't be verified, yet they tantalize and terrify us with the prospect that, supposing that they do exist, they depict a reality so horrific that it can't be publicly shown.[13] Snuff films present us with a paradoxical singularity in cinema: a documentary kernel truth shorn of any and all special effects, and yet a subgenre whose own elusiveness makes it seem the stuff of myth, the ultimate special effect. "The idea is to make it as real, as totally real as I can get it," says the director of the film-within-the film in Larry Cohen's 1984 film *Special Effects*. The director, Chris Neville, is referring to a movie he's working on which re-enacts a recent sex slaying. What no one but the viewer realizes is that in his "documentary" Neville has used footage of the actual murder which he's filmed himself committing. In order to achieve his "totally real" ideal, Neville has to resort to an actual snuff sequence which, in the context of a staged film, appears as the absolute limit in special effects.

Given the uncertainty as to whether snuff films exist, it's as if fictional films are striving to *give reality* to snuff films themselves—no doubt to arouse terror or produce a horror effect, but also to play on people's suspicions that there is a subculture out there in which such films are made, marketed, and enjoyed. The mythic status of snuff films has spurred underground filmmakers and, increasingly, mainstream filmmakers to incorporate simulated snuff scenes in their movies, employing all manner of special effects—prostheses, camera angles, and so on—to produce the illusion of reality. As horror and slasher movies strive toward increasing realism in their depictions of violence, it's inevitable that a subgenre of fictional films has come into existence that plays with the ambiguous reality of snuff films either by incorporating staged versions of such films or by documenting the making of such films.[14]

For the mainstream filmmaker aware of his role as a purveyor of violent imagery and as a murderer manqué, the only option may be to abandon his craft and go underground. This is what the Hollywood film producer Mike Max (played by Bill Pullman) does in Wim Wenders's

The End of Violence (1996). Having established himself as a major Hollywood player by making violent, commercially successful movies such as *Creative Killing* and his present project, *The Seeds of Violence*, Mike abruptly abandons his career after coming face-to-face with actual violence: he barely escapes being killed after inadvertently learning about a top-secret satellite surveillance project. Cutting off all contact with the world, the Hollywood filmmaker who made a fortune from exploiting and simulating violence is forced by the threat of *real* violence to go into hiding—in effect, outer-space surveillance drives him literally underground.

It turns out Mike's near-death experience has been observed by a man involved in the project whose job is to monitor such violent crimes and who also happens to be indirectly responsible for Mike's plight. Ray Bering (Gabriel Byrne), a former NASA technician, has been hired to work on the secret surveillance network, which is supposedly intended to eliminate crime and bring an end to violence. Instead of scanning the heavens from his lab in Los Angeles's Griffith Park observatory, Ray relies on his eyes-in-the-sky to view criminal activity on earth. All the while, he himself is closely watched by surveillance cameras in his lab that transmit his every move to the project's paranoid directors, who are wary of any leaks that might compromise their Orwellian undertaking. Ray, it turns out, has had second thoughts about the project, which he once attempted to share with Mike, whom he met at a surveillance equipment trade show. Considered a security risk, Ray is shot to death outside the observatory. (One assumes his death was recorded by the same satellite cameras he had been monitoring.) The surveillance project brings about the very violence it was designed to end.

It is commonly assumed that the commercial media tend to promote violent behavior while surveillance media prevent crimes or provide information leading to the identification and apprehension of criminals and terrorists. Thus, in the case of the 1993 murder in Liverpool of two-year-old James Bulger, a shopping-mall security camera recorded Bulger's abduction by two older boys; the discovery that one of the boys' fathers had just rented *Child's Play 3*—the horror film about the children's doll Chucky that comes to life and starts killing people—prompted investigators to study that film as a possible factor in the killing. *The End of Violence* turns this conventional wisdom on its head. Wenders seems to suggest that even if commercial filmmakers such as Mike Max renounce fictional violence in their pictures, they will have little effect on reducing violent crime in real life. This is because the "filmmakers" who have the greatest interest in and the closest relation to actual violence are not movie directors or producers but the under-cover police and intelligence agencies that have appropriated the most advanced film-recording technology for "security"/surveillance purposes. U.S. federal authorities and intelligence agencies have been using Global Positioning System (GPS) devices for years: whenever buildings and installations in Belgrade, Sudan, Iraq, or Afghanistan are targeted and hit, these operations are made possible by information—which often turns out to be inaccurate or incomplete—provided by satellite cameras trained on the earth. And GPS-aided surveillance is increasingly being used in local criminal investigations.[15]

While *The End of Violence* examines the relation between violence and surveillance, most mainstream movies ignore the connection or cover it up. A case in point is the movie *The Silence of the Lambs*, which, notes Martin Rubin,

> balances its superpsychos not with supercops but with a super institution: the FBI, depicted as an organization of dedicated professionals with a quietly overwhelming arsenal of high-tech communications, octopus-like aerial connections, and elaborate profiling and surveillance systems. These types of weapons easily can be turned to other, less commendable, more covert and political uses (and, in the FBI's history, often have been). Whatever the intentions of its makers may have been, *The Silence of the Lambs*, by trafficking in super criminals and super organizations, opens a Pandora's box of exalted institutional power that other elements in the film do not sufficiently counteract.[16]

In contrast, *The End of Violence* leaves no doubt as to the violent abuses of power that are all too likely when supersecret intelligence agencies employ state-of-the-art surveillance technologies. These institutions themselves need to be monitored and subjected to forms of countersurveillance. To some extent, Wenders's film begins to do this simply by calling attention to the problem. Few other films so clearly expose the violation of individual privacy by high-tech surveillance and contrast the diversionary artifice of Hollywood movies about serial violence with the reality of panoptic imaging directed by paranoid spymasters in the name of corporate, national, and global security.

Far from being Wenders's own paranoid fantasy, the dystopian vision of a panoptic future presented in *The End of Violence* is already a reality. The expectation, epitomized in the '60s mantra "The whole world is watching," that the presence of television cameras serves to deter violence through its coverage of news stories such as the suppression of the civil rights movement and the horrors of the Vietnam War, has given way a half century later to the realization that the whole world is being watched, and that to be watched is to be targeted. As the precision-guided "smart bombs" of the Gulf War made clear, whatever enters the camera's field of vision is subject to elimination. And in twenty years, the whole world—or rather the whole earth—will literally be on film in round-the-clock surveillance.[17]

The fact that the most sophisticated surveillance systems are by no means foolproof offers only cold comfort, as in the case of the mistaken NATO bombing of the Chinese embassy in Belgrade during the 1999 Kosovo conflict. Indeed, the more advanced such surveillance systems become, the more their limitations are evident. Yet we've also seen in the same year how bogus, politically motivated questions about the ability of monitoring devices to detect nuclear testing by rogue nations led the U.S. Senate to scuttle the Comprehensive Test Ban Treaty.[18] (This is much the same tactic that is used when politically motivated attacks on fictional violence in movies distract public attention from the "real" issue of gun control.) The scuttling of the test ban treaty, combined with the present administration's efforts to dismantle the Anti-Ballistic Missile Treaty and to restart the movie-president Ronald Reagan's "Star Wars" program—the ultimate surveillance project of all time—are almost certain to lead to a post–Cold War global nuclear arms race. In the cases of the Chinese embassy bombing, the Senate's rejection of the test ban treaty, and the likely implementation of the National Missile program, the actual cause of violence in the world has less to do with what is shown on movie or television screens than with what is—or is not—detected on surveillance cameras.

The Year of Filming Dangerously

In the late twentieth century, another kind of movie emerged that blurred the boundary between actual and staged violence. Although based on fictional stories, these films had a documentary quality because they were shot in (or gave the impression that they were shot in) one of the post–Cold War world's political hot spots, where military violence was always imminent. Directors in search of extreme realism might set their films in the midst of an ongoing conflict, as Volker Schlöndorff did in *Circle of Deceit*, shot in Beirut in 1980, during the civil war there. A more typical and less risky approach involved re-creating the conflict well after the fact. Thus Peter Weir's depiction in *The Year of Living Dangerously* of the swashbuckling adventures of an ingenuous Australian news reporter caught up in the failed Indonesian revolution of 1965 was made seventeen years after the events it portrays. (It would take another seventeen years for the film—banned by President Suharto who succeeded Indonesia's founding president Sukarno who was ousted in 1965—to be shown publicly in the country.[19]) Although the movie was not shot in Indonesia—the world's largest Muslim nation—but in

Australia and the Philippines, the cast and crew received death threats from Islamic extremists who feared the movie would be anti-Muslim.

Ziad Doueiri's *West Beirut* is set in 1975, during the Lebanese civil war, but wasn't made until more than two decades later, after Doueiri served as Quentin Tarantino's cameraman on *Reservoir Dogs*, *Pulp Fiction*, and *Jackie Brown*. Here is a striking instance of fiction mediating reality to create a filmic event: a filmmaker grows up in his native country amid the slaughter of civil war, goes to Hollywood with these images of real violence in his mind to work on shooting scenes of simulated violence, and finally returns to his native land to direct a semifictional, semidocumentary film about his country's war-torn past. Moreover, a key sequence in this picture centers on a film-within-the-film: the risky attempt of some boys to reach a shop just beyond the checkpoint in order to get developed some home-movie footage that they have shot.

Of course, shooting films under difficult or dangerous circumstances is hardly new. One thinks of Marcel Carné's *Children of Paradise* (1945), with its extravagant sets of nineteenth-century Paris, amazingly produced during the German occupation. The romantic world of the theater and boulevard life portrayed in the film seems infinitely removed from the turbulent events unfolding at the time of the shooting.[20] In contrast, the new genre of pseudodocumentaries makes every effort to integrate a volatile area's current crisis into the fictional story.

The Balkan conflict of the '90s has proven an especially fertile ground for guerrilla filmmaking. While Goran Paskaljevic's 1998 film *Cabaret Balkan* presents a surreal picture of ethnic tensions in Belgrade before the NATO bombing, Srdjan Dragojevic's *The Wounds*, released the same year, portrays the absurdist story of two boys coming of age in Belgrade from 1991 to 1996, during Serbia's self-destructive campaign when kids "have no hope for the future, no heroes except for criminals."[21] The plight of Bosnian children was the focus of Michael Winterbottom's commercial venture of the previous year, *Welcome to Sarajevo*. This film, about the 1992 siege of the Bosnian capital, records the ravages of a contemporary war while pursuing two quite distinct documentary objectives. Originally, Winterbottom was hired to film a screenplay of British television correspondent Michael Nicholson's book *Natasha's Story*, which describes his experience of smuggling an eleven-year-old girl out of a Sarajevo orphanage and bringing her to England as an adopted member of his family. In the face of international indifference to the Bosnian crisis, however, Winterbottom saw fit to use Nicholson's narrative as a framework for an expanded presentation of the siege that would "tell other people's stories rather than just Nicholson's own."[22] Nicholson's original account was accordingly interspersed with the activities of several of his fellow television war correspondents during their year of living dangerously. In the tradition of *The Troubles We've Seen*, Marcel Ophüls's 1995 documentary on correspondents during the Sarajevo siege, Winterbottom's mock documentary shows journalists encamped in the bombed-out shell of the Sarajevo Holiday Inn, bringing the horrors of the war to the attention of a seemingly indifferent world. By re-creating the correspondents' ordeal, Winterbottom continues their crusade, revealing the perils as well as the necessity of documentary journalism in a work that is itself neither a "true" documentary of war nor simply a fictional film portraying scenes of realistic violence.

The movie was shot on location in 1996, four years after the siege it depicts and six months after the end of the fighting and the arrival of NATO peacekeeping forces. Actual video recordings of the war provided by the local Saga Film Company that show civilians being shelled in the streets were intercut with scenes shot for the film, making it all but impossible to distinguish the two. Some of the documentary material (which takes up a tenth of the film) had been considered "too horrific" by news agencies to be seen on television and had been, in Nicholson's words, "on our cutting-room floor." Defending his use of the news footage, Winterbottom argued that "it seemed crazy not to use it ... the general principle was to re-create as little as possible. It wasn't a stylistic thing. It just seemed to be much more honest to use real footage." Yet one may question the honesty of a movie in which a seamless weave of existing news footage and original fictional material makes it appear that the actual documentary images are seen and shot by the fictional television reporters in the film. Curiously, as Alan Riding reports, Winterbottom insisted "that while he intentionally blurred fact and fiction, his purpose was to make things as real as possible, not to make some large metaphorical statement." One might have expected the opposite reasoning—that as an artist, a director would blur fact and fiction precisely to produce a "metaphorical statement" rather than "to make things as real as possible." But for Winterbottom and other directors, it is both necessary and acceptable to resort to special effects and fictional sleight of hand in order to make things (appear) real. It's not that Winterbottom is making excuses for himself or indulging in creative doublespeak. He may well feel justified in taking artistic liberties that border on deception when he's trying to reach audiences far removed from the conflict that either seem remarkably unaffected by straightforward documentary reporting of the truth or would otherwise never get to see the more gruesome and "horrific" images of the siege that wind up on the "cutting-room floor."

Welcome to Sarajevo isn't an artistic success. It sacrifices much of the coherence that would have resulted from a straightforward adaptation of

Nicholson's narrative as originally planned. Yet the film's achievement in publicizing the horrors of the Bosnian war is evident from the fact that it was endorsed by no less a publicist than Richard Holbrooke, the chief architect of the 1995 Dayton peace agreement. In Holbrooke's judgment, "the film really captures" the fact that "Bosnia was the greatest collective security failure of the West since the 1930s." But the film conveys this insight almost as an afterthought. What it really captures is the efforts of a ragtag group of journalists to document the sufferings of the Sarajevan people—and especially of the children—during the siege, and the need of those journalists to go to ever greater lengths, and to expose themselves to ever greater risks, in order to bring the cruelty endured by a besieged people to the attention of a world that has become increasingly desensitized to actual violence. When a United Nations official can dispassionately rank Sarajevo fourteenth among the world's most dangerous places, as is shown in one scene in the film, journalists clearly have their work cut out for them if they are to get outsiders to take notice of the Sarajevans' terror. Yet as much as the reporters covering the siege may welcome the fact that their story has finally been told in the powerful medium of commercial film, they may also experience a degree of resentment. Admitting that "the film is very real" despite the fact that "a lot of events are compressed into a short time," Nicholson has expressed amazement "that people like me spent four years trying to tell people what it was like and it takes a movie for people to get it."

Hidden Figures: The Assassination Scene from Antonioni to Zapruder

REPORTER: "I guess you prefer New York anyway. Things are more real?"

FILM DIRECTOR CHRIS NEVILLE (ERIC BOGOSIAN): "Any place real when you're making movies?"

REPORTER: "What characters influenced you the most?"

NEVILLE: "Abraham Zapruder."

REPORTER: "Who?"

NEVILLE: "Honest Abe."

REPORTER: "Can you spell that?"

NEVILLE: "Honest Abe."

—Dialogue overheard during opening credits
to Larry Cohen's *Special Effects*

I would venture to say that you could take the best expert today on moviemaking and he wouldn't be able to tell if it's real or not. The only thing is if you find the victim.

—Israeli investigative journalist Yoran Svoray on snuff films

Now that the recording media of film and video regularly present communal spectacles of violence, sensation, or humiliation (one thinks of President Clinton's nationally broadcast confession and grand jury testimony about his affair with Monica Lewinsky), it is no longer necessary to be directly present at such events, or even to be alive when they take place. No event shows this more clearly than the filmed assassination of President Kennedy, which marks a decisive turning point in the project of putting the twentieth century on film.

Throughout its history, film has had an affinity for assassination scenes. From *The Assassination of the Duc de Guise* of 1907 and D. W. Griffith's meticulous reconstruction of Lincoln's murder in Ford's Theater in *The Birth of a Nation* to *The Manchurian Candidate*'s presentation (only a year before the JFK assassination) of a brainwashed veteran's attempt to kill a presidential candidate, such scenes have become memorable cinematic moments. The suspense and drama that they generate seem ideally suited for cinematic representation and invite innovative techniques of editing and slow motion. Yet a profound change occurred in the depiction of such scenes after the assassination of John F. Kennedy. The focus shifted from the suspense leading up to the event, as the known killer is shown stalking his victim, to the drama *following* the assassination—the investigation into the identity, location, and motives of the unknown assailant or assailants. No longer merely a dramatic event in itself, assassinations were increasingly depicted as obscure and problematic, as events that entailed a laborious search for documentary evidence of what had taken place, and why. In its capacity as a recording rather than as a representational medium, film played a critical role in such investigations, particularly through the techniques of slow-motion and close-up photography—the retarding and even reversal of time, and the vast enlargement of minute details.

The change in the movies' portrayal of assassination since the Kennedy assassination stems from the fact that the filmed record of this event raised more questions than it settled. One reason for this ambiguity was the absence of authoritative coverage by professional photographers. The best visual evidence of the assassination in the prevideo period of the early 1960s was produced by amateurs using Polaroid cameras (Mary Moorman and David Miller) or 8 mm movie cameras (Mary Muchmore and Orville Nix).[23] Abraham Zapruder, who produced the most famous movie images, was not a professional cameraman but a dressmaker, and it was only by chance that he happened to shoot the twenty-six-second film that has been called "the most famous amateur footage in the history of cinema."[24] Because of overcast conditions on the morning of November 22, 1963, he had left his camera at home, and he retrieved it only toward noon, when his secretary noticed that the skies had begun to clear. In addition to this fortunate turn of events, one must marvel that this amateur filmmaker managed to keep his camera running for the entire duration of the tragedy, even as he saw and heard the impact of the shots.[25]

Although the record of the assassination that was inadvertently produced by Zapruder and other amateur photographers was invaluable as evidence, it was by no means comprehensive and comprehensible. Professional journalists and investigators were obliged to assemble some sort of coherent picture from these jumbled fragments. The Zapruder film in particular was subjected to intensive scrutiny by official governmental agencies for any evidence it might yield about the nature of the assault. It was not until the entire film entered the public domain, however—which didn't happen until twelve years later, when it was nationally broadcast in March 1975 on Geraldo Rivera's show *Goodnight America*—that assassination buffs studied these images of death with the same obsessive, voyeuristic fascination that other viewers respond to pornography or snuff films. "Indeed," observes Art Simon,

> the head snap in frames 313 through 315 [of the Zapruder film] became the site of an investigatory fetish, not only because they fixed a vision of the wound, but because interpretations differed as to the causes and meaning of the "involuntary spasm." Was Kennedy's body driven backwards by the force of the bullet fired from the front, or was its motion determined by a neuro-muscular reaction to a blow to the brain area?[26]

Assassination and sexual imagery are linked, suggests Simon, by the fact that they were (and are) both perceived as types of "dangerous knowledge" that could conceivably harm the impressionable minds of minors and of citizens accustomed to believe the government's official version of truth in those pre-Watergate days. But, as Simon reminds us, it's important to note that while the government chose "to make the infliction of [the president's] wounds public, if only through the printing of black-and-white Zapruder stills in Volume 18 of the Warren Commission exhibits, ... it chose to keep the images of death private" by "refrain[ing] from publishing any of the photographs taken during the autopsy."[27] Even today, it is primarily the dramatic images of "the infliction of wounds" that are in the public domain; most of "the images of death" represented by the autopsy photographs remain off-limits, and are "missing"—as, indeed, are slides of tissue sections of the president's wounds, and even his brain itself, which mysteriously disappeared from the National Archives.

Given the unavailability of such crucial images and evidence, it has been up to journalists, assassination critics, and conspiracy buffs to fill in the gaps in the historical record with their own images and interpretations of the Kennedy assassination. All the media attention given to sensational stories such as the death of JFK and, more recently, the brutal murder of O.J. Simpson's ex-wife, Nicole Brown Simpson, and Ronald Goldman (one thinks especially of the camera's presence in Judge Ito's courtroom, which turned the trial into a public spectacle and the country into a nation of voyeurs) can't make up for the media's absence from the actual murder scenes and their failure to record what "really" happened at the crime scene.[28] Precisely the opposite situation was involved in Princess Diana's death in 1997; the presence of the paparazzi at the crash site gave rise to suspicions that they recorded the event and may even have caused it. But in the case of murders such as the Kennedy assassination and the Simpson-Goldman killings, the *lack* of photographic documentation was the problem. (Then there is Pier Paolo Pasolini's claim in the case of the Kennedy assassination that even if we had access to other filmed records of the event, shot at the same time but from different vantages and angles, we would still only have a series of separate sequence shots that would contribute nothing to our understanding until they were edited into a meaningful montage.)[29] In an effort to compensate for this lack of photographic documentation, the news media devoted all their resources to "covering" these events, as if a surplus of media analysis and commentary could uncover or recover the truth by reconstructing the missing murder scene in a responsible, convincing, authoritative way. Especially in the investigation of the Kennedy assassination, the numerous reconstructions and interpretations inevitably conflicted, and often obscured more than they revealed.

Amid—and perhaps adding to—this confusion, the task of making sense of the assassination has ultimately fallen to, of all people, artists and narrative filmmakers. On one hand, Oswald is portrayed in DeLillo's documentary novel *Libra* as a man acting out the assassination scenarios of movies he happened to see on TV a few days before JFK came to Dallas—*Suddenly* and *We Were Strangers*.[30] (The last film Kennedy is believed to have seen before his death was *Tom Jones*.) On the other hand, there are all the films to which the assassination itself gave rise. In his discussion of five movies related directly or indirectly to the JFK assassination/conspiracy (*Executive Action*, *The Parallax View*, *Winter Kills*, *Blow Out*, and *JFK*), Art Simon notes that despite their differences, the films "are thoroughly inscribed by the discourses of investigation" and "make the investigation process the defining concept for their narratives."[31] The earliest of the films discussed by Simon appeared in 1971; yet five years before this, and only three years after the Kennedy assassination, Michelangelo Antonioni's *Blow-Up* appeared—a film that, while making no mention of the event and bearing no direct relation to it, was marked by the assassination in several important ways.[32] *Blow-Up* went on to have a major influence on filmmakers such as Francis Ford Coppola in *The Conversation* and Brian De Palma in *Blow Out* and *Snake Eyes*, whose movies called attention to the analytic or investigatory use of recording media. Moreover, *Blow-Up* even presaged the growing use of documentary evidence in criminal investigations; as examples, we might note the proliferation in the past few decades of surveillance cameras in public as well as private areas and the installation of video cameras in police cruisers, in local TV-news helicopters, in cockpits of commercial aircraft, and even at major traffic intersections to record drivers running red lights.

Although *Blow-Up*'s credits state that it was inspired by Julio Cortázar's story "Las babas del diablo" ("Devil's Drool"), the principal source for the film is arguably the Kennedy assassination. Antonioni admitted that he "was not so much interested in the events [of Cortázar's story] as in the technical aspects of photography. I discarded the plot and wrote a new one in which the equipment itself assumed a different weight and significance."[33] Specifically, Antonioni borrowed Cortázar's idea of making his protagonist a still photographer who believes he's basically in control of whatever shot he takes, and whose aspirations to express his own vision of things in this supposedly representational medium are undercut by its recording function that exposes his own perceptual limitations. In both Cortázar's story and Antonioni's film, the photographer takes a candid picture or series of pictures in an idyllic setting of what appears to be an amorous couple, only to discover, after he develops the pictures in his studio and studies the enlargements, that he's recorded a very different, far more sinister situation. Cortázar's amateur photographer, Michel, realizes that the seduction he thinks he's witnessed (and interrupted)—namely, of a boy by an older woman—is actually a different kind of seduction. The woman was procuring the boy for an accomplice, an older man in a nearby car who had been watching the scene that Michel was photographing, but with quite a different interest. In contrast, the photographer in Antonioni's film (played by David Hemmings) takes not just a single shot but a series of photographs of a couple consisting not of a boy and an older woman but of a young woman (Vanessa Redgrave) and an older man. In the wake of the Kennedy assassination, Antonioni altered the woman's accomplice, who is concealed in the margin of the frame. Instead of the lecherous old man in Cortázar's story, who is outside the frame of Michel's photograph, the montage of enlargements in *Blow-Up* reveals an assassin hidden in the bushes—possibly a lover closer to her own age than the man she has lured into the gunman's range of fire. Antonioni transforms

Cortázar's scenario by making the old man the victim rather than the assailant, the young man (presumably) the assailant rather than the victim, and the "crime" a murder rather than a sexual setup. Only the woman's role remains constant in both works: as in Hitchcock's *Vertigo*, she is a decoy, in this case luring her male companion into striking range of her accomplice waiting in the wings (the libertine in the car in Cortázar's story, the gunman in the bushes in Antonioni's film).

In both works, however, there is a second individual outside of the frame: the photographer himself. An implicit link is drawn between the two marginal figures watching the couple—the photographer and the libertine in Cortázar's story, the photographer and the gunman in Antonioni's film. Stalking the couple, the photographer is either the gunman's or the libertine's double; in Cortázar's story, the camera becomes the equivalent of the libertine's phallus, while in Antonioni's film the camera is the equivalent of the assassin's gun.

Antonioni goes to great lengths to emphasize the parallel between the photographer and the gunman, both of whom are simultaneously stalking the couple in the park, each without the other's knowledge. At one point, the photographer jumps behind the picket fence bordering the park and snaps off a few pictures of the couple from the dense bushes behind the fence. He is then shown moving from his left to his right behind the fence, edging closer to the couple, taking a few more pictures, and then jumping back over the fence into the park. Later, when he develops and enlarges the pictures in his studio and discovers the gunman situated further along behind the same fence, it becomes clear that had the photographer continued his progress behind the fence, he would have run directly into the assassin. Unaware of each other, both men are shown converging on the same vantage point from which to shoot either photos of or bullets at the couple.

All of which leads us back to Zapruder's home movie of JFK's assassination. Although this film did not become generally available until 1975 and thus could not have been seen by Antonioni, its existence was well known, and individual frames had appeared in *Life* magazine only a week after the assassination occurred, as well as subsequently in the Warren Commission report. As the best documentary evidence of the assassination, the Zapruder film was used by critics of the commission to support their thesis that the fatal shot that killed Kennedy in frame 313 was fired by someone other than Oswald. This second gunman, it is argued, would have been positioned on the grassy knoll behind Zapruder and to his right, concealed by a wooden picket fence that has been the focus of conspiracy theorists' investigations and that figures so prominently in Oliver Stone's film *JFK*. If the fatal shot was fired by a gunman on the grassy knoll, as many believe—relying in part on evidence provided by the Zapruder film itself—Zapruder would have been standing in a relation to this gunman behind the picket fence that was analogous to the one between the photographer in *Blow-Up* and the shooter behind *that* picket fence. As the older man in the company of his wife or lover was the killer's target in Antonioni's film, so Kennedy was seated next to his wife when he was shot. With uncanny prescience—knowing, no doubt, of the Zapruder film, but not having seen the film in its entirety, nor yet aware of the conflicting theories it was to incite—Antonioni replicated in *Blow-Up* the precise triangular configuration of gunman-target-cameraman that characterizes the grassy-knoll scenario in the Kennedy assassination.

The most important parallel to JFK's murder in *Blow-Up*, however, concerns the extended sequence in the photographer's studio when he discovers the gunman by developing his pictures of the lovers in the park, enlarging them, and pinning them up around his studio in a montage that enables him to reconstruct the entire event as if he had made a movie rather than a succession of stills. Only after he greatly enlarges a small section of one of the pictures is he able to discern the gunman behind the fence. Antonioni thus has his protagonist anticipate the technique that investigators such as optics technician Robert Grodon would use two years later in his analysis of a bootleg copy of the Zapruder film. Based on the "enhanced view of the shooting" afforded by "enlarg[ing] those images depicting the head wound," Grodon would conclude that the footage "provided 'absolute, incontestable proof of cross-fire and conspiracy.'"[34] Even more relevant to *Blow-Up* are the enhancements and enlargements that were made not of Kennedy in the Zapruder film but of suspicious figures in other photographic evidence collected from the assassination site. Blurry shadows and lights in these photographs—especially those taken of the grassy knoll, to the left of and behind the spot where Zapruder was filming—have been scrutinized as evidence of possible gunmen, though without any definitive results. All this meticulous analysis of the filmed record is an attempt to discover the presence of the gunman within the frame, when the significant feature so intensely sought in much photographic evidence often lies outside the frame.

While certain narrative and thematic elements of *Blow-Up* were influenced by the known circumstances of Kennedy's assassination, Antonioni's film may in turn have affected the attitudes, and even the approach and technique, of investigators examining photographic evidence of the assassination. This is one aspect of a general phenomenon that Ralph Rugoff calls a "forensic aesthetic": as photographers and filmmakers increasingly emulate the themes and procedures of criminal investigation, professional criminalists routinely investigate and prosecute cases on the basis of "aesthetic" or media evidence.[35] Such evidence is often inadvertently recorded by amateurs with access to cheaper and more sophisticated media technology—George Holliday's videotape of the Rodney King beating, for example, or photographs sought by the FBI in connection with the bombings at Atlanta's Centennial Park during the 1996 Olympics. And since Mark David Chapman's murder of John Lennon in 1980 and John Hinckley Jr.'s 1981 assassination attempt against President Reagan, we've become familiar with the possibility that spectacular acts of violence may be mediated by literary and cinematic fictions.[36] Criminal investigators now routinely treat literary narratives as potential evidence of illicit activity; thus, the Unabomber's published manifesto provided crucial clues to his identity, and investigators subpoenaed the list of Monica Lewinsky's reading material for information it supposedly revealed about her relationship with President Clinton.

Evidence is one thing; interpretation of that evidence is something else. After Antonioni's photographer discovers the figure of the gunman in one of the pictures he has taken in the park, he believes that he has prevented a murder from occurring, just as Michel in Cortázar's story takes credit for having saved the boy from his female companion's wiles and her accomplice's sexual predations. But the photographer in Blow-Up is mistaken. When he's able to look at the pictures from the park from a fresh perspective—namely, after the famous orgy scene with the two girls, which apparently helped to clear his head—he notices a splotch in one of the last pictures in the sequence. An extreme enlargement reveals a grainy shape that could be a corpse under a bush, but which the photographer can verify only by revisiting the park and seeing for himself. Far from having prevented a killing, the photographer has witnessed and indeed recorded a murder. But he is unable to prove anything, because all the evidence he has compiled suddenly vanishes: returning to his studio, he finds his equipment smashed and all the prints and negatives stolen. And when he returns to the park with his camera the following day to take pictures of the corpse, it's no longer there. No trace of the murder is left except for a single print that the thieves have inadvertently left behind—the enlargement of the grainy image of the corpse. Yet this image is so unintelligible that when the wife of his abstract-artist friend sees it, she comments, "It looks just like one of Bill's paintings." The one remaining piece of photographic evidence of the murder has the appearance of an abstract painting, an artistic representation that is useless as recorded evidence.[37]

The two scenes in which the photographer returns to the park to document the corpse are precisely analogous to the two confession scenes in Polanski's Death and the Maiden in which Dr. Miranda admits his role in Paulina's torture. In *Blow-Up*, the photographer first returns to the park at night *without his camera* and discovers the corpse; when he returns *with his camera* the following day, the corpse is gone. Similarly, whereas Dr. Miranda's first videotaped "confession" in Polanski's film is useless as evidence because it is so obviously staged, the second confession on the cliff appears "true," but it is unrecorded—or perhaps it appears true *because* it is unrecorded. In both films these sequences clearly show the limitations of the recording media in documenting evidence of truth and violence. It's one thing to use the recording medium of film to *discover* the truth as the photographer does in *Blow-Up*; it's something else, he learns, to use that same medium to *document* the truth and to establish it as public record.[38]

As in the case of the Zapruder film of JFK's assassination, the photographic evidence of the killing in *Blow-Up* provides visible documentation of a murder that is nevertheless fraught with ambiguity, and ultimately it doesn't prove very much at all. But the documentation of Zapruder and Antonioni's photographer fail for different reasons. Antonioni's photographer had been able to obtain a relatively complete cinematic sequence of the murder in the park, and he had even inadvertently recorded a picture of the shooter on the border of the park, in the margin of one of his pictures of the "lovers." Only the fact that the photographs happen to be stolen from his studio makes them unavailable as comprehensive evidence of the murder. In contrast, although Zapruder's film preserves a record of JFK's death, that record is incomplete because the figure of the gunman (or gunmen) in the act of shooting remains missing. Zapruder's film fails to lay to rest the conspiracy theories about JFK's death because while it shows the president being shot, it doesn't show, and can't even establish, who is doing the shooting. Its significance lies outside the frame. Antonioni's fictional film suggests that the photographic apparatus can provide a complete record of events as long as contingent factors don't intervene, while Zapruder's real-life film raises doubts that such a complete account is ever possible.

In either case, film's documentary function ultimately fails. When in *Blow-Up* the photographic evidence of the murder disappears and the photographer is left with only a greatly enlarged, grainy photo of the corpse, his documentary endeavor collapses. His use of film as a medium of reproduction, a means of recording reality, is undercut by film's artistic function as a medium of representation. Instead of showing a slice of real life, the photographer has only produced a work of artistic appearance and illusion. What's particularly ironic about this is that throughout *Blow-Up*, the protagonist has been striving to rise above his job as a commercial fashion photographer and become an art photographer. He had been hoping to include the shots of the lovers in the park in a book of photographs he'd taken in a dosshouse; the grim poverty and violence of the lives of the homeless were to have been rounded off by the peacefulness of the pictures in the park. Behind the obvious irony that his presumably idyllic shots of lovers in a park unwittingly document a violent murder lurks a deeper paradox. As an aspiring art photographer, Antonioni's protagonist has striven to give artistic expression to banal reality in an honest way—that is, raising the documentary (and commercial), reproductive nature of his medium to the level of artistic representation. With his candid photos in the park he achieves this artistic goal only too well: on the one occasion when he needs to use a photograph as documentary evidence, it is regarded *as* art. Having struggled so long against having his lofty artistic intentions undercut by the documentary nature of his medium (representation undercut by reproduction, the illusion of art undercut by the reality of life), he finds that when he requires the medium to live up to its documentary expectations, it is treated as art without any evidentiary value. If the documentation and the investigation of crimes are based on the belief, as Art Simon writes, that "camera vision asserts its superiority over the power of the human organ" of the eye, the value of the knowledge provided by the recording apparatus, and the long-standing assumption of the connection between knowledge and the visible, seems forever open to question.[39]

In contrast to the convention of the missing scene discussed in chapter 1, *Blow-Up* establishes the convention of the hidden figure. According to this convention, viewing a photograph or a film under normal conditions fails to reveal what is really going on in the scene—a murder committed by a hidden assassin. This only becomes visible when the photograph is greatly enlarged, or when the film is slowed down or stopped and studied one blown-up frame at a time. But taken together with the Zapruder film, *Blow-Up* also suggests that such intense scrutiny of the magnified image does not necessarily bring the viewer any closer to the truth. In fact, since the optical principle behind the filmic medium is the use of still images to create the illusion of movement, intensive frame-by-frame analysis of a given cinematic sequence often reveals that significant movements or events are *not* actually in the film, as the viewer supposed, but in the viewer's mind. Such scenes are not so much "missing" as they are *filled in*.[40]

Surprise Executions

Filmed assassination scenes tend to evoke responses either of surprise or acute suspense. When an actual murder is unexpectedly recorded, as in the case of Zapruder's inadvertent filming of JFK's death, viewers may be startled even after repeated showings. Suspense is a more likely response in the case of narrative films when viewers have privileged foreknowledge of the assassin's actions, as in the reconstruction of Booth's murder of Lincoln in *The Birth of a Nation* or the depiction of a brainwashed veteran stalking his victim in *The Manchurian Candidate*. In these films in which the assassination scene takes place before a crowd in a public arena (a theater or hall), tension is generated by the viewer's privileged knowledge; only the viewer knows what is about to take place and, as if in a dream, is powerless to communicate that knowledge. When the shots finally ring out, everyone in the film reacts with horrified surprise except the viewer, who feels utterly isolated.

While assassinations are generally secret operations that take people off guard, everyone knows what's coming in execution scenes. Here suspense combined with anticipation or dread is the order of the day. Executions—which Sara Knox has called "the last great secular ritual surrounding death in American culture," a ritual that is "important, if not critical, to that culture's sense of its own *life*"—lend themselves to film even more than assassinations because they are spectacles, staged events with their own ritual and ceremony.[41] It was, after all, not President William McKinley's 1901 assassination that Thomas Edison's studio reenacted on film, but the execution that same year of his killer, the anarchist Leon Czolgosz. With its depiction of the condemned man approaching the electric chair, being strapped down, blindfolded, and finally electrocuted while staring directly into the camera, *Execution of Czolgosz with Panorama of Auburn Prison* elicited a voyeuristic response in the viewer rather than surprise at a time when cinema was a "medium of shock and excitement and stimulation."[42] "Spectacle films" like this—or like the one two years later that showed a Coney Island circus elephant being electrocuted after it went on a rampage, "the first real death filmed for entertainment purposes"[43]—flourished before settling into a narrative form.

In a narrative context, however, the spectacle of execution became an especially prominent feature. One of the most frequently dramatized historical subjects in the history of cinema, after all, is the story of Joan of Arc, culminating in the nineteen-year-old girl's trial and immolation in the marketplace at Rouen. Six films had already been made about the Maid of Orléans by the end of World War I, most notably Cecil B. DeMille's *Joan the Woman* (1916). Numerous remakes followed throughout the century, the most famous being Carl Dreyer's *Passion of Joan of Arc* (1928), with Maria Falconetti; Victor Fleming's *Joan of Arc* (1948), starring Ingrid Bergman; Otto Preminger's *Saint Joan* (1957), featuring Jean Seberg; Robert Bresson's *Trial of Joan of Arc* (1962), with Florence Carrez; Jacques Rivette's *Joan the Maid* (1994), starring

Sandrine Bonnaire; and most recently the sensationalistic *The Messenger: The Story of Joan of Arc* (1999), directed by Luc Besson of *La Femme Nikita* fame. Three more films about Joan were in production at the century's end.[44]

As a spectacle, executions have elicited antithetical responses from observers, appealing to people's voyeuristic appetites or compelling them to turn away. During the Reign of Terror, Robespierre refused to watch any of the beheadings he ordered, declaring that public executions brutalized character; in contrast, the painter Jacques-Louis David, Robespierre's admirer and a great promoter of public spectacles, had no such qualms and sketched Marie Antoinette and others on their way to the guillotine. A similar divergence of attitudes was evident in the United States in the early 1990s when the issue arose of whether executions ought to be televised, ostensibly as a way of deterring crime. The decision not to allow actual executions to be broadcast publicly, while staged murders of the most brutal kind continued to be routinely shown on television and film, might seem a contradiction in popular attitudes regarding what is viewable and what is not. And yet a work such as Kieslowski's *A Short Film about Killing* points up the difficulty in making such determinations: after an excruciating, extended murder sequence, the film concludes with an even more horrific legal execution.[45]

Although executions aren't likely to occasion surprise in the manner of assassinations, writers and filmmakers have found ways to provoke such a reaction from their audiences. A well-known example is Robert Enrico's *An Occurrence at Owl Creek Bridge* (1962), based on Ambrose Bierce's 1891 short story set during the Civil War. The film depicts a regiment of Union soldiers in the process of hanging the southern planter Peyton Farquhar from a bridge he had tried to burn. Both Bierce's story and Enrico's film open at sunrise with an objective account of the ritual preparations for the execution on the bridge; gradually the narrative shifts to Farquhar's subjective point of view. As the fatal instant approaches, his perceptions become heightened and distorted; the ticking of his watch, for example, becomes increasingly audible while seeming to slow down. When the order is finally given in the film for the hanging to take place, the rope breaks and Farquhar plunges into the river. A slow-motion sequence ensues, showing the escaped planter struggling underwater to free his hands from the ropes and his feet from his boots, and then gasping for air as he returns to the surface. Only when he desperately swims away to escape the soldiers firing at him from the bridge is the world shown returning to normal speed. The rest of the film follows Farquhar's flight home during the course of the day. Exhausted by his ordeal, he finally catches sight of his wife and runs to her embrace. Just as they meet, the music stops and the scene abruptly shifts back to the bridge, where the hanging is shown taking place without a hitch.

Even if the attentive viewer has followed the visual and auditory cues (the slowing down of motion and sound, the musical accompaniment) indicating that the entire daylong flight sequence is actually an extended fantasy experienced by Farquhar a minute or so before his death, the abrupt return to reality at the very peak of the fantasy still comes as a shock. What had seemed to be a graphic document of an objectively observed public spectacle is revealed to be the compelling escape fantasy of a condemned man. As a result, the viewer experiences the inevitable moment of execution as an unexpected, jolting turn of events.

In its impact on the viewer, the film version of *An Occurrence at Owl Creek Bridge* actually surpasses the story on which it was based. Written only a few years before the invention of film, Bierce's story is ideally suited for the new medium as Enrico's adaptation demonstrates. The shift from objective presentation to subjective fantasy—itself portrayed as intensely real—followed by the abrupt return to the reality of the execution scene seems made for cinematic treatment. Anticipating Schwartz's story "In Dreams Begin Responsibilities," Bierce's tale is an allegory of the cinematic experience itself: the viewer leaves his or her own reality behind to enter the realistic dream world of the film, only to return to reality at the end. In adapting Bierce's story to the screen, Enrico exploits the cliché whereby time seems to slow down in the instant before one's death. Once again, the pretense of making reality more visible by slowing it down, and even stopping it so that it can be more closely inspected and its truth revealed, is exposed as film's grandest illusion of all.

The surprise in *An Occurrence at Owl Creek Bridge* consists in the reader's or viewer's discovery that an execution that appeared *not* to have taken place actually did. In most cases in which executions involve surprise, the unexpected outcome is the execution's nonoccurrence, or its failure to proceed as planned. The viewer of Polanski's *Death and the Maiden* is led to expect that Paulina's interrogation of the doctor who she suspects is her former torturer will culminate in his execution. Indeed, this seems to be what happens in Ariel Dorfman's original stage version, although the outcome remains ambiguous. Polanski's graphically realistic film is unable to resort to such theatrical ambiguities, and its climactic scene clearly shows Paulina resisting the impulse to push her prisoner—who has just confessed his crimes to her—off the cliff. In contrast to the scenario in *An Occurrence at Owl Creek Bridge*, the condemned man in Polanski's film is spared at the last instant by his would-be executioner. Yet the sight of this execution survivor in the final scene attending a performance of "Death and the Maiden" at which

Paulina and her husband are also present is nearly as much as a shock as the sight of Peyton Farquhar hanging from the bridge at the end of Enrico's film.

Polanski might fittingly have given his film the title of John D. MacDonald's 1957 novel *The Executioners*—a particularly ironic title for both works. Indeed, the word *execution* occurs only once in MacDonald's novel. When attorney Sam Bowden, driven to desperation by the failure of the police and the legal system to protect his family from ex-convict Max Cady's harassment, tells his wife, Carol, that he is prepared to take the law into his own hands and kill Cady himself, she encourages him by saying, "Not murder. Execution."[46] Sam resists the word, preferring not to rationalize murder, however justified it may be. As events turn out, he is right to avoid applying the term to himself. The trap he has set for Cady is bungled, the officer assisting him is killed, his wife is nearly raped, and Cady is brought down only by a wild shot that Sam fires into the darkness. So much for execution. In fact, the notion of Sam as an executioner is so ludicrous that J. Lee-Thompson abandoned MacDonald's title when he adapted the novel to film in 1962. The new title, *Cape Fear*—named after the North Carolina river where the film's climactic scene takes place—proved so compelling that it was used not only by Martin Scorsese thirty years later in his 1991 remake, but by the publishers of the reissued novel, despite the fact that this location is never even mentioned in the book.

If the title of the films is inappropriate for the novel, the novel's title, *The Executioners*, doesn't fit the films, in both of which the scene of Bowden killing Cady—like the scene of Paulina killing Dr. Miranda in Polanski's *Death and the Maiden*—fails to occur. In Lee-Thompson's version, Sam (played by Gregory Peck) resists the impulse to shoot Max (Robert Mitchum), who dares him to do so; as a result, Max faces the worse fate of returning to prison—this time for life, since he's killed the deputy assisting Sam. In Scorsese's hyperbolic ending, although Sam (Nick Nolte) smashes Cady's head with a rock, Cady (Robert De Niro) seems unaffected by the blow and appears to will his own death, drowning while speaking in tongues and singing about the promised land as Sam watches from the shore. Both film versions emphasize the Bowden family's fear of Cady by depicting him as a merciless rapist and killer who seems immune to punishment, pain (especially in Scorsese's film), and execution. MacDonald's novel, in contrast, while describing the ineffectiveness of Sam's efforts to dispose of Cady, at least shows Sam finally shooting and killing his intended target, even if it is just by chance. Moreover, this "execution" takes place at the Bowden home; the climactic scene in the two film versions is set on the family houseboat. This key change of scene in which the home is literally deprived of its foundation offers a compelling visual image of the family in peril: while the houseboat merely drifts downstream in Lee-Thompson's film, in Scorsese's film it careens out of control in a flood—a visual dramatization of domestic crisis.

From MacDonald's novel to Lee-Thompson's adaptation to Scorsese's remake, the possibility of resolving an intolerable crisis through firm, decisive action—namely, execution—is shown to be increasingly remote. Taken together, these works portray Sam's progressive loss of control with respect to Cady, his family, and himself. This diminishing control is even evident in such a small detail as Sam's grip on his gun. In the novel, Sam maintains a hold on his weapon even as he shoots wildly into the darkness. The films show Sam losing his grip: Lee-Thompson shows him groping for the gun on the ground, while Scorsese features a slow-motion close-up of the gun flying through the air. Lee-Thompson's suspense (who will get the gun?) gives way to Scorsese's staged spectacle (the gun's choreographed flight). Scorsese was unable to resist including this over-the-top shot of the flying gun in the film, even though it doesn't create suspense and is largely gratuitous. Where Lee-Thompson offers "gripping" drama, Scorsese aims at putting more of the world on film and overwhelming the viewer with spectacular effects.

Films that Kill

No one seems more successful at integrating the roles of lawyer and novelist than John Grisham, who has been called "the most successful legal-thriller novelist on the planet."[47] Every year since 1991, when he gave up his law practice to write full time, at least one new best-selling novel appeared—*The Firm, The Pelican Brief* (which premiered at the White House), *The Client, A Time to Kill*—focusing on some sensational aspect of the judicial system, often based on actual events. Each novel spawned yet another blockbuster movie. Then in 1996, Grisham apparently forgot his own affiliation with Hollywood and launched a crusade against one of its most prominent directors, Oliver Stone. What began in the spring as a literary critique of Stone's 1995 film *Natural Born Killers* soon escalated into an all-out, real-life legal battle.

In an essay called "Unnatural Killers" that appeared in *The Oxford American*, a southern literary journal of which he is copublisher, Grisham blamed Stone's film for the March 7, 1995, murder of a personal acquaintance, Mississippi cotton-gin manager William Savage, and for the shooting the following day in Ponchatoula, Louisiana, of Patsy Ann Byers, which left this part-time convenience-store clerk paralyzed from the neck down. A teenage couple from Oklahoma was arrested for the crimes, and the girl, Sarah Edmondson, testified that she and her boyfriend Benjamin Darras had seen *Natural Born Killers* numerous times before driving off in the direction of Memphis with the vague notion of attending a Grateful Dead concert. Sarah reported that during the drive Ben couldn't stop thinking about Stone's film and "spoke openly of killing people, randomly, just like Mickey spoke to Mallory," before those two fictional lovers in *Natural Born Killers* began the killing spree that resulted in more than fifty deaths.[48] Diverted from their Memphis destination, Ben and Sarah wandered into Hernando, Mississippi, where Ben allegedly shot and robbed Savage in his office. Then, according to Grisham, just as "Mickey encouraged Mallory to kill" (4), Ben urged Sarah to do the same. Grisham took Sarah's explanation for shooting Patsy Byers as further evidence of the influence of Stone's film (an influence that Sarah herself subsequently rejected): just as Mickey and Mallory were pursued by demons, Sarah "didn't see a thirty-five-year-old woman next to the cash register" when she pulled the trigger, but a "demon" (4).[49]

Grisham seems to have been doing his own bit of demonizing.[50] Alleging that Stone's film was made "with the intent of glorifying random murder" (4), he argued that the director and the studio executives who produced the film were legally responsible for Ben and Sarah's crime. "A case can be made," he wrote, "that there exists a direct causal link between the movie *Natural Born Killers* and the death of Bill Savage" (5). Grisham then proposed a legal remedy that the families of victims might seek in cases of media-mediated violence—that is, cases of murder at a distance or homicidal speech that actually entail an *indirect* "causal link" between a media statement and the murderous act.

> Think of a movie as a product, something created and brought to market, not too dissimilar from breast implants, Honda three-wheelers, and Ford Pintos. Though the law has yet to declare movies to be products, it is only one small step away. If something goes wrong with the product, whether by design or defect, and injury ensues, then its makers are held responsible. (5)

In June 1996, an attempt was made to take the "one small step" recommended by Grisham: Patsy Byers brought a lawsuit against the "Hollywood defendants" (Stone and the film's producers and distributors) for damages reported to be between $20 million and $30 million.[51] After a Louisiana judge decided that Byers's family could proceed with her suit (Patsy died of cancer in 1997), attorneys for Stone and Warner Bros. appealed the ruling, but in March 1999 it was upheld by the Supreme Court. Even if the film was found to be only one of several contributing factors in the crime, and a small one at that, Stone and Warner Bros. would be liable under Louisiana law for 50 percent of the damages.[52]

The case hinges on the legal and aesthetic issue of whether a commercial film should be considered as an instance of artistic expression protected by freedom-of-speech arguments, or whether it is more appropriately seen as a manufactured and potentially dangerous commodity covered by product liability laws. Aside from the legal arguments relevant to the case, several related issues are worth noting.

Grisham's attack on *Natural Born Killers* is hardly the first time that a movie has been blamed for influencing one of its viewers to commit a real-life act of violence. In the fall of 1991, a man drove a pickup truck into a cafeteria window and started shooting after seeing the newly released film *The Fisher King*, about a media-mediated mass murder. And Michael Carneal, a fourteen-year-old boy charged with opening fire in the lobby of his Paducah, Kentucky, high school in 1997, killing three girls and wounding five other students, was said by prosecutors to have been influenced by the 1995 film *The Basketball Diaries*. Based on the life of New York poet and former high school basketball player Jim Carroll, the film includes a dream scene in which Carroll shoots his classmates and a teacher. "These movies are a factor," declared attorney Timothy Kaltenbach. "People come up with some of these ideas."[53] But while the possible role of such films in the commission of violent crimes might be considered in determining the degree of the alleged assailant's culpability, the films themselves have not been held directly accountable. Indeed, there has never been a case in the United States in which an artist, author, or movie company has been found liable for inciting murder. In the aftermath of the 1999 Columbine High School shootings, however, and amid the massive legal campaign against the tobacco industry for cigarette-related deaths, the motion-picture industry appears more vulnerable than ever.

Natural Born Killers is hardly an original work in its own right, but was loosely based on the story of Charles Starkweather, who went on a rampage with his teenage girlfriend in the Midwest during the 1950s. The "rock-and-roll killers," as they came to be known, had already been the subject of Terrence Malick's critically acclaimed 1973 movie *Badlands*. Since *Natural Born Killers* was a remake of a film that was itself based on actual events, can Malick and Starkweather also be considered culpable in the Byers case? Why single Stone out as the liable party? Was it because *Natural Born Killers* happened to be the film that Benjamin Darras and Sarah Edmondson watched shortly before committing their crimes and is therefore more directly responsible? (They had also seen the Disney animated feature *Fantasia*.) Producers of books and movies, however, cannot be prosecuted simply because their products are imitated in copycat crimes; it must be shown that the producers intended their products to result in violence. Stone's intentions in making *Natural Born Killers* (which may have to be determined solely on the basis of outtakes and rough cuts of the film, since Warner Bros. has refused to disclose Stone's psychological and medical records) might have to be compared to Malick's intentions in making *Badlands,* or even Starkweather's "intentions" in killing his victims in the first place.

Grisham's use of *Natural Born Killers* as the most glaring example of the movies' responsibility for acts of violence is especially ironic since Stone considered this film to be an *attack* on the media. He wanted, as he put it, to "mak[e] the point that the killers have been so idealized and so glorified by the media that the media become worse than the killers."[54] Indeed, the tabloid-TV host Wayne Gale (played by Robert Downey Jr.), who turns Mickey and Mallory (Woody Harrelson and Juliette Lewis) into celebrities as a way of boosting his own ratings, comes off as the real villain in the piece.[55] Viewers feel little sympathy for him when he is blown away at the end of the film by Mickey, who says, "Frankenstein killed Dr. Frankenstein"—the monster slays its creator. (When Gale, in desperation, reminds Mickey of his policy to spare one victim in his murder sprees to be a witness, Mickey dryly explains that the tape in Gale's camera, which has been running incessantly, makes the best witness of all.) While nearly all the characters in *Natural Born Killers* use the media to promote themselves—the manic TV host out to make television history, the warden eager to sell his soul to TV, the sleazy cop hawking copies of his book—Mickey sees himself as a scourge of the media. In fact, he is as much a creature of the media as anyone, and is less interested in condemning than manipulating the media to enhance his celebrity image.[56] Instead of asking the hackneyed psychological question of the old media—"What made Mickey and Mallory murderers?"—Stone poses the postmodern query "What made them celebrities?" to which the movie's advertising slogan, "The media made them superstars," provides the obvious answer. While Grisham cites Stone's film in order to argue that the media *cause* violence, the film itself shows, both thematically and aesthetically, how the media *celebrate* violence—leaving it up to viewers to draw their own conclusions and to assign blame where they see fit. Stone himself would almost certainly insist that the movies themselves can't be blamed; like Mickey, they are a "natural" product of media-driven culture.[57]

Grisham himself is hardly immune from his attack on the producers of violent films. Citing his novel *A Time to Kill,* in which a man "murders with clear premeditation two young racists who raped his ten-year-old daughter (a rape which Mr. Grisham writes about in horrifyingly graphic detail), Stone has facetiously argued that "according to Mr. Grisham's logic, the next time a 'righteous' revenge murder takes place (or, for that matter, the rape of a child) [Grisham] will be happy to assume liability if it can be shown that the offender had read or seen *A Time to Kill*."[58] And in fact, one reader responded to Grisham's *Oxford American* essay by citing a recent case in which a California woman killed a man who had molested her son. The respondent quipped that he expected Grisham to accept "responsibility for this killing, since it resembles the plot of his fine novel, *A Time to Kill*, and [to pay] a huge amount of money to the family of the child molester."[59] Of course, this was unlikely because, as First Amendment lawyer Floyd Abrams has pointed out, Grisham's "books, modest from a literary perspective, are not like breast implants. They are fully protected First Amendment speech, and the notion of judging them from some almost undefinable negligence standards is very troubling."[60] Given the graphic nature of the medium, are films to be held to a different standard than literary works and to be considered more like breast implants than exercises of free speech?

The fact remains that murder scenes are by no means absent from Grisham's novels or their cinematic adaptations. So the question then arises as to what distinguishes scenes of violence in his work from those in Stone's film. One key difference is that Grisham's violent episodes are placed in (and subordinated to) a judicial context, a narrative about the law in which the killers are invariably exposed and brought to justice by the system. No such moral resolution is depicted in Stone's film, and this is no doubt what really got Grisham's goat. What he found intolerable about *Natural Born Killers* was not Mickey's and Mallory's mindless violence but their escape from prison. As he described the film's ending, "they free themselves, have children, and are last seen happily rambling down the highway in a Winnebago" (3). The obvious problem with Grisham's aesthetic and legal perspective in this regard is that it is informed by a rigidly conservative, law-and-order ideology. He falls into the same trap that troubled Bob Dole during his 1996 presidential campaign when he selectively blamed Stone and other Hollywood filmmakers for fomenting social violence but was careful not to include the *Terminator* films, starring Republican stalwart Arnold Schwarzenegger, in his indictment.

Grisham's double standard is even more blatant in that he saw fit to assail Stone's film without assessing the impact on viewers of the hugely popular movies based on his own novels. Grisham's call for commercial filmmakers to exercise artistic restraint while he reaps windfall benefits from the unregulated marketplace for producing books of dubious artistic merit is wide open to attack.[61] As Stone points out, "Mr. Grisham has become a very rich man off a body of work which utilizes violent crime as a foundation for mass entertainment."[62] And the spirit of corporate capitalism frequently not only fails to support but flagrantly contradicts the Protestant ethic promoted by religious conservatives.

Indeed, the moralizing ethic that informs Grisham's argument is more troubling than its conservative ideology. According to this ethic, displays of physical violence and abuses of justice are acceptable as long as the law reestablishes and reasserts itself in the end. Eager to expose this ethic as a fiction, and "tired of making high-minded movies like 'Born on the Fourth of July' and 'Platoon,'" Stone was drawn in the case of *Natural Born Killers* to a nihilistic script that subversively revealed the irrelevance, if not the fictionality, of the law in a media-saturated culture.[63] This vision of the law as fiction was bound to outrage a lawyer-turned-writer such as Grisham, much as many journalists and historians had been infuriated by Stone's earlier film *JFK* for suggesting that official "historical" accounts of events such as President Kennedy's assassination were for the most part fabrications.[64] That being the case, Stone seemed to believe, he was entitled to offer his own version of events, mixing fact and fiction as he later did with the personal life and political career of another president in *Nixon*. If Grisham were to succeed in arguing that *Natural Born Killers* was directly responsible for William Savage's death and Patsy Byers's paralysis, could similar suits be brought against *JFK* and *Nixon*, alleging these films to be acts of character assassination—products that irreparably distorted the reputations of public figures, falsified the historical record, and warped the minds of young, impressionable viewers?

This isn't to say that Stone didn't engage in such distortions or that *Natural Born Killers* doesn't have its flaws. However, its shortcomings have less to do with its depiction of violence than with its claim to satirize the media.[65] Stone's critique of mass-mediated violence remains shallow because he fails to explore his own role in this regard, especially in making a film such as *Natural Born Killers* in the first place. Ultimately, Stone is indistinguishable from the butt of his satire against the media, his character Wayne Gale. Stone glamorizes the murderer Mickey in his movie as much as Gale does in his live broadcasts. And it's not only their use of violent images that Stone and Gale have in common, but their violent manipulation of those images. Despite the difference between Stone's sophisticated editing in *Natural Born Killers* and Gale's mindless hack work on tabloid TV, the *effects* they produce are strikingly similar. When Gale supervises the promo of his interview with Mickey, he and his editor accuse each other of butchery. "We've really raped and pillaged the first show to do this," the editor protests after Gale criticizes him for making the promo look "like it was cut by a fucking meat cleaver."

Stone's precision editing of *Natural Born Killers* was hardly done with a meat cleaver, yet with its unremitting alternation of color and black-and-white images, its long shots and close-ups, its use of newsreel, animation, and video footage, and its bewildering array of film stocks, filters, and camera angles, it was deliberately designed to have a meat-cleaver look, as if to make the point that all filmmaking is basically a matter of "shooting" and "cutting." As cut-up artists, Stone and Gale are both drawn to the subject of murder, but their imaginary identification with the murderer underscores their actual identity with each other—an identity that Stone disingenuously prefers not to acknowledge.

Ironically, it's when Stone shows Gale at his most inane that his resemblance to Gale as a media purveyor is most striking. During the scene of the prison riot, Gale joins Mickey in the shoot-out, giving up any pretense of journalistic neutrality as he experiences "the feeling"—an ecstatic sense of purity. Mickey's response to Gale's frenzied shooting is to take his gun away. "You're not centered, Wayne," he says as he hands Gale the camera and tells him, "Here, shoot this." Guns are for natural born killers who are cool and centered, while cameras are for hotheaded, decentered media artists. As expected, Gale wields the camera as erratically as he handled the gun. The images of violence he records are as jerky and disjointed as many of the shots in *Natural Born Killers*—indeed, it's impossible to distinguish Gale's shots from Stone's during this part of the film. Stone's "hot" shooting and editing techniques are a good deal closer to Gale's erratic aesthetic of violence than to Mickey's cold, deliberate ethic of violence. Far from having a distancing effect on his viewers, Stone's frenetic cutting all but eliminates the possibility for critical reflection.

If Grisham contradicts himself by criticizing the violence in Stone's film while glossing over violent episodes in his own books and in the films based on his books, Stone falls into the trap of assailing the media for celebrating violence in a film that seems to do just that. But it's one thing to call attention to this contradiction in Stone's film and something else to hold Stone liable for acts of violence committed by the film's viewers. Grisham evidently believed he had found a way with his movies-qua-product argument to get around David Denby's assertion that "there is no way *in law* of curtailing exploiters without also curtailing artists."[66] While the law determines whether, in cases such as that of Patsy Byers, Hollywood movies are to be considered primarily as instances of artistic expression or as commercial products like cigarettes that are legally liable for the harmful effects they have on consumers, the question remains whether the law itself has a conflict of interest when it tries to adjudicate films such as *Natural Born Killers* in which it doesn't prevail in the end.

Returning to the question of what distinguishes scenes of violence in Grisham's work from those in Stone's film, we should note that in addition to ideological and moral issues, there are basic matters involving the role of the media itself. In his editorial, Grisham predicted that an eventual "large verdict against the likes of Oliver Stone, and his production company, and perhaps the studio itself ... will come from the heartland, far away from Southern California, in some small courtroom with no cameras" (5). Originating in Tangipahoa Parish, Louisiana, Byers's suit indeed seemed to fulfill this real-life script. Evidently Grisham expected such a rural venue to deter the presence of cameras in the courtroom and to prevent Stone and his cohorts from playing the media card the way that other controversial Hollywood defendant, O.J. Simpson, did in his criminal trial. But this line of reasoning is hopelessly entangled in contradictions and in Grisham's own conflict of interest. Apparently it is acceptable for his own dramatic courtroom-centered novels to be staged before Hollywood's cameras, but it is forbidden to broadcast real-life courtroom proceedings in which Hollywood filmmakers are on trial for their allegedly irresponsible camerawork. Now that the news media have lost the right to film actual executions and are facing the prospect, strongly supported by Grisham, of having their cameras banned from sensational trials, the entertainment media can look forward to enjoying exclusive rights to present compelling courtroom and death-row dramas—albeit of a fictional or simulated nature—to eager audiences. That prospect seems to meet with Grisham's approval, as long as competing Hollywood products such as *Natural Born Killers* that feature graphic depictions of violence are kept off the screen.

Grisham's view finds support in the media criticism of forensics expert and prosecutorial advisor Park Dietz. "When I get to the bottom of each problem I look at," Dietz has commented, "I keep finding television, Hollywood, the media, an unregulated industry standing behind the First Amendment, and gaining power despite their harmfulness, because they—unlike everyone else—needn't be accountable or compensate their victims."[67] Unfortunately, Dietz's case against Hollywood, like Grisham's, is weakened by the fact that he has profited from, and indeed joined forces with, the entertainment industry. Dietz would no doubt argue that in his role as consultant for the TV series *Law and Order* as well as for sensational Hollywood thrillers, he has worked to change the industry for the better. Yet his claims about his effectiveness in getting producers to avoid scenes of graphic violence may puzzle viewers of *Kiss the Girls*, one of the movies on which he served as a consultant. Oliver Stone could make a similar claim regarding his role in improving Quentin Tarantino's original script of *Natural Born Killers*, which was a good deal more violent than his own film version.

Because of its graphic nature and its penchant for scenes of violence, film is bound to elicit ongoing criticism, much of it quite justified. It's hard, however, to give serious credence to attacks on the industry from critics who belong to and profit from it. (Ironically, this includes Stone himself, who belongs to the very media establishment he trashes in *Natural Born Killers*.) And it's not easy to follow the reasoning of such critics when they discriminate between "artistic" depictions of violence, which are acceptable, and "graphic" depictions, which supposedly incite copycat crimes and therefore should be regulated in some way—especially when such content-focused reasoning ignores the all-important issue of context. Should text-based, symbolic media (books and film scripts such as Grisham writes) have a broader license to represent violence than the audiovisual, iconic medium of film? (This seems unjust when a movie such as Mary Harron's *American Psycho* plays down the excessive violence of Bret Easton Ellis's slasher novel on which it was based in order to focus instead on the novel's satirical side "as a critique of male misogyny.")[68] And if a movie based on a book, such as one of Grisham's, is found liable in accordance with his own arguments, should the writer still be exempt from liability? Numerous examples can be cited of literary works that have influenced individuals in the commission of violent deeds, and there's no reason why books should be treated differently than films in this regard, or authors and screenwriters should hide behind filmmakers who adapt their works to the screen.[69] Yet the fact that an author such as Grisham was prompted to make a case against the visual medium of film as an agent of social violence rather than against the verbal medium of literature is another indication of the anxiety felt by many not only as the visual media become increasingly graphic in their depiction of violence, but as actual events continue to look suspiciously like "effects" resulting from a cinematic cause.

Telling
Stories

"I Want You to See with My Eyes"

We seem to belong to a culture in which seeing ever more clearly the very objects that we want to know (objects we can never fully reach) leads to moral ambiguities.

—Gavriel Moses

One of the most obvious ways in which the visual medium of film differs from the verbal medium of the novel is that while the latter consists in large part of story*telling*, films *show* stories directly to a viewing audience. When words that are merely spoken or thought by characters in the novel are acted out on the screen and presented directly to the film viewer as staged performance, they tend to take on a vivid life of their own. Situations and events that are merely spoken or written about are made to appear as if they actually happened—yet another example of the reality effect of film.

In *The Birth of a Nation*, D. W. Griffith presented his own racist version of American history in which the Ku Klux Klan is depicted as saving the South and, indeed, America itself from the depredations of the newly freed black slaves and the vengeful policies of northern politicians in the aftermath of the Civil War. Griffith discovered how history could be revised through the power of cinematic spectacle—"writing history with lightning" was how Woodrow Wilson described it. Specifically, he discovered that motion pictures made it possible to foist his own vision of history onto his audiences, to make viewers see events as he saw them, to turn people into spectators who experienced history and life itself as a series of filmic events.

Griffith's vision was hardly original. His screenplay was based on the novels of the racist minister Thomas Dixon, particularly his 1905 work *The Clansman*. Even in this verbal form, the strategy of visual persuasion that Griffith was to use so effectively in *The Birth of a Nation* is already evident. In the process of courting the young northerner Elsie Stoneman after the end of the Civil War, the former Confederate colonel Ben Cameron gives her a revisionist history lesson that lays the blame for slavery on Yankee slave traders. Although Elsie resists Ben's story at first, after listening to him "for hours" as he would "confess to her the secrets of his boyish dreams of glory in war, recount his thrilling adventures and daring deeds," and proclaim his "love for his native state," she

> began to see for the first time how the cords which bound the Southerner to his soil were of the heart's red blood.
>
> She began to understand why the war, which had seemed to her a wicked, cruel, and causeless rebellion, was the one inevitable thing in our growth from a loose group of sovereign states to a United Nation. Love had given her his point of view.[1]

Listening to her lover, Elsie is able to "see" and "understand ... his point of view" that the Civil War and the South's struggle for secession was justified as necessary for a new united nation—White America—to be born.

Ben's verbose lesson in Dixon's novel is reduced in Griffith's silent film to the two brief vignettes, ripped from their historical context, which open the movie. The first scene shows New England merchants importing slaves from Africa during the colonial period, while the second scene shows nineteenth-century northern abolitionists decrying slavery. Thus the history lesson that Ben gives to Elsie well into Dixon's novel is presented directly to the viewer in Griffith's film even before the main storyline begins. A digression in the novel becomes the frame narrative of the film; no longer a mere history lesson, the tale of black/northern oppression of the white South is presented directly to the viewer as historical truth. It is in this authenticated context that the "historical romance" of the Klan and the fictional Stoneman and Cameron families is set.

More than a hundred pages after Elsie comes to see Ben's "point of view" in Dixon's novel, her brother Phil, a former soldier in the Union army, undergoes a similar conversion. "The sight of the Black Hand on [the white Southerners'] throats now roused his righteous indignation.... He began now to see that it was reverence for authority as expressed in the Constitution under which slavery was established which made Secession inevitable" (276–77). Throughout the novel, deluded northerners—Elsie, Phil, and finally even their abolitionist father himself—eventually come round to seeing events from the perspective of the southern characters. (Elsie is able to see the "light" well before her resistant brother and father not because she is more perceptive or intelligent but because, as a woman, she is more impressionable—a gender distinction appearing throughout the novel.)[2] The northerners' conversion is less a rational response to what they are told than an emotional response to what they feel and see. Thus, Elsie and Phil adopt the southern point of view not through reasoning or research, but because of their respective infatuations with the southern siblings Ben and Margaret Cameron.

In one scene late in the novel, Phil looks out his window one night and happens to see the Klan in full regalia on horseback secretly assembling in preparation for the final ride. "By George," Phil exclaims, "it stirs the blood to see it! You can't crush men of that breed!" (340). What really wins Phil over is the spectacle that he watches in the dark through a window frame—a clear prefiguration of the cinematic experience that Griffith offered millions of viewers a decade later. Whereas Dixon indirectly foists his version of history onto his readers by manipulating the perspective of the northern characters in his novel, all of whom eventually come round to the southern viewpoint as a result of the lessons they are taught and the events they witness, Griffith directly manipulates his viewer by presenting them with spectacles calculated to "stir the blood."

The Clansman is a rudimentary example of a novel in which characters tell extended stories within a frame narrative—in this case, Ben's revisionist lesson about American history that he tells Elsie during their courtship. It's one thing, however, to adapt a novel containing verbal subnarratives into the visual medium of film; it's something else to base a movie on a novel in which a character tells stories that are themselves based on movies. Such is the case in Manuel Puig's 1976 novel *The Kiss of the Spider Woman*, adapted to the screen nine years later by Hector Babenco. The challenge confronting Babenco and other would-be adapters of Puig's novels is that they are what Gavriel Moses calls "film novels"—literary works in which movies are a key structural and thematic element.

The Kiss of the Spider Woman, which Moses calls "Puig's most extensive attempt to incorporate film into his writing," is written almost entirely in dialogue form without the guiding presence of a narrator.[3] As a way of passing the time, a gay prisoner named Molina tells his cellmate, the political activist Valentin, the plots of a number of melodramatic movies he has seen, occasionally embellishing them to suit his fancy. At first Valentin scoffs at these recitations, denouncing them as sentimental bourgeois fantasies that distract him from his serious political readings. After listening to one of Molina's narrations—a Nazi propaganda film called *Her Real Glory*—Valentin admits that "somehow I'm intrigued," but quickly adds that "it interests me as propaganda, that's all. In a certain sense it serves as a document."[4] While Molina responds to movies purely as romantic fantasies in which he identifies with the female lead, from Valentin's masculinist point of view the only value of such movies is as documents of political and historical reality.[5] It is the movies' social context that interests him, not their content, which he regards as nothing more than seductive illusions to be avoided at all costs. "No food and no naked girls," he warns Molina, who in turn asks, "Why break the illusion for me, and for yourself too? What kind of trick is that to pull?" (14). Over the course of the novel, however, Valentin succumbs to the spell of Molina's diverting performances as a welcome escape from the dreariness of prison, and acknowledges that the films have "really been entertaining" (205). Thus he allows himself to be seduced—both figuratively and literally—by Molina, whom he ultimately identifies as a kind of exotic cinematic persona in his own right: the spider woman, a spinner of captivating webs/tales (260).

Besides *Her Real Glory*, Molina rehearses a number of other movie narratives in Puig's novel, including a film about a panther woman (based on the actual movie *Cat People*), a movie about a race car driver in Europe who returns to the family plantation in South America to help his father during an uprising, and a horror movie about a girl from New York who travels to a Caribbean island to meet her fiancé only to discover that he is married to a zombie woman. Babenco eliminates all these movie plots from his adaptation except *Her Real Glory* and, at the end of the film, a brief scene from a movie called *The Kiss of the Spider Woman*. (In the novel, this is not a movie narrated by Molina, but a hallucination that Valentin experiences during a drug-induced delirium.) Rather than simply have Molina recite the plot of *Her Real Glory*, as he does in Puig's novel, Babenco actually shows portions of the silent, sepia-tinted film accompanied by Molina's voice-over narrative. Obviously this film-within-a-film can be seen directly only by viewers of Babenco's movie; the only way the two prisoners can experience it is either as a memory (in Molina's case) or as an imaginative construct (in Valentin's). Thus, Babenco's viewers actually see footage from the film that Valentin and Puig's readers only hear about. (And don't even hear very much about: a detailed description of the central section of the film appears in the novel not as part of Molina's narration, but in a footnote extending over several pages that contains an excerpt from the studio "press-book" [82].) Babenco places the viewer of his film in a position that is at once privileged and highly ambiguous. Is the viewer of *The*

Kiss of the Spider Woman seeing segments of the "actual" film *Her Real Glory* that Molina is describing (which, after all, is not really a German film from the '40s but a Babenco simulation)? Or is the viewer seeing Molina's reconstruction of that film as he remembers or fantasizes it? Or, finally, is the viewer seeing Valentin's construction of his own vision of the film based on Molina's recitation?[6]

Matters are further complicated by the fact that we must deal not simply with a film-within-a-film, but with a film *within* the film-within-a-film. *Her Real Glory* is the tragic love story of a French cabaret singer named Leni and Werner, a high-ranking German official. Leni is about to help the Resistance, "but then along came the offer to make films in Germany" (87). And how does her Nazi lover finally win her over and convince her of the rightness of his cause? He shows her what he claims to be a documentary film but which is in fact blatant propaganda. (In the novel, the studio press book describes this film as "a long documentary on famine, world famine" whose agonies are everywhere preceded by the appearance of "two or three implacable beings, always the same ones, wandering Jews bearing death's fateful tiding. All of it accurately registered by the unmistakable camera eye" [91].) After seeing this film, Leni wholeheartedly embraces both Werner and his mission, having been completely misled by the prospect of a career as a movie actress and by the gross distortions of the camera reality presented in the pseudodocumentary.

In Babenco's film, Molina's voice-over narration explains that Werner "wanted to make Leni see with his eyes," which is precisely what he achieves by showing her the falsified documentary. This phrase doesn't appear in Puig's account of the scene (which in any case appears in a footnote and is not narrated by Molina), but a similar phrase does appear in the novel in another context. During Molina's narration of the movie *The Panther Woman* near the beginning of the novel, Valentin objects that Molina isn't giving an accurate account but is "inventing half the picture." Molina responds by saying, "No, I'm not inventing, I swear, but some things, to round them out for you, so you can see them the way I'm seeing them ... well, to some extent I have to embroider a little" (18). This statement summarizes the craft of any good artist, storyteller, or filmmaker, but in the context of the novel it also suggests an affinity between the artist and the lover, or the artist and the seducer. What is love, after all, if not getting the beloved to see the world as you do, making the beloved see with your eyes? And what do filmmakers finally achieve—to a much greater degree than writers—if not making their audiences see what they want them to see? Through his explicit treatment of the theme of showing as seduction or seduction by showing, Babenco imparts an insight about his own medium *in* his own medium that is left implicit in Puig's novel. What makes film more powerful than literature or any other medium is that it quite literally compels viewers to see the world as the director wants them to see it. In the film *Her Real Glory*, Werner (who we may assume has himself been seduced by Hitler's vision of the Third Reich) seduces Leni by showing her the false documentary about world famine; Molina in turn has been seduced by the Nazi propagandists who produced *Her Real Glory*; and finally Molina the spider woman seduces Valentin by retelling the stories of films he has seen, one of which is *Her Real Glory*.

The bulk of Puig's novel deals with the process of converting the visual experience of movies into words: Molina's retelling the plots of movies in his prison cell. This procedure reverses the customary practice of making literary works into movies, as in Babenco's own adaptation of Puig's novel. Once Babenco decided to make a movie out of Puig's book, it was inevitable that Molina's verbal retellings of film plots would end up as films-within-the-film—a return to the conventional operation of turning stories into movies. This process of adaptation seems at odds with Puig's purpose in writing a film novel in which, through the discursive acts of retelling, criticizing, and reimagining the plots of movies, the antithetical characters of Molina and Valentin are shown entering into a homoerotic relationship that otherwise probably never would have happened. It's not surprising, then, that the adaptation of *The Kiss of the Spider Woman* to the screen has struck some as co-opting Puig's intramedial literary endeavor, and to be yet another instance of the relentless, irresistible process whereby the whole world seems destined to appear on film.[7] The logical next step (which did indeed happen) was for Puig's novel to be turned into a musical—the ultimate spectacle.

It may be that the only way to escape the dire effects of mass-mediated film culture is to be locked up in a prison cell; at least that would be one way of avoiding direct exposure to the movies. The attempt to recollect and reenact the plots of movies one has seen—to put those visual images into words—is the first step in counteracting the inherent passivity of moviegoing by beginning an active process of reflection and re-creation. In one scene in Babenco's film, the prisoners are sitting on the floor of their cell with the camera facing them; as Molina narrates a movie for Valentin both men are gazing up at a point well above the camera. The viewer is unable to see what the two men are absently staring at, but it is evident that their gaze is directed to the small, barred window of their cell. Gazing up at that illuminated rectangular opening is the closest either prisoner can approach the experience of watching a movie, with the key difference that in the absence of an actual film each man must project his own images upon that bare/barred screen. The problem arises when one of the men tries to validate his image by describing it to the other and making him see it the way he does, with his own eyes. Then the line between unconditional love and seduction, mediation and manipulation, becomes very tenuous indeed.

Screening the Holocaust

I've always believed that people construct for themselves some kind of world they live in that they reveal through language.... In "The Thin Blue Line," one witness, Emily Miller, says: "Everywhere I go, there's murders, even around my house." It tells us a lot about Emily Miller. Not that everywhere she goes there are murders, but that she sees herself as a protagonist in a crime drama. She is living in some whacked-out Boston Blackie movie.

—Errol Morris

Werner's use of the "documentary" film on world famine to brainwash Leni in *Her Real Glory*, and the Nazis' use of propaganda films such as *Her Real Glory* to promote their version of history among the masses, suggests that the need for persuasion and the capacity for distortion are nowhere greater than in filmed accounts of the Holocaust—especially those that use the pretense of documentary to depict this historical debacle as a fictional filmic event.

This is what Fred Leuchter did when he went to Poland in 1988 to make a videotape record of his inspection of the death camp at Auschwitz-Birkenau. Leuchter had undertaken the journey on behalf of the neo-Nazi Ernst Zündel, on trial in Toronto. A manufacturer of execution equipment, Leuchter sought to demonstrate that the Nazi gas chambers never existed and that Zündel therefore couldn't be found guilty of disseminating a "false fact" in his published denials of the Holocaust. Leuchter's videotape recorded his meticulous inspection of the buildings at Auschwitz, which found no evidence of ventilation systems. Back in the United States, Leuchter sent his collection of fragments chipped off the walls of the more-than-forty-year-old crematoria to an independent laboratory. After pulverizing the masonry, the lab found no evidence of cyanide contamination. The only significant findings of cyanide were in the delousing building, a finding that supported revisionist claims that "only lice were gassed at Auschwitz."[8] The videotape became part of "The Leuchter Report," which was accepted as an "information exhibit," although not as evidence, at Zündel's 1988 trial. Although Zündel was found guilty, the report—which has been called "one of the most treacherous documents ever generated by the Holocaust-denial movement"—went on to have a life of its own on his Web site.[9]

Leuchter's videotape "documentary" became the centerpiece of Errol Morris's 1999 nonfictional film ("don't call them documentaries," he has said of his work) *Mr. Death: The Rise and Fall of Fred A. Leuchter Jr.*, which reconstructed the Auschwitz expedition a decade earlier.[10] By reproducing Leuchter's journey to Poland, Morris undertook "to make a Holocaust movie without reference to what other people have done." In contrast to Steven Spielberg's exploration in *Schindler's List* of "the interesting thesis that anybody can be a hero," Morris found that Leuchter illustrated "the far more interesting thesis that anybody can *think* he's a hero."[11] Leuchter was an instance of a "lovable idiot," one of those people who "sometimes commit truly despicable acts while convincing themselves they're good." Morris was clearly fascinated by Leuchter as a deluded documentarian who revealed the limitations of the genre and, indeed, of film itself as a recording technology.

> Fred sees himself in various ways. He sees himself as a humanitarian, the Florence Nightingale of Death Row, the man who took the ouch out of the death penalty. He's a concerned citizen, seeker of truth, civil libertarian. Who would speak for people like Zündel if not for him? Finally, he sees himself as ultimately a Christlike figure, hounded and persecuted and reviled, as he sees it, because of his inherent goodness and correctness.[12]

The irony of making a nonfictional film about Leuchter's documentary project, retracing his journey and even reshooting his film, did not escape Morris. "Because Fred uses a handheld camera and shoots with available light," he said, "his film is somehow authentic, vérité-in-a-nutshell, 'true' cinema.... The irony here is that his cinéma vérité is in the service of falsehood. And my contrived material, I like to think, is in the service of the underlying truth ... but, of course, I could be wrong."[13] Despite Leuchter's pretense of authenticity, Morris called his videotape "the most surreal piece of film I've ever seen."[14] By incorporating the videotape within his own film as a kind of kernel documentary, and by juxtaposing Leuchter's original shots with his own reenactments, Morris calls the videotape's purported truth into question and exposes its camera-reality as an effect. Had Morris made a documentary that merely contested Leuchter's claims and that set forth his own filmed counterevidence, his debunking of Leuchter would not have been nearly as effective. By *doubling* and *reduplicating* Leuchter's enterprise, however, Morris destabilized Leuchter's truth claims, exposing them as a fiction, a story. Instead of appearing in the quasi-heroic role he assumes in "The Leuchter Report"—a man in possession of a secret truth who wants the world to see what he sees—Leuchter comes across as a man who *thinks* he is a hero, an expert on gas chamber design who knows such devices (never existed) when he sees them.[15]

The destabilizing effects of documentary doubling are evident in another filmic event of 1999. As part of the festivities in celebration of Goethe's 250th anniversary, the city of Weimar constructed an exact copy of the writer's Garden House, the architectural epitome of German classicism, one hundred yards from the original. The idea was conceived by Lorenz Engell, dean of media studies at Bauhaus University, who envisioned the project as a practical way of questioning accepted notions of authenticity and originality. Sixty years earlier, Walter Benjamin observed that the cult of originality was already being challenged by the new quasi-artistic medium of film. The construction of an exact duplicate of Goethe's Garden House within sight of the original—much like Morris's duplication of Leuchter's Auschwitz tape and juxtaposition of that documentary with his own—was intended to call the authenticity and authority of the original into question. "The copy has become an original," suggested Volker Laier, who supervised the construction of the second Garden House and oversaw the meticulous reproduction of every detail, inside and outside, "from the threshold to the roof ridge," even down to traces of age and use. (Laier designed the replica house to be easily dismantled and rebuilt so that it could tour the world after the Weimar exposition.) But for the more theoretically inclined Engell, "the original is itself a copy, since it represents only the way people understand the house at this point in time."[16] To underscore the point, an on-site installation fitted out with multimedia technology made it possible for visitors to "tour" a third, virtual-reality replica of the Garden House complete with computer-generated pictures, smells, and sounds. As the Web site for the Garden House described the visitor's experience: "and so you will stand in front of the spitting image of the second Goethe Garden House and ask yourself: How real is reality? What does the original mean to us today, the handed-down form, the suggestion of the auratic space—from Chartres to the Cathedral in Cologne to Weimar—when everything thanks to the new technologies can be simulated, copied and virtualized?"

Benjamin had written his famous essay "On the Work of Art in the Age of Mechanical Reproduction" on the eve of the Holocaust. More than half a century after that event, questions of the original and the real have taken on new urgency, especially in postwar Germany, where, as Jan Otakar Fischer has observed, "great tracts of the national heritage were destroyed and have had to be rebuilt.... Few other countries have such expertise in reconstruction. Gutted ruins like the Charlottenburg Palace in Berlin and the Wuerzburg Palace were immaculately restored to glory, as if the bombing had never happened." All the more need, it would seem, for the planning and construction throughout Germany of Holocaust memorials when all traces of wartime devastation were being thoroughly erased.

Nowhere is the issue of "reproduction restoration" more acute than in the preservation of the Nazi death camps themselves: should they too be rebuilt in their original condition or should they be left intact and allowed to decay? Which alternative would serve the interests of historical memory and which would serve the interests of revisionists such as Leuchter, chipping away pieces of the crematoria walls for use in his dubious analysis? "Is there not an irony involved in the retrieval of history with a simulation?" asks Fischer regarding the construction of a second Garden House a short distance from the rusting gates of Buchenwald. "Is memory served at a concentration camp when the very methods used to preserve it inevitably lead to the diminution of the 'real'?" As Weimar took stock of its tumultuous past at the end of the twentieth century, Goethe's second Garden House may have been "the most quietly subversive provocation of the year."

Screening Hollywood

The verbal activity of storytelling might not be expected to play much of a role in movies set in Hollywood dealing with the film industry. Such, however, is the case in John Schlesinger's 1975 movie *The Day of the Locust* and in Joel and Ethan Coen's 1991 production *Barton Fink*. The former film is based on Nathanael West's 1939 novel, in which the aspiring actress Faye Greener loves to make up stories and to tell them to anyone willing to listen.

> She often spent the whole day making up stories.... She would get some music on the radio, then lie down on her bed and shut her eyes. She had a large assortment of stories to choose from. And getting herself in the right mood, she would go over them in her mind, as though they were a pack of cards, discarding one after another until she found the one that suited. On some days she would run through the whole pack without making a choice.[17]

Faye's storytelling is actually a form of daydreaming, and she is, quite literally, a dream machine: "While she admitted that her method was too mechanical for the best results and that it was better to slip into a dream naturally, she said that any dream was better than no dream and beggars couldn't be choosers" (104). But Faye is not content merely to dream. Living in the big dream machine of Hollywood, she plans to make money by teaming up with her neighbor Tod Hackett, a painter turned set designer. Her scheme is to tell him her "swell ideas for pictures" and for Tod to "write them up and then we'll sell them to the studios" (105).

Faye seems unaware that her "swell ideas for pictures" are themselves derived from films she has already seen or otherwise absorbed in the movie culture she inhabits. When Tod asks her to tell him one of her ideas, she starts fantasizing while gazing at a movie poster for a Tarzan picture; Tod knows that "when she told her story … this photograph had a lot to do with inspiring it" (105). The story she narrates based on the poster is an exotic romance on the high seas: a spoiled, wealthy girl aboard her father's yacht is engaged to a Russian count who is traveling with her and urging her to set a date for their wedding. She finds him boring, however, and begins flirting with a handsome young sailor who at first resents her haughty manner and her wealth. Eventually they fall in love, but a storm destroys their ship, leaving them stranded out at sea. As improbable as it sounds, this tale (minus the ending) eventually made it to the screen as Hollywood's biggest blockbuster to date—the 1998 film *Titanic*. Evidently Faye's plans to make money as a Hollywood screenwriter weren't so outlandish after all. Her romantic story is also the sort of exotic fantasy narrated by Molina in *The Kiss of the Spider Woman*. Just as Molina "remember[s] lots of lovely, lovely films" that he is eager to tell Valentin (*Kiss* 37), so Faye boasts to Tod that "I've got just hundreds and hundreds more" stories to tell (106).

Like Molina, Faye is another spider woman, a film enthusiast who (re)tells hackneyed film scripts, spinning weblike yarns that entangle and entrap her listeners despite their better judgment. However, Molina tells his movie stories not with any expectation of financial gain but in order to divert himself and his listener and, beyond this, to communicate with the listener and ultimately to bond with him. His aim is to make the listener "see [things] the way I'm seeing them," to see what he sees, as if the listener were looking through his eyes and indeed becoming one with him. For Faye, in contrast, storytelling is a far more mundane, mechanical process in which communication and communion play no part. There's not even anything seductive about her storytelling; her attraction consists not in what she says but in how she performs with her body. Thus Tod "earnestly" responds to Faye's romantic tale, telling her "it's sure-fire" when he's hardly been listening to it at all; all the while he has been "staring at her wet lips and the tiny point of her tongue which she kept moving between them" (106). (Schlesinger and his screenwriter, Waldo Salt, find an apt visual image for this passage by having Karen Black in the role of Faye tell one of her stories while licking an ice-cream cone.) "The strange thing about her gestures and expressions," West writes, "was that they really didn't illustrate what she was saying. They were almost pure. It was as though her body recognized how foolish her words were and tried to excite her hearers into being uncritical" (159). Instead of making others see through her eyes, Faye simply puts herself on display before an audience of male admirers. Her facility in coming up with ideas for movies—which are in fact derived from existing motion pictures—is hardly surprising considering that her entire life is a movie-mediated construction. (Her father, played in the film by Burgess Meredith, is a former vaudeville performer.) Like Ilse and Bianca in *Gravity's Rainbow*, she too is a movie child.

In his adaptation, Schlesinger follows West's novel by including the film-within-a-film scene of the stag film shown at a Hollywood party. But Schlesinger also incorporates a film-within-a-film not found in the novel in a scene that adds another dimension to West's analysis of a culture increasingly enthralled by movies. Tod accompanies Faye and her friend Earle to see the 1937 Eddie Cantor film *Ali Baba Goes to Town*, in which Faye has a bit part. (Intercut with the original movie are several black-and-white shots of Karen Black in harem costume.) As they leave the theater, Faye complains to her companions about her fleeting appearance in the film. With her back turned to the screen, she walks out on the newsreel that immediately follows the *Ali Baba* feature and that reports the arms buildup on the eve of the Second World War. The announcer's ominous voice can still be heard from the theater lobby, but Faye is utterly oblivious to the newsreel. Instead her attention is taken up by a publicity photo showing the one scene from the picture in which she appears, and she goads Earle into stealing the photo for her.

In this incisive comment on film culture, Faye is shown dragging her two male companions, who are interested only in her, to a movie that has aroused her interest only because she has a role in it. The act of going to the movies has become for her a spectacle in which she plays the part of the Hollywood star among her adoring fans. Moreover, the exotic *Ali Baba* picture that is being shown couldn't be further removed from reality, and the contrast between it and the succeeding newsreel couldn't be greater. Yet Faye is utterly enthralled by the movie fantasy, in which she plays a bit part, and she has no interest in—indeed, she seems completely unaware of—the momentous, all-too-real events subsequently reported in the newsreel. We are left to wonder about the stories that Faye delights in making up, screen fantasies that literally shut out the real world. Although the content of Faye's movie fantasies is much the same as that of Molina's movie narratives, their reasons for telling such stories are sharply different. Molina, after all, tells stories to distract himself from the horrors of prison life; telling fanciful stories has much the same purpose for him and Valentin that the stories in

Boccaccio's *Decameron* have for the speakers and auditors quarantined by the plague who must find some way of passing time. Faye's stories don't provide a temporary respite from an unbearable reality as much as they become a substitute, secondary reality that permanently screens off real life. So great is Faye's delusion that she credits herself for making up stories *for* the movies, when she merely recycles predictable story lines already *in* the movies. Molina never makes such a grand claim; the most he says about his creative role in retelling the plots of movies he has seen is that he sometimes finds it necessary "to embroider a little" (*Kiss* 18).

As closely as Schlesinger's adaptation follows West's novel, there has been a significant shift in emphasis. Writing at the height of the Hollywood dream machine, in the year of both *The Wizard of Oz* and *Gone with the Wind*, West plays up the distinction between the self-delusions of film culture and the possibility of self-discovery and self-revelation offered by the traditional representational art of painting, and, by extension, literature. Having been co-opted by Hollywood for the purpose of entertainment, the graphic medium of film has not only lost its ability to reveal reality and to tell the truth, but has become entirely devoted to fabricating illusions that conceal reality and distort the truth. Incapable of critiquing itself, film requires the artist's iconoclastic vision to explode its deceptions. This is what West does in his novel, and what he has his protagonist Tod Hackett do as a break from his hack work as a set designer—on a wall of his apartment he fashions an apocalyptic painting called *The Burning of Los Angeles* inspired by the grotesque social caricatures of Goya and Ensor. Schlesinger's mid-'70s adaptation fine-tunes West's rather broad, literary critique of film culture. Instead of contrasting the false world of movies to the true world of art, Schlesinger distinguishes the diverting and diversionary dream cinema typically turned out by Hollywood from a more realistic, documentary cinema capable of reporting events of great consequence, recording events for posterity, and even reflecting on film's cultural function.

And yet in a scene such as Faye's visit to the movie theater, Schlesinger calls into question those documentary and revelatory aspects that promise to redeem film from its role of mere entertainment. Historical reality comes to look more and more like an artificial effect (the newsreel as a preview of coming attractions), and cinematic special effects look increasingly real (Faye recognizing herself in a film fantasy about Ali Baba, while the 1970s actress Karen Black is shown appearing in a film from the 1930s). For Hollywood movie children like Faye, the problem is not that they, in Gavriel Moses's words, "belong to a culture in which seeing ever more clearly the very objects that we want to know (objects we can never fully reach) leads to moral ambiguities"; the problem is rather with the sort of clearly visible objects they *want* to know in the first place. Movie children can no longer distinguish vividly delineated cinematic objects that aren't worth knowing from those that are.

This is certainly not the first time we have seen doubts raised about film's documentary capabilities. While newsreel footage of preparations for war is ignored by Faye and her companions in Schlesinger's *The Day of the Locust*, the Nazi official Werner in Babenco's *Kiss of the Spider Woman* uses pseudodocumentary footage of global famine to seduce Leni with a distorted picture of the world as seen through his eyes. In Polanski's *Death and the Maiden*, Paulina is unable to record Dr. Miranda's "true" confession on videotape, while the photographer in Antonioni's *Blow-Up* is unable to produce an identifiable photograph of the murder victim. (The more he enlarges his picture of the corpse and seems to get closer to the "truth," the more the photograph looks like an artistic illusion.) And of course, haunting *Blow-Up* and numerous other films is the documentary specter of the Zapruder footage of the Kennedy assassination, the crucial piece of cinematic evidence in the crime of the century, which has frustrated the most determined efforts to uncover the truth.

The Death of the Mind

This is the best part of life. The life of the mind.
This is not killing kudu.
                    —Ernest Hemingway, *Green Hills of Africa*

Like *The Day of the Locust*, *Barton Fink* is set in Hollywood at the peak of the studio era (while West's novel takes place in the late '30s, the Coen brothers' film is set in 1941), when East Coast writers were lured out to Los Angeles to work for the film industry. Both Tod Hackett, the Yale-educated artist in *The Day of the Locust*, and the New York playwright Barton Fink ingenuously think they are immune to the blandishments of Hollywood, and Barton even believes he can restore artistic integrity to the movies. All too soon, however, their artistic ideals are challenged by an industry dedicated to producing mass entertainment for profit. Trained in the traditional representational art forms of painting and the theater, Tod and Barton are not prepared to work in the recording medium of film and to accept the ethical cost of a technological aesthetic grounded in reproduction and reproducibility.

We expect these idealistic young men to run up against a system personified by profiteering producers and fast-talking executives, and this certainly is the case. But it isn't the studio bosses who pose the most formidable challenge to the artist protagonists in these works. That challenge comes instead from a quite unexpected type of character who is also a creature of the system, and who is in a way its most revealing representative. Storytellers such as Faye Greener in *The Day of the Locust* mindlessly reproduce film scenarios that they then mechanically proceed to act out in real life. (Predictably, Tod's attempt at a relationship with Faye goes nowhere; he's making love to an illusion.) The storyteller that John Turturro's character of Barton Fink encounters also happens to be his neighbor—a jovial insurance salesman named Charlie Meadows (John Goodman) who lives in an adjacent room in the seedy hotel that Barton has moved into in order to be close to "the common man." Charlie has plenty of stories to tell and is eager to share them with Barton ("I could tell you stories"), especially after learning that he's come to Hollywood to write for the movies. The problem is that Barton doesn't let Charlie tell his stories, despite the fact he's suffering from writer's block and is supposed to be writing a script for a wrestling picture about which he knows nothing and Charlie knows a great deal. Barton sees Charlie only as a character type, an emblem of the common man, whom he has big plans to celebrate in the new "living theater" that he wants to create. Absorbed as he is in what Charlie calls "the life of the mind," Barton has little interest in hearing what his fellow lodger might have to say about his own life, which, it turns out, is anything but common. Unlike *The Kiss of the Spider Woman*, in which a bond is able to develop between two incompatible cellmates because Valentin indulges Molina in his penchant for telling movie plots, no such connection takes place between the two principal characters in *Barton Fink* because Barton is incapable of listening to what Charlie has to say.

There *is* someone, however, whose stories Barton is quite eager to hear. Audrey Taylor (Judy Davis) can provide Barton with the wrestling stories he desperately needs, having been accustomed to do this for the celebrated alcoholic writer Bill Mayhew. ("Bill's wrestling scenarios are morality tales," she tells Barton. "He'd have the wrestler protecting an idiot man-child.") Audrey is an able, though unacknowledged, storyteller who supplies blocked screenwriters with scripts for which she not only receives no credit, but—after spending the night with Barton—gets herself killed. How she dies is not clear, but her assailant appears to be Charlie Meadows, the common man who turns out to be leading a double life as the vicious serial murderer "Madman" Mundt. And although no reason emerges for Mundt's murder of Audrey or his other victims, we may infer from his apocalyptic outburst during his final rampage in the hotel's blazing hallway ("Look upon me, I'll show you the life of the mind!"), and from his irate response to Barton's baffled query "Why me?" ("Because you just don't *Listen!*") that he holds Barton personally responsible for his own violence. In his self-absorbed quest to create "a living theater of, about and for the common man," Barton has failed to provide an outlet or sounding board for the anonymous common man's pent-up real-life "stories," although he had been willing enough to listen to Audrey's contrived film scenarios.

The explanation that Charlie's violence results from his inability to find anyone to listen to his stories is not as facile as it may seem. In fact, it helps to account for the proliferation of spectacular scenes of mindless violence in the movies at a time when less importance is given to writers (storytellers) *for* the movies. Movies about writers such as *Barton Fink*—especially movies about writers who come to Hollywood to ply their trade in the movies—inevitably depict their sufferings and humiliation. As Morris Dickstein has suggested, such films tend to take the form of "the revenge movie, where the writer has been called to Hollywood and isn't properly used and appreciated, despite the gigantic amount of money he receives."[18] But while Hollywood may get its pound of flesh out of the writer, the writer in his bitterness may strike back, unleashing violence that is beyond his control—and even beyond his awareness—against innocent victims. Thus in the 1950 movie *In a Lonely Place*, Humphrey Bogart plays a writer embittered about selling out to Hollywood. When he hires a girl to read a book to him that he is supposed to develop into a screenplay, the girl is killed.[19] Although Bogart's character, like Barton Fink, is not directly responsible for the girl's murder, a pattern emerges in which women who offer their services to angry young writers are putting their lives at risk. *Barton Fink* and *The Day of the Locust* are revenge movies in which the writer avenges himself against Hollywood as much as Hollywood avenges itself against the writer. Both films culminate, after all, in surreal scenes of apocalyptic violence in which Hollywood-Babylon goes up in flames. One can't help but think of such scenes as the revenge fantasies of screenwriters who dream of making the industry pay for their years of ill-treatment.

In the end, the mayhem that destroys nearly everyone in Barton's life doesn't destroy him, but actually empowers him. Audrey's murder releases him from his writer's block, much as Bill Lee, the writer in David Cronenberg's 1992 adaptation of *Naked Lunch*, is only able to work after killing his wife.[20] Murderous violence provides the artist with the creative impetus he desperately needs. Some innocent victim must be sacrificed to release the artist-murderer's creative wellspring as well as to appease his rage. Despite their differences, Barton and Charlie, the artist and the killer, are doubles of one another: blocked storytellers who find release only in violence. Yet their differences cannot be overlooked. When all is said and done, *Barton Fink* is not just another film about the antagonism between the humiliated artist (writer or director) and the commercialism of Hollywood, but a dramatization of the conflict between the unrecognized, private storyteller with plenty of material (Charlie, Audrey) and the celebrated public writer who has nothing left to say (Barton, Bill).

A number of critics have been put off by the Coens' surrealism, which can seem gratuitous and sophomoric (the oozing, peeling wallpaper; the camera's descent down the rabbit hole of the bathroom sink). Jonathan Rosenbaum has described *Barton Fink* as a "festival of fancy effects" with an "arty surface" but a banal message—a "funhouse ride" that we're invited to take "through the effects rather than ponder too much what they're supposed to mean."[21] Such a description could easily be applied to most of the contemporary blockbusters churned out by Hollywood. (In fact, Rosenbaum's characterization of *Barton Fink* as a "string of sensations that alternates among styles and moods like a kind of vaudeville" is equally applicable to Schlesinger's carnivalesque view of Hollywood in *The Day of the Locust*.)[22] Although *Barton Fink* has its share of sensational special effects—indeed, the Hotel Earle portrayed in the film bears a striking resemblance to the eerie Hollywood Tower Hotel reproduced in Walt Disney World's Twilight Zone Tower of Terror thrill ride—it belongs to a tradition of novels and films inaugurated by West and Fitzgerald that make a point of exposing Hollywood's artificiality and false consciousness. *Barton Fink* stands out among such works in that it not only satirizes the film industry, but unabashedly presents itself as a product of the industry and culture it deplores. The over-the-top special effects that Rosenbaum condemns as "adolescent" in *Barton Fink* are themselves evidence of the impact of film on culture. And that impact is not entirely negative: even as the Coens show the popular mass medium of the movies co-opting the traditional representational art form of the theater and neutralizing its capacity for social criticism, they use the medium to expose some of the pretentiousness associated with such high-minded art—Barton Fink's vaunted "life of the mind."

Barton Fink demonstrates the positive and negative impact of film not just on culture, but on life. In the film's final scene, Barton finally escapes the overheated confines of his hotel and visits a pristine beach, where he comes upon a girl seated with her back toward him, looking out to sea—an ordinary scene, except for the fact that it's identical to a picture on the wall above his typewriter in his room in the Hotel Earle. Throughout the film he has blankly stared at this picture while trying to write his script. Offhandedly, he tells the girl she's beautiful and asks if she's in pictures. Her only response is to laugh, as if the idea of connecting her life and the reality of the moment to the artificial world of the movies is absurd. Of course, the viewer of *Barton Fink* knows what she can't know: that she *is* in pictures, although perhaps not *motion* pictures. Having abandoned for the moment his project of using art to imitate life, Barton has one of those uncanny experiences in which life seems to imitate art. It's no longer a modernist, Joycean matter of a young man seeing a girl on the beach and having an epiphany that prompts him to become an artist, but rather a postmodernist, Finkian matter of recognizing that the scene on the beach has not only already been artfully represented, but mass-(re)produced in the quotidian form of hotel "art." Without even knowing it, the girl on the beach is already in pictures. She is already on film, though whether she is still in the world or in a world apart from film remains an open and perhaps undecidable question.

Showing
the Obscene

Time and the Unthinkable

Twentieth-century cinema was based on the illusory perception of continuous movement out of a succession of photographic "stills." The counterpart of this illusion—actually a second and possibly more profound illusion—was the belief that the "reality" of that movement can be observed when the film is broken back down into its component stills and studied one frame at a time. The otherwise invisible truth of the horse's stride is revealed, and the fallacy exposed in an entire pictorial genre of horses in midgallop. But what happens when different movies of the same story are made at different times, separated by a number of years? Wouldn't a kind of metafilm emerge offering a time-lapse view of the century and an insight into certain truths about this period that might otherwise go unnoticed?

This curious phenomenon concerning cinematic remakes has been noted by Brian McFarlane, who cites the example of the 1962 and 1991 versions of *Cape Fear* directed by J. Lee-Thompson and Martin Scorsese.[1] Along with their original source, John D. MacDonald's 1957 novel *The Executioners*, these movies document the transformations in the American family during the second half of the twentieth century. Only four years after MacDonald's portrayal of the close-knit 1950s household, bravely confronting the external threat posed by the vindictive ex-convict Max Cady, that family shows distinct signs of internal stress in Lee-Thompson's film, specifically in the antagonism that develops between Gregory Peck's resolute Sam and his terrified wife, played by Polly Bergen. Three decades later in Scorsese's treatment, the family is fully dysfunctional, to the point where Robert De Niro's Cady is less a threat from outside than a catalyst who simply exploits the turmoil already in the family—the enmity between Sam and his wife, on one hand, and between Sam and his daughter, on the other.

The question raised by MacDonald's, Lee-Thompson's, and Scorsese's inadvertent collaboration on this metadocumentary of the disintegration of the American family is whether it depicts an actual societal change that occurred over a thirty-year period from the 1950s to the 1980s, or whether it only provides evidence of a change in the mass media's depiction of the family during this time. After all, the media went through a series of major corporate, technological, and aesthetic changes of their own during this period, and much more can be said and shown in the literature and film of the 1980s than was possible in the 1950s. Was the typical American family of the 1950s so much more well-adjusted than its counterpart in the 1980s, or was it filled with its own tensions that were just not as readily expressed or recognized and which literature and film were simply not licensed to record?

The question can perhaps best be approached by considering how the concept of "the unthinkable" applies to each of the three works under discussion. In MacDonald's novel, this word appears late in the work, after the ordeal is over and as Sam reflects on the death of Kersek, the officer assigned to protect his family from Cady. "It was hard to believe that Kersek was dead. Tough, competent, efficient Kersek. But, in dying, he had prevented the unthinkable from happening. There was that much."[2] For Sam, and evidently for MacDonald's narrator as well, the word *unthinkable* refers to the possibility of Carol's rape by Cady, which Kersek's fatal intervention managed to prevent. Apparently, Kersek's death is thinkable, but Carol's rape is not. In fact, it's literally unthinkable. Like the marquise's rape in Kleist's "The Marquise von O——" or the love scene in *Casablanca*, it is a missing scene that can only be hinted at by this word. In Lee-Thompson's film, the unthinkable has been subtly transformed. The character of Sam's teenage daughter Peggy (renamed from Nancy in the novel) emerges as a more significant figure; indeed, the two sons in the novel have disappeared. It is Cady's pedophilia, his all too likely molestation of Peggy rather than his imminent rape of Carol in the novel, that is now presented as the unthinkable event.

Taking his cue from the 1962 film, Scorsese greatly expands this theme in his 1991 remake. One need only compare Peggy's flight from Cady in the school building in Lee-Thompson's film with Scorsese's scene of Cady's seduction of Danielle (Nancy/Peggy's newest guise) in the school auditorium, culminating in the notorious thumb-sucking scene. But times have changed, and the fact that Scorsese nearly shows an actual sexual liaison between Cady and Danielle suggests that such an act is no longer unthinkable. In fact, as McFarlane notes, both Sam's wife and daughter now demonstrate, "in their dealings with Cady, an element of complicity *unthinkable* in either the MacDonald or Lee-Thompson versions thirty-odd years earlier."[3] So if a sexual relation between Cady and Sam's wife or between Cady and Sam's daughter is no longer unthinkable in the world presented by Scorsese, then what is? McFarlane leaves no doubt: "unthinkable is the word for the incestuous overtones in the scenes between Sam and Danielle."[4] In effect, the MacDonald/Lee-Thompson/Scorsese "collaboration" traces the transformation of the unthinkable from rape to pedophilia to incest. Does this mean that with the passage of time we are increasingly able to think about topics previously considered unthinkable, or does it mean that topics that were formerly *unrepresentable* in literature and film have become increasingly visible as more and more of the world is finding its way onto film, with the result that they *appear* to be thinkable for the first time? Is film actually recording the emergence of the unconscious into consciousness, or is it merely registering its own inexorable technological and sociocultural development?

The question of the relation between the thinkable and the representable, and of their vicissitudes over time, has important implications for cinematic adaptations of literary works. When Jane Campion adapted Henry James's 1881 novel *The Portrait of a Lady* to the screen in 1996, she was assailed by critics—many of them women—for having made a feminist, postmodernist travesty of the novel. Jesse Green declared Campion's film to be "one of several recent adaptations ... in which 19th-century women are improperly exposed in the ironic light of 20th-century values." Green particularly objected to the film's opening series of shots of contemporary young "ladies" lounging in a park accompanied by their voice-over accounts of the sensation of kissing; she compared this scene to "a commercial for a feminine-hygiene product."[5] The only sense that novelist Cynthia Ozick could make of this "extraneous ... prologue" was that it was "plainly offered as a key to the director's sensibility. Self-oriented eroticism (or call it, more generally, a circumscribed interest in one's body), a current theme of a certain order of feminism, here replaces James's searching idea of a large and susceptible imagination roiling with world-hunger." "What crudity," Ozick wrote of Campion's portrayal of James's heroine Isabel Archer, "compared to what the novelist saw!"[6]

Actually, Campion's "prologue" is not necessarily as extraneous or foreign to James's vision as Ozick believes. After all, in 1907 James himself added a preface to his novel in which he expressed his views on a number of artistic issues concerning the work's composition. Comparing the novel to a great edifice, he observes that construction began with nothing more than the "single, small corner-stone, the conception of a certain young woman affronting her destiny." He then proceeds to ask a crucial question regarding the character:

> By what process of logical accretion was this slight "personality," the mere slim shade of an intelligent but presumptuous girl, to find itself endowed with the high attributes of a Subject?—and indeed by what thinness, at the best, would such a subject not be vitiated? Millions of presumptuous girls, intelligent or not intelligent, daily affront their destiny, and what is it open to their destiny to *be*, at the most, that we should make an ado about it?[7]

James is concerned here with how the artist individuates his or her subject into a compelling character. But he also seems to suggest that a perceptive artist could single out any one of the "millions of presumptuous girls" who in real life "daily affront their destiny," and show the distinctive way in which that particular one does so. Alternatively, he could be saying that of the millions of presumptuous girls daily affronting their destiny, only one is really worth "organising an ado about" in the form of a novel, and that Isabel Archer is such a girl. In either case, James is clearly preoccupied with the question of what sets a particular individual off from the millions of her counterparts and makes her worth writing about. Whether or not Campion had this passage from James's preface in mind, her opening series of vignettes of modern women is a striking visual image that seems remarkably attuned to James's artistic concerns and that enables her to compare the situation of contemporary young women with that of their counterparts in James's time.

Critics such as Green and Ozick reject such a comparison, arguing that it reduces James's nineteenth-century heroine's naive but grand quest to conquer the world to a stereotypical twentieth-century young woman's exploration of her sexuality. Ozick takes particular exception to Campion's portrayal of Isabel's 1873 world tour, on which she embarks after receiving an unexpected inheritance. The trip is presented anachronistically as a surreal black-and-white home movie that Ozick considers a "burlesque":

> Isabel's first and buoyant choice is to voyage around the world, the bold outward sign of her valued new freedom—a freedom that Ms. Campion burlesques in a series of scenes (Isabel riding a camel, visiting the Pyramids) rendered playfully but reductively in silent-film style. Yet James recounts Isabel's worldly education as a serious enrichment: "She had ranged ... through space and surveyed much of mankind, and was therefore now, in her own eyes, a very different

person from the frivolous young woman from Albany who had begun
to take the measure of Europe."

To be sure, Campion's treatment of Isabel's tour differs substantially
from the account provided by James, who "recounts Isabel's worldly
education as a serious enrichment"; he does this by presenting the tour
from Isabel's point of view, how it appeared "in her own eyes." Ozick is
put off by Campion's more ironic account, achieved through the use of
the film-within-the-film, which distances the viewer from Isabel and
casts doubt on the value of the experience that she has acquired on her
journey.

An even greater difference between the film and the novel concerns
their depiction of Isabel's thoughts during her tour, specifically of
Gilbert Osmond and his ardent declaration of love. All the reader of the
novel is told is that Isabel was silent about Osmond at this time,
although it is enigmatically hinted that this silence "was in direct
proportion to the frequency with which he occupied her thoughts"
(347). In contrast, the film-within-the-film employs a hallucinatory
series of graphic and erotic images to show that Isabel is obsessed with
Osmond and has little else on her mind during her travels. On the one
hand, such sharply different treatments can be attributed to the different media involved: the verbal medium of the novel emphasizes Isabel's
silence about Osmond, while the visual medium of film—and especially
of the *silent* film-within-the-film—shows how haunted she is by his
image. On the other hand, it's possible that Isabel *did* think a great deal
about Osmond during her travels, but either she wasn't aware of this
fact or refused to admit it, or else James simply chose not to describe her
thoughts. For James, Isabel's thoughts about Osmond are not necessarily unthinkable or even unrepresentable; they simply do not serve his
artistic project. Campion's aim, in contrast, is precisely to depict Isabel's
most private thoughts and to make her feelings and fantasies about
Osmond fully accessible to the viewer. In doing so, Campion may well
appear to be burlesquing what Ozick calls Isabel's "buoyant choice ...
to voyage around the world, the bold outward sign of her valued new
freedom." Yet such a caricature is an inevitable result of film's objective
pretense, which presents Isabel's quest for freedom as the illusion it is.
After all, her bold voyage around the world is already in the process of
being undermined by her unspoken thoughts, which lead directly to her
imprisonment as Osmond's wife.

Publishing his novel fourteen years before the Lumière brothers
projected their first film, James is credited with developing a technique
of "cinematic narrative" in which the principal events of the story are
presented through a character's perceptions.[8] Such a technique antici-

pated the subjective use of the camera in cinematography, and especially the point-of-view shot that depicts characters' thoughts and feelings. There is no evidence, however, that James had any intention of extending the protocinematic technique of registering characters' perceptions to include their unconscious fantasies, as later modernists such as Joyce and Faulkner were to do through the use of stream of consciousness. It's not surprising, then, that Campion's critics have been especially put off by a scene in her film that has no counterpart in the novel. Lying supine on her bed, Isabel (Nicole Kidman) is approached by Caspar Goodwood, her persistent suitor from America. Inexplicably, she submits to the caresses of this man, whom she has just expelled, as well as to the attentions of two other rejected suitors who suddenly appear around her bed. The three men simultaneously begin to fondle her in a dressed-up, buttoned-down orgy until a mock scuffle ensues between the rivals and one by one they vanish into thin air. It may be asked whether such an erotic fantasy, while certainly an accepted convention in late-twentieth-century film, is appropriate in an adaptation of a late-nineteenth-century novel in which no such scene occurs, and in which, it could be argued, such a scene is indeed unthinkable. Did the fact that James didn't include any reference to Isabel's erotic fantasies in his novel indicate that Isabel simply didn't have any, or did it mean that she may have had them but they were wholly irrelevant to the portrait of Isabel he wanted to create? Or was it rather that those fantasies were both unthinkable and inexpressible in the pre-Freudian and precinematic age in which James lived and in which his novel was situated? Is Isabel's fantasy of an orgy with her lovers really her own fantasy, or is it Campion's, which she anachronistically imposes upon James's nineteenth-century heroine?

The problem is complicated by the fact that James was writing not only on the eve of modern filmmaking, but on the eve of psychoanalysis, which recognized that every individual has a fantasy life that is an integral, albeit largely hidden, part of his or her personality. (It was in the 1880s, as we have seen, that Freud's teacher Charcot carried out his pioneering work with female hysterics and arranged for their "stagings of sexual truth" to be recorded in a photographic series.[9] And in 1895 not only did Freud and Breuer publish *Studies on Hysteria*, but the Lumières projected their first cinematographic effort.) Campion may have given not so much a feminist portrait of James's lady as a Freudian interpretation. Living in a post-Freudian age when sexual fantasies are no longer unthinkable or unrepresentable, could she really have done otherwise in her film without adopting the pretense that such fantasies play no part in the lives of young women? The medium of film has proven to be uncannily revealing of characters' (and actors') fantasies, apart from the intentions of authors and directors. One need only think of the notorious shot in *The Birth of a Nation* of Lillian Gish seated on her bed and thinking of her lover. When the camera cuts to an outdoor shot of the lover and then back to a close-up of Gish, she excitedly caresses the tip of a very phallic-looking bedpost, ultimately giving it an adoring kiss. Such a scene—unthinkable as well as unrepresentable in Dixon's novel—must give pause to critics inclined to repudiate cinematic depictions of characters' sexual fantasies as the fantasies of Freudians or feminists.

The very liberties for which Campion has been criticized in her adaptation of James's novel have enabled her to produce an illuminating "commentary" on the novel (to use the term McFarlane applied to Scorsese's *Cape Fear*) that suggests how the world has changed over the past century.[10] Unlike his brother William, Henry James had little inclination to investigate or portray the fantasies of his characters in any great detail; his interest was rather in depicting their often illusory perceptions and their manner of responding to their disillusionment. *The Portrait of a Lady* vividly points up the dangers of artistic illusions by showing how seductive they can be, especially as embodied in a character such as the aesthete Gilbert Osmond. More than a century after James wrote his novel, in a world that has become fully aestheticized (or anaesthetized)—in large part as a result of the new medium of film and its (re)production of reality as artistic effect—Campion shifted the focus of James's narrative to the dangers and delights posed by inner sexual fantasies as well as by external aesthetic illusions. And she reveals an unsuspected stratum of Isabel's psyche by showing that of the four men who pursue her, she gives herself to the one who doesn't take part in her orgy fantasy, a man whose only attraction is his own utter absorption in the seductive illusion of art.

Releasing the Unreleasable

Total use of media instead of total literacy: sound film and video cameras as mass entertainment liquidate the real event.

—Friedrich Kittler, *Gramophone, Film, Typewriter*

Stealing Childhood: Lolita *and JonBenét*

Whereas James's portrait of Isabel Archer as a young lady consists for the most part of her own perceptions of the world, acute but woefully limited as they are, Nabokov's portrait of a pubescent girl in *Lolita* consists almost entirely of the narrator's erotically charged perceptions of her.[11] The issue is no longer a young woman's illusions about the world, but an older man's fantasies about a girl—a subject that would seem to be ideally suited to the voyeuristic medium of film. Too much so, it turns out. A novel that makes "the reader empathize with a narrator who's a pedophiliac rapist"[12] and that raises the "urgent question of the writer's choosing to find his aesthetic bliss in a scandalous subject"[13] is an especially problematic work to adapt to the visual medium of film. What is to keep heterosexual male viewers from identifying with Humbert and their aesthetic experience of the film from turning into an erotic—and even a pedophilic—desire for the title character? Although critic Michael Wood may be right that "the book is more shocking than either of the movies [adapted from the novel], or than a movie could be," the mere prospect of putting *Lolita* on film is enough to panic censors and distributors, since such an adaptation is bound to link the culturally acceptable scopophilic experience of watching movies with the taboo desire of the pedophile (especially such a nonthreatening and sympathetic pedophile as Humbert Humbert), unmediated by the buffer zone of Nabokov's alternately lyrical and ironic language.[14]

Of course, the novel itself met with formidable resistance when it first appeared. Turned down by five American publishers after its completion in 1953, it only became available two years later in Paris (where it was banned the following year), and it wasn't published in the United States as a complete work until 1958. And although it became an instant best-seller and had acquired literary respectability by the time Stanley Kubrick adapted it to the screen in 1962, studio censors forced a number of modifications to be made. Departing both from the novel and Nabokov's own meticulously prepared screenplay, Kubrick toned down the sexual relation between the twelve-year-old Lolita (played by a seventeen-or-so-year-old Sue Lyon) and thirty-six-year-old Humbert (played by a sedate, fifty-two-year-old James Mason). With Lyon's lurid performance as Lolita, Shelley Winters as her overbearing mother, and Peter Sellers's antic portrayal of Humbert's rival Clare Quilty, the film was not erotic or even melodramatic but rather a piece of black comedy. (Kubrick remained dissatisfied with the result, regretting that "in the film, the fact that [Humbert's] sexual obsession could not be portrayed tended to imply from the start that he was in love with [Lolita]," whereas "the important thing in the novel is to think at the outset that Humbert is enslaved by his 'perversion.' ... Not until the end, when Lolita is married and pregnant and no longer a nymphet, do you realize—along with Humbert—that he loves her."[15]) Thirty-five years later, Adrian Lyne's *Lolita*—with Jeremy Irons and a pigtailed Dominique Swain in the principal roles—was less a remake of Kubrick's film than an attempt at a faithful adaptation of the novel. Without being overly explicit, Lyne restored a sense of Humbert's intense sexual yearning and obsession. Yet despite the fact that there are few sexual scenes in the film in comparison with Lyne's earlier films (*Fatal Attraction, Indecent Proposal, 9 1/2 Weeks*)[16]—especially after Lyne spent nearly six weeks cutting the film to meet the demands of the 1996 Child Pornography Prevention Act, which forbids "any visual depiction" that "is or appears to be of a minor engaging in sexually explicit conduct"—no U.S. distributor would touch the film for more than a year.[17]

Why was there so much more resistance to a film version of *Lolita* in 1997 than in 1962, when Kubrick actually advertised his film with the tag "How did they ever make a movie of *Lolita?*" Lyne's film is no more shocking than Kubrick's, particularly when one considers how much more sexually explicit films had become since the early 1960s. So why all the fuss, especially in the United States? One answer, no doubt, is that pedophilia had been so widely publicized since Nabokov wrote his novel or Kubrick made his film, and it had emerged as the ultimate taboo subject. Child pornography and the sexual abuse of children became such scandalous topics at the end of the century, not necessarily because they were more prevalent than in previous decades (although the Internet had made child pornography far more accessible) but because they were now such obsessive topics in the media's increasingly graphic discourse. Indeed, the fact that there *was* so much more graphic sexual content in films of the '90s than in films of the '60s must have made distributors uneasy. They must have shuddered to think what a new adaptation of *Lolita* might show that previously would have been unshowable, if not unthinkable.

But Lyne's film was not explicit, and the public's heightened awareness of pedophilia doesn't entirely explain American distributors' resistance to his film. The picture was released without any difficulty in Italy, France, and Germany; and even the British Board of Film Classification granted it an eighteen-or-over certificate after determining that it wasn't likely to have a corrupting influence or to encourage pedophilia. (As Lyne said, "If you go into *Lolita* a pedophile, you come out a pedophile. But nobody is going to go and watch *Lolita* and come out a pedophile if they weren't one before they went in. It's just such nonsense.")[18] Yet the president of the Cincinnati-based National Coalition for the Protection of Children and Families declared that showing the film in America "will increase child molestation and have a harmful effect on pedophiles and healthy men."[19] It may well be the case that Europeans tend to be less shocked than Americans by sex between middle-aged men and young women, or even barely pubescent girls: witness their surprise at America's hysterical reaction to reports of President Clinton's affair with a White House intern, and their hospitality toward filmmaker Roman Polanski when he was permanently banned from the United States in 1977 after molesting a thirteen-year-old girl.[20] Yet Europeans are hardly indifferent to brutal sexual crimes against children: in the 1990s they were horrified by a wave of pedophilic killings in Belgium and a massive child pornography operation uncovered in France. No event of such magnitude had occurred in the United States that would have offered a compelling reason to block the release of Lyne's remake in 1997. Or had it?

The sensational beating, strangulation, and possible sexual assault of the six-year-old beauty queen JonBenét Ramsey on Christmas day 1996 continues to make headlines years after it occurred.[21] At least six books have been written about the case, one of which was made into a television movie. Despite the numerous reasons that have been offered to explain why the case remains unsolved—the incompetence of the police, the laxity of the district attorney, the connivance of the lawyers involved in the case, the killer's ingenuity, the lack of any clear leads—many have come to suspect, with or without the media's prompting, that the investigation reached an impasse because the truth was too terrible to disclose and was therefore squelched: the parents had some involvement in their daughter's abuse and murder. The police and media seemed inclined to believe John and Patsy Ramsey to be more likely suspects than some outside intruder, and will probably continue to do so until such a killer surfaces. (Justice Department statistics suggest a twelve-to-one probability that the assailant was a family member or caregiver, and the parents' behavior since the murder has only fueled suspicions.)[22] In short, the Ramsey case cannot be put to rest (solved or forgotten) because it touches upon the ultimate taboo, not of pedophilia but of incest.

A case can be made that incest is also the underlying issue in *Lolita*, despite all the brouhaha one invariably hears—now more than ever—about pedophilia in connection with this work. After all, Humbert was Lolita's stepfather when he seduced the girl (although, to be sure, he became her stepfather in order to have the opportunity to seduce her).[23] And as the previous comparison of Lee-Thompson's 1962 and Scorsese's 1991 versions of *Cape Fear* suggested, a father's incestuous desire for his daughter is even more unthinkable—but also a more compelling factor—than a nonrelative's "merely" pedophilic desire for a child. Humbert is closer to Sam Bowden than to Max Cady in the *Cape Fear* films; he bears much more of a paternal, and therefore incestuous, relation to Lolita than the kind of crude, pedophilic desire that Max feels toward Sam's child.

Although John and Patsy Ramsey may well have had nothing to do with their daughter's abuse and murder—indeed, a grand jury investigation lasting more than a year found insufficient evidence to indict them—they were presumed guilty by the mass media. Their suspicious conduct since the tragedy and lack of cooperation in the investigation no doubt contributed to this negative portrayal, but possibly the most significant factor was JonBenét's hypervisible public image as a beauty-contest queen who had been Little Miss Colorado in 1995. The press ran titillating photos of the child-woman in lurid lipstick and sequined outfits next to stories hinting that the Ramseys had exploited their daughter, pressuring her to enter beauty contests and to follow the example of her mother, who in 1977 had been crowned Miss West Virginia. Despite their own practice of marketing adult products to preteen consumers and using preteen models to market the youth look to older consumers, the media portrayed the Ramseys as parents who showed no compunction about turning their six-year-old child into an adult and depriving her of a childhood.

This is the very crime that Michael Wood accuses Humbert of committing against Lolita, that he "has stolen her childhood, taken from her the years when she should still have been a child."[24] The issue is certainly a timely one, and it made headlines in the fall of 1998 when the seventeen-year-old American gymnast Dominique Moceanu leveled much the same charge against her Romanian gymnast-parents, from whom she sought a divorce. Indeed, the chief offense of parents against children in the 1990s seemed to be that of robbing them of their childhood by making them become little adults. But what Humbert did to Lolita, and the Ramseys did to their daughter, is symptomatic of what the new graphic culture has done to the myth of childhood innocence in general. Advertising, fashion, and film have eroticized childhood in the sense that adults have made children into erotic objects for other adults. For adults living in film culture, childhood hardly appears to have been lost; on the contrary, it's everywhere one looks, glamorized and fetishized by the advertising and entertainment media. And the children whom one might expect to feel the loss of childhood most acutely may not even know what they are missing. Before they know it, they find themselves living in a world in which everything has become explicit and in which, as Neil Postman has suggested, nothing is any longer secret:

> With the new technologies, television being at the forefront, there are fewer and fewer secrets—medical secrets, sexual secrets, political secrets.... Adults used to reveal secrets to you, the child, in stages, in school, in books. When you knew all the secrets, you became an adult. But now all of that is available on the Internet or TV.[25]

One consequence of this "disappearance of childhood" has been noted by Anthony Ramirez: when the information media have turned all the children into adults, Lolitas will abound. "Today there seem to be so many real-life counterparts to Humbert and his 'Lo' ... ranging from the buffoonish to the discomforting to the horrifying: Amy Fisher and Joey Buttafuoco, Soon-Yi Previn and Woody Allen, JonBenét Ramsey and her murderer." (Note the assumption that JonBenét was killed by an adult male.) In fact, however, none of these late-twentieth-century Lolita figures (among whom some might even include Monica Lewinsky) is a true Lolita precisely because they are all so grown-up and "informed." Lolita's charm for Humbert was that she was decidedly *not* a fully (in)formed adult, but a nymphet who still retained the innocence of childhood.

No doubt Adrian Lyne's decision to follow Nabokov in setting his film in the late 1940s rather than in the 1990s stems from the fact that there are no more Lolitas in the graphic age of "new technologies." An alternative explanation, however, has been offered by the film's screenwriter, Stephen Schiff—namely, the perceived omnipresence of Humberts in today's culture: "I didn't set Lolita in contemporary times for a simple reason.... It would be absurd. Parents today would be looking for Humbert Humbert everywhere."[26] The same graphic culture that has made childhood (and Lolitas) all but disappear finds pedophiles everywhere. Rather than recognize film, television, and the new information technologies as being responsible for the theft of childhood, society finds it simpler and more satisfying to scapegoat pedophiles as a source of corruption and to blame suspected Humberts for the "sins" of graphic culture. As we shall see, this is also what happened to Bill Clinton during his presidency. First, however, we need to consider the full impact of the new technologies on sexuality, and the fact that not just has childhood been eroticized by technology, but technology has become fully eroticized in its own right. To see that this is the case, we need to turn to yet another unreleasable film with parallels to yet another dead princess.

Death Imitates Art: Crash and Princess Diana

I can't believe there won't be another photograph.

—A news commentator referring to Princess Diana after her death

"They're trying to reduce the number of accidents here, not increase it."
"I suppose that's a point of view."

—J. G. Ballard, *Crash*

In retrospect, all the controversy over the release of David Cronenberg's *Crash* seems beside the point. Despite the fact that this film—adapted from British writer J. G. Ballard's 1973 novel about car crashes as a peak erotic experience—won a jury prize at the Cannes Film Festival in 1996 and opened as number one at the box office in France and Canada, its American release was delayed until the following year, largely because of the scruples of Ted Turner at Fine Line, the U.S. distributor. "People with warped minds are going to love this movie," he said. "I worry about the first teens that try it."[27] As it turned out, Turner needn't have fretted. The film was neither a commercial nor a critical success: those teenage Americans who did see the film seem to have found it boring, while those reviewers who didn't condemn the film out of hand were simply baffled. Most critics were unable to make sense of the characters' voyeuristic interest in car crashes. Stephen Holden, for example, simply lumped *Crash* together with two other pictures that appeared around the same time—Lynne Stopkewich's *Kissed* and Kirby Dick's *Sick: The Life and Death of Bob Flanagan, Supermasochist*. "These films," Holden claimed,

> arrive at a time when not only has eroticism been discussed to death on talk shows but biomedical research has reduced sex to a science. In the age of the organ transplant, the sex change, the testosterone patch and Dr. Ruth, it is increasingly difficult to imagine erotic fulfillment as a mystical fade-out at the end of a movie.[28]

Given this level of desensitization, the erotics of technology hardly seemed a matter for concern; rather, it was all too easy to ignore. Far from revealing technology to be the last, and perhaps the most intense, bastion of eroticism in postindustrial society, and far from exploring the link between technology's seductive appeal and the death wish, *Crash* was simply seen as confirming the sad (but perhaps reassuring) truism set forth by directors in the '60s and '70s of the *end* of eroticism in the age of mechanical reproduction.[29]

Half a year after its American release, however, the film's unheeded thesis of the erotic frisson associated with car crashes was spectacularly demonstrated for all the world to see by the deaths on August 31, 1997, of Princess Diana, her companion, Dodi Fayed, and their drunken chauffeur in a Paris underpass. In what has been called "the most obscene celebration to date of a celebrity's death and of the media's power," news agencies went into a frenzy to cover (or create) a tragedy of enormous public interest—ratings for entertainment news shows on TV shot up by as much as 30 percent—even as they were widely perceived as being responsible for the crash.[30] The paparazzi (a term itself derived from film culture) tailing Diana and Dodi's Mercedes, and apparently setting off a high-speed chase, had been desperate to photograph the celebrated couple, preferably in some form of amorous contact.[31] Having been involved in the events leading up to the disaster, some of the paparazzi were alleged to have committed the truly unforgivable offense of taking photos of Diana and Dodi *after* the crash, while Diana was still alive in the wreckage. Under different circumstances the tabloids might have paid vast sums to acquire these photos; indeed, a photograph surfaced on the Internet apparently showing Diana in the crushed Mercedes, although this was later denounced as a fake. Now any such photo was potentially damning evidence of the photographers' guilt. Only after an investigation that lasted over a year were the photographers finally cleared of all charges and responsibility for the tragedy placed exclusively on the inebriated driver of the Mercedes, who perished in the crash.

Although few made the connection, the circumstances of Diana's death ought to have been a stunning vindication of Cronenberg's film after the reactions of corporate shock and critical neglect it had incurred. One commentator who did make the connection was Pat Kane in the British paper *The Herald*. Referring to the crushed Mercedes, Kane wrote, "If sex, death, and technology were ever compacted into one object, this would be it." In Kane's view, the only person who could have anything "original to say about this century defining event" was "J. G. Ballard, controversial author of *Crash*."[32] The link to Ballard's *Crash* was developed at greater length the following week by Salman Rushdie in the *New Yorker*'s special issue on Diana. Rushdie noted as "one of the darker ironies" of the tragedy that "the themes and ideas explored by Ballard and Cronenberg, themes and ideas that many in Britain have called pornographic, should have been lethally acted out" in this event. He went on to identify the "two erotic fetishes" in our culture that Ballard had revealed in his novel, the combination of which had elicited a perverse fascination in Diana's death.

> We live in a culture that routinely eroticizes and glamorizes its consumer technology, notably the motorcar. We also live in the Age of Fame, in which the intensity of our gaze upon celebrity turns the famous into commodities, too—a transformation that has often proved powerful enough to destroy them. Ballard's novel, by bringing together these two erotic fetishes—the Automobile and the Star—in an act of sexual violence (a car crash), created an effect so shocking as to be thought obscene.[33]

So it seemed that, contrary to the views of many of Ballard's readers and Cronenberg's critics, eroticism was far from dead in postmodern culture after all. Rather, as Georges Bataille had observed decades earlier, it flourished precisely at the site of violent death.[34] Ballard had merely brought Bataille up to date, further specifying the erotic imaginary by introducing the additional elements of celebrity and technology into the equation: the events that left the most lasting impression on the public's collective fantasy life in the latter half of the twentieth century were the deaths in a motorcar of a president, a princess, and a movie star.

Already in his 1970 work *The Atrocity Exhibition*, Ballard had hinted that no events reveal the voyeuristic fascination with violence more vividly than automobile disasters involving the death of a celebrity: "the car crash may be perceived unconsciously as a fertilizing rather than a destructive event—a liberation of sexual energy—mediating the sexuality of those who have died with an intensity impossible in any other form: James Dean and Miss Mansfield, Camus and the late President."[35] If "the motorcade assassination of JFK" stood apart from these other celebrity deaths as "the most extreme auto disaster of our age" (44), this was not simply because of its historic magnitude; what made Kennedy's assassination seem larger than life was the fact that it happened to be recorded on film, however imperfectly and amateurishly. Kennedy became the "victim of the first conceptual car crash" (25) because it was possible to reexperience the trauma of his death again and again, to slow the event down mercilessly, and to subject it to endless frame-by-frame analysis.

A generation after Kennedy's assassination, the death of Diana became the subject of similar scrutiny and speculation. Ballard's analysis helps us to understand its significance. For example, the reason that the death of Princess Grace of Monaco (a princess *and* a movie star) wasn't as erotically charged as that of Princess Diana was because Princess Grace didn't die with her lover and—perhaps as a consequence—wasn't surrounded by picture-taking onlookers at the scene of the crash. JFK's assassination met both of these conditions, but even his death, which occurred in an open car in a public space at midday, lacked the elements of intimacy and secrecy associated with the scene of Diana's death—the closed car and the tunnel. (The virtually invisible death two years after Diana of John F. Kennedy Jr., along with his wife and sister-in-law, in the plane he was piloting at night, was neither an erotic nor a filmic event—the plane didn't crash so much as it vanished, leaving little for the media and thus for the imagination.) The combination of celebrity, intimacy, visibility, and violence associated with Diana's death made it not only a filmic event, but also the most captivating erotic event in the public imagination at the time.

Above all, it was the presence of cameras at the crash site, and their proximity to the dying princess, that was the key eroticizing element that transformed Diana's death from a sexual spectacle to a virtual sexual assault in which every viewer became an accomplice. Rushdie elaborates this point:

The object of desire, in the moment of her death, sees the phallic lenses advancing upon her, snapping, snapping. Think of it this way, and the pornography of Diana Spencer's death becomes apparent. She died in a sublimated sexual assault.... The brutal truth is that the camera is acting on our behalf. If the camera acts voyeuristically, it is because our relationship with the Beauty has always been voyeuristic. If blood is on the hands of the photographers and the photo agencies and the news media's photo editors, it is also on ours.... We are the lethal voyeurs.[36]

Once the camera quite literally enters the picture—once it is drawn into the frame that it so carefully constructs—its intrusive, phallic, mediating role is suddenly revealed, raising a host of ethical issues concerning privacy, decency, voyeurism, and greed. With the camera in the picture, we pass (as Rushdie's diction attests) from the benign realm of erotic spectacle to the malign domain of pornographic assault. (Is it Norman Bates's knife or the intrusive presence of Hitchcock's camera that constitutes the assault on Janet Leigh in *Psycho*'s shower scene?) The question of moral responsibility returns with a vengeance as soon as we are made aware, as happened in the case of Diana's obscenely publicized and public death, of the media's (and our own) voyeuristic intrusion into those enclosed spaces, such as the interior of an automobile, where the private intimacies and death agonies of real people occur. Rushdie leaves open the question whether "we can collectively accept that our insatiable, voyeuristic appetite for the iconic Diana was ultimately responsible for her death"; indeed, the public outpouring of grief in the weeks following the tragedy may have been both a vocal disavowal and a tacit admission of collective complicity.[37]

The media's coverage of Diana's death, and of their own role in that event, dramatically brought Ballard's and Cronenberg's marginalized explorations of technoeroticism and celebrity culture onto center stage. The erotic allure of car crashes, especially those involving celebrities, was no longer a pathological subject of satiric or exploitative fiction that corporate moguls could deplore and mainstream critics could ignore; suddenly it was revealed as a defining fact of contemporary life. Ballard and Cronenberg had heralded the crisis of a society given over to spectacle in which privacy was elusive and intimacy illusory, a society in which "reality" was thoroughly mediated by the media and in which the boundary between fantasy and real life was increasingly susceptible to violent collapse.

The 1973 novel *Crash* portrayed this crisis through its relentless focus on the violent violation of borders, specifically the all-too-palpable interface between artifice and nature—"the erotic collision of technology and the human body."[38] The automobile provided Ballard with an apt metaphor for making his readers aware of their contradictory responses to technology. At once familiar and disturbing, auto accidents elicit both a sense of awe (as an index of power, speed, and mastery) and a sense of dread (as a brutal violation of privacy and bodily integrity). Ballard's novel describes a nearly total loss of intimacy in a brave new world mediated by technology, and nowhere more visibly than by the automobile, that most familiar and seemingly personal of machines.

As Michel, the first-person narrator in André Gide's *L'Immoraliste*, is never so much alive, sexually sensitized, and free from customary social and moral ties as he is after his recovery from a nearly fatal illness, so a new and unsuspected world of erotic possibility and perverse sexuality opens itself up to the first-person narrator of *Crash* after he survives a serious collision in which a man is killed. Before the accident, the relationship between the narrator—"a 40-year-old producer of television commercials" named "James Ballard"[39]—and his wife, Catherine, had deteriorated to the point where he felt that he had become for her "a kind of emotional cassette, taking my place with all those scenes of pain and violence that illuminated the margins of our lives—television newsreels of wars and student riots, natural disasters and police brutality which we vaguely watched on the colour TV set in our bedroom as we masturbated each other" (37). After the accident, however, Catherine takes a new interest in James, becoming "fascinated by the scars on my chest, touching them with her spittle-wet lips" (51). The scars are not only simulations of orifices, new erogenous zones that promise unsuspected sexual experiences, but visible signs of visceral violence that are far more stimulating—because they're so much more immediate and "real"—than the mass-mediated "violence experienced at so many removes [that] had become intimately associated with our sex acts" (37) in the masturbatory bedroom sessions prior to the crash. This is the most obvious significance of car crashes in the novel: the media's endless aesthetic of violence and disaster had anaesthetized the senses of James and Catherine to the point where it took nothing less than the unmediated violence of an automobile collision to snap them out of their media stupor. In a grotesque parody of a conventional aesthetics based on restful contemplation of the beautiful or on controlled exposure to the sublime, only experiences of unmediated violence will henceforth seem real to James and Catherine. The shock associated with James's car accident represents an initial incursion of the marginal realm of the pornographic into intimacy's inner sanctum. Hereafter, sex will be possible only in cars, as James discovers during his affair with Dr. Helen Remington, a fellow survivor in the collision that killed her husband: "only in the car could she reach her orgasm" and could he "mount an erection" (120, 82). With the loss of intimacy, sexual arousal is possible only in that most public, cramped, and potentially lethal of places—the automobile.

The idea of automobiles as a sexual turn-on is hardly a new insight. The "revelation of man's sex relation to the motorcar" was already a cliché when it was pointed out by Marshall McLuhan early in the 1960s,[40] and "the blending of cars with sex and violence has been a staple of the advertising world for most of this century."[41] Still, Ballard's novel was sufficiently shocking for him to feel it necessary to write an introduction to the French edition, within a year of its original publication, in which he stressed the cautionary nature of the work. This supplementary, critical frame had the express didactic and moral purpose of warning about a strange world beyond the border of our daily existence that threatens to intrude on our private intimacies—a "brutal, erotic and overlit realm that beckons more and more persuasively to us from the margins of the technological landscape," and that has encroached upon the intimacy of the dimly lit bedroom, itself an echo of the paternal bedchamber, the site of the primal scene. Sacred, secret, sexual mysteries that had formerly been the occult focus of cult worship had become profane spectacles pornographically displayed before an increasingly jaded public that had seen everything many times before.

With the release of Cronenberg's film a quarter century later, when the advent of video and Internet technologies had further demystified sexuality by making pornography not only widely available but inescapable, Ballard found it necessary to provide further commentary for his novel.[42] Unlike Anthony Burgess's preface added to later editions of *A Clockwork Orange* that repudiated Stanley Kubrick's cinematic adaptation, Ballard praised Cronenberg's *Crash* for being even more extreme than the book.[43] Because it is so extreme, however, Ballard felt obliged to reiterate the distinction between the reality of car crashes and their artistic representations. He insisted, for instance, that "I've never said crashes are sexually exciting. I've been in a car crash, and I assure you it did nothing for my libido.... All I've said is that the idea of car crashes is sexually exciting, and that's very different and, in a way, much more disturbing, because it is curious that we should attach to this violent and mutilating event any sort of exciting possibility."[44] Or as Claudia Springer succinctly puts it, "Technology has no sex, but representations of technology often do."[45]

The problem is that this key critical distinction between the nonsexuality of technology and the sexuality of representations of technology— or Ballard's distinction between the nonerotic nature of car crashes and the hypereroticism of the *idea* of car crashes—is virtually absent from the text of the novel itself. That's because the novel is presented from the postcrash perspective of the narrator, James Ballard, who has become exclusively attuned to (or warped by) the marginal zone of pornographic technology. Adopting Ballard-the-narrator's perspective, Jean Baudrillard claimed in 1981 that "in *Crash*, there is neither fiction nor reality—a kind of hyper-reality has abolished both."[46] Reading the novel from Ballard-the-narrator's traumatized perspective of the world as a hyperreal domain beyond moral judgments and ontological distinctions, Baudrillard deliberately ignores the framing context of Ballard-the-author's extraliterary remarks. Indeed, Baudrillard willfully ignores *any* context beyond the text of the novel, treating the text as lacking external limits or internal distinctions. In short, he contests Ballard-the-author's claim that *Crash* is a cautionary tale. "*Crash* is hypercritical," he writes, "in the sense of being beyond the critical (and even beyond its own author, who, in the introduction, speaks of this novel as 'cautionary.')"[47]

Baudrillard's willful neglect of Ballard's extratextual perspective enables him to read the novel as a limitless, hypercritical text, but only by adopting the limited perspective of the traumatized narrator. The narrator's initiation into the hyperreal doesn't come about by itself, but is supervised by the character Robert Vaughan. Variously described by the narrator as a "hoodlum," a "TV scientist," or "renegade scientist" (19, 63, 110) who "seemed to hover like an invigilator in the margins of my life" (65), Vaughan leads a fully transgressive, transmarginal existence of "complete confinement in his own panicky universe" while remaining "at the same time open to all kinds of experiences from the outer world" (123). Ballard-the-narrator plays Marlow to Vaughan's Kurtz, following him into the heart of darkness of the postindustrial "age of the automobile accident" (57), meticulously studying "imaginary automobile disasters and insane wounds" as "the keys to a new sexuality born from a perverse technology" (13). In this phantasmagoric world governed by the play of simulacra, one can no longer distinguish between the real thing and its representation, reality and fantasy. Wounds sustained in wrecked automobiles are presented as new sexual organs in the body, "templates for new genital organs, the moulds of sexual possibilities yet to be created in a hundred experimental carcrashes" (177). Given such hallucinatory visions on the part of Ballard-the-narrator, it's understandable that Ballard-the-author has found it necessary to provide contextual frames and marginal commentaries for his highly unstable text—frames that Baudrillard perversely refuses to recognize. The valiant attempts by critics such as N. Katherine Hayles and Vivian Sobchack to defend Ballard's novel from Baudrillard's intervention by insisting that it *does* present clear-cut borders between reality and simulation and between nature and technology are unable to dispel the need for contextualization and commentary—including, of course, their own.[48]

Unlike Baudrillard, Cronenberg acknowledges a distinction in the novel between the narrator's inner world and external reality: "In the book you're in the head of the character James Ballard. There's that interior monologue thing that fiction does so beautifully, and which movies cannot do at all."[49] The literary distinction between subjective experience and external reality is difficult to maintain in film, given what Cronenberg calls the "immediacy of movie reality." The ostensibly reliable mediating perspective of the documentary camera makes it difficult to repudiate the film's transmarginal content as the warped viewpoint of an unreliable narrator. And while it's still possible for most readers—even if not for Baudrillard—to read Ballard's novel as presenting car crashes as a metaphor for humans' relation to technology, and as presenting the visceral impact of wreckage on the body as a metaphor for the effect of an increasingly technologized world on the psyche, this relation becomes far more ambiguous in the medium of film, where signifier and signified become interchangeable. Is the car crash a metaphor for intercourse (what the Germans aptly call *bumsen*)—after all, the two principal styles of car crashes are head-on and rear-end, corresponding to the two favored sexual positions—or is intercourse a metaphor for car crashes?[50] Neither sex nor car crash is given precedence in the film, but each is presented as being equivalent and equivocal in a Baudrillardian implosion of value.[51]

Scenes of sex and car crashes abound in commercial film; in Cronenberg's film, these two conventional types of scene are conflated, producing a disturbing but strangely logical effect. For one thing, the crash scenes are not shot in the manner of most Hollywood action pictures. In contrast to big-budget car crashes, which are often shot in slow motion, using multiple cameras from various angles to prolong the instant of the crash into an elaborately choreographed spectacle, Cronenberg intended his crashes "to be fast, brutal and over before you knew it. There's not one foot of slow motion. No repeated shots. I wanted to make them realistic in a cinematic way, because it's the *aftermath* that is delicious: that can be savoured and apprehended by the senses."[52] The sex scenes are also presented unconventionally, not as isolated moments that are embedded in and separable from the narrative—what Cronenberg calls "lyrical little interludes" that can "be cut out and not change the plot or characters one iota." Rather, in *Crash* "very often the sex scenes are *absolutely* the plot and the character development. You can't take them out."[53] The disequilibrium of a film constructed around a series of sex and collision scenes is reinforced by the way the scenes are framed. Cronenberg explains how he would put the camera "more *outboard* of the car body so that the windshield pillar was halfway through the frame, and the other half is looking right down the car body."[54] By alternating such partial, external shots with close-ups in the dim, confined space of cars, any overview or total view of the whole is left undisclosed. (Only in the final scene does the camera move back from a close-up of the couple James and Catherine beneath her wrecked car.) We are merely given glimpses of body parts, fragments that always seem to exceed whatever frame might contain them. Perhaps this was Cronenberg's way of tapping into a book that he found to be "hermetically sealed."[55]

Ballard's insistence that it is the *image* of car crashes that is eroticized in his novel, rather than actual car crashes themselves, somewhat begs the question since the difference between the two has become so blurred in contemporary culture. That this blurring between image and reality is itself a key concern in the novel is shown by the pervasive references to celebrity. Anticipating the paparazzi's hot pursuit of Princess Diana's Mercedes, Vaughan endlessly rehearses his big project, which is to arrange a collision with Elizabeth Taylor's Rolls-Royce. All of his bizarre automotive and sexual rituals throughout the novel are presented as foreplay leading up to this final consummation. "[E]verything lies in the future for her," Vaughan tells the narrator. "With a little forethought she could die in a unique vehicle collision, one that would transform all our dreams and fantasies. The man who dies in that crash with her ..." (130). Vaughan's obsession with Taylor is the key dynamic in the novel and illustrates Ballard's often expressed view about the crucial role that media icons play in people's fantasy lives: "Celebrity uncontaminated by actual achievement has enormous liftoff capacity.... This puzzles us and triggers a curiosity about the real nature of these people whose fame you can't justify."[56]

Cronenberg treats the celebrity motif more obliquely in his adaptation. Gone is any reference to Vaughan's obsession with Taylor, or for that matter, any reference to the actress at all. In part, this significant departure from the novel is explained by the fact that the film was made and set a quarter century later, at a time when Taylor was no longer the erotic icon she once was. In 1973 the possibility of Taylor's death in a car crash could be presented as a vivid erotic fantasy; this was hardly possible in the late '90s, when the aging actress was campaigning for AIDS research and waging her own battle against cancer, two debilitating illnesses that couldn't be further from the sudden, violent spectacle of automobile disasters. Of course, Cronenberg could have substituted a contemporary actress possessing some of Taylor's former glamour and appeal as the object of Vaughan's fantasy—Liv Tyler for Liz Taylor—

but such a revision would inevitably have run into legal and security problems in these times of celebrity stalkers and celebricides. Instead, Cronenberg found a way to incorporate the theme of the public's fascination and obsession with celebrity that did not involve Vaughan's prospective crash with a living movie star—namely, by playing up the novel's references to Vaughan's *retrospective* project of meticulously studying *past* celebrity deaths in automobiles. The film is filled with references to the violent deaths of such celebrities as Jayne Mansfield and Grace Kelly, of literary figures such as Camus and Nathanael West, and, of course, of President Kennedy. Vaughan studies these disasters in the way that documentary filmmakers research a subject—for the purpose of reenacting them, of making them real again. Yet Vaughan's interest in re-creating these scenes goes beyond restoring the fading reality of these luminous events; he seems to be looking for a way to channel their auratic hyperreality into a derealized and mundane present.

One of the film's most memorable scenes doesn't even appear in the novel: Vaughan and a veteran stunt driver named Seagrave are shown reenacting James Dean's 1955 fatal collision with student Donald Turnupseed down to the most minute detail before an avid audience at an abandoned sports stadium at twilight. After the crash, which Seagrave barely survives, the event is raided—not by the police, Vaughan explains, but by the transport authorities, who have "no idea of what any of this is all about." What it is about, at least in the short term, is Vaughan's next collaboration with Seagrave, which is to re-create the gruesome crash that killed Jayne Mansfield. Later Vaughan is devastated when Seagrave kills himself by reenacting her death on his own, thus depriving Vaughan of the satisfaction of directing and witnessing the event he has so carefully planned. (In the novel Seagrave dies while impersonating Elizabeth Taylor in a car commercial in which the actress was to play a crash victim; his simulation of Taylor's death unnerves Vaughan because it seems to preempt his own project of dying with the movie star in real life.)

Neither the simulated crash scene of Dean nor that of Mansfield appears in the novel. By giving such prominence to these reenactments of celebrity deaths, Cronenberg departs significantly from Ballard's work. Instead of making Vaughan's obsession with the living actress Taylor the focus of the narrative, Cronenberg emphasizes Vaughan's obsession with celebrities who have already died. Vaughan is portrayed as a connoisseur of such deaths, as a kind of documentary filmmaker who uses body doubles to reconstruct these fatalities before an audience. As someone who consciously and deliberately reenacts famous car accidents in the past, Vaughan appears in Cronenberg's adaptation as a conscious artificer of the real who reveals reality to be not what simply (i.e., accidentally) happens only once, but a special (i.e., deliberately caused) effect that can be endlessly repeated. Vaughan is an artist who doesn't simply imitate scenes of life or death, but stages violent "accidents" based on well-known celebrity deaths, rewriting those accidents as aesthetic experiences produced by artistic effects, revealing the virtuality and intentionality of what appear to be actual and accidental events.

After the Mansfield crash scene Cronenberg's film falters, having nowhere to go. Without the fiery consummation to look forward to of perishing with the living celebrity Taylor—a grotesque parody of fans stalking a media icon—Vaughan's project of making the car crash into a fecundating technique or "fertilizing event" lacks specificity and suspense. Elias Koteas's portrayal of Vaughan loses its edge and merely unravels toward the end with the Lincoln's uncontrolled flight into the roof of a tour bus. That leaves James Spader and Deborah Unger (as James and Catherine), who have come under Koteas's spell, to try rather pointlessly to work out their own autoerotic consummation by themselves. In the novel, the narrator's fantasy about his wife's death in a car crash is directly linked to Vaughan's obsession with Taylor's death (181)—a linkage lost in the film, where Spader's consoling words to his wife after her car overturns in the final scene make it seem that automobile accidents are just a way for the two to get their kicks.

And yet, in shifting his focus onto Vaughan's obsessive re-creations of bygone celebrity fatalities, Cronenberg manages not only to remain true to Ballard's original vision, but to update it for the postmodern '90s. The filmmaker simply takes the writer at his word in his 1974 introduction when he comments on the reversal that has taken place between fiction and reality: "We live inside an enormous novel. For the writer in particular it is less and less necessary for him to invent the fictional content of his novel. The fiction is already there. The writer's task is to invent the reality."[57] As a filmmaker engaged in adapting a work of literature for the screen, Cronenberg found the novel *Crash* "already there" for him in a literal sense. But he also recognized that certain sensational events—technological disasters such as the explosions of the space-shuttle *Challenger* and TWA flight 800, or the violent deaths of celebrities such as the JFK assassination (which Ballard has called "a peculiar kind of car accident") or the car crash that killed Princess Diana—are no longer real occurrences upon which the artist bases his or her fictions.[58] Mass-mediated society seizes on and sensationalizes these violent accidents and disasters, bestowing upon them a quasi-fictional, mythic status. It then becomes the task of the writer and filmmaker to provide the inside story—the secret history behind these filmic events, or their genesis *as* filmic events—thereby restoring a semblance of their reality. There is always the possibility, however, that these events may be thoroughly derealized as in those auratic, cult spectacles staged by Vaughan that hypostasize car crashes and other "accidents."

It is all too easy for audiences to dismiss Vaughan and the other characters in Cronenberg's film (like the paparazzi in pursuit of Diana) as sociopaths even as reality TV routinely captivates those same mass audiences with graphic news images of live police chases, shoot-outs, and horrific accidents at air shows and car and boat races, as well as celebrity tragedies—all of which are calculated to elicit a precise erotic frisson. Executions may not be televised, but the public is endlessly treated to live news broadcasts of images of disasters and violent death that can be scrutinized and studied in much the same way that Vaughan investigates car crashes. In one dreamlike, nocturnal sequence in Cronenberg's film, Vaughan photographs a highway accident and even interferes with the rescue workers in their attempt to reach the victims trapped inside the wrecked vehicle. In this grotesque scene that anticipates the real-life nightmare of the paparazzi swarming around the site of Diana's accident, Cronenberg extends Ballard's metaphor of automobile technology to the camera itself, the apparatus that confers celebrity much as the fatal car crash paradoxically ensures the victim's immortality. After all, celebrity is a modern phenomenon that is conceivable only in the recording age; there have been famous people throughout history, but there could be no celebrities—people famous merely for being visible—before the invention of photography.[59]

By showing Vaughan's meticulous but modest simulations of the car crashes of dead celebrities such as James Dean and Jayne Mansfield, and avoiding any reference to the hubristic project of staging his own spectacular end with a living cultural icon such as Elizabeth Taylor, Cronenberg is truer to Ballard than Ballard is to himself. Ballard may have written, "The fiction is already there, the writer's task is to invent the reality," but in Cronenberg's film, "idealization and fantasy are shown to precede reality and to give it shape."[60] Carrying connoisseurship to the extreme, Vaughan in Cronenberg's film stages actual fatal collisions on the virtual model of famous celebrity deaths; Ballard's Vaughan, in contrast, is a parodic version of the traditional image of the creative artist who studies the past in order to produce something wholly new and unprecedented. The characters in Ballard's novel seem to be nostalgic for a reality that they can attain only through violence; as the narrator says, "The crash was the only real experience I had been through for years." Cronenberg's damaged cinematic characters, in contrast, seem fully at home in the Baudrillardian hyperreal, against which there is no "real experience" to long for or to look forward to. As Fred Botting and Scott Wilson note, far from bringing the crash victim into contact with the real, "crashes become, for the hypermodern subject, simulations of the traumatic (missed) encounter with the real. Which is why they must be photographed. The photograph functions as a scar in time, freezing the moment when the mortal being becomes Other, fully transformed into pure image."[61] The close encounter with the real that takes place in the crash event must be reproduced both graphically as photo-images and virtually in the reenactment of celebrities' deaths.

If Cronenberg's *Crash* seems more a Baudrillardian than Ballardian work, it is because he has followed the Baudrillardian implications of Ballard's insight that Ballard himself may not have entirely accepted.[62] In the scenes in which Vaughan re-creates the Dean and Mansfield crashes, Cronenberg follows Baudrillard's program "to put in place 'decentered' situations, models of simulation, and to give them the colors of the real, the banal, the lived."[63] In the hyperreal world of Cronenberg's *Crash*, body (and body part) doubles not only abound, but they regularly cross gender lines: not only does Seagrave die as Jayne Mansfield, but Catherine arouses her husband during sex by "tak[ing] Vaughan's place for James, becom[ing] Vaughan's anus for him."[64] This rampant erotic substitution is unable to sustain itself, however, with the result that Cronenberg's narrative soon peters out. Without the goal of Vaughan's anticipated *Liebestod* with Taylor in Ballard's novel, and without the external frame of critical commentary that Ballard has provided in his introductions and interviews, Cronenberg's film has trouble standing on its own. Its lack of any formal or structural center highlights the absence of any moral center. In the end, Ballard's novel and Cronenberg's film need each other to convey a more focused and nuanced picture of car crashes as erotic spectacles and of celebrity deaths as filmic events.

Wagging the Dog: Sex, Lies, and the Clinton Videotapes

If I thought I was going to publish a book, I would have been taking pictures.... I would have been documenting this relationship.

> —Linda Tripp testifying about her reasons for secretly taping
> conversations with her friend Monica Lewinsky
> about Lewinsky's relationship with President Clinton

It's like *Fatal Attraction*. Ken Starr is Glenn Close.

> —Actress Sharon Stone on Starr's investigation of Clinton's
> relationship with Lewinsky

In a study of filmic events in the late twentieth century and of the tendency toward ever greater explicitness in the already literalist medium of the movies, it's hard to avoid commenting on a "real-life movie" made and released amid much controversy in 1998.[65] The September broadcast on all the major television networks of the videotape of President Clinton's August 17 testimony to a federal grand jury about his relationship with former White House intern Monica Lewinsky was truly, as Clinton himself acknowledged, an "unprecedented" event. If the twenty-six-second Zapruder film had been the first visual recording of a president's assassination, the four-hour Clinton videotape gave the whole world its first unedited glimpse of a sitting president's humiliation—his sworn testimony about the most intimate details of his private life.[66] Since FDR, presidents had recorded many of their private conversations and consultations, and it was such a tape, of course, that compromised Nixon and led to his removal from office.[67] Never before, however, had the private been made so glaringly public as with the worldwide broadcast of the videotape of Clinton's testimony following the equally precipitous release, first over the Internet and then in the print media, of independent counsel Kenneth Starr's report meticulously documenting the lurid details of each alleged sexual encounter between the president and the intern. Together, the Starr Report, the videotape of the president's grand jury testimony, and the second, even more evasive videotape of his January 17, 1998, deposition in the Paula Jones sexual harassment case that was made public during the House Judiciary Committee hearings on impeachment in December all but undermined Clinton's claim in his apology to the nation that even presidents have a right to a private life.[68]

The decision by Congress to release the Starr Report and the videotape of Clinton's grand jury testimony was intended to provide the American people with evidence of "wrongdoing"—whether such misconduct was the actual adulterous affair or the act of lying about that affair under oath—that could be used as grounds for initiating impeachment proceedings. Ironically, the tape had been made only because the president's lawyers had maintained that it would hurt the dignity of his office for him to testify in federal court before the grand jury. But by permitting Clinton's testimony to be videotaped in the White House Map Room, they unwittingly cleared the way for the release of salacious material before the entire world on the Internet and on television, creating a media frenzy not seen since the O.J. Simpson trial four years earlier.[69]

Aside from Clinton's and his attorneys' legal hairsplitting about whether his relationship with the intern could be termed "sexual," the most preposterous aspect of the investigation was the fact that the very same conservative politicians who just two years before had decried pornography in the arts and on the Internet and who had pushed for the

Communications Decency Act were now insisting that the most lurid details of the affair be made public, regardless of the consequences. Concerned that "the revolution of graphic communication" that caused people to be "moved much more by moving pictures than by words" had kept "most Americans" from reading the Starr Report and "getting the full flavor of Clinton," conservative commentator George Will provided readers of his *Newsweek* column with a juicy sampling: a bit of pillow talk reported by Lewinsky and the image of Clinton "seen in Starr's report masturbating in the West Wing after an episode with the intern."[70] It's as if Will was trying to conjure up a *visual* image of Starr's verbal account, to use the report as a script for a porn film. And so it was that a columnist who was quick to condemn as obscene depictions on the Internet of ordinary anonymous individuals engaged in sex had no qualms about foisting upon the public the most graphic accounts of the sexual affairs of the president of the United States.

No doubt Will would argue that the public not only has a right but a need to know the details of the president's relationship in order to judge his character and his fitness to remain in office. But as Jeffrey Rosen has observed, Starr's decision to fill "his report with gratuitous, X-rated details about Clinton's intimate moments with Lewinsky" was a strategic move to "shore up a questionable legal case with reams of graphic sexual material." The problem with such a strategy, notes Rosen, is that by "its very nature, explicit sexual material overwhelms all other arguments and ideas ... it's hard to have a calm debate about legal guilt or innocence when you're distracted by lurid and graphic sexual information."[71] No wonder, then, that the president was adamant in his testimony that he would not go into details about his relationship with Lewinsky. In a prepared statement at the outset of his testimony, he declared that "I am right to answer all the questions about perjury, but not to say things which will be forever in the historical annals of the United States because of this unprecedented videotape, and may be leaked at any time."

As it turned out, of course, the ensuing chain of events was even worse than Clinton had anticipated: the videotape was not only leaked, but broadcast in its entirety around the globe. Yet Clinton was well aware at the time of the taping that by giving testimony before a video camera that could therefore be made public, he was, in Caryn James's words, "making a movie," and so he refused "to provide sexually explicit details." But, as James points out, this was no conventional film. For one thing it was unedited: "most documentaries don't unfold in real time the way this did." For another thing, it lacked a director. Despite all the efforts or Starr and his colleagues to guide the proceedings, it "was decidedly Clinton's show ... he was the Bill Clinton who knows how to play to the camera."[72] If the broadcast of the videotape was not immediately as damaging to Clinton as Starr had anticipated, this was in large part because the president, by refusing to provide the graphic sexual information that the grand jury requested, did not make the movie that his offscreen questioners wanted him to make. Instead, he forced them to continually and obsessively return the subject of the proceedings to sex. This made the prosecutors' repeated declarations that the charges against the president had nothing to do with sex sound as absurd as Clinton's continued denials that his relations with Lewinsky were sexual. Of course, from a Foucauldian perspective both Clinton and his prosecutors were right: the issue was never sex per se, but "the over-all 'discursive fact,' the way sex 'is put into discourse,'" often for purely political purposes of power/knowledge.[73]

If Clinton and his prosecutors assumed the role of competing film-makers in the production and distribution of the videotaped testimony, the news media and political pundits were quick to assume the role of movie critics. Countless headlines and TV special reports at the time of the tape's broadcast dubbed the story "sex, lies, and videotape," after the title of Steven Soderbergh's 1989 film. But the press had already made its most pointed cinematic allusion regarding the scandal the previous month when the president had ordered military attacks on suspected terrorist sites in Sudan and Afghanistan, ostensibly in response to bombings of U.S. embassies in Tanzania and Kenya. Numerous news commentators at the time had invoked the recent release of Barry Levinson's 1997 film *Wag the Dog*, in which a U.S. president seduces an underage "Firefly Girl" in a room off the Oval Office. In an attempt at damage control, the president's aides call upon a savvy political consultant named Conrad Brean (Robert De Niro), who in turn enlists the services of a Hollywood movie producer, Stanley Motss (Dustin Hoffman). Using an array of special effects, Stanley arranges for fake news footage to be made of a nonexistent war in Albania. The press and the public are distracted by the sensational story, and a potentially fatal scandal on the eve of a national election is narrowly averted.

After *Wag the Dog*'s unexpected success at its release in January 1998, which coincided with the initial reports of the Lewinsky affair and the president's threat of an air strike against Iraq, the film enjoyed a second boost in publicity that summer when Clinton ordered the strikes against Sudan and Afghanistan three days after his grand jury testimony, and on the very day that Monica Lewinsky was called back for a second round of testimony about her relationship with him. Inevitably, comparisons were made abroad and at home between the movie *Wag the*

Dog and Clinton's real-life situation as a president who seemed inclined to "let loose the arsenal in a time of personal crisis."[74] State-controlled Iranian radio declared that the president's decision to attack sites in Africa and the Near East was "aimed at covering up and overshadowing his problem." This view was echoed at home by conservative commentators such as Arianna Huffington, who wondered whether Hollywood producer and Clinton crony Harry Thomason might have had a hand in the military operation. Republican senator Dan Coats called the timing of the mission "suspect," while Arlen Specter saw reason to ask "whether there was any diversionary motive involved."[75] But despite the need for caution voiced by leaders such as House Speaker Newt Gingrich, who said it was "sick" to suggest that the president acted out of motives other than national security, or by commentators such as Jay Carr, who lamented "that a Hollywood movie should figure in any discussion" of the military action—a turn of events that showed "how skewed our collective sense of so-called reality has become"[76]—many continued to "wonder if life is imitating a certain movie."[77] That speculation became especially credible in mid-December when, on the eve of the House of Representatives' vote on impeachment, Clinton ordered an all-out strike against Iraq. The suspicious timing of this attack and the August bombings left many incredulous and prompted House majority leader Trent Lott to announce he could no longer support the president.

Because the "phrase 'wag the dog' is now embedded in the political lexicon," it's worth asking how accurately this cinematic reference describes political and military reality.[78] The phrase has come to refer to a president's use of a diversionary tactic to distract the press and the public from a personal scandal that threatens to undermine his authority. In a democratic society, the military leader may be less concerned with fooling the enemy than with distracting his own voting constituency. In the film *Wag the Dog*, the diversionary tactic is not a real war but a fake one, the *appearance* of an international conflict (hostilities between the United States and Albania) triggered by a wholly invented incident (the story that an Albanian agent had brought a nuclear device onto U.S. territory). In the case of the December 1998 attack on Iraq, President Clinton maintained that America's real military action had been in response to an actual military threat (Richard Butler's report of Iraq's refusal to open suspected weapons sites to UN investigators). And as one Democratic congressman reminded colleagues who raised the specter of *Wag the Dog* after the August attacks on sites in Afghanistan and Sudan, "The bombing of our embassy was very real. That 260 people were murdered in Kenya and Tanzania was real. The movie was fiction."[79]

Yet even this retort to the life-imitates-movies adherents (should this group be considered excessively credulous or excessively skeptical?) neglects the fact that not only was the movie fiction, but so was the war-within-the-movie. In contrast, both the embassy bombings and the U.S. military response were real. If Clinton were really enacting the script of *Wag the Dog*, he would have staged a fake military operation rather than a real one, much as President Reagan had done in 1983 in Grenada to divert public attention from the 230 U.S. marines killed two days earlier in Beirut in a terrorist attack. What made Clinton's diversionary tactic, if that's what it was, so much more sensational than Reagan's was, first, that it involved actual bombings and missile strikes rather than a staged military rescue, and, second, that it was supposedly intended to divert public attention from a personal—and especially a sexual—crisis rather than a national tragedy. But how is one to determine what was the greater scandal—a mock military action designed to distract the nation from a truly grievous national injury or a real military action that may have been timed to divert attention from what many considered a media-driven pseudoevent? Or were the media and the nation so capti-vated by the (porno)graphic nature of Clinton's behavior that it took nothing less than a military strike to restore a sense of reality?

One reason why Clinton's military operations were widely seen as a political ploy while Reagan's equally blatant machinations went rela-tively unnoticed was the fortuitous appearance of Levinson's fictional film at the height of Clinton's troubles. *Wag the Dog* provided the pres-ident's critics with a convenient label with which to tag him, and enabled those critics to recast his military operations as filmic events. Yet the film's depiction of a president staging a fake war was actually closer to the kind of diversionary tactic that the movie-star-turned-president Reagan had pulled off in Grenada—a feat to which the film alludes—than to Clinton's military actions in Africa and Asia. But without a popular cinematic reference available to them at the time, commentators on the Grenada diversion were unable to draw a connection between movies and real life or to get a handle on events, despite Reagan's embarrassing tendency to confuse movie roles and fictional characters with the real thing.[80] The fortuitous release of *Wag the Dog* at the time that the Lewinsky story broke made it appear that Clinton was acting out the scenario depicted in the film and that he was the first president to do such an unheard-of act as stage a military operation in order to divert public attention from a crisis.

Wag the Dog is less an instance of an artistic fiction that somehow took on a reality of its own than an exemplary illustration of the reality effect. Not only does the movie show how thoroughly Washington-based political life is already mediated by Hollywood-based fictions, but it exemplifies the way in which such fictions are perceived as uncanny anticipations and even logical explanations of actual events, when the grounds for making such connections are tenuous and fortuitous at best. Thus only a year after the false war in Albania shown in the film—what could be more ludicrous, or so it seemed at the time, than American troops at war in such an insignificant country?—a real war took place in the region when U.S. and NATO forces launched an air campaign against the Serbs for their policy of driving ethnic Albanians out of Kosovo. Yet no one would claim that the makers of *Wag the Dog* foresaw or predicted this conflict. In fact, the movie was dead wrong on this point: the bogus war it portrayed in Albania turned out to be anything but bogus. Nevertheless, based on coincidental similarities between the plot of *Wag the Dog* and the Clinton sex scandal, a number of supposedly objective observers suspected a connection and were led to question whether Clinton, by ordering strikes against suspected terrorist or military sites, was taking his cue from this film. In effect, these commentators were asking whether the strikes in Afghanistan, Sudan, and Iraq were staged events, a diversionary tactic like the bogus war with Albania in the movie.

In making such a suggestion, the commentators may themselves have been following the movie's cues. By relying on a ready-made cinematic "fiction" as an "explanation" for complex real-life events, Clinton's critics were actually the individuals who were most closely enacting Levinson's script. In the very act of invoking *Wag the Dog* as the key to Clinton's policy, they were unwittingly performing the film's preposterous story line: far from showing themselves to be media-savvy, they were as much media dupes as the credulous citizens in the film who readily accepted ludicrous scenarios cooked up by a Hollywood producer as the gospel truth. And so we may ask whether a movie gave Clinton an idea that he proceeded to act out in real life, or whether the "insight" of Clinton's critics into his supposed diversionary stratagem was planted in their heads by the same movie. Whose dog indeed was being wagged?

As for the videotape of Clinton's grand jury testimony, its ultimate significance may be its role in defining his presidential legacy. Ironically, the man who modeled his life and presidency on John F. Kennedy is likely to have his memory indissolubly associated with the videotape of his testimony about the Lewinsky affair, just as Kennedy's memory is indelibly associated with the Zapruder film of his murder. These two pieces of film footage may well serve as the century's most spectacular examples of obfuscation and assassination, and of the increasingly graphic and public display of film culture's twin peaks of sex and violence.

part three

film dreams

From
Dream Work
to DreamWorks

The stuff that dreams are made of.
  —Humphrey Bogart as Sam Spade, *The Maltese Falcon* (1941)

Unreal Estate: Fake Towns, Real People

Nowadays when a person lives somewhere, in a neighborhood, the place is not certified from him. More than likely he will live there sadly and the emptiness which is inside him will expand until it evacuates the entire neighborhood. But if he sees a movie which shows his very neighborhood, it becomes possible for him to live, for a time at least, as a person who is Somewhere and not Anywhere.
  —Walker Percy, *The Moviegoer*

Besides *Wag the Dog*, two other noteworthy movies about the media appeared in 1998. In Gary Ross's *Pleasantville*, two contemporary siblings are transported back into a 1950s-era TV show, experiencing and exposing the blandness of that artificial world. And Peter Weir's *The Truman Show* presents the ultimate paranoid scenario: Jim Carrey's character, Truman Burbank, is a man whose entire life is a staged, ongoing soap opera, filmed by five thousand tiny hidden cameras and watched by millions on TV. Reality triumphs over artifice at the end of both movies: the TV characters in the *Pleasantville* series wake up to the unpredictability of real life, and Truman discovers the elaborate deception in which he has been both dupe and star, whereupon he abandons his closed sound-stage world in order to live an authentic life beyond the cameras' myriad probing eyes.

  The Truman Show and *Pleasantville* are movies whose stories play on the unprecedented power of the visual media of television and, by extension, film at the end of the twentieth century. They especially call attention to Americans' obsessive fascination with "the surreal ordinariness" of life as embodied in the character of Truman or in the town of Pleasantville, and they self-reflexively examine the willingness of viewers "to find the most nondescript ... experiences" of a character such as Truman "more poignant and meaningful than one's own."[1] But why do viewers find the ordinary so fascinating? Perhaps because it's become so rare in a society of the spectacle where more and more of life is mediated by the mass media. Or perhaps because in such a society the "ordinary" is anything but natural, but is itself the most surreal and extraordinary effect of all.

It's worth noting in this regard that both *The Truman Show* and *Pleasantville* are situated in towns that look like sets staged for movies or television. Oddly, the fake town of Seahaven portrayed in *The Truman Show* was *not* a set, but the actual planned community of Seaside on Florida's panhandle. The film's producers had simply reversed the customary practice of building an artificial set that looks real; instead they used a real town that looked like a set to evoke "a setting that becomes a character in its own right."[2] Viewers unaware of the fact that Seahaven is not just a set but the real town of Seaside miss the irony in the film's premise that enormous effort, incalculable expense, and ingenious special effects have been used to provide Truman with the illusion of reality—that he is living a normal life in an ordinary town—when the film was in fact shot in an actual (although thoroughly movie-mediated) town. If, as J. G. Ballard said, "the fiction is already there" for the writer whose only "task is to invent the reality," the setting for Peter Weir's film already existed as the town of Seaside. Rather than create a fake town as an "effect," Weir merely had to give this ready-made town a slightly altered name.

It's not often that the real thing suits Hollywood's artificial purposes. When an existing historical monument figures prominently in a movie, it's usually necessary to construct a fake alternative. Thus when a film about the Alamo was being made in Texas, moviemakers considered the real landmark "small and unprepossessing." As a result, they arranged for "a bigger and better Alamo" to be built in a nearby town, and today it is as much a tourist attraction as the genuine Alamo.[3] (One is reminded of the exact copy of Goethe's Garden House built a hundred yards from the original in Weimar to celebrate the writer's 250th birthday.)

Similarly, in seeking set locations, Hollywood production designers routinely settle on small, historic American towns to create a feeling of authenticity—for example the Rhode Island towns of Wickford in *Meet Joe Black* (1998) and Jamestown in *Me, Myself, and Irene* (2000). Yet although these traditional towns would seem to be utterly unlike the artificial fantasy worlds of Hollywood or the synthetic sprawl of Los Angeles, they increasingly seem quaint and unreal, as if they were constructed as movie sets. In fact, a growing number of residential communities have so assiduously simulated the pristine towns portrayed in the movies that they themselves take on the appearance of movie sets. And so the producers of *The Truman Show*—a movie satirizing the media's idealized depictions of post–World War II American life—were able to use a real-life town as a set precisely because it looked so artificial. The logical next step was for the movie companies themselves to construct new "real" communities that replicate the appearance of the few remaining towns of yesteryear, and then to use these new-old, fake-real hybrid towns as movie sets.[4]

The fact that real and fake towns can no longer be distinguished in the movies is another sign that the traditional distinction between narrative films and documentaries has been thoroughly blurred. After Michael Moore's *Roger & Me* documented the ravaged economy of Flint, Michigan, in the aftermath of General Motors plant closings and layoffs, it was only a matter of time before a virtual documentary such as Russ Hexter's 1997 movie *Dadetown* would portray the economic woes of a fake town.

> The film unrolled like an as-it-happened documentary of a small town where the factory economy was dying and giving way to the software business. Not until the credits rolled was it revealed that the town, the citizens and the upheaval were entirely fictional.
>
> Any critic who raced out at the close of the final scene reviewed a documentary they only thought they saw.[5]

While *Roger & Me* depicts the decline of an actual industrial city, a fin-de-siècle documentary such as James Marsh's *Wisconsin Death Trip* insidiously suggests that the apparent prosperity of the rural farming community of Black River Falls is deceptive, and that the pleasant rituals of small-town life—parades, beauty contests, high-school football games—mask occasional eruptions of criminal violence that are painfully reminiscent of the town's harrowing gothic past.

These documentaries about decaying cities and troubled towns are giving way to a new phenomenon: real towns whose survival depends on their becoming an artificial film set, a theme park, or even an advertisement. Take the small Cascade Mountain town of Cashmere, Washington, which recently faced economic ruin when its principal business, a candy company that had been based there since 1918, threatened to move to a nearby "Bavarian theme town." The company, Liberty Orchards, would agree to stay in Cashmere only if a list of demands were met that would effectively turn the town into an advertisement for its business—changing road signs and renaming streets to refer to Liberty Orchards' products, and even letting the company buy the town hall.

"It is not surprising," writes architecture critic Ada Louise Huxtable, "that much of the most popular and profitable development of the [theme park] genre is spearheaded and bankrolled by the masters of illusion; the movie and entertainment businesses have become the major innovators and investors in theme parks and related enterprises."[6] But it should also come as no surprise to learn that the media company most adept in constructing amusement parks and entertainment complexes as well as movie sets simulating small-town life in America would enter the real estate business and build actual residential communities. This is what the Walt Disney Company did when it created the town of Celebration in Florida on land acquired in the 1960s for Walt Disney World. Disney himself had wanted to create "a real town with real citizens" in central Florida to be called Epcot, the Experimental Prototype Community of Tomorrow.[7] But the Epcot that eventually opened in the early '80s as part of Disney World was a futuristic theme park that hardly conformed to the original project. Disney's dream had to wait until the company came under the management of Michael Eisner, who agreed to develop a five-thousand-acre tract of land that wasn't needed for the park's expansion into a town that he hoped "would be a model for development in the next millennium."[8] But far from being a futuristic town, Celebration—which was designed by the same architects who planned Seaside, that other artificial-looking Florida site where *The Truman Show* was filmed—is an example of "New Urbanism," a style modeled on Savannah, Georgia, and other pre-1940s southern towns. The exterior appearance of the homes are carefully regulated, from the landscaping to the pastel shades of paint to the white and off-white color of the window curtains.[9] It's fitting that the town's central feature is its movie house, designed by Cesar Pelli in the style of 1930s theaters.

For critics such as Neal Gabler, Celebration's nostalgic creation of a movie-mediated past is a sign of its unreality. Celebration is *The Truman Show* come true—a town in which all the inhabitants "were cast members on the set of their own life movies."[10] But the New Urbanist invocation of an earlier period in American culture can also be seen as a move toward a new reality. In contrast to Disney's futuristic Epcot, Celebration may be, as Kurt Andersen suggests, "the real EPCOT—the quasi-democratic, postmodern fulfillment of Walt's totalitarian, late-modern vision." To those critics who would sneer at Celebration's "picturesque fakery," Andersen responds,

Isn't the obligatory American lawn a form of fakery? Isn't air-conditioning a fake? Aren't the crazy architectural mongrels built every day in every city in America—all the tarty Mediterranean-Colonial-Norman-Palladian raised ranches—thoroughly (and wretchedly) fake? ... Celebration's "fakery"—its small scale, its density, its hidden garages, its pre-mall commercial core—is in the service of a coherent vision, as opposed to the accumulation of developers' cost-efficient short cuts and aesthetic bad habits that produce the random, sprawling, ghastly "real" suburbs of the late twentieth century.[11]

For end-of-the-century advocates of New Urbanism, planned fakery has become preferable to a ruthlessly unregulated reality. And Celebration's particular brand of fakery is also preferable to all the other forms of artificiality that characterize modern American life, not so much because it is more picturesque or more up-front about its pretense, but because its coherent vision of small-town life (which is really a cinematic vision à la Capra and Disney) comes closest to creating the ultimate reality effect—the illusion of "a real town with real citizens." According to this logic, the only place in late-twentieth-century America to find real people who can be spontaneously and genuinely themselves is in fake towns, communities deliberately designed to recapture the supposed simplicity of a bygone era before the advent of the very technology that transformed reality into—or revealed it as—an effect.

Ants Wars

While families were moving into Celebration's movie-set community in an attempt to (re-experience real life at the close of the twentieth century, another building project of a different kind was under way on the other side of the country that was intended to challenge Disney's media hegemony. (Under Eisner's leadership, the Disney corporation had acquired the film company Miramax, allied itself with the software company Pixar, and was once again producing cutting-edge feature animation as in the days of its founder.) On a 1,087-acre stretch of marshland on the California coast, the first new Hollywood studio in sixty years was being planned by DreamWorks SKG. The complex was to be a state-of-the-art technological marvel, constructed on the very site where former film mogul Howard Hughes had built his "Spruce Goose" seaplane. Headed by director Steven Spielberg, former Disney movie chief Jeffrey Katzenberg, and record mogul David Geffen, the company was valued at $2.7 billion before it even produced its first product.[12] A project of this size had to be more than just a complex of sound stages; DreamWorks was to be the anchor tenant of the projected

Playa Vista development, which, with thirteen thousand new condos and commercial space including a new marina, and at least $75 million in city and state tax incentives, was intended to be a self-sufficient residential community with an estimated worth of $6 billion to $8 billion.

From the start, however, the ambitious project was headed for trouble. Environmentalists charged that Playa Vista threatened the Ballona wetlands, the last undeveloped tract in Los Angeles County. Ultimately, financing difficulties led DreamWorks to pull out of the project in 1999. There are limits, it seems, to the joint business ventures envisioned by dream movies and "real" estate.[13]

Nevertheless, DreamWorks was—and still is—clearly positioning itself to give Disney, one of the world's largest media companies, a run for its money. Specifically, it has sought to challenge Disney in the domain where it reigns supreme—animation—and especially in the new generation of computer-generated animation that Disney had inaugurated with its partner Pixar (the software company that Apple Computer cofounder Steve Jobs bought from George Lucas in 1986). Since the huge success of the first computer-animated feature, *Toy Story*, Pixar's staff focused exclusively on making movies, entering into a five-picture partnership with Disney and building its own base of operations on sixteen and a half acres in Emeryville, California.

Competition between DreamWorks and Disney/Pixar came to a head in the fall of 1998 with each studio's release of a blockbuster computer-generated animation feature dealing with the unlikely subject of ants. Although DreamWorks started work on *Antz* in 1995, a full year after Pixar began developing *A Bug's Life*, the film was rushed into production so that it could be released more than a month ahead of its competitor. Pixar protested that its idea for an ant movie had been stolen by Katzenberg when he quit his post as chairman of Disney Studios to join DreamWorks in August 1994—two days before the idea was pitched to Disney by Pixar director John Lasseter. (Katzenberg has denied knowing about the project.) But while DreamWorks scooped Disney in the ants animation war, *A Bug's Life* held its own and was widely hailed as a superior achievement. Besides, the technical innovations of *Antz* did not go without criticism. Film critic Anthony Lane complained about the movie's "decorative uniformity," its shiny surfaces that show no trace of

> the random ways on which physical surfaces are rubbed and scarred. This was no problem with "Toy Story," where the natural sheen of the animation coincided happily with the fact that the heroes were molded from plastic; it is more of a letdown in "Antz," which is, by definition, set in a universe of trash and crap.[14]

The movie's key scene in a garbage dump dubbed "Insectopia" fails to come off "because the garbage cannot help but suffer from the same spooky, enhanced cleanness in which computer design has wrapped the entire movie." The contradiction Lane finds between computerized cleanliness and a sort of sanitized filth that appeals to humans and vermin alike would seem to be an inevitable result of the new technology which is incapable of simulating oldness and waste.

And why two ant films anyway? The life of insects, typically the subject of nature documentaries, became the ideal subject for filmmakers eager to demonstrate the new capabilities of the most artificial of cinematic forms—animation—to reproduce the natural world. What better subject, as Edward Rothstein observes, to display "texture, character, individuality, nuance and other un-antlike characteristics" created by the new technology? "Computer animation was once the sign of artificiality; now it is humanized, naturalized, and we are meant to see it at work bringing a human touch to the inhuman realm of the ant. Nature is transformed by artifice into seeming more natural."[15] Computer animation, the latest breakthrough in cinematic special effects, was used to produce the illusion not of the supernatural but of nature at its most ordinary, familiar, and homely. The greatest technical feat in *Toy Story 2* wasn't the lifelike animation of the toy characters but the digitized portrayal of the dachshund Buster; the four million hairs on his body are visual effects made possible by fur software developed during the movie's production. It's as if nature presents the computer-animation wizards not only with the greatest challenge, but also with an unprecedented opportunity to re-create it into something altogether new, artificial, and supremely graphic—to make reality over once and for all as an effect.

Back to the Future: Movies, the Ride

At the end of the twentieth century, Neal Gabler's claim that life has become "the biggest, most entertaining, most realistic movie of all, one that played twenty-four hours a day, 365 days a year, and featured a cast of billions" itself became the subject of movies.[16] In *The Truman Show* one man's life is nothing more than a cinematic illusion; the following year *The Matrix* revealed *all* life to be an illusion. The latter film is based on the Kabbalistic premise that the world as we know it is no longer real but a "computer-generated dream" that only a few select individuals can penetrate to the reality beyond. The irony here, of course, is that the movie *The Matrix* is itself a computer-generated dream that envelops its viewers, sealing them off in its own substitute reality. It doesn't take much imagination to see *The Matrix* as an allegory of the pervasive power of movies—especially movies loaded with special effects—to create an alternate, substitute, but ultimately false reality. A key problem with such movies is that they are utterly incapable of critically looking at or reflecting upon new developments in digital media and virtual-reality technology because for the most part they are themselves a product of that technology. A better title for the movie might have been *The Möbius Strip* since the mediated reality it depicts loops back into its own production. The use of all the advanced special effects—especially the well-hyped "Flo-Mo" sequences—give the movie the look not of real life, but of a spectacular sci-fi comic book.

The explicit thematization of virtual reality machines in movies such as *The Matrix* calls attention to the fact—already anticipated by early-twentieth-century writers such as Pirandello and Schwartz—that the ultimate machine of this kind, the ideal dream machine, is the cinematic apparatus itself and its more recent televisual derivatives. Most of today's commercial films do not encourage such reflection, however, but rather employ a powerfully synchronized combination of digital audio and visual effects to plunge the viewer into an all-encompassing, somnambulent state that all but screens out the real world. Caught up in the overwhelming imagery of Tony Scott's 1998 thriller *Enemy of the State*, *Newsweek*'s Jack Kroll describes the

> scary fun of the movie ... embodied in a brilliantly filmed and edited chase sequence in which [Will] Smith tries to escape the ubiquitous cyber-eyes that see every inch of his flight. In such passages Scott ... creates a new cinematic landscape out of hurtling satellite images and flashing computer screens, turning the whole earth into a claustrophobic space that affords no escape.[17]

Scott's creation of a "new cinematic landscape" is an instance of the Kuleshov effect taken to the extreme: now not merely does the swift sequencing of scenes shot at different locations serve to create an artificial space for the viewer, who remains outside the action, but the film surrounds the viewer with a total surveillance space in which there is no escape from remote cameras, bugging devices, and concealed monitoring systems. The wording of Kroll's description leaves it unclear whether it is the actor Smith or the viewer who is unable to escape the "claustrophobic space" of the "cinematic landscape" into which "the whole earth" has been transformed—the world made film. Whether viewers want it or not, they are along for the ride.

Many of Hollywood's blockbuster films are really no longer movies, but are better described (and evaluated) as rides or games. Some movies, such as *Raiders of the Lost Ark* or *Back to the Future*, become actual rides in theme parks such as Walt Disney World and Universal City, where visitors are no longer passive spectators but have the sense of being interactive participants in cinematic events. Yet there is also a sense in which some of the most entertaining special-effects movies are more than mere rides, providing graphic, documentary evidence or even proof of a reality that has never been, and can never be, recorded on film. One thinks of the prehistoric dinosaurs reconstructed in Steven Spielberg's *Jurassic Park*: although this movie itself became a ride, and is itself *about* a ride in a futuristic theme park, it also presents a vivid picture of a "lost world" that no human being has ever witnessed, let alone documented. In contrast to Disney's talking-dinosaur movie a few years later, Spielberg endeavored to use special effects to reconstruct the most realistic visual simulation possible of these prehistoric creatures. Like all those cinematic reconstructions of JFK's assassination that tried to fill in the gaps left by the spotty film record, Spielberg was making up for the absolute absence of cameras, recording technology, or eyewitnesses during the Jurassic period. Beyond providing a graphic "record" of that lost world, he may have been giving it a kind of reality. For as the real is increasingly identified with recorded audiovisual "evidence" that dates back only to the twentieth—or the first filmed—century, there is a chance that history may appear to future generations as *beginning* with the twentieth century, or at least with what was graphically recorded at that time. (This was, after all, the logic behind the Kansas Board of Education's 1999 decision to drop evolution and the big bang theory from the state's science curriculum since such unobserved and unrecorded events are open to doubt.) The corollary of the literalist belief that the whole world is on film is the view that there's every reason to doubt the reality of whatever *isn't* on film. Given such a view, events in earlier times will have to be photographically reconstructed through dramatization and special effects if they are to appear real. A popular commercial filmmaker such as Spielberg may find himself as a documentarian not only preserving history (as in his project to record the recollections of Holocaust survivors), but also creating history as he and others face the daunting task of having to fill in the yawning gap of all of unrecorded history with realistic, graphic reconstructions.

The longest running back-to-the-future ride is George Lucas's *Star Wars* series. In a curious temporal twist, *Episode I: The Phantom Menace*—the 1999 sequel to the trilogy of movies that appeared in the 1970s—purported to be a *prequel* that depicted events a generation before those shown in the earlier films. The first three movies dealt with the aftermath of a great debacle that reduced the former Galactic Empire (derived from Isaac Asimov's *Foundation* stories) to a primitive condition of nomadic warriors working with salvaged weaponry; the new film introduced viewers to the period preceding the debacle, when the Empire was at the height of its technological glory.[18]

In fact, this was all an ingenious strategy on Lucas's part to showcase the special-effects wizardry of his company Industrial Light and Magic, effects that were necessary to bring the pre-debacle Empire to the screen in the first place. Twenty years earlier, when the original *Star Wars* movies appeared dealing with the Empire's aftermath, a movie about the Empire could not be made because the special effects needed to represent—and, indeed, create—it did not yet exist. And so Lucas found it necessary to put the series on hold. The depiction of a lost world of marvelous but dangerous technology had to be postponed until end-of-the-century computer technology could catch up with his own imaginative scenarios. (The contradiction between the antitechnological thrust of Lucas's films and his love of special-effects technology has not gone unnoticed.)[19] As late as 1990, Lucas still didn't consider computers sufficiently cost-effective to create the effects he wanted. But with the release of his friend Spielberg's *Jurassic Park* he realized that "we can create a photo-realistic, digital character that can look as real as any actor.... I was just so desperate to have an alien character that I can turn into a real character who interacts with other humans." Here was a case in which a certain spectacle—in this case, the world of the Empire—could not be "recorded" on film until the special effects needed to represent that spectacle became available.

But the epic saga doesn't end here. The images of the Galactic Empire with their vast scale that Lucas's FX-driven movies made so popular have gone on to generate our very conception of the actual cosmos. It's now common to hear the three-dimensional universe described cinematically, as a thin membrane in which we are trapped like "characters playing out their lives within the confines of a movie screen. Unknown to these shallow, two-dimensional players, a larger universe spreads into numerous extra dimensions, like theaters in a multiplex."[20] Or, as Dick Teresi puts it more dramatically, "With its fiery explosions, wormholes, white dwarfs, red giants and black holes, the big bang universe satisfies our Lucasfilm sensibilities.... It is the biggest-budget universe ever, with mind-boggling numbers to dazzle us.... Who wants to live in a smallish, low-budget universe?"[21]

From the Moon to Mars: *2001* Then and Now

In his use of special effects to realize his dreams of space travel and extraterrestrial life, Lucas was building on a long cinematic tradition that goes back to the origin of the medium itself when Georges Méliès produced *Le Voyage dans la lune* (*A Trip to the Moon*, 1902). Credited with being "the cinema's first narrative artist" who "discovered that film need not obey the laws of empirical reality, as his predecessors had supposed, because film was in some sense a separate reality with structural laws of its own," Méliès also devised the first special effects that have since become standard cinematic practices (fade-ins, fade-outs, "laps," dissolves, and stop-motion photography).[22] The techniques and mise-en-scène used in *Le Voyage dans la lune*, however, were derived from a theatrical tradition and produced a purely fantastic effect that no one could mistake for reality. Much the same could be said of nearly all the science-fiction movies about adventures in outer space made over the next half-century with their absurd gimmicks and preposterous illusions. Things began to change in the 1950s, the "high-water mark for science-fiction films," when directors of movies like *Destination Moon* (1950) and *The Conquest of Space* (1955) "ransack[ed] the special effects departments in attempts to create authentic-looking space technology consistent with the scientific ideas of the day."[23] But it was not until the race to the moon between the Americans and the Russians in the 1960s that an unprecedented degree of realism in the use of special effects was expected of filmmakers who tackled the subject of space travel.

As is well known, the challenge was spectacularly taken up by Stanley Kubrick in his four-year-long project to make *2001: A Space Odyssey* (1968). For this perfectionist and master at making special effects look real, there could not be the slightest sign of anything fake in the film. As noted by the team of reviewers in the *Harvard Crimson* (in what is said to be the longest film review ever published in that paper), Kubrick's "triumph, both in terms of film technique and directorial approach, is in the audience's almost immediate acceptance of special effects as reality: after we have seen a stewardess walk up a wall and across the ceiling early in the film, we no longer question similar amazements and accept Kubrick's *new world* without question."[24]

Thirty-three years after the film's release—in the actual year 2001—such hyperbolic claims about the authenticity of its special effects still hold up for the most part. The film is far off the mark, however, in its depiction of the state of space exploration today. (The original 1965 press release for the movie—then titled *Journey Beyond the Stars*—predicted that the year 2001 would be a time "when permanent bases have been established on the Moon, manned expeditions have visited Mars, and automatic probes have been sent to all the major planets of this Solar System.")[25] But while Kubrick and his co-scenarist, science-fiction author Arthur C. Clarke, may have been wildly over-optimistic about what the state of space technology would be like in 2001 ("We didn't project the devastating economic effects of the Vietnam War, and the changing priorities of the country," says former NASA engineer

Frederick Ordway who served as technical adviser to the film),[26] they actually underestimated the state of special-effects film technology that is now widely available. And although the pathbreaking special effects that Kubrick and his team of specialists painstakingly came up with more than thirty years ago in the pre-digital age of filmmaking have been rendered obsolete by today's standards, the comparatively primitive state of special-effects technology in the 1960s may in fact have been a blessing. For we are now in a position to recognize that the unavailability of digital effects served as an imaginative, visionary spur to Kubrick and his associates that is sadly lacking in most filmmaking— especially futuristic filmmaking—today.

Consider what is without doubt the most enigmatic and debated feature in the film: the mysterious black slab. The idea for the monolith has a long history that began with Clarke's 1948 short story "The Sentinel." In this story the monolith is not an upright black slab but a crystal pyramid that astronauts discover in 1996 on a cliff ledge on the moon. Unable to pursue their investigation of the pyramid because of the powerful force-shield it emits, the astronauts blast it with nuclear energy. Eventually the astronaut telling the story comes to the realization that the pyramid is one of many left throughout the galaxy by an alien civilization that evolved long before any others. The tetrahedron is one of many "sentinels" or alarms scattered throughout the galaxy by these advanced beings to alert them when other living beings have reached a certain stage in their evolutionary development. Now that the astronauts have penetrated the sentinel's shield, they have in effect "set off the fire alarm" that will soon bring back those advanced beings.

The story "The Sentinel" was the germ of *2001*, a work that Clarke wrote as a novel in consultation with Kubrick during the same period that Kubrick, in consultation with Clarke, was making the film. (Small wonder, then, that *2001* is a very literary film since the movie was conceived and produced at the same time it was being written as a novel; Kubrick was quite literally giving filmic expression and embodiment to Clarke's mental imaginings.)[27] As the novel and film progressed, the crystal pyramid in "The Sentinel" underwent a number of transformations before becoming the monolith—a black tetrahedron (an idea that was rejected because it risked eliciting "wholly irrelevant associations with the pyramids"), a transparent cube, and a rectangular block of lucite which at three tons was the largest ever cast. (Indeed, this is the form the monolith takes in its initial appearance to the ape-men in Clarke's novel.)[28] Finding this form "unconvincing," Kubrick finally came up with the idea of a black slab of the same dimensions as the lucite block.[29] Structurally and thematically, it is the device that unifies a picture that sprawls millions of miles across space and spans millions of years over time into a coherent whole. The monolith—or rather, the monoliths—punctuate the picture, appearing four times to mark each of its four major sections. It first appears in the opening "Dawn of Man" section where it turns up one day before the cave of a group of pre-human ape-like creatures, enabling one of them to achieve the first technological breakthrough of using bones as tools—or rather weapons since it is soon used to kill a member of a rival group. The monolith next appears three million years later in the year 2001 when it is discovered by American astronauts near their base camp on the moon. Although the monolith appears two more times in the film, this second appearance is especially critical since it is the moment when contemporary humans are confronted with the first evidence of extraterrestrial life—a discovery that the Americans treat with utmost secrecy.

The lengthy sequence showing the astronauts' descent into the excavation site where the monolith has been uncovered is pervaded by a sense of awe and almost religious reverence. The research team approaches the monolith as if it were a sacred object. The sequence culminates with a close-up of the lead astronaut's hand making contact with the slab. The ponderous mood eases up somewhat as the astronauts assemble to have their picture taken before the monolith as if it were some tourist site. But the relaxed moment breaks off abruptly when—just as the moon, the earth, and the sun are shown lining up—the monolith emanates a disorienting high-pitched signal. Thus ends the movie's second section; the next section, which takes place eighteen months later, is the manned mission to Jupiter to investigate the monolith's magnetic force which has been found to be directed toward that planet. (Kubrick had wanted to follow Clarke's scenario in having Saturn be the mission's objective, but he was dissatisfied with his special-effects team's attempt to simulate this planet's rings.)

It's instructive to compare the mystery of the monolith in *2001* with a similar enigma in Brian De Palma's 1999 space film *Mission to Mars*. In several respects this movie —as well as, to a lesser extent, Anthony Hoffman's contemporaneous Mars film, *Red Planet* (2000)[30]—is a homage to Kubrick's film. For one thing, *Mission to Mars* has basically the same plot as *2001*, and actually follows Clarke's story "The Sentinel" even more closely than Kubrick's film, although no credit is given to either Clarke or Kubrick. A group of astronauts on the first manned mission to Mars discover a curious glinting pyramid-shaped object atop a mountain near their base. (In Clarke's story, the crystal pyramid is found on a terrace hewn out of a mountain, not buried beneath the lunar surface as in *2001*.) On an expedition to investigate the object, the team of astronauts direct radiation at the mountain, much like the nuclear energy that penetrates the force field of the pyramid in Clarke's story.

But while that beam merely neutralized the pyramid's force field (and supposedly signaled the aliens that the human species had evolved to the point of developing nuclear technology), the astronauts' experiments on the alien object in *Mission to Mars* unleash catastrophic forces in the mountain which destroy all but one of the team—Luke Graham, played by Don Cheadle. (In a very graphic scene one of the astronauts is shown being whirled about in the Martian storm until his limbs fly off.) The storm sequence ends with the viewer catching an aerial glimpse of the mountain on which the pyramid was perched. Now that the dust has cleared the mountain turns out to be something quite different—a giant stone face.

The next section of the film depicts a rescue mission sent to Mars headed by astronauts played by Tim Robbins and Gary Sinise. Robbins's character perishes en route (his corpse floating in space in a scene that echoes the one of the dead astronaut Poole in *2001*), but the rest of the crew arrives and makes contact with the survivor Graham, who by now has discovered in the aftermath of its explosion that the mountain is a giant face. When Graham shows his discovery to his would-be rescuers on his computer monitor, they are astounded by what they see. This is the moment of wonder that corresponds to the quasi-religious procession of the astronauts to the moon-based monolith in the scene from Kubrick's film. Although both movies tell basically the same story—a group of astronauts' encounter with an alien artifact—the most important difference between the two films is the nature of these artifacts: the mysterious monolith in *2001* and the great stone face in *Mission to Mars*. A comparison of these two entities tells a great deal not only about the different interests of the two filmmakers, but about a pervasive aesthetic transformation that has taken place between 1968 when Kubrick released his film and 1999 when De Palma released his.

The opposed forms used by Kubrick and De Palma to evoke in viewers a sense of awe at the prospect of otherworldly intelligent life in the universe is not merely a difference of cinematic technique and effect, but reenacts one of the oldest debates about artistic representation. This debate is vividly presented by the early third-century Greek sophist Philostratus in *The Life of Apollonius of Tyana* in which Apollonius argues with Thespesion about the proper way to portray the gods. Apollonius advocates the high mimetic approach of Greek sculptors who combined imitation and imagination to depict the gods in the most beautiful and noble human forms, and mocks the low mimetic approach of the Egyptians who depict their gods as animals. Thespesion responds that Apollonius has entirely missed the point; the Egyptians have shown more respect for the gods than the Greeks by not even making the attempt to depict them mimetically as they are; instead they have adopted a symbolic mode of representation, fashioning the gods' "forms as symbols of a profound inner meaning, so as to enhance their solemnity and august character." According to this argument, the greater the distance or disparity between the image and the divine referent, the more awe-inspiring and superhuman the gods will appear. Apollonius comes across as a literalist and ridicules Thespesion's argument, declaring that there is nothing "august or awe-inspiring" in animal images. However, he then proceeds to suggest that the Egyptian gods "would have met with much greater reverence, if no images of them had ever been set up at all, and if you had planned your theology along other lines wider and more mysterious." Ultimately, Apollonius proposes a minimalist or conceptual aesthetic that supersedes the symbolic aesthetic of the Egyptians as well as the mimetic aesthetic of the Greeks. In depicting the gods, the best approach is not "introducing any image at all, but leaving it to those who frequented the temples to imagine the images of the gods; for the mind can more or less delineate and figure them to itself better than can any artist."[31]

What happens when this ancient debate about the most awe-inspiring way to represent the gods is translated to film—at once the most realistic and mimetic of media, and yet a medium capable of producing the most dazzling special effects? Working with the most advanced special effects available to him in the 1960s, Kubrick followed the logic of Apollonius's argument by settling on the minimalist form of the monolith as the image of alien, if not divine, intelligence. Thirty years later, working with vastly improved production technology, De Palma falls back upon the venerable mimetic program, teasing viewers at first with a glimpse of Clarke's tetrahedron atop a cliff, but then in some colossal cosmic joke revealing this mysterious object to be the tip of the nose of a great anthropomorphic stone face after centuries of accumulated dust are blown away in a violent storm.

In opting for the mimetic simulacrum rather than the minimalist tabula rasa, De Palma is hardly alone. He represents the general tendency of the graphic imperative in present-day cinema whereby everything must be shown and as little as possible must be left to the viewer's imagination. This tendency is especially evident when we compare the latter part of Kubrick's film with De Palma's. Like nearly every other contemporary filmmaker depicting space exploration—most famously, George Lucas in the *Star Wars* film cycle and Steven Spielberg in *Close Encounters of the Third Kind* (1977) and *E.T.* (1982)—De Palma actually "takes us inside" to give us a glimpse of at least one alien who turns out to be an anthropomorphic superbeing who differs from humans only in being smarter, more exotic, or more cute and cuddly. We should be grateful to Kubrick for resisting this now rampant, mimetic, special-effects driven impulse in cinema, and *not* showing us any alien beings.[32] To be sure, the impossibility of producing "a truly believable-looking extraterrestrial" with the special effects available in the 1960s was also a significant factor in this regard.[33] Kubrick simply couldn't make aliens look "real"—a bizarre notion since who knows what a real alien looks like? Nevertheless, the key principle guiding him in making the film was his disdain for nearly all space movies made before *2001* which, according to Clarke, he regarded as "trash." He "was determined to create a work of art which would arouse the emotions of wonder, awe ... even, if appropriate, terror" rather than mere "schoolboy excitement."[34]

Today, of course, in the post–*Star Wars* era of digital filmmaking, it's commonplace to portray believable alien worlds and aliens themselves, and De Palma didn't shirk from availing himself of these advances. (Indeed, given this special-effects crazed era in filmmaking, he probably couldn't afford *not* to.) And so he gives us the absurd scene at the end of his film showing three astronauts' encounter with the alien who gives a brief nonverbal lesson (actually a visual demonstration) about the history of the solar system, the evolution of life on earth (in which creationism plays a key role), and the Martian colonization of Earth and ultimately of the entire galaxy. One can't help wondering if something hasn't been lost in the process, and access to more advanced special-effects wizardry hasn't meant a decline in imaginative vision on the viewer's as well as the director's part.

In his study *The Philosophy of Horror*, Noël Carroll, expanding upon H. P. Lovecraft's concept of "cosmic fear," refers to the sense of awe provoked by supernatural phenomena "which confirms a deep-seated human conviction about the world, viz., that it contains vast unknown forces."[35] This type of awe is readily aroused by *2001*, but not by *Mission to Mars* (although a sense of supernatural terror that comes close to awe is evoked by De Palma's earlier work—especially in *Carrie*). Yet there is one poignant and powerful scene in *Mission to Mars* which recalls early De Palma and conveys a sense of cosmic fear. Curiously, this scene also involves a stone face. About midway through the film, the spacecraft sent to find out what happened to the astronauts on the first mission is itself critically damaged, and the four astronauts on this second mission are forced to abandon their spaceship. During their space walk Tim Robbins's character Woody Bate leaves his companions in order to try to hitch up with a module orbiting Mars that is their last hope. He fails to snag the module and is left suspended in space, in sight of his companions (one of whom is his wife Terri, played by Connie Nielsen), but without the fuel necessary to rejoin them. Terri begins to propel herself in his direction in order to help him, but when it becomes clear that by doing so she would exhaust her own fuel supply and perish as well, Woody stops her by ending his own life in a gruesome manner. After a few last affectionate words he removes his helmet, effectively freezing his head which turns to stone.

There is little to link Woody's stone face with the aliens' stone-face monument on Mars. If anything, Woody has become the true alien in the film: he has become his own grotesque stony monument before his wife's anguished gaze. In its own way, De Palma's nightmarish grotes-querie in this scene is far more poignant and "real" than the dreamlike rapture viewers are absurdly expected to share with Gary Sinise's char-acter at the end of the movie as he leaves his fellow astronauts in order to fly off into the unknown with his Martian mentor.[36] Had De Palma been content to end his film with the all-too-realistic scene of Woody's sacrificial suicide in space, he may have achieved an image as memorable as—albeit far more unsettling than—Kubrick's unforgettable, upbeat image of a dying astronaut's transcendence into a cosmic Star-Child.

The Color of Dreams

Everything looks worse in black and white.

—Paul Simon, "Kodachrome"

The curious logic behind special effects dictates that in order to more closely simulate the ordinary, the effects need to become more sophisti-cated and "special." This was already apparent with the introduction of color cinematography, an innovation intended to make the movies more lifelike in comparison with black-and-white pictures. Yet in *The Wizard of Oz*, one of the earliest films to exploit the new technology, black-and-white film was used to depict the drab reality of Kansas at the beginning and the end of the film, while color was reserved for the extended central sequence set in the rich dreamworld of Oz. (Actually, in L. Frank Baum's original 1900 tale, Dorothy's trip to Oz is real and *not* a dream, as in the movie.) One might have expected the depiction of the land of Oz in colors familiar from everyday life to have made this appear the more realistic section to the screen audiences and the black-and-white Kansas sections to seem unreal in comparison. Yet for view-ers accustomed to black-and-white movies, the vivid colors of the dream section made it seem not so much real as hyperreal. "Contrary to what should be expected," Kracauer observed, "natural colors, as recorded by the camera, tend to weaken rather than increase the realistic effect which black-and-white movies are able to produce."[37] The paradox is espe-cially apparent now, nearly a half century later, when color has become the norm in moviemaking and black-and-white seems strange and artificial. Thus in *Pleasantville*, the black-and-white scenes depict the "perfect" but deadly dull and artificial world of 1950s suburban life as portrayed by the media, while the color segments portray life in all its unmediated and unedited reality—precisely the opposite use of the technique in *The Wizard of Oz*.

Actually, the technique used in *Pleasantville* of showing the real world in "living" color and the fantasy world in black and white had been implemented only seven years after the release of *The Wizard of Oz* in Michael Powell's 1946 fantasy *A Matter of Life and Death* (released in the U.S. as *Stairway to Heaven*). In this film the black-and-white segment is set in heaven, where a court deliberates the fate of David Niven's character, a British squadron leader in World War II who undergoes brain surgery after the crash of his aircraft. The color section depicts the pilot's romance in the surreal setting of the war with a woman (Kim Hunter) who works at the U.S. Air Force base in England. Communicating with him by radio, she was the last person he spoke to in the moments before he lost consciousness in the crash. It's left unclear whether the romance that develops between these characters, who did not know each other before the crash, is really taking place, or whether it's just his fantasy while he's unconscious. The alternation between the colorful romance on earth and the austere black-and-white realm of heaven contribute to the film's dreamlike quality; this is especially evident in those scenes in which the heavenly world impinges on the earthly in cinematic effects involving abrupt time shifts and sudden stop-action, such as a Ping Pong match frozen in midserve. Ultimately Powell's color scheme subverts conventional wisdom, making transitory life on earth seem more heavenly (i.e., colorful) than an eternity in heaven. Thus, when the angel assigned to escort the pilot to heaven happens to descend into a brilliantly hued rhododendron grove, he remarks, "One is starved for Technicolor up there."

The angel's appreciation of living color has been echoed by Martin Scorsese, who finds Powell's "use of Technicolor" admirable for being "so romantic and spiritual"—that is, not for depicting life as it is customarily experienced, but for presenting a vision of life as "a place that's so beautiful to be alive in." Powell manages to combine two conflicting genres. On one hand, *A Matter of Life and Death* is "a fantasy and a love story that plays out in the mind of Niven"; on the other hand, "what happens to him is totally realistic."[38] (In fact, the film was based on the actual story of a Royal Air Force pilot who somehow survived after jumping from his downed plane without a parachute.) Rather than oppose a real world of living color to a fantasy world in black and white, Powell sets two fantasy worlds against one another (the beleaguered pilot's fantasy of earthly life and the viewers' collective fantasy about the heavenly afterlife), and leaves it to the viewer to choose which is more "real." As the heavenly court assembles to decide the pilot's fate, the movie's color code has already cued the viewer to decide in favor of the pilot's dream of love.

Although *The Wizard of Oz* and *A Matter of Life and Death* may both use the technical innovation of color to depict dream fantasies, the latter movie valorizes the dream (if that's what it is) as desirable and (therefore) real, while the dream in *The Wizard of Oz* is presented as a beautiful but dangerous fantasy that is ultimately renounced for Kansas's familiar black-and-white security. Looking decades ahead to *Pleasantville* rather than a few years behind to *The Wizard of Oz*, *A Matter of Life and Death* declares that "reality" really is a matter of special effects—a matter of graphic vividness—and that a dream in heavenly Technicolor is preferable to a dream in black and white.

Back to the Drawing Board: Movies, the Game

There's a kind of dream that movies sell to people: You can start as the lowliest person and rise to the top. [I don't] sell this fantasy.

— Director Steven Shainberg

Made at the end of the 1930s in the heyday of the Hollywood "dream factory," *The Wizard of Oz* popularized what has become one of the most familiar cinematic conventions: the protagonist suddenly awakening to discover that the experiences she thought were real were actually only a dream. Viewers sharing the protagonist's sense of the reality of her experiences are jolted into a similar recognition. (Published two years before the release of *The Wizard of Oz*, Schwartz's "In Dreams Begin Responsibilities" uses the same convention, although the dream from which the narrator awakens in the final sentence of that story is, as we have seen, itself a visit to the movies.)

Sixty years after *The Wizard of Oz*—at the close of the filmed century that pioneered the recording of reality, and at the dawn of the digital age of the virtually real—the convention of the abrupt awakening from a bad dream has been reversed: the dream *is* the reality. In 1999 the heroine's nightmares of a psychotic killer turn out to be true in Neil Jordan's film *In Dreams*, Kevin Bacon's character in *Stir of Echoes* has nightmares about a corpse in his house that turn out to be real, and the boy in *The Sixth Sense* has visions of the dead that prove to be valid. Also in the same year, the besieged heroine of Satoshi Kon's animated psychothriller *Perfect Blue* undergoes what seems to be a mental breakdown in which her nightmares begin to take on a reality of their own and to become an actual threat. The question is raised of whether in the fantasy world of animation dreams are different from reality. Are dreams (or nightmares) just dreams, or are they as real as anything else in the film? Is it possible to dream in animation, and if not, how is it possible to ever wake up?

In order to make the dreams of characters accessible to viewers in a medium that "is as close to a dream as you can get," filmmakers have relied on special effects to provide audiences with the illusion that they can peer into the dreams of characters.[39] The new innovation of Technicolor, we have seen, was used to portray Dorothy's dreamworld in *The Wizard of Oz* and the downed pilot's dream of life and love in *A Matter of Life and Death*. In the era of virtual reality, however, the idea of peering into characters' dreams, or even of influencing their dreams, seems no longer a matter of special effects, but a prospect that is only too real. Movies today are increasingly concerned less with showing the dreams of characters than with thematizing the apparatus itself that makes such oneiric eavesdropping possible. Story lines of films such as *The Manchurian Candidate*, *True Lies*, *Total Recall*, and *Virtuosity* typically trace the development and refinement of mind-reading or brainwashing technology, and show the abuses to which such technology lends itself.

The movies' sci-fi obsession with the recording apparatus as a way of documenting psychical as well as physical reality is particularly evident in two films made in the early 1990s but set in 1999, on the eve of the new millennium. In *Until the End of the World* (1991), Wim Wenders updated Marshall McLuhan's idea of media technology as an extension of the senses. In this postmodernist Oedipal scenario, Sam Farber (William Hurt) records images of his global wanderings on a special camera, which he delivers to his father (Max von Sydow), a neuroscientist who attempts to transmit those images to his blind wife, played by Jeanne Moreau. After she dies from the exhausting process, Sam and his companion, Claire, join Dr. Farber in a new project in the latter's underground laboratory in the Australian outback. Instead of transmitting recorded images of physical scenes to the blind by bypassing the sense of sight, the new team of researchers work on a technique for making visual recordings of dream images that can be played back and observed. But the project is a disaster, since experimental subjects become addicted to the self-absorbed activity of repeatedly watching their recorded dream images—a rather heavy-handed allegory of the seductive power of the cinematic image and its complicity with the viewer's dream life.

In the dystopic world imagined by Kathryn Bigelow in *Strange Days* (1995), most of the population of Los Angeles in the final days of 1999 is addicted to "clips"—virtual-reality recordings that are produced and played back on Superconducting Quantum Interference Devices

(SQUIDS). When these devices are attached to the user's scalp, they "put the viewer into the head of the person having a particular experience," in Bigelow's words, much like the dream recordings in *Until the End of the World* that enable conscious users to replay their own unconscious experiences as well as those of others. The protagonist of *Strange Days* (played by Ralph Fiennes) is a dealer in such illegal clips named Lenny Nero, or, as Bigelow calls him, "a kind of director-producer of heightened-reality documentaries." In order to show these clips, Bigelow simulated the SQUID apparatus with helmet cameras that approximated her subjects' visual experiences. Viewers of *Strange Days* experience these heightened-reality documentaries at a third remove, imagining the SQUID user's reaction to the original subject's sensations and fantasies recorded on the clips. Bigelow's use of kernel hyperreal documentaries and Wenders's use of kernel dream documentaries in their cinematic fictions are an attempt to extend the recording possibilities of film to the subjective and unconscious realms, and to transform film into a fully interactive medium like video games or virtual-reality machines. In both cases, the attempts are more interesting than the results, which are neither movies nor games but something in between.

Wenders and Bigelow set their movies in 1999, a year when they imagined film moving beyond being a mere recording medium and becoming fully interactive. Ironically, it was in 1999 that movie revenues were surpassed by the video game industry for the first time—surely a sign of things to come. In September of that year, moreover, Sega set the stage for "a new era of console gaming in the United States" when it introduced a 128-bit video game system that was four times more powerful than the Pentium II processors in general use at the time.[40] (Sony and Nintendo quickly followed with their own state-of-the-art systems.) Sega's fully interactive system was the first to include a modem so that new games could be accessed on the Internet and even played online. In contrast to films, in which all the animation is prerecorded and simply played back the same way every time during projection, the animation in video games is computer-generated during play, giving it a degree of realism and autonomy that, as Sony boasted of its new graphics chip, is "capable of generating emotions in people who play them."[41] (Indeed, the "Emotion Engine," as Sony called its PlayStation 2, aimed at nothing less than "break[ing] the visual barrier so people can identify with the [game's] characters.")[42] With the movies' teenage target audience turning increasingly to the emotionally stimulating interactive hyperrealism of video games, it seemed a propitious moment for Disney, Lucasfilm, and DreamWorks to reassess their plans for future films.[43] Appropriately, Sega's new system was called Dreamcast.

Dream Worlds

Whether we like it or not that war destroyed a kind of privacy, perhaps the privacy of dream.... Our Vheissus are no longer our own, or even confined to a circle of friends; they're public property.

—Thomas Pynchon, *V.*

All my films are dreams.

—Ingmar Bergman

A hundred years after the publication of the *Interpretation of Dreams*, in which Freud elaborated his theory of dream work as a system of arcane mechanisms mediating the individual's conscious and unconscious modes of existence, dreams need to be reexamined, no longer from a psychological perspective as products of the individual's unconscious, but in a sociocultural or psychotechnological context, where they may be studied as carefully designed, produced, and massmarketed corporate products. The image of the Hollywood "dream factory" has even greater relevance today than it did in the 1930s, when Depression-era Americans were distracted by its brilliant spectacles, as does the flip side of Hollywood's image as the "dream dump" described in West's *The Day of the Locust*. Not that there is any conspiracy here on the part of the Hollywood dream (or media) machine, or any secret agenda on the part of industry insiders to use mass entertainment to influence entire populations. The recognition that people's dreams and fantasies are no longer their "own" but are mediated by media that are more powerful than ever is now openly acknowledged by the media moguls themselves, as shown by the choice of a name for Spielberg's, Katzenberg's, and Geffen's new movie company, and by the titles of such end-of-the-century movies as *What Dreams May Come* (1998), *In Dreams* (1999), *The Dreamlife of Angels* (1999), and Stanley Kubrick's 1999 film *Eyes Wide Shut*, adapted and updated from Arthur Schnitzler's 1926 morality tale *Traumnovelle* (Dream Story).

Although the affinity of films and dreams, the idea of movies as a kind of dream, was recognized by early theorists of the medium, the practical consequences of this parallel have taken on greater urgency in recent years. Noting that in dreams "we create, behind our own backs, so to speak, a 'reality' that we then experience as objective," Jonathan Schell has recently restated the crucial question regarding the relation between dreaming and media technology as world-making activities. "Is it possible," he asks, "that because of the rise of the new media, which have given us the ability to manufacture what we call virtual reality, we are now able, without quite knowing what we are doing, to create a secondary world that we are liable to mistake for the primary world given to our senses at birth?" Schell hypothesizes that the masses' fascination with the media's fictions is motivated by the same principle that produces dreams according to Freud—wish fulfillment. But it was one thing, Schell argues, for the media to "manufacture ... dramas out of real events," as they did with the O.J. Simpson trial and numerous other forms of infotainment; it is something else for the media to engage in reification, as they did in the Clinton impeachment proceedings, abruptly turning what had seemed a "soap opera into something terrifyingly actual."[44]

Actually, as Pirandello was quick to recognize, movies had been giving reality to dreams and fantasies from the start. Moreover, Schell's distinction between the media's activities of infotainment and reification is by no means as sharp as he suggests. After all, before the "Monica and Bill story" became a diverting soap opera or a terrifying political crisis, it was an actual incident. The subsequent reification of the story as a filmic event by the Starr Report and the impeachment proceedings was a vain attempt at a *return* to reality that the news and entertainment media had hopelessly obscured; inevitably this attempt to *recover* the story's factual basis only made it thoroughly hyperreal. As makers of fictional films routinely fabricate dramatic narratives out of sensational (and even banal) real events, heightening and hyperbolizing our sense of reality in the process, so makers of nonfictional films increasingly find it necessary to rely on special effects to create the illusion of a reality that appears less and less self-evident and authentic and which requires ever more sophisticated forms of artifice to appear convincing.

For Neal Gabler, there is no doubting Schell's hypothesis about the new media's capacity "to create a secondary [dream] world that we are liable to mistake for the primary world given to our senses at birth"; entertainment, "arguably the most pervasive and ineluctable force of our time ... has finally metastasized into life."[45] Like the turn-of-the-millennium Los Angelinos addicted to virtual-reality clips in *Strange Days*, most Americans in Gabler's view are addicted to "lifies"—movie scenarios that are more absorbing and compelling than real life itself. More than mere entertainment or infotainment, a diversion from life's exigencies, the movies as a mass-mediated, collective dream life are now constitutive of "life" itself.

Apart from the fact that this reduction of all media to entertainment ignores the impact on people's lives of art, news, documentary, and other communication technologies—not to mention the unmediated experience of life itself—the question remains whether it is only the public lives of Americans addicted to "lifies" that are molded by the media, or their private lives as well. And what about people who do not passively absorb the movies' images and the media's messages but interact with them, either creatively, by artistically refashioning their own imaginative insights and visions, or destructively, by publicly acting out "their" private fantasies and affecting others' lives in the process? When an individual lives a life based on his or her own dreams, as critic Nicholas Lemann observes, that life is bound to wind up foundering on the shoals of reality. But if the fantasy life of that individual attracts public attention and becomes a public issue, as happens with increasing frequency in the era of mass-mediated "postreality," then it acquires its own reality and "quite often pushes issues of objectively greater importance off the stage."[46] Like Schell, Lemann cites Monica Lewinsky's affair with President Clinton as an example, suggesting that the White House intern's fantasy that the president would leave his wife for her was "an example of a 'lifie' that didn't come true precisely because it was so unrealistic," having been based on the artificial genres of the Hollywood or Harlequin romance; however, "the public drama of the affair and its discovery did become the driving force in American politics for quite a while."[47]

Related examples crop up in recent history. Two of the most notable are John Hinckley Jr.'s obsession with the actress Jodie Foster in the 1976 movie *Taxi Driver*, which led him to attempt to take the life of President Reagan in 1981, and Mark David Chapman's slaying of John Lennon four months earlier, an act motivated in large part by his reading of J. D. Salinger's novel *Catcher in the Rye*.[48] The 1999 rampage by Eric Harris and Dylan Klebold at Columbine High School represents a particularly ominous development in media-mediated violence: more than books or films, interactive video games appear to have played a major part in fueling the killers' fantasies, not to mention sharpening their shooting reflexes. But Harris and Klebold also had certain cinematic models in mind in the weeks leading up to their attack, and they already envisioned their exploits dramatized by a high-profile director such as Steven Spielberg or Quentin Tarantino. Lemann may be right that individuals are able to live out their private fantasies only for a limited time before running up against the reality principle, but those fantasies may remain alive long enough to impose themselves violently in the public sphere. What meaning does the reality principle have for individuals living in a dreamworld increasingly mediated and constituted by the mass media, and by movies in particular—whether they embrace that mediated dreamworld willingly, or unwillingly find it imposed upon them?

For those of us affected and afflicted by the private fantasies of the Lewinskys, Chapmans, Hinckleys, Harrises, and Klebolds after they become a public issue that "pushes issues of objectively greater importance off the stage," we might ask how their fantasy lives so suddenly and shockingly become part of our public reality in the first place. If the private dreams and fantasies of individuals can so easily dominate the public agenda, this is because in what Mark Seltzer calls the "pathological public sphere" there is very little private life left where people can simply "be themselves."[49] The supposedly private fantasies of individuals are already stamped by the mass media; when a person's fantasy life suddenly seems to burst upon the stage of public life, it has really been there all along. Attempts by critics to salvage some semblance of normative reality in a media-saturated age by invoking distinctions between news and entertainment, documentary and narrative film, and public and private life inevitably fail to recognize that such distinctions are increasingly difficult to maintain as the media play an ever greater role in people's daily existence; as previously hidden, intimate, and personal aspects of the world show up publicly on film and screen; as filmmakers' collectively crafted and calibrated products become our individual, spontaneous dreams; and as the mass-mediated fantasies of certain troubled individuals become our waking nightmares.

Afterword
on the Afterlife

What lies before me is my past. I have got to make myself look on that with different eyes, to make the world look on it with different eyes, to make God look on it with different eyes.

—Oscar Wilde, *De Profundis*

First learn to write as if you were already dead, and then you will discover that you can write as if you were still alive.

—Niccolo Tucci

Oh. That is how angels up in heaven must look down upon us, the way I look in this picture.

—Barbara La Marr, movie actress heroine
of Arnolt Bronnen's 1927 novel *Film and Life*

If private life has all but disappeared in the public domain of film culture, maybe we need to look for it in the afterlife.

Earlier in this study I suggested that we sometimes have the feeling while watching films that we are reviewing events that happened to us at another time, or in another life, or possibly in a life we no longer live. Maybe that's also why a number of films—from Frank Capra's *It's a Wonderful Life* and Billy Wilder's *Sunset Boulevard* to Woody Allen's *Love and Death* and Wim Wenders's *Wings of Desire*—are either narrated from the beyond or else depict the world from a posthumous or angelic perspective as a place that is vividly real and yet dreamlike, indeterminate, and uncanny. (A related genre is movies narrated by a protagonist awaiting his or her imminent death.[1]) Four films released at the tail end of the twentieth century are noteworthy in this regard.

In the 1999 film *After Life*, the Japanese documentary filmmaker Kore-eda Hirokazu portrays a fantasy situation in which the newly dead are asked to select a single memory of pure happiness in their lives. A heavenly film crew then makes that moment—which may be only the briefest sensation of pleasure—into a movie the deceased can relive forever. Through this self-reflexive device, Hirokazu presents the experience of eternity as a filmic phenomenon. As critic David Denby writes, "the picture raises a marvelous, fanciful question: Are all movies simply the favorite dreams of the dead?"[2]

Released just a few months later, DreamWorks' *American Beauty* seemed to answer this question in the affirmative, moving Denby to hail the film as a "miracle."[3] The aerial shot that opens and closes the film, in which the camera glides just above the roofs and treetops of what could be any affluent American suburb, is accompanied by the voice-over narration of a dead man, Lester Burnham, played by Kevin Spacey. From his angelic perspective, Lester good-naturedly guides the viewer in seeing the desolate reality behind the rose-covered white picket fence compulsively tended by his image-obsessed real-estate-agent wife and behind the silence of his moody teenage daughter, who can't stand him. Yet the cynicism with which he lays bare the falseness of his life is interrupted by hyperrealistic glimpses of breathtaking beauty and even sublimity, followed by an abrupt return to the banal and the phony. Lester's fantasies are signaled by visions of blood-red rose petals whenever he sees or dreams about his daughter's girlfriend—a seductive nymphet horrified at being perceived as ordinary.

An even more profound, neglected beauty that lurks behind—or rather *in*—appearances is registered by the young man whose family moves next to the Burnhams. Ricky records virtually everything he sees on videotape, in effect putting his life on film. One of his recordings stands out as a documentary kernel qua work of art; the videotape depicts nothing more than an empty white plastic bag dancing among some windblown leaves against the backdrop of a brick wall. A recording of the most banal and meaningless sort that everyone is bound to overlook, the video is presented in the film as an artifact of deep mystery and beauty precisely because of its indeterminacy and contingency, and because it reveals "the ability of the particular, the detail, the incident, to take on a life of its own, to precipitate processes in the viewer that may not be entirely controlled by the film."[4] It is not just that this "young man with a camera ... sees what others can't"; like the documentary auteurs discussed in chapter 5, he wants others to see what he sees, but as a gift of genuine vision and not as a distortion of reality or self-serving fabrication of the truth.[5] Ricky's record of a banal moment that extends into a fifteen-minute epiphany harks back to the dawn of motion pictures and the films of Lumière, which were praised by early viewers for showing "the ripple of the leaves stirred by the wind."⁶ It is the kind of memorable film that is made and then played back endlessly for the dead souls in *After Life*. It also anticipates Lester's revelation at the instant of his violent death—his sense of wonder that his life not only slows down, but extends for all eternity, during which he can revisit and reenvision, if not revise, all the meaningless moments and minutiae of his life, much like a connoisseur lovingly savoring a favorite film one frame at a time. Improbable as it may seem, suburbs that have been exposed as even more fake than Celebration somehow become a cause for celebration.

Although not set in the afterlife or narrated from the beyond, Atom Egoyan's *The Sweet Hereafter* (1997) and Thomas Winterberg's *The Celebration* (1998) present the posttraumatic perspective of characters whose abuse by their fathers and by patriarchy in general gives them access to worlds other than the one they've had to endure. In *The Celebration*, the outwardly successful entrepreneur Christian Klingenfeldt is tormented by the recent suicide of his twin sister, Linda. He finds relief—and possibly avoids his sister's fate—only by revealing a shocking secret at a family reunion at his father's country estate on the occasion of his sixtieth birthday. Toasting his father, Helge, Christian stuns the assembled company by announcing that Helge has repeatedly raped him and his sister and been the cause of the latter's death. Denounced by the guests as a lunatic, branded a fantasist by his mother, beaten and ejected from the party by his younger brother, Christian is ultimately vindicated by his dead sister's "return." In one sense, this reappearance is merely symbolic, taking the form of a discovered suicide note in which Linda explains that she took her life to escape Helge's molestation, which she had begun to experience in her dreams. But Linda also reappears quite literally to Christian, physically comforting him in the depths of his torment and preventing him from joining her by taking his own life. At this updated Elsinore, an aggrieved Hamlet overcomes his demons by confronting his lecherous and murderous father with the truth. But whereas Hamlet is doomed from the moment he is visited by his father's ghost, Christian is saved by the timely visitation of his twin sister's visible image.

The fate of the character Nicole (Sarah Polley) in *The Sweet Hereafter* is a good deal more ambiguous. Like Christian, she is a survivor of paternal incest, but she is also the survivor of a school-bus accident that has taken the lives of most of the children in her small British Columbia town. The accident has made her an invalid and seemingly even more vulnerable to the depredations of both her father, Sam, and the high-powered, out-of-state attorney, Mitchell Stephens (Ian Holm), who tries to involve her and the grieving parents of the dead children in a negligence lawsuit, milking their tragedy for all it's worth. In her helplessness, Nicole retreats into an imaginative dreamworld based on the fable of the Pied Piper, who spirits the children of Hamlin away from their selfish parents. This dreamworld enables Nicole to escape the abusive reality of her patriarchal tormentors: she thwarts Stephens's case by implicating the bus driver as the cause of the accident and puts herself out of Sam's reach by attaching herself to Billy—the one good father in the film, whose own children died in the accident. "We live in a different community, the sweet hereafter," she says, counting herself among the dead children in the accident and the fable.

It is left unclear whether Nicole's decision to live in the sweet hereafter is a retreat into fantasy from an unwelcome reality in which she is merely an exploited victim or a release into a virtual reality where she is truly empowered. The viewer doesn't know if Nicole is ultimately one of the dead or one of the saved.[7] The highly ambiguous final scene depicts Nicole in Billy's home on the eve of the accident, walking into the brilliant glare of the headlights of an arriving car; we do not learn whether the car belongs to the liberating surrogate father, Billy, or to the repressive real father, Sam, who has come to take her home. Like the cause of the school-bus tragedy, the film's presentation of Nicole's angelic viewpoint from "the sweet hereafter" is altogether indecipherable. Matters are a good deal clearer in *The Celebration*: Christian shatters the hypocritical pretense adopted by his family by telling the truth, and thereby brings about a return to reality. By directly confronting his father, Christian vanquishes him and avoids his twin sister's fate. The women in these films have more difficulty confronting the abusive father, or at least do so less directly. Nicole foils Stephens's lawsuit in *The Sweet Hereafter*, but only by telling what seems to be a lie, in contrast to Christian's clearing the air in *The Celebration* by declaring the truth. Moreover, she seems to have escaped her father's bonds, but only by retreating into the vague fantasy of "the sweet hereafter." Either a supreme reality or a supreme illusion, that fantasy is what Nicole needs to survive—a dreamworld of real virtuality. In *The Celebration*, Linda's father has haunted her *in* her dreams; her only refuge is the literal hereafter of death. Yet in the graphic medium of film, both Nicole's fantasy world and Linda's experience of death are presented as secret, unrepresentable realms that, as such, are comforting alternatives to the harsh explicitness of reality.

Films such as *After Life*, *American Beauty*, *The Celebration*, and *The Sweet Hereafter* invite the viewer to see them not only in relation to real life, but with respect to the afterlife—either an imagined state of being directly presented to the viewer, or an angelic perspective on worldly existence. Yet despite their evocations of transcendence, these films make only the most minimal use of cinematic effects, a pleasing alternative to movies such as *What Dreams May Come*, which overwhelm the viewer with special effects and spectacular visions of heaven as a brilliantly colored, digital landscape that somehow looks real. Of course, the movies' use of special effects to portray heaven is hardly original; it continues a long and venerable history of medieval and Renaissance painting and literature. Indeed, so powerful is the reality effect of the arts that leaders in the Catholic Church recently found it necessary to make clear that the vivid visual and literary depictions of artists and writers such as Dante, Michelangelo, and Milton were intended not as actual physical locations but as metaphorical representations of one's spiritual condition. Hell was "more than a physical place," Pope John Paul II told pilgrims visiting Rome in the summer of 1999; rather, it "is the state of those who freely and definitively separate themselves from God, the source of all life and joy."[8] This wasn't to say that hell wasn't real; the Pope insisted it was. Its reality, however, was not that of a *visible* place of punishment and eternal damnation, the conception familiar to most people through the images found in art and literature. (As might be expected, evangelical Protestants took exception to the Pope's remarks on the grounds that "the dire warnings in Scripture to respond to Christ in faith—while there is time—make sense only if hell is a very real place of very real torment.")[9]

Presumably the Pope's observations about hell are also true of heaven, the popular view of which has similarly been determined in large part by literary and pictorial representations, usually as a blissful abode in the clouds. One would expect the Church to remind its worshipers that heaven too is not a physical place but a spiritual condition in which the soul is open to God. As one commentator observes, however, "the church has declared thousands of people to be saints and therefore in heaven" while insisting that it has never declared a person damned.[10] It would seem that the Church tends to regard heaven as being more real—in the sense of having a graphic, physical existence—than hell. The reality effect is especially powerful with respect to heaven, no doubt because if there is an afterlife, most people count on spending it there rather than in hell.

Like the representational arts of literature and painting that preceded them, movies occasionally undertake to provide artistic visions of the afterlife. As a recording medium in a modern, secular, and skeptical age, however, film faces an especially daunting task in giving a graphic picture of the afterlife as something real while differentiating it as much as possible from everyday reality. Too often movie studios have relied on special effects to dazzle and defraud viewers with otherworldy spectacles such as those that appear in biblical epics like *The Ten Commandments* and *The Greatest Story Ever Told*, or more recently in such high-tech, secular, New Age exercises as *What Dreams May Come* and *Ever After*.[11] But it isn't necessary for movies to use special effects to depict heaven as a supersensible realm because the movies themselves are its closest graphic equivalent. Thus when John Coffey, the gentle giant in *The Green Mile*, tries to imagine what heaven will be like as he awaits his execution on death row, he recalls Fred Astaire singing Irving Berlin's "Cheek to Cheek" ("Heaven, I'm in heaven ...") in the famous dance number from the movie *Top Hat*. For others, heaven might call up quite different cinematic images, such as the dancing plastic bag in *American Beauty*, the ferris wheel in *The Sweet Hereafter*, or any of the ephemeral glimpses of life portrayed in *After Life*. Rather than continue to create grandiose and far-fetched pseudo-religious spectacles of heaven and hell, or sci-fi spectacles of the matrix of physical existence, filmmakers can use the most graphic of all media to provide glimpses of the heavenly and hellish aspects of the here and now—to reveal reality at its most transitory and ordinary where it is often also most extraordinary, but where it is also all too often most overlooked.[12]

Notes

Introduction

1. James Gleick, "Seeing Faster," *New York Times Magazine* (Oct. 3, 1999).
2. *The New York Times Magazine* (Oct. 3, 1999). Yet as Luc Sante notes in the same issue, artists provide a very distorted image of the past since "[f]or most of this millennium, art was reserved for the rich and the religious," and its "first task with regard to history [was] to celebrate and commemorate the great" ("Triumph of the Image").
3. Siegfried Kracauer, *Theory of Film: The Redemption of Physical Reality* (Princeton: Princeton University Press, 1997), 28.
4. Stephen Prince, "True Lies: Perceptual Realism, Digital Images, and Film Theory," *Film Quarterly* 49 (1996): 28. See also Dudley Andrew, *Concepts in Film Theory* (New York: Oxford University Press, 1984), 22.
5. Heidi G. Dawidoff, *Between the Frames: Thinking about Movies* (Hamden, Conn.: Archon Books, 1989), 131.
6. Thus Siegfried Kracauer states from the outset that his approach to film "rests on the assumption that film is essentially an extension of photography and therefore shares with this medium a marked affinity for the visible world around us. Films come into their own when they record and reveal physical reality" (*Theory of Film*, xlix). Cf. Friedrich Kittler: "A reproduction authenticated by the object itself is one of physical precision. It refers to the bodily real, which of necessity escapes all symbolic grids" (*Gramophone, Film, Typewriter*, trans. Geoffrey Winthrop-Young and Michael Wutz [Stanford: Stanford University Press, 1999], 12).
7. See Sari Thomas, introduction to S. Thomas, ed., *Film/Culture: Explorations of Cinema in Its Social Context* (Metuchen, N.J.: Scarecrow Press, 1982), 1. Again, the counterargument to those critics who embrace the film-as-art idea is voiced by Siegfried Kracauer, who insists that film's photographic nature makes it

   > impossible to accept the widely sanctioned belief or claim that film is an art like the traditional arts. Works of art consume the raw material from which they are drawn, whereas films as an outgrowth of camera work are bound to exhibit it.... If film is an art, it is art with a difference. Along with photography, film is the only art which leaves its raw material more or less intact. (*Theory of Film*, l)

8. Noël Carroll, *Theorizing the Moving Image* (Cambridge: Cambridge University Press, 1996), 78. Stephen Prince finds formalist (in contrast to realist) theorists promoting the view of cinematic realism

> as an *effect* produced by the apparatus or by spectators positioned within the Lacanian Imaginary. Cinematic realism is viewed as a discourse *coded* for transparency such that the indexicality of photographic realism is replaced by a view of the "reality-effect" produced by codes and discourse. ("True Lies," 30)

But if *cinematic* realism, especially in the age of digital imaging, is an effect, the question remains: *what about reality itself?*

9. Cf. Geoffrey Winthrop-Young and Michael Wutz: "What distinguishes the post-Gutenberg methods of data processing from the old alphabetic storage and transmission monopoly is the fact that they no longer rely on *symbolic mediation* but instead record, in the shape of sound and light waves, visual and acoustic *effects of the real*" ("Translator's Introduction" to Kittler, *Gramophone, Film, Typewriter*, xxvii–xxviii).

10. Among the recent attempts to reformulate the discipline of film studies in the "postfilm era" are Christine Gledhill and Linda Williams, eds., *Reinventing Film Studies* (New York: Oxford University Press, 2000); David Bordwell and Noël Carroll, eds., *Post-Theory: Reconstructing Film Studies* (Madison: University of Wisconsin Press, 1996); and Deborah Knight, "Reconsidering Film Theory and Method," *New Literary History* 24, 2 (1993): 321–38.

11. Ross Pudaloff, "Celebrity as Identity: Richard Wright, *Native Son* and Mass Culture," *Studies in American Fiction* 2 (spring 1983); see also Hayden White, *The Content of the Form* (Baltimore: The Johns Hopkins University Press, 1987). Kracauer describes his "*material* aesthetics," as opposed to the conventional formal variety, as being "concerned with content" (*Theory of Film*, xlix).

12. Kracauer, *Theory of Film*, l.

13. Harold Bloom, quoted on *The Charlie Rose Show*, WGBH-TV (July 11, 2000).

14. N. Katherine Hayles, "Simulating Narratives: What Virtual Creatures Can Teach Us," *Critical Inquiry* 26 (1999): 15.

15. Kittler, *Gramophone, Film, Typewriter*, 151.

16. John Johnston, "Machinic Vision," *Critical Inquiry* 26 (1999): 40.

17. As Betsy McLane, executive director of the International Documentary Association, notes,

> basically, the only stable moving-image visual medium is black-and-white separation film. That's why we can look at the very first films that have ever been projected and we know they'll last, because they've been properly stored and cared for.... What's frightening is that we'll have no record of the century we're entering. The media that people are creating as the current record, whether it's video or computed digitalization, are not stable. We've already lost the eighties and nineties to bad video.

(Quoted by Cliff Rothman, "Reality Programming," *The Nation*, Nov. 22, 1999, 32.)

18. On the one hand, one need only imagine the inhibiting effect that the proliferation of recording and surveillance devices have on people's willingness— or even on their daring—to express themselves "on the record" given their awareness that any documented admission, intimation, confession, or suggestion they may make is instantly subject to worldwide broadcast. On

the other hand, the pervasive presence of recording devices can just as easily have the opposite effect on people who use Web sites and other new media-technologies to exhibit, publicize, and market themselves. In either case, the distinction between the intimate and the global has largely been rendered meaningless.

19. See Mark Crispin Miller, "Hollywood, The Ad," *The Atlantic Monthly* (April 1990), 41–68. The product placement in the James Bond film *Golden-eye* and the merchandising associated with the 1999 *Star Wars* prequel *The Phantom Menace* are two of the most extreme examples.

20. Neal Gabler, *Life The Movie: How Entertainment Conquered Reality* (New York: Knopf, 1998).

21. For critic Wendy Lesser, the Hollywood version of *Awakenings* altogether failed to convey the "devastatingly affecting" ordeal of the real-life patients depicted in the British documentary. Against the "fashionable" view "that the borderline between fact and fiction is blurry," Lesser insists that "some experiences make you realize how hard and distinct that edge really is. This film is one of them" ("Seeing 'Awakenings' with Its Real-Life Cast," *New York Times*, Jan. 21, 2001). Yet the fact that the documentary was largely eclipsed by its sentimentalized Hollywood simulation (it wasn't shown on American television because Columbia Pictures didn't want the competition) is one more example of a cinematic fiction usurping the place of recorded reality.

22. "A Century of Reality" was the title of a monthlong series shown by Turner Classic Movies in November 1999 of some of the foremost documentary films of the twentieth century. For a survey of the varied uses of documentary during the century, see Jane M. Gaines and Michael Renov, eds., *Collecting Visible Evidence* (Minneapolis: University of Minnesota Press, 1999).

23. Reported by Nancy Gibbs and Timothy Roche, "The Columbine Tapes," *Time*, Dec. 20, 1999, 42.

24. Don DeLillo, *Mao II* (1991; rpt. New York: Penguin, 1992), 43.

25. Kittler, *Gramophone, Film, Typewriter*, xxxix-xl.

26. Of course, as Gavriel Moses has shown, literature's incorporation of cinematic topics and techniques has enabled it to become more conscious of its own artistic strategies and conventions:

> To the power of a particular way of seeing the world that belongs to all genres ... the incorporation of the discourse of extraliterary media adds the ability to question the very status of that "way of seeing" (its *truth*, its *validity*) from within the structure of the individual text.

(*The Nickel Was for the Movies: Film in the Novel from Pirandello to Puig* [Berkeley: University of California Press, 1995], 124.)

27. At least according to documentary filmmaker Barbara Kopple: "We're calling what was formerly documentaries nonfiction films now. Like fiction and nonfiction books" (as reported in Rothman, "Reality Programming," 31).

28. Roland Barthes, Jean Baudrillard, and Michel Foucault have each theorized about reality effects and truth effects. Barthes and Baudrillard both refer to "the effect of the real"—the former as the mode of naturalist writing ("L'Effet de réel" (*Communications* 11 [1968]: 84–89), the latter as "the structural effect of the disjunction between two terms." For Baudrillard, "the opposition between the real and the imaginary" is undone through the act of symbolic exchange which "*puts an end to the real*" (*Symbolic Exchange and Death*, trans. Iain Hamilton Grant [London: Sage, 1993], 133). As Baudrillard dismantles the opposition between the real and the imaginary, Foucault deconstructs the distinction between truth and fiction: "It seems

possible to me to make fiction work within truth, to induce truth–effects within a fictional discourse, and in some way make the discourse of truth arouse, 'fabricate' something which does not as yet exist, thus 'fiction' something" ("Interview with Lucette Finas," trans. Paul Foss and Meaghan Morris, in Meaghan Morris and Paul Patton, eds., *Michel Foucault: Power, Truth, Strategy* (Sydney: Feral, 1979), 74.

29. Kurt Andersen, "Blunt Trauma," *The New Yorker*, Mar. 30, 1998, 13–14.

30. Ibid.

31. James Sterngold, "For Artistic Freedom, It's Not the Worst of Times," *New York Times*, Sept. 20, 1998.

32. Chad Finan, president of the American Booksellers Foundation for Free Expression, cited in Sterngold.

33. On the distinction between referential and perceptual realism, see Stephen Prince, "True Lies," 32, which notes that "unreal images can be referentially fictional but perceptually realistic."

34. Quoted by Lisa Belkin in "The Making of an 8-year-old Woman," *New York Times Magazine* (Dec. 24, 2000). Herman-Giddens also describes an experience with her twelve-year-old granddaughter in a checkout line:

> I happened to notice that her eye level is exactly on the level with *Cosmopolitan* magazine. The headlines were "10 Ways to Drive Your Man Wild in Bed," and my granddaughter was standing there, reading, looking at this half-naked woman. I'm thinking to myself, I wonder what in God's name is going through this child's mind. It's in their face, all the time, literally. (ibid)

Herman-Giddens is not alone in suspecting that puberty may be triggered by the media. Drew Pinsky, a physician and former cohost of MTV's *Loveline* advice program, has declared MTV to be "absolutely one of the factors in early puberty" (quoted by Michael D. Lemonic in "Teens Before Their Time," *Time* [Oct. 30, 2000]).

35. Dawidoff, *Between the Frames*, 132.

36. Galyn Susman, quoted in Michael Mallory, "Creating a New Buzz" (*Los Angeles Times*, Nov. 18, 1999, Weekend Section, 8, 10).

37. See Cynthia A. Freeland, "Realist Horror," in Cynthia A. Freeland and Thomas E. Wartenberg, eds., *Philosophy and Film* (New York: Routledge, 1995), and my essay "Real(ist) Horror: From Execution Videos to Snuff Films," forthcoming in Steven Jay Schneider and Xavier Mendik, eds., *Underground U.S.A.: Filmmaking beyond the Hollywood Canon* (London: Wallflower Press, 2002).

38. The unprecedented speed, availability, and authenticity of digital sound recording that have made piracy programs such as Napster such a threat to record companies may paradoxically bring about a return to a time prior to the invention of recording technologies. Digitalization may compel musicians to make a living like their eighteenth- and nineteenth-century predecessors—through live concert performances. The difference, of course, is that composers and virtuosos were formerly obliged to perform their work because recording technologies were unavailable; now musicians may have to devote more time to live performances *because* such technologies have become so advanced and accessible. The dynamics of the music industry may be overturned so that live performances will no longer provide an incentive (or an occasion) for listeners to buy recordings, but free recordings will increasingly be used to promote paid live performances.

39. Johnston, "Machinic Vision," 31.

40. Miriam Bratu Hansen, introduction to Kracauer's *Theory of Film*, viii.

41. Thus, for the 1999 release of the DVD version of his 1992 movie *The Last of the Mohicans*, Michael Mann introduced a number of substantial changes of the kind that are "ordinarily made before the movie is released in theaters" (Peter M. Nichols, "Back for Fixes on the Frontier," *New York Times*, Dec. 3, 1999).

42. Stuart Klawans has described the recent films of Zhang Yimou, Abbas Kiarostami, and Mohsen Makhmalbaf as fictions that take "on the immediacy of documentary, a documentary that shows you how real people would behave in fictive situations" ("To Her, with Love," *The Nation*, Feb. 28, 2000, 33).

43. See my distinction between "key" and "prize texts" in detective fiction in "(De)feats of Detection: The Spurious Key Text from Poe to Eco," in P. Merivale and S. E. Sweeney, eds., *Detecting Texts: The Metaphysical Detective Story from Poe to Postmodernism* (Philadelphia: University of Pennsylvania Press, 1999), 75–98. In "Real(ist) Horror," I discuss simulated and even real snuff-film sequences in narrative films as kernel texts embodying kernel truths.

44. A variation of this procedure are documentaries about the making of major feature movies. Thus Eleanor Coppola's *Hearts of Darkness* documented her husband's—and her own—ordeal in shooting *Apocalypse Now*, while Werner Herzog's trials during the making of *Fitzcarraldo* are recorded in *Burden of Dreams*. Such parasitic documentaries provide a measure of insurance in the event that the movies that are their subjects fail. And sometimes these documentaries achieve cult status themselves and are even of greater interest than the films they are about.

45. A good example is Dariusz Jablonski's 1998 documentary *Photographer*, which reconstructs the experience of life in the Lodz ghetto during World War II based on four hundred color slides discovered in a Viennese used-book store in 1987. The slides were taken by the amateur photographer Walter Genewein, the Nazis' chief accountant in the ghetto, who wanted the photographs to document his administrative success to his superiors; ultimately those slides became the basis for Jablonski's own cinematic documentary of Nazi atrocities. By shooting the present-day sections of the film in black and white (and often in slow motion) while using color for the images of the past recorded in the slides, Jablonski succeeds in making the past appear more real than the present.

46. Stephen Holden, "'Wisconsin Death Trip': How a Town in Wisconsin Went Mad," *New York Times*, Dec. 1, 1999.

47. John Leland, "The Blair Witch Cult," *Newsweek*, Aug. 16, 1999, 49.

48. Stuart Klawans, "Bewitched," *The Nation*, Sept. 6/13, 1999, 34. *The Blair Witch Project*'s Net-driven success was repeated the following year with Greg Harrison's 2000 independent film *Groove* about the San Francisco rave scene.

49. Charles Herold, "Tracking an Elusive Film Genre Online," *New York Times*, May 3, 2001.

50. Jonathan Schell, "Land of Dreams," *The Nation*, Jan. 11/18, 1999, 6–7; I've substituted "real virtuality" for Schell's term "virtual fiction." Regarding the practical implications of this crisis for art museums as a site for the collection and interpretation of "real" objects, see Selma Thomas and Ann Mintz, eds., *The Virtual and the Real: Media in the Museum* (Washington, D.C.: American Association of Museums, 1998). The distinction between simulation and duplication of phenomena has emerged as a key issue in debates

about artificial intelligence. John R. Searle has repeatedly maintained that it is a "mistake to suppose that when a computer simulates the processes of a conscious brain it is thereby conscious" ("I Married a Computer," *New York Review of Books*, Apr. 8, 1999, 37).

51. Examples of such crossovers are Frank Biondi (Universal Studios to Water-View Advisors), Michael Ovitz (Disney to the entertainment search company Scour), Warren Littlefield (NBC Entertainment to the online music business LaunchMedia), Michael Fuchs (HBO to Autobytel.com), and Rob Fried (Savoy Pictures to WhatsHotNow.com). See John Geirland, "I'm Ready for My Startup, Mr. De Mille," *Wired*, Apr. 2000, 150–66.

52. In 1998 video game industry revenues (software and hardware) were $6.3 billion, slightly less than the movie industry's record $6.9 billion box-office earnings. Two years later, at the time of this writing, video game software and hardware sales are about $8.9 billion per year, while box office receipts are around $7.3 billion. See Steven Poole, *Trigger Happy: Video Games and the Entertainment Revolution* (New York: Arcade Publishing, 2001).

53. Statement by Colonel Grossman, a consultant hired by the parents of three girls killed in fourteen-year-old video game player Michael Carneal's 1997 rampage in Paducah, Kentucky; quoted on *60 Minutes*, Apr. 25, 1999. Describing the war-simulation game Kessen, N'Gai Croal writes that it "combines the pageantry of Akira Kurosawa's epic 'Ran' with the in-the-trenches combat of 'Saving Private Ryan'" ("The Art of the Game," *Newsweek*, Mar. 6, 2000, 61). There are limits, however, to video game makers' emulation of the movies. The enhanced cinematic qualities of Warp's action-adventure game D2—whose "cut scene" animation sequences are the length of a feature film—detract from its gaming features. "Failing miserably as a game," writes Charles Herold, "D2 succeeds remarkably well as a movie. The script would have made an excellent Japanese anime cartoon" ("A Video Game with Cinematic Aspirations," *New York Times*, Sept. 28, 2000). See also Herold's review of Clive Barker's 2001 game "Undying," which "manages to combine enough story for a movie with enough action for a game" ("A Horror Movie Adds Shudders to a Shooter," *New York Times*, March 15, 2001).

54. Bob Schwabach, "Don't Bet Your Cybersavings on Video-Game Spinoffs," *New York Times*, May 13, 2001.

55. Johnston, "Machinic Vision," p. 31.

56. Albert Borgmann, *Holding on to Reality: The Nature of Information at the Turn of the Millennium* (Chicago: University of Chicago Press, 1999).

57. Quoted by Eric Alterman, "A Euro without a Europe," *The Nation*, Oct. 11, 1999, 10.

58. Neal Gabler, "Molding Our Lives in the Image of Movies," *New York Times*, Oct. 25, 1998.

59. See Bill Kovach and Tom Rosenstiel, *Warp Speed: America in the Age of Mixed Media* (New York: The Century Foundation Press, 1999).

60. Thus Sterngold observes that "real life, as portrayed on television, has grown so graphic that the people who write teleplays and screenplays have been forced into greater luridness just to keep up" ("For Artistic Freedom, It's Not the Worst of Times"). Don DeLillo has contrasted "choreographed movie violence" with the surveillance videos of bank robberies and shoot-outs that are shown and reshown on television news programs, commenting that while such television images are "produced in a mass-market kind of fashion," they're "also real, it's real life. It's as though this were our last experience of nature: seeing a guy with a gun totally separate from choreo-

graphed movie violence. It's all that we've got left of nature, in a strange way. But it's all happening on our TV set" (quoted in David Remnick, "Exile on Main Street," *The New Yorker*, Sept. 15, 1997, 48).

61. Examples of medical reality shows are the Discovery Health Channel's *Operation*, the Health Network's *O.R.: Behind the Mask*, and the Learning Channel's *Trauma: Life in the E.R.* See Craig Tomashoff, "When the Reality Is inside the Body," *New York Times*, June 11, 2000.

62. Quoted in James Sterngold, "Bruce Nash: Seeking to Go Beyond the 'Shockumentary,'" *New York Times*, Jan. 25, 1999.

63. Lincoln Caplan, "The Failure (and Promise) of Legal Journalism," in J. Abramson, ed., *Postmortem: The O.J. Simpson Case: Justice Confronts Race, Domestic Violence, Lawyers, Money, and the Media* (New York: Basic Books, 1996), 199–207.

64. Tarleton Gillespie, "Narrative Control and Visual Polysemy: Fox Surveillance Specials and the Limits of Legitimation," *The Velvet Light Trap* 45 (Spring 2000): 40.

65. Interview with Mandalit Delbarco on NPR's "Morning Edition" (Feb. 9, 2001).

66. Peter Benedek, quoted in Bernard Weinraub, "Sudden Explosion of Game Shows Threatens the Old TV Staples," *New York Times*, Feb. 9, 2000.

67. Bill Carter, "Space: Network TV's Commercial Frontier," *New York Times*, Sept. 21, 2000.

68. John Leland, "Why America's Hooked on Wrestling," *Newsweek*, Feb. 7, 2000, 48.

69. The unreliability of video evidence in the courtroom became especially apparent in the 1999 antitrust case against Microsoft; a videotape demonstration that the corporation had prepared in its defense backfired when troubling inconsistencies on the tape prompted the judge to reject it as evidence.

70. In a marketing ploy devised by producers of the film *The X-Files*, ads for the video version advised viewers who had already seen the movie in theaters that "if you've seen it once, you haven't seen it all; now you can look closer, dig deeper." While this promotion ostensibly referred to the fact that the video—like many DVD releases—included additional scenes that weren't shown in theaters, it also hinted that *The X-Files* was a kind of hermetic text with hidden clues that required endless study, and that the video was a medium more conducive to in-depth research than the movie's theatrical presentation.

71. Luigi Pirandello, *The Notebooks of Serafino Gubbio or (Shoot!)*, trans. C. K. Scott Moncrieff (1915; Cambs, UK: Dedalus, 1990), 106.

72. Pirandello's insight is dramatically illustrated in the climactic episode of his novel, in which Gubbio is filming a scene of an actor shooting a tiger that goes horribly wrong. The figure of speech that Gubbio has employed throughout his narrative of machine/beasts devouring life is grotesquely and graphically literalized when the tiger overpowers and proceeds to feast upon the hapless actor Aldo Nuti. (Instead of shooting the tiger, as the script called upon him to do, Nuti's final act is to fire his rifle at his lover, who has spurned him.) All the while Gubbio continues to crank his camera and record the grisly scene. It's not that Gubbio just happens to film a disaster that happens by chance to occur, nor that the violence is the result of the tiger's savage nature. The tragedy occurred during the making of a movie when a real tiger was introduced into an artificial set that was made up to look like a natural jungle; the confusion and collapse of the relation between nature and artifice, reality and representation, is inevitably marked by

violence. As for Gubbio, he can't help but be aware of his own complicity in a tragedy that so spectacularly demonstrates his own insight into film's power to turn fiction into reality. After all, it was his act of shooting the scene, and the mediating presence of the devouring recording apparatus, that turned the scene of staged violence into one that was all too real.

In our own time we have become familiar with the phenomenon that as disaster movies strive for increasing verisimilitude, they run the risk of creating *actual* disasters. The issue has been explored in films such as *The Stunt Man* and *FX*, and has become a reality in the case of the accidental deaths that occurred in the filming of *The Twilight Zone* and *The Crow*. In this last film, actor Brandon Lee was shot and killed by a dummy bullet three days before the end of filming. The scene leading up to Lee's death appears in the finished film, although the footage of the actual death itself was destroyed.

73. These and other examples are cited by Phillip W. D. Martin, "Did 'Prisoner of the Mountains' Help End the War in Chechnya?," *New York Times*, Feb. 2, 1997.

74. Television dramas in the 1990s such as *Law and Order* routinely dramatize material"ripped from today's headlines." Even a series such as NBC's *Homicide* which strove to present original dramatic situations also borrowed freely from current news stories. Thus, the idea for the famous "subway episode" involving the final hours of a man fatally injured in a subway accident was based on an anecdote about an actual fatality told by a detective to a cab driver in a TV documentary that one of the *Homicide* writers had happened to see. The genesis of the subway episode itself became the subject of a PBS documentary by Ted Bogosian. So a TV documentary gave rise to a fictional episode on a TV series, which in turn gave rise to another TV documentary. Bogosian's documentary incidentally helped to get *Homicide* renewed for another year despite the series's sagging ratings.

75. Lawrence Wechsler, "Artist in Exile," *The New Yorker*, Dec. 5, 1994, 99.

76. Pierre Huyghe is somewhat of a "parasitic" filmmaker whose productions are less remakes of classic motion pictures than quasi-documentary revisitations that reexamine the "host" movie's constructedness and its underlying reality conditions. Thus, Huyghe's 1994 video "remake" of Hitchcock's *Rear Window* features amateur actors on a suburban construction site; his 1998 documentary on Andy Warhol's 1963 *Sleep* includes commentary by the film's original protagonist, poet John Giorno; and his 1998 video *Blanche-Neige Lucie* documents the legal battle of the woman who dubbed Snow White's voice in the 1962 French version of the animated classic. (She won her suit against Disney for failing to pay her royalties, thereby recovering her voice, which "she felt belonged equally to her and to Snow White.") See Holland Carter, "Films that Keep Asking, Is It Fact or Fiction?" *New York Times*, Jan. 19, 2001.

77. Quoted by Arthur C. Clarke in an interview with Steven Levy, "The Past Future," *Newsweek* Special Issue, Dec. 2000–Feb. 2001, 53.

78. Ruling that TV cameras would be barred from the courtroom in the wrongful-death suit against O.J. Simpson, Judge Hiroshi Fujisaki stated "the court's belief that history will repeat itself" (*Newsweek*, Sept. 2, 1996, 19). See Jeffrey Abramson, "The Pros and Cons of Televising Trials," in *Postmortem*, 195–98, and Toby Miller, *Technologies of Truth: Cultural Citizenship and the Popular Media* (Minneapolis: University of Minnesota Press, 1998), 197–200.

79. See Wendy Lesser, *Pictures at an Execution* (Cambridge, Mass.: Harvard University Press, 1993), which examines the implications of public TV

station KQED's unsuccessful 1991 suit for the right to broadcast an execution at San Quentin prison.

80. Sara L. Knox, *Murder: A Tale of Modern American Life* (Durham, N.C.: Duke University Press, 1998), 194. Cf. 193: "When an execution is televised there is no guarantee that the *documentary* nature of the broadcast will make the death of the condemned man actually believable." Contrast Gary Indiana's contention that the "courtroom camera reduces all other media coverage to interpretation, slant, spin, in other words, to fiction. There is nothing to 'report' about an event witnessed by everybody" ("The O.J. Papers: Muddied Waters," *The Village Voice*, Nov. 15, 1994, 23). On the contrary, nothing is more open to interpretation and debate than a recorded event that can be seen by everyone any number of times.

81. See "Court Explores Media, Police Link," Associated Press, Mar. 24, 1999.

82. Gabler, *Life The Movie*, 236.

83. Dawidoff, *Between the Frames*, 132.

84. Walter Kendrick, *The Secret Museum: Pornography in Modern Culture* (New York: Viking, 1987), 221.

85. Carl S. Kaplan, "Supreme Court to Consider Digital Images," *New York Times*, Jan. 26, 2001. See also Adam Liptak, "When Is a Fake Too Real? It's Virtually Uncertain," *New York Times*, Jan. 28, 2001.

86. As Gilberto Perez observes, despite Aristotle's dictum that tragedy "is the imitation of an action 'in the form of action, not of narrative,' ... not much happens on the stage [in Greek tragedy] that an audience today would call action: the action imitated is the action of speaking. What was made present on the Greek stage was not primarily a visual scene but the speech of human beings" (*The Material Ghost: Films and Their Medium* [Baltimore: The Johns Hopkins University Press, 1998], 59).

87. See Sylviane Gold: "Plays—serious, mainstream works by serious writers that shed light on the role of sex in the human drama—are actually few and far between.... our theater has for the most part been more comfortable laughing at this crucial subject than exploring it" ("One Place Sex is Seldom Taken Seriously," *New York Times*, June 27, 1999, Arts and Leisure section, 5, 7).

88. See René Girard, *Violence and the Sacred*, trans. Patrick Gregory (Baltimore: The Johns Hopkins University Press, 1977). Sylviane Gold notes that "the first theatrical performance may well have been a crude and lewd representation of the sex act in some tribal ritual" ("One Place," 7).

89. Perez, *The Material Ghost*, 59.

90. Kurt Andersen, "Sore Winner," *The New Yorker*, Mar. 16, 1998, 29. See also David Denby, "The Moviegoers," *The New Yorker*, Apr. 6, 1998.

91. James Atlas, "The Loose Canon," *The New Yorker*, Mar. 29, 1999, 63.

92. Ibid.

93. The uncertainty regarding the truth of female sexual enjoyment became a matter of some controversy when the actress who played the character of Linda Lovelace in the classic '70s pornographic film *Deep Throat* published her book *Ordeal* (Secaucus, N.J.: Citadel Press, 1980) in which she denounced the abuse she suffered during her years in the porn industry. All the scenes in *Deep Throat* in which she appeared to be enjoying sex, she maintains, were done under coercion. So depending on whether one judges her performance in the film as simulated or real, the same cinematic record could be cited as evidence either for or against abuse.

94. Atlas, "The Loose Canon," 64.

95. I borrow the term "techno-primitivism" from Mark Seltzer, *Serial Killers: Death and Life in America's Wound Culture* (New York: Routledge, 1998), ch. 9, and the phrase "crash aesthetic" from Bradley Butterfield's article "Ethical Value and Negative Aesthetics: Reconsidering the Ballard-Baudrillard Connection," *PMLA* 114, 1 (1999): 64–77.

96. Bill Nichols demonstrates the similarities of ethnography and pornography as documentary genres in *Representing Reality: Issues and Concepts in Documentary* (Bloomington: Indiana University Press, 1991).

97. See Lynn Hunt, ed., *The Invention of Pornography: Obscenity and the Origins of Modernity, 1500–1800* (New York: Zone Books, 1993), and Michel Foucault, *The History of Sexuality, Vol. 1: An Introduction*, trans. Robert Hurley (New York: Vintage, 1980).

98. *Newsweek*, Nov. 30, 1998, 33.

99. Kurt Andersen, "Blunt Trauma," 14.

Chapter one: Pornographic Science

A shorter version of this section appeared in the *Yearbook of Comparative and General Literature* 40 (1992): 83–89.

1. Cf. Stephen Heath's reference to the fade-out on the love scene in Max Ophuls's *Letter from an Unknown Woman* (1948):

> Evidently, this is convention, its context the Hays Code, the awareness of what can and cannot be shown. But convention is never simply a fact outside a film: what can and cannot be shown, the determining confines of image and look, is in *Letter from*, is part of its film action and meaning. The fade, the image absent, is *Letter from*'s momentary and fundamental figure.

(Stephen Heath, "The Question—Oshima," *Wide Angle* 2, 1 [1977]: 49.) In the case of the fade-out that follows James Stewart's and Kim Novak's kiss in Hitchcock's *Vertigo* (1958), William Rothman infers that "presumably they make love for the first time" ("*Vertigo*: The Unknown Woman in Hitchcock," in Joseph H. Smith and William Kerrigan, eds., *Images in Our Souls: Cavell, Psychoanalysis, and Cinema* [Baltimore: The Johns Hopkins University Press, 1987], 72). The circular movement of the camera around the lovers that *precedes* the fade-out in *Vertigo* invites comparison with the corresponding movement of the beam from the beacon in *Casablanca* that *follows* the fade-out on Rick and Ilsa's embrace.

2. Robert Coover, *A Night at the Movies, or, You Must Remember This* (New York: Linden Press/Simon and Schuster, 1987), 164. Page references will hereafter follow quotations.

3. Peter Lehman, "Oshima: The Avant-garde Artist without an Avant-garde Style," *Wide Angle* 9, 2 (1987): 19. If hard-core pornography is linked to the fade in classical cinema, soft-core pornography exploits the limitations of the cinematic frame. Thus Stephen Koch describes Andy Warhol's technique in *Blow-Job*—a film that consists of a sustained shot of the facial expressions of the actor who is being sexually serviced—as one in which "the real action is taking place very much out of frame." Koch finds this "exercise in the evidence of things unseen" to be characteristic of "Duchampian pornography":

> The Duchampian context invariably involves a displacement of interest from what is being seen into a visually marginal, imagined concern created within us by the shadow-play of perception, by the activation of thoughts and alternate responses, even when the thing before us is truncated, un-

interesting in itself, or absurd.... Duchamp's art is involved in trans-
vestism, castration, sadomasochism, the refusal to give, the deprivation of
the senses—the stuff of pornography, in short.

(Stephen Koch, *Stargazer: Andy Warhol and His Films* [New York: Praeger,
1973], 9, 51.)

4. Michael Medved, *Hollywood vs. America: Popular Culture and the War on
Traditional Values* (New York: HarperCollins, 1992), 282–83.

5. Martin Amis, "Blown Away," *The New Yorker*, May 30, 1994, 49.

6. Quoted by Austin Bunn, "The Dead Celebrity Who Comes Back to Life,"
The New York Times Magazine, June 11, 2000, 92. There have already been
several instances involving the digital resuscitation of dead actors. As Bunn
points out, Oliver Reed, who died during the filming of *Gladiator*, was "resur-
rected ... for a pivotal scene," and the film *StarWay* stars "two of India's
most famous dead celebrities, M.G.R. and Raj Kapor.... Death may no
longer mark the conclusion of a star's career, just a pause before rebooting."

7. Quoted in *Parade*, Dec. 19, 1993, 16.

8. Umberto Eco, "*Casablanca*, or, the Clichés Are Having a Ball," in Sonia
Maasik and Jack Solomon, eds., *Signs of Life in the USA: Readings in Popular Culture for Writers* (Boston: Bedford Books, 1994), 260–64.

9. Edmund White, "Splice Memory," in *New York Times Book Review*, Feb. 1,
1987, 15.

10. Michiko Kakutani, review of Coover, *A Night at the Movies*, in *New York
Times*, Jan. 7, 1987, C24.

11. John Blades, "A Night to Remember in Coover's 'Casablanca,'" *Chicago
Tribune*, Jan. 18, 1987, 3.

12. Heidi G. Dawidoff, *Between the Frames: Thinking About Movies* (Hamdem,
Conn.: Archon Books, 1989), 133. Dawidoff's chief example of an adaptation
"in which visible sex lessens the sexiness of the atmosphere" (135) is the
1981 remake of James Cain's novel *The Postman Always Rings Twice*.

13. For Dawidoff, pornography itself is "a kind of parody of sex" (ibid., 140).
On the problematic relation between parody and pornography, see Carolyn
J. Dean's reading of Sade (*The Self and Its Pleasures: Bataille, Lacan, and the
History of the Decentered Subject* [Ithaca: Cornell University Press, 1992],
(182, no.30). If parody redeems pornography, politics may be required to
redeem parody. Reviewing Coover's 1996 novel *Joan's Wife*, Paul Levine
writes that the banality of Coover's pornographic parodies ("screwing in
Coover tends towards *Popular Mechanics*: sexual performance as mechanical
parody. After a while the joke is thin and the heavy breathing tedious"
["Copulating Fictions," *The Nation*, June 24, 1996, 32]) is redeemed by the
strain of political satire in his writing. Similarly, it was as a political satirist
rather than as a pornographer that *Hustler* publisher Larry Flynt was acquit-
ted in the landmark Supreme Court decision that overruled a $200,000 jury
award to Jerry Falwell for his "emotional distress" at Flynt's "ad parody" in
which the Baptist preacher is shown recalling his "first time" in an outhouse
with his mother.

14. Cited in Anthony Lake, "American Diasporist," *The New Yorker*, Mar. 13,
1995, 90–91.

15. See Manohla Dargis, "Peep Show," *LA Weekly*, July 16–22, 1999, 43.

16. The story of the making of *Casablanca* has become a drama in its own right,
with film historians billing the movie "the happiest of happy accidents"
(Andrew Sarris, *The American Cinema* [New York: Dutton, 1968], 176) and
"one of Hollywood's luckiest accidents" (Aljean Harmetz, *Round Up the*

Usual Suspects [New York: Hyperion, 1992]). Bogart and Bergman never warmed up to the project, and far from carrying on a wild real-life affair, they barely got along with each other.

17. In Allen's takeoff, Bogart's character Rick is an immortal being who provides a role model for Allen's all-too-mortal neurotic protagonist, an actor-in-search-of-(a)-character. With the help of the transcendent figure of Rick/Bogart, the all-too-real Allen succeeds in seducing a woman and then in giving her up in a mock-heroic act of renunciation.

18. In his psychoanalytic reading of the film, Harvey Roy Greenberg shows how the romantic illusion is sustained through the displacement and disavowal of erotic reality. Rick is haunted by a repressed Oedipal "crime," while Ilsa is "not quite the innocent she seems (or believes herself to be). She has actually been unfaithful to Rick *and* to Lazslo, although *Casablanca* will go to great lengths to justify her infidelity" and make her appear "worthy, pure and guiltless, exciting admiration rather than censure" (*Screen Memories: Hollywood Cinema on the Psychoanalytic Couch* [New York: Columbia University Press, 1993], 49, 53, 58).

19. The overwhelmingly favorable response to the 1997 film *Titanic* suggested that Hollywood may have finally hit upon the right formula. But it was a telling sign of the times that when Kate Winslet, appearing as a guest on *The Tonight Show*, referred to the film's discreet love scene, she couldn't refrain from making a tasteless comment about some dark makeup that appeared on the tip of her nose during the shooting.

20. Steven Marcus, *The Other Victorians: A Study of Sexuality and Pornography in Mid-Nineteenth-Century England* (New York: Basic Books, 1966).

21. Ernest Becker, *The Denial of Death* (New York: Free Press, 1973), 44.

22. As Steven Marcus describes, the "governing tendency" in pornography

> is toward the elimination of external or social reality. And although on first inspection pornography seems to be the most concrete kind of writing—concerned as it is with organs, positions, events—it is in reality very abstract. It regularly moves toward independence of time, space, history, and even language itself.

(*The Other Victorians*, 44–45.)

23. Actually, *Blow-Up* established the convention not of the missing scene but of the hidden figure. See chapter 4.

24. Slavoj Žižek, *The Plague of Fantasies* (London: Verso, 1997), 174–75.

25. In Rohmer's film, the scene fades out on a reaction shot of the count (Bruno Ganz) who is transfixed by the sight of the marquise, shown in the preceding shot stretched voluptuously on a makeshift bed under the influence of a sleeping potion she's been given to calm her after her ordeal. Whereas in Kleist's story the marquise faints in the count's arms during the attack on the castle, Rohmer sets the scene away from the heat of battle, leaving little doubt in the viewer's mind that the count has both the motive and the opportunity to have his way with the drugged marquise. With everything spelled out and no "whodunit" mystery as to what happens after the fade-out, the missing rape scene in the film is not nearly as effective as its concealed-by-the-dash counterpart in Kleist's story.

26. Dorrit Cohn, "Kleist's 'Marquise von O . . . ': The Problem of Knowledge," *Monatshefte* 67 (1975): 129. See also Susan Winnett, "The Marquise's 'O' and the Mad Dash of Narrative," in Lynn A. Higgins and Brenda R. Silver, eds., *Rape and Representation* (New York: Columbia University Press, 1991), 67–86.

27. As in his analysis of Hollywood romances such as David Lean's *Ryan's Daughter*, which attempt "to conceal [the] deadlocks" involved in representing physical intimacy "by expressing sexual ecstasy through metaphors, musical accompaniment, and so on," Žižek would probably regard the musical number "As Time Goes By" itself as "the phantasmic screen obfuscating the Real of the sexual act" (*The Plague of Fantasies*, 182).

28. He may also have been aware of a similar fiction by Léon Gozlan—his best-selling novel *Le médicin de Pecq* (1839) in which a young neurotic impregnates a woman while in a somnambulic state and cannot recall the event when he awakes. (See Dider Anzieu, *Freud's Self-Analysis*, trans. Peter Graham [London: Hogarth Press, 1986], 85.) Wilkie Collins's *The Moonstone* (1868) and Robert Louis Stevenson's *Strange Case of Dr. Jekyll and Mr. Hyde* (1886) both deal with crimes committed in altered states of consciousness, not to mention the entire tradition of literature about vampires and werewolves, which is also based on this theme.

29. See Joyce McDougall, *The Many Faces of Eros: A Psychoanalytic Exploration of Human Sexuality* (New York: Norton, 1995), xxi.

30. While Freudian analysis would describe Coover's takeoff on *Casablanca* as a reconstruction of the film's repressed sexual scene (screened by the phallic image of the airport beacon), Lacanian analysis, which has proven so congenial to film theory, would further specify that Coover supplies the missing phallus itself in its most visible form. See below.

31. Heinrich von Kleist, *"The Marquise of O—" and Other Stories*, trans. David Luke and Nigel Reeves (London: Penguin, 1978), 110.

32. Ibid., 113.

33. Two examples are *Reservoir Dogs* (which director Quentin Tarantino has described as a heist film without the heist) and the 1957 film *Sayonara*. As Robert Osborne has pointed out, the Japanese actress Miiko Taka won an academy award less for her actual performance in the film than for the character she played, Hana-ogi. Audiences were affected by this character's experiences—her being sold into marriage by her parents, the loss of her family in the Allied bombing, her rise to becoming the premier Matsubayashi artist—none of which were shown in the film.

34. When the laser-disc version of Disney's semianimated film *Who Framed Roger Rabbit* was released in March 1994, several lewd frames of the cartoon character Jessica were discovered. Invisible under normal conditions, the images were detected when viewers were able to examine the film frame by frame.

35. See Stephen Heath, "Notes on Suture," *Screen* 18, 4 (1977–78): 48–76, and Rosalind E. Krauss, *The Optical Unconscious* (Cambridge, Mass.: MIT Press, 1993).

36. Theodore Roszak, *Flicker* (New York: Bantam, 1991), 418.

37. Marcus, *The Other Victorians*, 22.

38. Cf. Charles Taylor: "My life always has this degree of narrative understanding, that I understand my present action in the form of an 'and then': there was A (what I am), and then I do B (what I project to become)" (*Sources of the Self: The Making of the Modern Identity* [Cambridge, Mass.: Harvard University Press, 1989], 47).

39. Evelyn Fox Keller, "The Biological Gaze," in George Robertson et al., eds., *FutureNatural: Nature, Science, Culture* (London and New York: Routledge), 109.

40. Ibid., 120.

41. Ibid., 111.
42. Peter Webb, *The Erotic Arts* (1975; New York: Farrar, Straus, Giroux, 1983), 1; my emphasis.
43. Jean Baudrillard, *Seduction*, trans. Brian Singer (New York: St. Martin's Press, 1990), 31.
44. Linda Williams, *Hard Core: Power, Pleasure, and the "Frenzy of the Visible"* (Berkeley: University of California Press, 1989), 53.
45. Ibid., 48.
46. I am following the Lacanian distinction between psychosis and neurosis here as succinctly set forth by Carolyn Dean: "Psychosis represents the unconscious made transparent, whereas neurosis manifests a series of symbolic codes that have to be deciphered. Whereas the neurotic 'occupies language,' the psychotic 'is occupied, possessed' by it" (*The Self and its Pleasures*, 116). The psychotic is unable or unwilling to resolve castration anxiety through symbolization, through a process of recognition that would allow him to integrate his primal fear into the symbolic network of his experience. Having rejected "castration as a signifier for the mother's absent phallus," the psychotic finds himself living "his fear of castration as 'real' (not as symbolized)"; since "the real can never, ever be 'seen,' even as it is apprehended," the psychotic experiences the maternal phallus in the form of hallucinations (115, 119). Shoshana Felman usefully describes symbolization according to Lacan as being "coincident with the constitution of the unconscious (the displacement of desire) ... to symbolize is to incorporate death in language, *in order to survive*" (*Jacques Lacan and the Adventure of Insight: Psychoanalysis in Contemporary Culture* [Cambridge, Mass.: Harvard University Press, 1987]: 134).
47. Gertrude Koch, "The Body's Shadow Realm," in Pamela Church Gibson and Roma Gibson, eds., *Dirty Looks: Women, Pornography, Power* (London: British Film Institute, 1993), 41.
48. Ibid., 43.
49. Stanley Cavell, *The World Viewed* [Cambridge, Mass.: Harvard University Press, 1979), 45.
50. See Lisa Cartwright, *Screening the Body: Tracing Medicine's Visual Culture* (Minneapolis: University of Minnesota Press, 1995).
51. James Monaco, *How to Read a Film: The Art, Technology, Language, History, and Theory of Film and Media* (1977; rev. ed., New York: Oxford University Press, 1981), 76.
52. See Bettyann Holtzmann Kevles, *Naked to the Bone: Medical Imaging in the Twentieth Century* (New Brunswick, N.J.: Rutgers University Press, 1997).
53. See Bill Nichols, *Representing Reality: Issues and Concepts in Documentary* (Bloomington: Indiana University Press, 1991).
54. Williams, *Hard Core*, 36. Williams's discussion of the relation between the "academic question" and the "pornographic answer" is inspired by Albert Goldbarth's poem "The Origin of Porno," which suggests that Stanford's query—"Is there ever a moment when all four feet leave the ground?"—leads inevitably to "a question, an academic question, of at / which point in a leap the female breast / is highest?" Photography/pornography provides the answer. In Williams's words, "Goldbarth's poem emphasizes the way in which hard-core, pornographic answers proceed from new 'academic questions' that can be asked in this intensified field of the visible" (36). The way in which the ostensibly scientific quest for knowledge and truth produces pleasurable discoveries that verge on the pornographic is evident in

Muybridge's career following his resolution of the debate about trotting horses. His public demonstrations of his primitive movie projector, the zoopraxiscope, "delight[ed] and amaz[ed] popular and scientific audiences alike" (38) with its pictorial simulation of lifelike movement, not only of animals but of human beings—both men and women.

55. Cf. J. G. Ballard:

> Motion picture studies of four female subjects who have achieved world-wide celebrity (Brigitte Bardot, Jacqueline Kennedy, Madame Chiang Kai-Shek, Princess Margaret), reveal common patterns of posture, facial tones, pupil and respiratory responses. Leg stance was taken as a significant indicator of sexual arousal.

(*The Atrocity Exhibition* [1972; San Francisco: Re/Search, 1990], 89.)

56. Thomas Pynchon, *Gravity's Rainbow* (New York: Viking, 1973), 407. Later page references are to this book.

57. It may be more than just an analytic impulse that film and rocketry share. In 1929 a German film company supplied a group of enthusiasts with money to launch a rocket to coincide with the opening of Fritz Lang's film *Die Frau in Mond* (Michael J. Neufeld, *The Rocket and the Reich: Peenemünde and the Coming of the Ballistic Missile Era* [New York: The Free Press, 1994]). In *Gravity's Rainbow*, Pynchon credits Lang's film for the "countdown as we know it, 10-9-8-u.s.w.," noting that Lang "put it into the launch scene to heighten the suspense" (753).

58. Richard Rorty, *Philosophy and the Mirror of Nature* (Princeton: Princeton University Press, 1979).

59. W. B. Carnochan, *Confinement and Flight: An Essay on English Literature of the Eighteenth Century* (Berkeley: University of California Press, 1977), 7.

60. While Muybridge used multiple cameras to record separate images of moving bodies, Marey used a single camera in his chronophotography that "included all of the recorded successive positions of a single subject within the same frame" (Mary Ann Doane, "Temporality, Storage, Legibility: Freud, Marey, and the Cinema," *Critical Inquiry* 22 [1996]: 327). Marey criticized Muybridge for the lack of scientific precision in his technique, which failed to measure the intervals between his recorded images; however, his method of multiplying images in a single frame had a tendency to make his pictures illegible, with "the blurred image" marking "the limit or failure of Marey's scientific endeavor" (Doane, 333, 335; see also Marta Braun, *Picturing Time: The Work of Étienne-Jules Marey* [Chicago: University of Chicago Press, 1993], and François Dagognet, *Étienne-Jules Marey: A Passion for the Trace* [Cambridge, Mass.: Zone, 1992].)

61. Doane notes Marey's preference for graphic over photographic methods of representation because the former type of "record of a movement left no temporal gaps" while chronophotography "entail[ed] a necessary temporal elision." "Chronophotography 'only gives an approximate idea of the sequence of the various phases of movement, because its record is one of intermittent indications, instead of the continuous record of a curve'" ("Temporality, Storage, Legibility," 333, 287).

62. This phenomenon was already being investigated before the invention of cinema. First studied in the 1870s by Felix Roubaud, it was further explored in the 1920s by Robert Latou Dickinson, who tried "to observe what happened in the vagina during intercourse. To do so he used a glass tube resembling an erect penis in size and shape while the woman masturbated to orgasm; in the process, he proved once and for all that women did have

orgasm involving physiological changes" (Vern L. Bullough, *Science in the Bedroom: A History of Sex Research* [New York: Basic Books, 1994], 111).

63. See Max Horkheimer's and Theodor W. Adorno's famous analysis of this episode in *Dialectic of the Enlightenment*, trans. John Cumming (New York: The Seabury Press, 1972), 32–36, and 58–60.

64. James Gleick, "Seeing Faster," *New York Times Magazine*, Oct. 3, 1999.

65. Doane (324–25) discusses Marey's protocinematic efforts to make time itself visible—specifically, "to make a 'lost time' visible" and "optically legible" through "chronophotography."

66. J. G. Ballard, interviewed by Ralph Rugoff in "The Atrocity Exhibitionist," *LA Weekly*, Mar. 21–27, 1997, 32–33.

Chapter two: Primal Scenes

1. Harvey Roy Greenberg, *Screen Memories: Hollywood Cinema on the Psychoanalytic Couch* (New York: Columbia University Press, 1993), 35, 2; see also 18–19.

2. Mary Ann Doane, "Temporality, Storage, Legibility: Freud, Marey, and the Cinema," *Critical Inquiry* 22 (1996): 334. Specifically, Doane writes that "Freud and Marey resisted the cinema because it adhered to the senses and was not amenable to the abstraction required either to illustrate the basic concepts of psychoanalysis or to produce scientific knowledge. In its hyper-indexicality it could not dissociate itself from the realm of the contingent or the material" (343). Yet Doane also points out that "Freud's and Marey's conscious rejection of the cinema was also accompanied by an unconscious complicity with its very aspirations"—namely, "the desire to store or represent time, the rejection of mortality (especially in the case of Freud, who continually attempted to demonstrate that death was accidental, contingent rather than inevitable)" (ibid.).

3. See Sarah Boxer's review of the 1999–2000 exhibition "Dreams 1900–2000: Science, Art and the Unconscious Mind" at the Equitable Gallery in Manhattan: "After a Freudian Century, There Are Good Dreams and Bad," *New York Times*, Dec. 3, 1999.

4. Stephen Heath, "Difference," *Screen* 19:3 (Autumn 1978): 51–112; 58.

5. Baudrillard, *Seduction*, trans. Brian Singer (New York: St. Martin's Press, 1990), 20. While Stephen Heath notes that the effect produced by Charcot's photographic record of hysterics "is of a kind of cinema," he is careful to distinguish this cinematic prototype from Freudian psychoanalysis in which "the spectacle gives way to the analytic situation ... Psychoanalysis is the anti-visible; significant in this respect, moreover, are Freud's distrust of projects for rendering analysis on the screen" ("Difference," 58). Cf. Laurence A Rickels: "Even while Freud was observing Charcot commence lending an ear to hysterics, a loan that would ultimately write psychoanalysis, asylum photographers were actively recording—and thus erasing—all signs or symptoms of hysterical conversion" (*The Case of California* [Baltimore: The Johns Hopkins University Press, 1991], 188–89).

6. See Friedrich A. Kittler: "When Freud 'unlocks images,' he does so not to store them, as Charcot does, but to decode the puzzles of their signifiers"(*Gramophone, Film, Typewriter*, trans. Geoffrey Winthrop-Young and Michael Wutz [Stanford: Stanford University Press, 1999], 143).

7. Linda Williams, *Hard Core: Power, Pleasure, and the "Frenzy of the Visible"* (Berkeley: University of California Press, 1989), 47.

8. Heath, "Difference," 58.

9. The question posed by André Breton to his fellow surrealists at the opening of the first of the sessions he organized to discuss sexual issues is also of interest in this regard: "A man and a woman make love. To what extent is the man aware of the woman's orgasm?" (José Pierre, ed., *Investigating Sex: Surrealist Research 1928–1932*, trans. Malcolm Imrie [London: Verso, 1992], 3). Lacan goes even further: not only may the man be in doubt about whether he has given his wife pleasure, or about whether he is the father of her children, but, like Oedipus, he may not even know his own relation to his wife, whose pleasure may be based on her awareness of his ignorance. Slavoj Žižek comments that such a scenario adds "a new, intersubjective dimension" to "the notorious thesis on the intimate link between feminine enjoyment and ignorance … : woman enjoys in so far as her *other* (man) does not know" ("Grimaces of the Real, or When the Phallus Appears," *October* 58 [1991]: 54, n. 11). As applied to heterosexual pornography, this paranoid scenario suggests that the male viewer's quest for visible knowledge of the woman's pleasure is stymied not only by his ignorance about the authenticity of her pleasure, but also by the suspicion that any pleasure she does feel is made possible by his ignorance.

10. Stanley Cavell, "Psychoanalysis and Cinema: The Melodrama of the Unknown Woman," in Joseph H. Smith and William Kerrigan, eds., *Images in Our Souls: Cavell, Psychoanalysis, and Cinema* (Baltimore: The Johns Hopkins University Press, 1987), 29, 32–33. This essay develops ideas in Cavell's earlier study, *Pursuits of Happiness: The Hollywood Comedy of Remarriage* (Cambridge, Mass.: Harvard University Press, 1981), and later received an expanded treatment in *Contesting Tears: The Hollywood Melodrama of the Unknown Woman* (Chicago: University of Chicago Press, 1996).

11. In Dorfman's original staged version he adds that even when he "became involved in more delicate operations" in which he was asked to advise the regime about how much torture, how much electric current, the prisoners could endure, he justified his action by telling himself "that it was a way of saving people's lives" (Ariel Dorfman, *Death and the Maiden* [New York: Penguin, 1991], 59).

12. One thinks of a somewhat analogous scene in Tom DiCillo's 1995 film *Living in Oblivion*. Steve Buscemi plays a frustrated independent film director who shoots the same simple scene over and over again because something always goes wrong with the actresses' performances. Eventually they play the scene to perfection, but during a break in the shoot when they're not being directed and the camera isn't rolling.

13. In the 1920s, shortages of film stock forced Kuleshov to devise exercises in his directorial workshop that were performed before an unloaded camera. See Ronald Levaco, introduction to *Kuleshov on Film: Writings By Lev Kuleshov* (Berkeley: University of California Press, 1974), 10.

14. Jacqueline Rose, *Sexuality in the Field of Vision* (London: Verso, 1986), 227.

15. Christian Metz, *The Imaginary Signifier: Psychoanalysis and the Cinema*, trans. Celia Britton et al. (Bloomington: Indiana University Press, 1982), 63–64. Others have gone even further in describing the viewer's experience during a film as a fantasy of participation in the primal scene. For Janine Chasseguet-Smirgel, "all vision, all spectacle is, in the unconscious, the primal scene, that is to say the relationships of the parents between themselves" (*Creativity and Perversion* [New York: Norton, 1984]).

16. Peter Baxter, "The One Woman," *Wide Angle* 6, 1 (1984): 36.

17. Well before Freud and the existence of motion pictures, another writer who strikingly anticipated both the cinematic aspects of pornography and the pornographic aspects of cinema was the eighteenth-century Chinese novelist Cao Xueqin. In a memorable scene in *The Story of the Stone*, Jia Rui's obsessive lust for his cousin Xi-feng leads him to peer at the forbidden front side of a magic "MIRROR FOR THE ROMANTIC" from the Land of Illusion. Confounding the unreal with the real, he becomes so addicted to his experiences of virtual sex with Xi-feng while looking at the forbidden mirror (an early form of computer porn) that he ultimately dies in "a large, wet, icy patch of recently ejaculated semen" (*The Story of the Stone*, vol. 1, trans. David Hawkes [London: Penguin, 1973], 251–52). Also, perhaps owing to his supernatural origins, the novel's youthful protagonist Bao-yu suffers from a deep-seated gender/identity crisis. On one occasion he makes the following outburst, supposedly about the magic jade found in his mouth when he was born: " 'None of the girls has got one.... Only I have got one. It always upsets me. And now this new cousin comes here who is as beautiful as an angel, and she hasn't got one either, so I *know* it can't be any good' "(104).

18. It is not surprising that as a scenarist, Freud should himself become the subject of film scripts, as in Sartre's scenario for Huston's film *Freud* or Herbert Ross's 1976 film *The Seven-Per-Cent Solution*, based on Nicholas Meyer's novel. Psychoanalytic readings of classic movies are of course legion. See, for example, Greenberg, *Screen Memories*.

19. Quoting Michelet, Michel de Certeau credits Freud with observing "that the dead are in fact 'beginning to speak.' " De Certeau adds, however, that in psychoanalysis, the dead "are not speaking through the 'medium' of the historian-wizard, as Michelet believed: *it is speaking [Ça parle] in the work and in the silences of the historian, but without his knowledge*" (*Heterologies: Discourse on the Other*, trans. Brian Massumi [Minneapolis: University of Minnesota Press, 1986], 8).

20. C. G. Jung, "The State of Psychotherapy Today" (1934), in *The Collected Works of C. G. Jung*, trans. R. F. C. Hull (New York: Bollingen Foundation, 1964), vol. 10, 167.

21. Reported by René Laforgue; quoted by Lisa Appignanesi and John Forrester, *Freud's Women* (London: Weidenfeld and Nicolson, 1992), 45.

22. The 1925 statement by the president of the American Association for the Advancement of Science that "psychoanalysis is not so much a question of science as a matter of taste" is misleading (quoted by John C. Burnham, "The Influence of Psychoanalysis upon American Culture," in Jacques M. Quen and Eric T. Carlson, eds., *American Psychoanalysis: Origins and Development* [New York: Brunner/Mazel, 1978], 61). Psychoanalysis's scientific status was very much *the* question. Regardless of whether, as Vern L. Bullough suggests, "Freud, sometime after 1900, either consciously or unconsciously abandoned the methods of science" (*Science in the Bedroom: A History of Sex Research* [New York: Basic Books, 1994], 150), he continued to insist upon the scientific character of his work.

23. Cf. Toril Moi's comment that it is "more than probable that the [fellatio] fantasy exists, not in Dora's mind, but in [Freud's] alone" ("Representation of Patriarchy: Sexuality and Epistemology in Freud's Dora," in Charles Bernheimer and Claire Kahane, eds., *In Dora's Case: Freud—Hysteria—Feminism* [1985; rev. ed. New York: Columbia University Press, 1990], 181–99, 190). Moi also detects Freud's own seduction fantasy behind his account of the scene in which Herr K. kisses Dora: in his identification with

the virile Herr K. whose erection, he imagines, was felt by Dora against her body, "Freud is completely in the grip of his countertransference" (189).

24. See the occasional references in the correspondence with Wilhelm Fliess—as in the draft enclosed with his letter of May 2, 1897, in which he writes, "The aim seems to be to reach the earliest [sexual] scenes [*Urszenen*]"—and Jeffrey Masson's annotations (*The Collected Letters of Sigmund Freud to Wilhelm Fliess, 1887–1904*, trans. Jeffrey Masson [Cambridge, Mass.: Harvard University Press, 1985], 239–40, 240 n. 1, 242 n. 1; hereafter *CL*). As early as April 1897, Freud had identified the source of hysteria in fantasies that "go back to things that children overhear at an early age and understand only subsequently" (*CL* 234). By the following year, as Didier Anzieu notes, "Freud had proof, based on his own evidence and that of others, that young children observe sexual scenes between adults with a mixture of curiosity and anxiety"; and in his analysis of two disguised autobiographical dreams that probably date from August 1898, he "describes the primal scene as a fact—but does not yet apprehend the primal phantasy produced in the child on that occasion" (Didier Anzieu, *Freud's Self-Analysis*, trans. Peter Graham [London: Hogarth Press, 1986], 356).

25. Whitney Davis, *Drawing the Dream of the Wolves: Homosexuality, Interpretation, and Freud's "Wolf Man"* (Bloomington: Indiana University Press, 1995).

26. *The Standard Edition of the Complete Psychological Works of Sigmund Freud*, trans. James Strachey (London: Hogarth Press, 1953–74), 17:35; hereafter *SE*.

27. Dorrit Cohn, "Freud's Case Histories and the Question of Fictionality," in Joseph H. Smith, ed., *Telling Facts: History and Narration in Psychoanalysis* (Baltimore: The Johns Hopkins University Press, 1992), 38.

28. Linda Williams observes that the "feelings and emotions" to which hard-core pornography appeals "are, almost by definition, infantile and regressive" (*Hard Core*, 232–33).

29. George Dimock, "Anna and the Wolf-Man: Rewriting Freud's Case History," *Representations* 50 (1995): 53–75.

30. Frederick Crews et al., *The Memory Wars: Freud's Legacy in Dispute* (New York: New York Review of Books, 1995), 46.

31. S. Viderman, *La Céleste et le sublunaire* (Paris: P. U. F. Viderman, 1977), 304. Cited in Patrick J. Mahony, *Cries of the Wolf Man* (New York: International Universities Press, 1984), 52. Lending support to Freud's view, however, is Linda Williams's observation, based on her study of hard-core films, that the "dorsal-ventral position ... is most favorable to visibility of the full frontal female body while simultaneously showing the insertion of penis in vagina" (*Hard Core*, 141).

32. Mahony, *Cries of the Wolf Man*, 52. Moreover, Mahony claims that Freud "suppressed" from his published case history any evidence of discussions with his patient about the reality of his experience (54). Allen Esterson similarly maintains that the primal scene existed only in Freud's imagination (*Seductive Mirage: An Exploration of the Work of Sigmund Freud* [Chicago: Open Court, 1993], 69, 89).

33. Crews et al., *The Memory Wars*, 214, 248, 187.

34. See Lynn Hunt, ed., *The Invention of Pornography: Obscenity and the Origins of Modernity, 1500–1800* (New York: Zone Books, 1993).

35. Freud, *Introductory Lectures on Psychoanalysis*, trans. James Strachey (New York: Norton, 1977), 369 [Lecture 23].

36. Donald Spence points out that it doesn't matter how "unlikely and even improbable" an event like "the Wolf Man's viewing of his parents coupling *a tergo*" is. Since "one cause is preferred to many," the event's uniqueness reinforces its reality: "*because* it was unusual, it probably happened only once; and *because* it was unusual, even though happening only once, it still might have reason to influence subsequent behavior" (*Narrative Truth and Historical Truth: Meaning and Interpretation in Psychoanalysis* [New York: Norton, 1982], 144).

37. In addition to—or perhaps underlying—the following alternating perspectives, is what Williams calls "a tension between pose and act" (*Hard Core*, 33).

38. Interview with Bill Margold, in Robert J. Stoller, *Porn: Myths for the Twentieth Century* (New Haven: Yale University Press, 1991), 62.

39. Lisa Katzman, "The Women of Porn," *The Village Voice*, Aug. 24, 1993, 33. Baudrillard finds a contradiction in pornography between the nonmeaning of the obscene body and the meaning expressed on the performers' faces; those faces must accordingly be effaced (*Seduction*, 33–34). Rather than efface the face, however, pornography typically juxtaposes facial and bodily images, often in the same shot. Through its juxtaposition with the face, the body's obscenity is maximized. See in this regard Slavoj Žižek, *The Plague of Fantasies* (London: Verso, 1997), 178–79:

  > The zero-level pornographic picture is that of a woman displaying her genitals *and* defiantly returning the gaze ... This elementary pornographic scene (a woman, twisted in an anamorphic way, displaying her sex to the camera as well as looking at it) also confronts the spectator with (what Lacan calls) the split between eye and gaze at its purest: the actress or model staring at the spectator stands for the eye, while the open hole of the vagina stands for the traumatic gaze—that is to say, it is from this gaping hole that the scene the spectator is witnessing *returns the gaze* to him. The gaze is thus not where one would expect it (in the eyes staring at us from the picture) but in the traumatic object/hole which transfixes our look and concerns us most intensely—the model's eyes staring at us here are, rather, to remind us: "You see, I'm watching you observe my gaze ..."

40. As Žižek (ibid., 177) describes this "paradox of pornography":

  > This genre, which is supposed to depict the most spontaneous of all human activities, is probably also the most codified, down to the most intimate details: the face of the actress during intercourse, for example, allows for four codified expressions: (1) indifference, signalled by ignorant, bored staring into space, chewing gum, yawning ... ; (2) the "instrumental" attitude, as if the subject is in the midst of a hard task which demands high concentration: eyes turned down, towards the region where things are happening, the tightened lips signalling concentrated effort ... ; (3) the provocative stare into the eyes of the male partner, whose message is: "Give me more! Is this all you can do?"; (4) ecstatic rapture, with half-closed eyes.

41. As Donald P. Spence notes, without documented confirmation Freud's explication of the Wolf Man's dream is purely a matter of interpretation and therefore fails to meet the criteria demanded by historical (or, for that matter, scientific) truth. Nevertheless—and here Spence as a psychoanalyst differs unexpectedly from literary critics of Freud such as Frederick Crews—the interpretation is compelling in its *narrative* truth (*Narrative Truth and Historical Truth*, 141–43).

42. Jay Martin suggests that Freud had second thoughts about his interpretation of the "wolf dream" after criticisms raised by Otto Rank in 1926. By asking his former patient at this time to confirm details of his dream—which he did—Freud revealed to the Wolf Man his "doubt about the truth of the narrative upon which the Wolf Man relied," and "started a process of refragmentation that brought back the patient's earlier borderline state. The shock to the Wolf Man must have been terrific. He had lost faith in his fiction" (*Who Am I This Time?: Uncovering the Fictive Personality* [New York: Norton, 1988], 182–83).

43. Karin Obholzer, *The Wolf-Man: Conversations with Freud's Patient—Sixty Years Later*, trans. Michael Shaw (New York: Continuum Books, 1982), 36.

44. Mahony observes that, given "the enormous wealth and aristocratic standing of [his] family and attendantly because of its palatial mansion, it is of the greatest unlikelihood that the boy would have slept in his parents' bedroom" (*Cries of the Wolf Man*, 51).

45. Obholzer, *The Wolf-Man*, 37. In direct opposition to Freud, George Dimock has taken Sergei at his word in considering his relations with his sister, and especially his reaction to her suicide, as the crux of his emotional and psychic life ("Anna and the Wolf-Man: Rewriting Freud's Case History," *Representations* 50 [1995]: 53–75).

46. Ned Lukacher, *Primal Scenes: Literature, Philosophy, Psychoanalysis* (Ithaca: Cornell University Press, 1986), 27.

47. Freud, *SE* 17:60. Peter Brooks has hailed Freud's decision, just prior to the publication of the case history, "to close the discussion of the reality of the primal scene with a *non liquet*" as "one of the most daring moments of Freud's thought, and one of his most heroic gestures as a writer" (*Reading for the Plot* [New York: Knopf, 1984], 277). Brooks goes too far, however, in seeing Freud as a forerunner of postmodernism; the *non liquet* admission is not a credo that "anything goes." Even if Freud could not be sure what primal scenes are, he knew what they were *not*—*merely* fantasies, or even "retrospective phantasies"; see below, n. 49.

48. Mahony adduces what he considers to be "strong indications that during the final months [of the case] Freud was driven to desperate lengths to find proof of the primal scene" (*Cries of the Wolf Man*, 102). Until the time he wrote up the case in 1915, Freud debated whether to characterize the scene as an actual event or a primal fantasy (see *SE* 17:62 n).

49. Failing to prove that his patient had actually experienced the primal scene, Freud was forced to fall back on the weaker phylogenetic argument that "scenes of observing parental intercourse, of being seduced in childhood, and of being threatened with castration are unquestionably an inherited endowment" that transcended individual experience. Although such scenes might not actually take place in the individual's life, Freud insisted that they were not *merely* fantasies—even displaced, adult "retrospective phantasies" as Jung suggested. They were *primal* fantasies, or *Urphantasien*, as Freud called them after 1915, that were based on real events in the history of the species, if not in the life of the individual. "It seems to me quite possible," he wrote in the *Introductory Lectures on Psychoanalysis* of 1916–17, "that all the things that are told us today in analysis as phantasy ... were once real occurrences in the primaeval times of the human family, and that children in their phantasies are simply filling in the gaps in individual truth with prehistoric truth" (*SE* 16:371). As late as 1920, in a note added to the *Three Essays of Sexuality*, Freud was leaning to the phylogenetic view, observing that the principal "sexual phantasies of the pubertal period"—namely, the primal,

seduction, and castration scenes—"are distinguished by their very gradual occurrence and by being to a great extent independent of individual experience" (*Three Essays on the Theory of Sexuality*, trans. James Strachey [New York: Basic Books, 1975], 92).

50. Sigmund Freud, *Introductory Lectures on Psychoanalysis*, trans. James Strachey (New York: Norton, 1977), 367 [Lecture 23].

51. See Slavoj Žižek's analysis of the scene in Hitchcock's *Vertigo* in which Scottie dresses Judy up (rather than undresses her) in order to make her resemble the dead Madeleine: "the very direction of the seduction process is inverted: instead of undressing his beloved, Scottie is dressing her up" (*The Plague of Fantasies*, 181).

52. I discuss this scene below, see chapter 7 (pp. 212–13).

53. Freud, *Three Essays*, 92 n.

Chapter three: Body Parts

1. James Gleick, "Seeing Faster," *New York Times Magazine*, Oct. 3, 1999. Gleick notes that Muybridge's horse pictures appeared on the cover of *Scientific American* in strips that could be cut out and viewed in the precinematic device of the Zoetrope.

2. Siegfried Kracauer, *Theory of Film*, 9.

3. Gleick, "Seeing Faster."

4. Kracauer, *Theory of Film*, 9.

5. Elaine Kilmurray and Richard Ormond, eds., *John Singer Sargent* (Boston: Museum of Fine Arts, 1999), 249.

6. This segment of the film is shot in such a way that the viewer does not see the cameras recording the sex scene until the last moment; for all the disoriented viewer knows, the entire staged music video could just be going on in Jake's head, a private video fantasy in anticipation of his sexual encounter with Holly. The spectacle could be nothing more than Jake's way of working himself up to perform with Holly before the camera. Or alternatively, Jake's participation in this spectacle could suggest that Jake not only is a voyeur who "likes to watch," but is himself an exhibitionist who enjoys *being* watched.

7. The older man in this film, played by Fernando Rey, appears not to notice that his beloved is really two different women played by two different actresses. Žižek proposes two alternative readings of this situation: Rey's character "*knows* there are really two women, yet he *acts* as if there is only one, since his fantasy determines his acts irrespective of his conscious knowledge," or there is actually only "one and the same 'real' woman [who] is (mis)perceived as two" (*The Plague of Fantasies* [London: Verso, 1997], 172).

8. Žižek, *The Plague of Fantasies*, 180. See also 191, n. 10: "In so far as drive relates to desire as partial object to subject, this 'desubjectivization' involves the passage from desire to drive: desire aims at the subject, as the void which is the core of other's [sic] subjectivity; while drive does not take into account the whole person, just the partial object around which it circulates (shoes, anus …)."

9. Dawidoff, *Between the Frames: Thinking About Movies* (Hamden, Conn.: Archon Books, 1989), 132.

10. Following this reasoning, Ilsa didn't so much choose between Rick and Victor Laszlo in the movie *Casablanca* as her desire led her to perceive them as one and the same person.

11. Like the dream rape in the shower, the actual rape follows a sexual fantasy. At the Metropolitan Museum of Art she is intrigued by a strange man who later lures her into a taxi where she is forcibly ravished. She spends the rest of the day making love at his apartment, and is killed on her way out of the building by another "stranger" in the elevator—another confined space not unlike a shower stall. See my discussion of the scene from *Dressed to Kill* in which Kate is slain in *The Aesthetics of Murder: A Study in Romantic Literature and Contemporary Culture* (Baltimore: The Johns Hopkins University Press, 1991), 63–64.

12. Some of De Palma's feminist critics have claimed that in place of Hitchcock's formula for horror where a helpless female becomes the involuntary victim of a male attacker's insane lust, De Palma depicts his women as nymphomaniacs who fantasize about being raped by unknown assailants in the sanctuary of their bathrooms. Instead of being victims of a psychopathic male's violence, they are the victims of their own erotic desire. And so the critical verdict spread quickly concerning De Palma's "contempt for women" (Joyce Sunila Holt in the *Los Angeles Times*, March 1984, cited in Susan Dworkin, *Double De Palma: A Film Study with Brian De Palma* [New York: Newmarket Press, 1984], 132; hereafter *DD*). As I show, Kate's "rape fantasy" is hardly an expression of her own desire.

13. Reviewing De Palma's career, Richard T. Jameson dismisses *Body Double* as "the reductio ad absurdum" that ended "his psycho-killer string" of films, finding nothing more in it than "a parody assault on his feminist critics that only backfired on the joker" ("Brian De Palma: Audacity, Mayhem and Images You Don't Forget," *New York Times*, April 29, 2001). Jameson echoes Pauline Kael's criticism years earlier that "the big, showy scenes recall 'Vertigo' and 'Rear Window' so obviously that the movie is like an assault on the people who have put De Palma down for being derivative." Kael adds that "these big scenes have no special point, other than their resemblance to Hitchcock's work" (*The New Yorker*, Nov. 12, 1984, 185). The basis of Kael's disappointment with *Body Double* (she had been enthusiastic about De Palma's earlier work) has to do with her view that De Palma's earlier films addressed "crude, real fears" that an audience can identify with— "dread of menstruation" in *Carrie*, "qualms that sexual pleasure would get you into trouble" in *Dressed to Kill*, "apprehensions that you were a coward and would fail those who counted on you" in *Blow Out*. Kael has a point when she suggests that in contrast to these real fears, Jake's claustrophobia in *Body Double* seems an artificial "plot contraption" (186). What she misses, however, is that while De Palma's earlier films may have exploited the Hitchcock formula of presenting a character's fears, his more recent films have been increasingly concerned with his character's fantasies and desires. The heavy-handed references to Hitchcock's work in *Body Double* were no doubt a joke on critics who accused him of being derivative and yet demanded more in the Hitchcockian vein. Actually, De Palma's interest had shifted away from a concern with "crude, real fears" to an investigation of the altogether *unreal* phenomenon of erotic fantasy, and so it's inappropriate to evaluate *Body Double* as Kael does, according to Hitchcockian conventions. While the treatment of Jake's claustrophobia fears is a throwback to the older director, the exposure of the mechanism of erotic fantasy through

Jake's voyeurism and the use of the body-double technique breaks new ground.

14. The most notable example is the menstruation scene in the girls' locker room at the beginning of *Carrie*, which is hyperbolically reenacted in the climactic scene in which Carrie is showered with pig's blood at the high-school prom. De Palma works his own twist on the Hitchcockian convention of the vulnerable woman alone in the shower in his film *Scarface*, where males are the victims of bathroom violence.

15. Acknowledging his obvious debt to Hitchcock who masterminded what has become the archetypal image of the solitary woman in her shower whose supposedly inviolable privacy is suddenly invaded by a maniacal killer, De Palma has observed that "Hitchcock discovered that people feel safe in the bathroom with the door shut. It's a place that when someone comes in, you really feel violated. To me it's almost a genre convention at this point—like using violins when people look at each other or using women in situations where they are killed or sexually attacked" ("'Double' Trouble," interview with Marcia Pally, *Film Comment* 20, 5 [1984]: 17). Where De Palma seems to work his own notorious twist on his master's model is in the woman's relation to her assailant. Hitchcock's female victim in *Psycho* recoils in terror from the advances of a real assailant; De Palma's contemporary woman in *Dressed to Kill* conjures up an imaginary rapist. (Later in the film, of course, she is attacked by both a real rapist and a real killer.)

16. Laura Mulvey, "Visual Pleasure and Narrative Cinema," *Screen* 16, 3 (1975): 6–18.

17. "'Double' Trouble," 15.

18. This point was not lost on other filmmakers in the years following *Body Double*'s appearance. In films such as David Lynch's *Blue Velvet* and Curtis Hanson's *The Bedroom Window*, both of which appeared in 1986, voyeurism plays a prominent part: the viewer is put directly in the situation of a witness to a violent sexual assault, and sees exactly what the witness sees. Where *Body Double* presents the doubling mechanism on the side of the exhibitionist and shows it to be a key element of erotic illusion (Jake thinks he sees Gloria when in fact he sees Holly), which is likely to provoke violence through deception, in films like *The Bedroom Window* (or Anthony Waller's 1991 film *Mute Witness* where the female protagonist is given the masculine name "Billy") the doubling rather occurs on the side of the voyeur himself. All these films suggest that the witness *in* the film and the viewer *of* the film are doubles, substitutes for each other by virtue of their voyeuristic roles.

19. Richard T. Jameson, "Brian De Palma."

20. A third scenario is developed in Larry Cohen's 1984 film *Special Effects*: a man accused of murdering his wife falls in love with an actress who plays her part in a film-within-the-film that reenacts the murder. Whereas in *Vertigo* Kim Novak plays two seemingly different characters (Madeleine and Judy) who are really one and the same, in *Special Effects* actress Zoe Tamerlis plays two different characters in the film—the dead wife and the actress who is made-up to look like her in the filmed reenactment. Released the same year as *Special Effects*, De Palma's *Body Double* inverts this arrangement by using two different actresses (Shelton and Griffith) to play the role of the same character, Gloria Revelle.

21. Actually, in an early version of the *Body Double* script, Holly *was* Sam's accomplice. However, Melanie Griffith apparently convinced De Palma that Holly would have been incapable of murder (*DD*, 53). It's as if Griffith— daughter of Tippi Hedren, Hitchcock's star in *Marnie* and *The Birds*—was

instinctively shying away from reenacting a Hitchcock plot.
22. Georges Bataille, *Death and Sensuality: A Study of Eroticism and the Taboo* (New York: Walker and Co., 1962), 17: "Toute la mise en oeuvre érotique a pour principe une destruction de la structure de l'être fermé qu'est à l'état normal un partenaire du jeu" (*L'Érotisme* [Paris: Minuit, 1957], 24).
23. Bataille, *Death and Sensuality*, 31.
24. Laura Mulvey, *Visual and Other Pleasures* (Bloomington: Indiana University Press, 1989), 20.
25. Greg Tate, "Making Betty Blue," *The Village Voice*, Dec. 30, 1986, 78. Tate claims that *Blue Velvet, Something Wild,* and *Betty Blue* "break new ground for mainstream cinema by having female sexual terrorism be the prod for the arousal of Wonder Bread males."
26. Friedrich A. Kittler, *Gramophone, Film, Typewriter*, trans. Geoffrey Winthrop-Young and Michael Wutz (Stanford: Standford University Press, 1999), 145.
27. Vladimir Nabokov, *Lolita* (New York: G. P. Putnam's, 1955), 82.

Chapter four: Documenting Violence

The section "Films that Kill" originally appeared in a condensed form as "Grisham's Demons" in *College Literature* 25, 1 (1998): 35–40.
1. Richard Rhodes, "Hollow Claims about Fantasy Violence," *New York Times*, Sept. 17, 2000.
2. Martin Amis, "Blown Away," *The New Yorker*, May 30, 1994, 48.
3. Reported by Katha Pollitt, "Natural Born Killers," *The Nation*, July 26/Aug. 2, 1999, 10.
4. I raise this second possibility in *The Aesthetics of Murder: A Study in Romantic Literature and Contemporary Culture* (Baltimore: The Johns Hopkins University Press, 1991), 25. As an example of the close relation between cultural illiteracy and mental incompetency, see Barbara Walters's interview of John Lennon's killer, Mark David Chapman (*20/20*, Dec. 4, 1992). Asked to describe *The Catcher in the Rye*, Chapman replies that it is a story narrated by a patient in a mental hospital. Later, when asked if he still reads the novel or believes it has a special meaning, Chapman says no, he never thinks about it, and doesn't even have a copy in his prison cell. But the fact that he believes Holden Caulfield to be a patient in a hospital suggests a continuing misunderstanding of, and identification with, J. D. Salinger's character—or rather, an identification of Caulfield with himself.
5. Sara L. Knox, *Murder: A Tale of Modern American Life* (Durham: Duke University Press, 1998), 195.
6. Stuart Klawans, "Artful Death, Fishy Art," *The Nation*, Feb. 5, 1996, 35.
7. According to Cynthia A. Freeland, "realist horror" is "a particularly postmodern phenomenon" that thoroughly blurs the distinction between fiction and nonfiction: "in the growing world of infotainment, realistic elements from news stories are easily, commonly, and quickly integrated into new feature film plots. Conversely, fictitious characters (like Hannibal Lecter) are alluded to in presenting or describing real ones (like Jeffrey Dahmer)" ("Realist Horror," in Cynthia A. Freeland and Thomas E. Wartenberg, eds., *Philosophy and Film* [New York: Routledge, 1995], 133–34).
8. See Black, *The Aesthetics of Murder*, ch. 1, and Steven Jay Schneider, "Murder as Art/The Art of Murder: Aestheticizing Violence in Modern

Cinematic Horror," in Andy Black, ed., *Necronomicon: The Journal of Horror and Erotic Cinema, Book Four* (London: Noir Press, 2001), 65–85.

9. For a more detailed discussion of this film as an instance of the murderer-as-corrupt-artist theme see Schneider, "Murder as Art/The Art of Murder."

10. Annalee Newitz, "Serial Killers, True Crime, and Economic Performance Anxiety," in Christopher Sharrett, ed., *Mythologies of Violence in Postmodern Media* (Detroit: Wayne State University Press, 1999), 80.

11. Thus, whereas Freeland's exemplary instances of "realist horror" are *Henry* and even *The Silence of the Lambs*, Rubin finds both of these films to be unrealistic in the way they exoticize their "monsters." See Martin Rubin, "The Grayness of Darkness: *The Honeymoon Killers* and Its Impact on Psychokiller Cinema," in *Mythologies of Violence in Postmodern Media*, 41–64. I discuss these differing views of realism at greater length in "Real(ist) Horror: From Execution Videos to Snuff Films," in Steven Jay Schneider and Xavier Mendik, eds., *Underground U.S.A.: Filmmaking Beyond the Hollywood Canon* (London: Wallflower Press, 2002).

12. Cynthia A. Freeland, "Realist Horror," 129.

13. See Black, "Real(ist) Horror."

14. Some notable examples are *Snuff* (1975), *Emanuelle in America* (1976), *Last House on Dead End Street* (1977), *Cannibal Holocaust* (1980), *Special Effects* (1982), *Videodrome* (1982), *Mute Witness* (1995), *Tesis* (1995), *Screen Kill* (1997), and *8mm* (1999). See David Kerekes and David Slater, *Killing for Culture: An Illustrated History of the Death Film from Mondo to Snuff* (London: Creation Books, 1995), and Julian Petley, " 'Snuffed Out': Nightmares in a Trading Standards Officer's Brain," in Xavier Mendik and Graeme Harper, eds., *Unruly Pleasures: The Cult Film and its Critics* (Guildford: FAB Press, 2000), 204–19.

15. Thus police in Spokane, Washington, relied on evidence obtained from GPS surveillance to arrest a man for the murder of his wife and daughter ("Cops Use Satellite to Track Suspect," Associated Press, Nov. 21, 1999).

16. Rubin, "The Grayness of Darkness," 59.

17. According to Peter McGrath, "Cameras will be everywhere, feeding visual data to the Internet, and some researchers believe that by 2020 we will be on camera nearly nonstop" ("If All the World's a Computer ...," *Newsweek*, Jan. 1, 2000, 72).

18. Pioneer nuclear physicist Hans Bethe has pointed out that "under almost all conditions, tests of weapons with more than a one-kiloton yield [as compared with the approximately twenty-kiloton yields of the bombs dropped on Japan in World War II] can be reliably detected," and "under ideal conditions we could now detect tests with nuclear yields as low as one pound" ("The Treaty Betrayed," *New York Review of Books*, Nov. 18, 1999, 6).

19. One Indonesian college student who saw the film when it was first shown at the Jakarta International Film Festival, and who admitted understanding only about 50 percent of the English dialogue of the non-subtitled film, nevertheless declared that the largely fictional movie "tells the true story of our history, and I think that every Indonesian should see it.... If the government had allowed Indonesians to view this film, they would have rebelled against the fascist dictators a long time ago" (Calvin Sims, "No Danger in Showing a Film Now in Indonesia," *New York Times* [Nov. 10, 2000]).

20. A different kind of pseudodocumentary filmed under difficult, if not dangerous, conditions was the fall 2000 PBS television series *Islam: Empire of Faith*. The director, Ron Gardner, was the first American filmmaker to be

allowed to work in Iran since the Islamic revolution in 1979. Far from depicting life in present-day Iran, however, Gardner's documentary presents the politically less sensitive subject of the history of Islam from the time of Muhammad in the seventh century to the glorious reign of the sixteenth-century Ottoman emperor Suleiman the Magnificent.

21. Quoted by Nancy Ramsey, " 'The Wounds': Growing Up in Belgrade with Suitably Black Humor," *New York Times*, Aug. 22, 1999.

22. Quoted by Alan Riding in "Bosnia Revisited, with an Eye on the Future," *New York Times*, Nov. 23, 1997. Subsequent citations are also taken from this article.

23. Barbie Zelizer, *Covering the Body: The Kennedy Assassination, the Media, and the Shaping of Collective Memory* (Chicago: University of Chicago Press, 1992), 68.

24. Art Simon, *Dangerous Knowledge: The JFK Assassination in Art and Film* (Philadelphia: Temple University Press, 1996), 35.

25. This raises an obvious question: What enabled Zapruder to keep filming for the entire duration of the assassination? One is reminded of the climactic scene in Pirandello's film novel *The Notebooks of Serafino Gubbio (Shoot!)* in which the professional cameraman Gubbio continues to film the scene in the tiger cage even after the actor Nuti fires his gun at Nestoroff and is himself attacked by the tiger. In response to the question why Zapruder and Gubbio fail to react to the horrible spectacle unfolding before them and stop filming, the answer that suggests itself is that they *become* the cinemato-graphic apparatus itself.

26. Simon, *Dangerous Knowledge*, 68.

27. Ibid., 55.

28. Even if photographic evidence of the Simpson-Goldman murders had turned up, questions would no doubt have been raised about the authenticity of the evidence. Thus, in the penultimate episode of the 1996 ABC series *Murder One*, which drew heavily on the Simpson criminal trial, the attorney of Neal Avedon, who has just been found guilty of the rape and murder of a fifteen-year-old girl, discovers a videotape that reveals the actual assailant. But the tape itself is not sufficient evidence to exonerate Avedon, and the final episode centers on a court hearing to determine the tape's authenticity. One defense witness is an expert video technician who can verify that the tape was not edited, but not that it was made at the time of the murder or that it was an actual murder and not a staged performance. This crucial testimony is provided only at the last moment when Richard Cross—the man who made the video and who is dying from AIDS, so he has no reason to conceal the truth—verifies its authenticity.

29. Pier Paolo Pasolini, "Observations on the Sequence Shot" (1967), in Louise K. Barnett, ed., *Heretical Empiricism* (Bloomington: Indiana University Press, 1988), 233–37.

30. Don DeLillo, *Libra* (New York: Viking, 1988), 370; see Black, *The Aesthetics of Murder*, 184–85.

31. Simon, *Dangerous Knowledge*, 163.

32. Simon only mentions *Blow-Up* briefly in passing as one of a number of works in which the Zapruder film is "a thinly veiled subject for the commercial movie industry" (ibid., 35).

33. Quoted in Roy Gerard Huss, ed., *Focus on Blow-Up* (Englewood Cliffs, N.J.: Prentice-Hall, Inc., 1971), 5; Huss's translation.

34. Simon, *Dangerous Knowledge*, 44.

35. Ralph Rugoff, *Scene of the Crime* (Cambridge, Mass.: MIT Press, 1997), 19.

36. See Black, *The Aesthetics of Murder*, ch. 4.

37. This scene invites comparison with one in Walker Percy's *Lancelot* in which the narrator uses hidden videocameras to document the sexual activities of his wife and daughter with a group of Hollywood filmmakers and actors. Because of the lighting, the images on the tape are completely distorted, and Lancelot must "fill in" what is taking place with his own feverish imaginings (1977; New York: Picador, 1999, 181–90).

38. Compare the case of Paulina in Polanski's *Death and the Maiden* who attempts to use recording devices not to discover the truth, but to document a truth she's convinced she already knows. Like the photographer in *Blow-Up*, however, Paulina fails to obtain documentary evidence of what she knows to be true: in her case, Dr. Miranda's guilt.

39. Simon, *Dangerous Knowledge*, 65.

40. See chapter one.

41. Knox, *Murder: A Tale of Modern American Life*, 19.

42. David Slocum, quoted in Holly Millea, "Voyeurs, Guns, and Money," *Premier*, March 1999, 65.

43. Ibid.

44. See Joan Acocella, "Burned Again," *The New Yorker*, Nov. 15, 1999, 98–106.

45. Stuart Klawans, "Artful Death, Fishy Art," *The Nation*, Feb. 5, 1996, 35–36.

46. John D. MacDonald, *The Executioners* (New York: Fawcett, 1968), 178.

47. Jesse Kornbluth, "Grisham, Yes, but a Far Cry From 'The Firm,'" *New York Times*, June 1, 1997. With respect to television, one should certainly mention former Boston lawyer David Kelley—writer for the show *LA Law* and creator of *Ally McBeal* and *The Practice*.

48. John Grisham, "Unnatural Killers," *The Oxford American*, spring 1996, 3. Subsequent quotations from this essay will be followed by the page numbers in parentheses.

49. Michael Shnayerson reports Sarah as saying, "As far as how much this case is leaning on *Natural Born Killers*, it is one of many elements.... It has its influence, but it is not as great as I would like to make it be.... And I wish I could say that it did. I wish I could point the finger at Hollywood completely. But that's not so, that's not honest" (quoted in "Natural Born Opponents," *Vanity Fair*, July 1996, 142.

50. And not just Grisham. Shnayerson writes that "*Natural Born Killers* remains in a class by itself, having been linked to more copycat killings than any film ever made" (ibid., 100).

51. Sam Gideon Anson, "Natural Born Litigants," *LA Weekly*, June 28–July 4, 1996, 11.

52. Shnayerson, "Natural Born Opponents," 106.

53. As reported in a *New York Times* update, "Prosecutor Says Movie's School Slaying Scene May Have Influenced Suspect," Dec. 4, 1997.

54. Stephen Schiff, "The Last Wild Man," *The New Yorker*, Aug. 8, 1994, 46.

55. In one scene in Stone's film, Gale pitches his idea to Mickey of doing a live prison interview immediately after the Super Bowl. "We're talking about nothing less than television history," he says, "the first sit down, in-depth interview with the most charismatic serial killer ever." When Mickey learns that he and Mallory were already featured in one of the most popular episodes on Gale's show, he asks how his ratings compared with episodes about John Wayne Gacy and Ted Bundy, and is assured that his ratings were

higher. Mickey then asks about Manson, and Gale has to admit that "Manson beat you." "Well," sighs Mickey, "it's pretty hard to beat the King."

56. For example, he and Mallory always leave one survivor at each murder scene to "tell the tale" to the press. During the prison riot triggered by his televised interview, Mickey orders Gale's cameraman to "shoot everything I do" as *he* shoots his way out of prison.

57. Needless to say, Stone's critique of the media in *Natural Born Killers* has not been universally endorsed. Jon Katz, who two years earlier in *Rolling Stone* had hailed Stone's *JFK* as "the most explosive assault the New News has made on the Old," panned *Natural Born Killers*, charging that the director has "defected" from his role as a cultural renegade. "He's switched sides, darting across our cultural Checkpoint Charlie to join the coalition of editorial boards, journalism school deans, religious fanatics, smug boomers, Charlton Hestonites and the other blockheads who have long held popular culture … responsible for the decline of America" ("Natural Born Killjoy," *Wired*, Dec. 26, 1994, 126).

58. Quoted in Shnayerson, "Natural Born Opponents," 144.

59. John Guntner, letter to *The Oxford American*, June/July 1996, 10.

60. Quoted in Shnayerson, "Natural Born Opponents," 143.

61. Especially since Grisham has expressed an interest in writing works that are "more literary" but has little motivation to do so as long as his legal thrillers remain so popular. "I keep waiting for people to get tired of legal thrillers and courtroom dramas, but there is no sign of a decrease in interest" (quoted by Mel Gussow, "For Grisham, Dream of Escape More Lucrative than Imagined," *New York Times*, Mar. 31, 1997).

62. Quoted in Shnayerson, "Natural Born Opponents," 144.

63. This is according to Jane Hamsher, one of Stone's producers, who reports Stone as saying, "Everyone expects me to be the guy with the message.... I just want to do something that's completely nihilistic." See Mark Miller, "Hollywood Goes On Trial," *Newsweek*, Aug. 2, 1999, 43.

64. Stone's portrayal of Oswald in *JFK* as someone who did not act alone in the assassination but was part of a CIA-directed conspiracy is analogous to his depiction of Mickey in *Natural Born Killers* as someone who doesn't really act alone in his murders but is a "natural" product of a media-driven culture.

65. Stone's view of the relation between violence and the media as expressed in his film is far more garbled than both his supporters and his critics give him credit for. Are Mickey and Mallory media celebrities or media critics? Are they natural born killers or media-mediated monsters? Wanting to have it both ways, Stone leaves his audiences bewildered. When Mickey tells Gale just before he shoots him that "killing you and what you represent is … a statement" but adds that "I'm not a hundred percent sure exactly what it's saying," it's tempting to hear this as Stone's ironic comment about his own message in *Natural Born Killers*.

Much of the incoherence of Stone's film stems from his imaginary identification with Mickey in the charismatic role of killer and media critic while denying his actual affinity with the media maniac Gale. Stone wants to give the impression that there's a world of difference between a socially and aesthetically conscious filmmaker such as himself and media "scum" like Gale, who refers to his own coverage as "filler, fodder … junk food for the brain," which he force-feeds to a nation of nitwits. If Stone goes out of his way to turn Gale into a caricature, it's not because he's lambasting the new media, as critics such as Katz believe (see above, n. 57, but because he needs to emphasize the difference between himself and Gale when it's not at all clear that such a difference exists. The real-life filmmaker and the fictional TV host both make a living by exploiting the masses' craving for images of murderous violence.

66. David Denby, "Buried Alive," *The New Yorker*, July 15, 1996, 57.

67. Quoted by Joyce Johnson in "Witness for the Prosecution," *The New Yorker*, May 16, 1994, 50.

68. Mary Harron, "The Risky Territory of 'American Psycho,'" *New York Times* (April 9, 2000). A copy of Ellis's novel reportedly found under Paul Bernardo and Karla Homolka's bed has been characterized as a "blueprint" for the series of rapes and murders attributed to this notorious Canadian couple (Stephen Williams, *Invisible Darkness: The Strange Case of Paul Bernardo and Karla Homolka* [New York: Bantam, 1998], 350–51; see also 172).

69. In the same special "crime" issue of *The Oxford American* in which Grisham's editorial appeared, novelist Donna Tartt speculates about the possibility that Jack the Ripper had read *Dr. Jekyll and Mr. Hyde* and had used Stevenson's novel "as a kind of blueprint for his own unprecedented crimes" ("Murder & Imagination: Further Reflections on a Fine Art," *The Oxford American*, spring 1996, 50). Noting that "the similarities are numerous and striking," Tartt proceeds to make a case for what, if true, would be the most sensational instance of literature-mediated-murder in history, far outstripping his precursor Jean-Baptiste Troppmann's 1869 slaughter of a family of eight after reading Eugène Sue's novel *The Wandering Jew*, Mark David Chapman's murder of John Lennon after poring over *The Catcher in the Rye*, or John Hinckley Jr.'s attempted assassination of President Reagan after seeing the film *Taxi Driver*. (See Black, *The Aesthetics of Murder*, ch. 4. Since *Taxi Driver* was itself based in part on Arthur Bremer's assassination attempt against George Wallace, Hinckley's assassination attempt can be considered a case of life imitating art imitating life, suggesting just how convoluted such trails of influence and imitation can be.) It's just as well that Tartt can't confirm her hunch about *Dr. Jekyll and Mr. Hyde*'s influence on Jack the Ripper; otherwise, following Grisham's argument, a case could be made—indeed, would *have* to be made—for taking legal action against the Stevenson estate. And following Grisham's implication that films are more likely than literary works to influence violent behavior, the producers and directors of all the cinematic adaptations of Stevenson's tale would also come under suspicion for their role in any crimes committed by viewers of those films.

Chapter five: Telling Stories

1. Thomas Dixon Jr., *The Clansman: An Historical Romance of the Ku Klux Klan* (Lexington: University Press of Kentucky, 1970), 149.

2. The visual sensitivity of women is most vividly demonstrated in the scene in which Dr. Cameron examines the bodies of Mrs. Lenoir and her daughter Marion, who took their lives after being attacked by a gang of blacks. Dr. Cameron detects the image of the women's principal assailant imprinted in the mother's eyes, but not in the eyes of the raped daughter. When Dr. Cameron instructs his son Ben to look at Mrs. Lenoir's eyes, he sees nothing. According to Dixon's fanciful physiology, women are more visually sensitive than men, and parents of both sexes are more sensitive than their sons and daughters.

3. Gavriel Moses, *The Nickel was for the Movies: Film in the Novel from Pirandello to Puig* (Berkeley: University of California Press, 1995), 247.

4. Manuel Puig, *Kiss of the Spider Woman*, trans. Thomas Colchie (New York: Vintage, 1991), 79.

5. See Moses, *The Nickel was for the Movies*: "the novel mostly juxtaposes Molina's view of film (the gender-centered passion for genre) to that of Valentin (a conventional view of film as social critique)" (255).

6. This ambiguity is especially acute near the end of Babenco's film at the point when the spider woman film-within-the-film begins. Moses criticizes Babenco for having Molina narrate this movie when in Puig's novel it is Valentin who invents the spider-woman persona, applies it to Molina, and then dreams up the spider-woman story. "[Valentin] learns his lesson well if he can ultimately choose the spider woman to personify Molina. It is, alas, symptomatic again of the failure in the film version that this choice is trans-posed to Molina himself" (249). But there is no reason to assume that because Molina is narrating the story, the spider-woman movie sequence in Babenco's film records what he is seeing in his mind's eye. In fact, Raul Julia's (Valentin's) pensive expression immediately before the spider-woman movie is shown suggests that it is he who is seeing/re-creating the film while listening to Molina's account. And, of course, Valentin "narrates" the prison-escape movie with which Babenco's film ends.

7. Describing the act of narrating films in Puig's novel as "a primary dialogic vehicle between two characters," Gavriel Moses declares it to be "important, in the economy of the novel, that these films *not* be seen. They must be mediated in elaborate ways by Molina and (eventually) by Valentin" (*The Nickel was for the Movies*, 247–48). These antithetical characters "use the retelling of movies as a means to communicate and, as the story advances, to grow as human beings in real life through the mediation of films" (246). Although Moses is certainly right to call attention to the problems entailed in adapting a film novel such as *The Kiss of the Spider Woman* to the screen, he goes too far in faulting Babenco's adaptation for actually showing films that Molina simply retells in the novel, and in claiming that Babenco thereby negates the dialogic and dialectical relationship that develops between the two cellmates. Such a view assumes that in order to be more than a diverting or seductive medium, films can't be shown or seen—and thus can no longer be movies—but have to be translated into the alternative medium of oral discourse, in which form they can mediate relationships through an active process of verbal exchange. Besides, even if Puig's primary concern was to demonstrate the desirability of such discursive interaction, a film version of the novel is ideally suited to explore Puig's implicit interest in the movies' seductive powers by actually making visible Molina's and Valentin's movie narratives and movie fantasies, and Babenco simply took full advantage of this opportunity.

8. Mark Singer, "The Friendly Executioner," *The New Yorker*, Feb. 1, 1999, 35.

9. Ibid., 34.

10. Quoted in Peter Applebome, "A Taste for the Eccentric, Marginal and Dangerous," *New York Times*, Dec. 26, 1999, Arts & Leisure, 9.

11. Errol Morris, quoted in Singer, "The Friendly Executioner," 36. Whereas Leuchter expected his report to discredit the presence of gas chambers at Auschwitz, Benjamin Wilkomirski expected his 1995 memoir *Fragments: Memories of a Wartime Childhood* to document his own presence in Auschwitz as a child and his hellish experiences there. Three years later, however, Wilkomirski's credibility was questioned by a Swiss writer who reported that Wilkomirski was not a Latvian Jew who survived the camps, but a Swiss citizen named Bruno Grosjean who spent the entire war in

Switzerland. In the aftermath of Ganzfried's revelations and Wilkomirski's persistent claims as to the trustworthiness of his memories, most commentators took the view "that his book, and his other activities as a survivor, could not be written off as conscious acts of fakery but should more properly be understood as expressions of the genuine conviction of a man who believed himself to be somebody that he probably was not" (Philip Gourevitch, "The Memory Thief," *The New Yorker*, June 14, 1999, 52). In October 1999, Suhrkamp Verlag, the original publisher of *Fragments*, which had maintained the work's authenticity, withdrew hardcover copies of the book from stores.

12. Quoted in Applebome, "A Taste for the Eccentric, Marginal and Dangerous," 12.

13. Singer, "The Friendly Executioner," 38. Despite Morris's insistence on the difference between his documentary and Spielberg's *Schindler's List*, his use of "contrived material ... in the service of the underlying truth" bears a striking resemblance to Thomas Keneally's method in composing *Schindler's Ark*, the novel upon which Spielberg based his film. In his author's note, Keneally claimed to have used "the texture and devices of a novel to tell a true story ... because the craft of the novelist is the only craft to which I can lay claim, and because the novel's techniques seem suited for a character of such ambiguity and magnitude as Oskar [Schindler]." Yet Keneally emphasized that in writing a novel about incidents that took place during the Holocaust, he had "attempted to avoid all fiction ... since fiction would debase the record" (*Schindler's Ark* [London: Hodder and Stoughton, 1982], 9–10). In short, Keneally had produced what Toby Miller has called "a seeming oxymoron—a novel that denied fiction," that "disarticulated genre from content, generating controversies over truth that mounted with the increased popularity and fame of the book and multiplied following its transmogrification into one of the most feted films of the decade" (*Technologies of Truth: Cultural Citizenship and the Popular Media* [Minneapolis: University of Minnesota Press, 1998], 10).

14. Singer, "The Friendly Executioner," 37.

15. Cf. Claude Lanzmann's 1979 documentary *A Visitor from the Living*, which consists of the director's conversation with Maurice Rossel, a Swiss member of an International Red Cross inspection party that visited the Theresienstadt concentration camp in 1944. Hardly a neutral observer, Rossel accepted the innocuous appearance of the camp at face value, oblivious to the fact that the Nazis had disguised the camp to look like a pleasant resort and had just killed five thousand Jews so that the camp would be less crowded. More than thirty years later, Rossel persisted in his belief that what he saw was real. Rather than confront Rossel directly with his collaboration in a monstrous fabrication, Lanzmann lets him reveal his own delusion to the viewer, much in the way Morris does in his documentary about Leuchter, or Dariusz Jablonski does in his 1998 documentary *Photographer* about Walter Genewein, the Nazis' chief accountant in the Lodz ghetto (see introduction, n. 45).

16. Jan Otakar Fischer, "Ask Not Which House Is Real, but Whether Reality Is," *New York Times*, Sept. 23, 1999. Subsequent citations in this section are taken from this article.

17. Nathanael West, *Miss Lonelyhearts and The Day of the Locust* (New York: New Directions, 1962), 104.

18. Quoted by Dinitia Smith in "Hollywood Loves Writers (if They Suffer)," *New York Times*, Sept. 27, 1998.

19. Ibid.

20. For all its extravagant surrealism and indulgence in the grotesque, *Barton Fink* draws heavily on real-life characters and events. William Burroughs's novel *Naked Lunch*, the source of Cronenberg's film, is based in part on the author's tragic killing of his wife and his relations with Paul and Jane Bowles, while the key characters in *Barton Fink* are based on real-life individuals: Barton on Clifford Odets, the writer Bill Mayhew on William Faulkner, and the studio chief Jack Lipnick on Louis B. Meyer. Jonathan Rosenbaum's criticism that *Barton Fink* fails to give an accurate account of the personalities on whom the principal characters are based, or of the era in which it is set, hardly seems to apply to a film in which the real and the surreal are shown to be inseparably linked (*Placing Movies: The Practice of Film Criticism* [Berkeley: University of California Press, 1995]).

21. Ibid., 250.

22. Also, as in *The Day of the Locust*, "the plot [of *Barton Fink*] suddenly veers into outright fantasy and metaphor, incorporating other styles and moods (mainly those of arty horror films)" (ibid., 250). And what Rosenbaum writes of Fink—that he seems unaware of and indifferent to the United States' entry into World War II at the end of the movie—is also typical of the characters in *The Day of the Locust*.

Chapter six: Showing the Obscene

1. Brian McFarlane, *Novel to Film: An Introduction to the Theory of Adaptation* (New York: Oxford University Press, 1996), 34, 171, 190.

2. John D. MacDonald, *The Executioners* (New York: Fawcett, 1968), 204.

3. McFarlane, *Novel to Film*, 190; my emphasis.

4. Ibid.

5. Jesse Green, "That Was No 'Lady': Pilfering Literature," *New York Times*, May 11, 1997.

6. Cynthia Ozick, "What Only Words, Not Film, Can Portray," *New York Times*, Jan. 5, 1997.

7. Henry James, *The Portrait of a Lady*, ed., Nicola Bradbury (Oxford: Oxford University Press, 1995), 10.

8. Gilberto Perez, *The Material Ghost: Films and their Medium* (Baltimore: The Johns Hopkins University Press, 1988), 88. Referring to James's technique of "restricted consciousness," McFarlane identifies James and Conrad as the chief literary forerunners of film in that they "may be said to have broken with the tradition of 'transparency' in relation to the novel's referential world so that the mode and angle of vision were as much a part of the novel's content as what was viewed" (*Novel to Film*, 6).

9. Linda Williams, *Hard Core: Power, Pleasure, and the "Frenzy of the Visible"* (Berkeley: University of California Press, 1989), 47.

10. McFarlane, *Novel to Film*, 188.

11. In her 1995 novel *Diario di Lo* (Venice: Marsilio Editori S.P.A.), the Italian writer Pia Pera attempted to reconstruct the girl's point of view, presenting her, rather than Humbert, as the seducer. When the book's U.S. publication was challenged on the grounds of copyright infringement by the Nabokov estate, Farrar, Straus and Giroux canceled its plans to bring it out. An agreement was later reached between the Nabokov estate and Foxrock, Inc., which published Pera's book in October 1999 as *Lo's Diary*, trans. Ann Goldstein (New York: Foxrock, Inc.).

12. Mim Udovitch, "Lo. Lee. Ta," *New York Times*, Oct. 31, 1999.
13. Michael Wood, "Revisiting Lolita," *New York Review of Books*, Mar. 26, 1998, 12.
14. Ibid.
15. Quoted by Jeremy Bernstein, "How About a Little Game," in Stephanie Schwam, ed., *The Making of 2001: A Space Odyssey* (New York: Modern Library, 2000), 75.
16. Celestine Bohlen has called the film "one of the least explicit treatments of a sexual passion, licit or illicit, to be screened in recent years" ("New 'Lolita' Is Snubbed by U.S. Distributors," *New York Times Book Review*, Sept. 23, 1997). Describing it as "downright demure" (9), Wood notes that "what's really shocking in the film is the deterioration of [Humbert and Lolita's] relationship rather than the sight of their sex acts" ("Revisiting Lolita," 10).
17. The film premiered in America on Aug. 2, 1998, on Showtime cable TV, and was released the following month by the Samuel Goldwyn Company. On July 15, a special screening of the film was presented at the Samuel Goldwyn Theater in Los Angeles by the American Civil Liberties Union of Southern California and Showtime.
18. Quoted in Holly Millea, "Voyeurs, Guns, and Money," *Premiere*, Mar. 1999, 100.
19. Quoted in Anthony Ramirez, "Lolitas Don't Shock Anymore, But 'Lolita' Still Does," *New York Times*, Aug. 2, 1998, sec. 4, 5.
20. Describing America at his film's debut at the 1997 San Sebastian film festival as "a country where 6-year-olds are sent home from school for kissing their classmates" and "where in Oklahoma, police raided video stores, seizing copies of 'The Tin Drum,'" Lyne claimed that he was "not altogether surprised" by the reluctance of American distributors. "The atmosphere in America has become very moralistic in the last three years, similar to the way it was in the 1950s" (Bohlen, "New 'Lolita' Is Snubbed").
21. Whether or not JonBenét was the victim of sexual abuse remains a murky issue. In March 1997 the *Rocky Mountain News* reported that although the partially released autopsy report found "chronic inflammation" and an "abrasion" in the area of the dead girl's genitals, "an unnamed, nationally known child abuse expert [who] had read the complete autopsy report … told investigators the slaying may not have included sexual abuse" ("Slaying May Not Be Sex Crime," Associated Press, Mar. 26, 1997).
22. They refused to talk to the police for four months after the murder, and declined to take a lie detector test while a number of their friends and neighbors have. "Instead, they mounted a defense team that includes eight lawyers, four publicists, three private investigators, two handwriting analysts and one retired FBI profiler" (James Brooke, "Did Boulder's Chummy Legal Culture Hinder Murder Investigation?" *New York Times*, Dec. 5, 1997). The case was further confused by the resignation in September 1998 of two detectives working on the case—the lead police detective, Steve Thomas, who denounced the Boulder County district attorney's office as "thoroughly compromised" in its treatment of the Ramseys, and Lou Smit, a homicide detective who concluded that the Ramseys were innocent. Smit's confidential resignation letter, which contained statements in support of the Ramseys, was made public only hours before a Sept. 27, 1998, report by the ABC news magazine *20/20*, which, relying on Thomas's testimony, cast the Ramseys in an unfavorable light.

23. The inverse scenario is depicted in *The Portrait of a Lady*, in which Lord Warburton contemplates marrying Isabel's stepdaughter Pansy as a way of being near to Isabel.

24. Wood, "Revisiting Lolita," 13.

25. Quoted by Ramirez, "Lolitas Don't Shock Anymore," 5. See Postman's book *The Disappearance of Childhood* (New York: Vintage, 1994). For a more recent view, see James R. Kincaid's *Erotic Innocence: The Culture of Child Molesting* (Durham: Duke University Press, 1998).

26. Quoted by Ramirez, "Lolitas Don't Shock Anymore," 5.

27. Quoted by Mark Danner, "Guardian Angels," *The New Yorker*, Nov. 25, 1996, 47.

28. Stephen Holden, "Unsettling Visions of the Erotic," *New York Times*, Mar. 30, 1997.

29. A good example are Pasolini's films of the early '70s celebrating the life of the body. As Millicent Marcus observes, the eroticism of the *Trilogy of Life* (*The Decameron* [1971], *The Canterbury Tales* [1972], and *The Arabian Nights* [1973]) "stands as an alternative to the compromised and fallen expressivity of the technological world. With the 'unreality of the subculture of the mass media and therefore of mass communication, the last bulwark of reality appeared to be "innocent" bodies in the archaic, dark, vital violence of their sex organs,' Pasolini wrote in the 'Abiura dalla *Trilogia della vita*'" (*Filmmaking by the Book: Italian Cinema and Literary Adaptation* [Baltimore: The Johns Hopkins University Press, 1993], 137).

30. Bradley Butterfield, "Ethical Value and Negative Aesthetics: Reconsidering the Ballard-Baudrillard Connection," *PMLA* 114, 1 (1999): 64.

31. As F. X. Feeney reports, "One of the extras playing a photographer in [Fellini's] *La Dolce Vita* was named Paparazzo. Fellini so loved that name that he coined a joking word to address the swarm of camera-bearing extras in shorthand: 'Paparazzi'" (*LA Weekly*, July 10–16, 1998, 70).

32. *The Herald*, Sept. 4, 1997, 17. Cited in Jenny Kitzinger, "Special Debate: Image," *Screen* 39, 1 (1998): 77.

33. Salman Rushdie, "Crash," *The New Yorker*, Sept. 15, 1997, 68.

34. Georges Bataille, *Death and Sensuality: A Study of Eroticism and the Taboo* (New York: Walker, 1962).

35. J. G. Ballard, *The Atrocity Exhibition* (1970; San Francisco: Re/Search Publications, 1990), 23.

36. Rushdie, "Crash," 68.

37. Ibid., 69.

38. Istvan Csicsery-Ronay, Jr., "Editorial Introduction: Postmodernism's SF/SF's Postmodernism," *Science-Fiction Studies* 18, 3 (1991): 307.

39. J. G. Ballard, *Crash* (1973; New York: Noonday Press, 1994), 101.

40. Marshall McLuhan, *Understanding Media: The Extensions of Man* (1964; New York: New American Library, n.d.), 56.

41. Garry Wills, "Dostoyevsky behind a Camera," *The Atlantic Monthly*, July 1997, 98. Wills adds that "no commentary on the phenomenon has had the biting wit" of a scene in Oliver Stone's 1994 film *Natural Born Killers* in which Mallory, having seduced and killed a gas station attendant on the hood of a sports car, is pursued by a police detective who, "intuiting Mallory's body in the lines of the car, strokes it erotically." Presumably Wills would find Cronenberg's commentary on the relation between cars, sex, and violence to be a good deal more extensive than Stone's.

42. See Frederick S. Lane, III, *Obscene Profits: The Entrepreneurs of Pornography in the Cyber Age* (New York: Routledge, 1999).

43. In subsequent editions of *A Clockwork Orange*, Burgess added an introduction faulting the film for following the truncated American edition of the novel, which omitted a final chapter showing the young protagonist as a mature man renouncing the violence of his youth. "The book does ... have a moral lesson," Burgess insisted, "and it is the weary traditional one of the fundamental importance of moral choice."

44. Quoted by Ralph Rugoff, "The Atrocity Exhibitionist," *LA Weekly*, Mar. 21–27, 1997, 32.

45. Claudia Springer, *Electronic Eros: Bodies and Desire in the Postindustrial Age* (Austin: University of Texas Press, 1996), 8.

46. Jean Baudrillard, "Ballard's *Crash*," *Science-Fiction Studies* 18, 3 (1991): 312.

47. Ibid., 319.

48. In the same issue of *Science-Fiction Studies* in which Baudrillard's piece on *Crash* appeared, Hayles and Sobchack roundly criticized his position, arguing that Ballard's novel establishes clear borders between reality and simulation, and between nature and technology that the French philosopher willfully overlooked. Sobchack makes the distinction between Ballard and Baudrillard most forcefully:

    > *Crash* is rigorously about the human body abstracted, objectified, and literalized as techno-body—and Ballard's vision sees this techno-body as driving us, quite literally, to a dead end. Baudrillard, however, refuses Ballard's condemnation, preferring his own immersed, supposedly value-free and objective "fascination" with scars, orifices, desireless and violent sexuality. He tells us that the "moral gaze—the critical judgmentalism that is still a part of the old world's functionality" has no relevance to the world of *Crash*, or to the postmodern, science-fictional world we live daily in all its "unpolished splendor of ordinariness and violence."

    Afflicted by a painful cancerous wound in her leg, Sobchack concludes by noting of Baudrillard, "The man is really dangerous" (Vivian Sobchack, "Baudrillard's Obscenity," *Science-Fiction Studies* 18, 3 [1991]: 328–29). For a defense of Baudrillard's reading of *Crash* and of his "radical aestheticism, which empties reality of all content by proclaiming a totally aestheticized world," see Bradley Butterfield: "[W]ho can reproach Baudrillard for occupying the extreme position of aesthetic liberty, without which art would lose its negative force and its power to challenge what is accepted as real?" ("Ethical Value and Negative Aesthetics," 71–72).

49. Chris Rodley, ed., *Cronenberg on Cronenberg* (1992; rev. ed., London: Faber and Faber, 1997), 194.

50. Asked about the preponderance of rear-entry or anal sex in the film, Cronenberg responded that he "liked the way it looked. It felt right, getting both the actors looking towards the camera and not at each other. It helped that sort of 'disconnected' thing" (ibid., 198).

51. See Butterfield: "Values implode on every page; the signifiers of the car and the body, of technology and nature, are virtually impaled on one another in every description and are left naked and without sin" ("Ethical Value and Negative Aesthetics," 70).

52. *Cronenberg on Cronenberg*, 203.

53. Ibid., 199.

54. Ibid., 202.

55. Ibid., 190.

56. Quoted in Rugoff, "The Atrocity Exhibitionist," 32.

57. J. G. Ballard, "Introduction to *Crash*," in V. Vale and Andrea Juno, eds., *Re/Search: J. G. Ballard* (1974; San Francisco: Re/Search Publications, 1984), 98.

58. Quoted in Rugoff, "The Atrocity Exhibitionist," 32. Noting that Vaughan drives a 1963 Lincoln—"the same make of vehicle as the open limousine in which President Kennedy had died" (64)—the narrator asks whether he sees "Kennedy's assassination as a special kind of car-crash," to which Vaughan responds "The case could be made" (130).

59. This point was underscored by the Getty Museum's 1999 exhibition of Nadar's and Warhol's celebrity photographs. See Gordon Baldwin and Judith Keller, *Nadar/Warhol: Paris/New York: Photography and Fame* (Los Angeles: Getty Trust Publications, 1999). See also Leo Braudy: "Film and the visual media display, enhance, and celebrate, but they domesticate and diminish as well" (*The Frenzy of Renown: Fame and Its History* [New York: Oxford University Press, 1986], 583, and esp. the concluding sections on "Hostages of the Eye," 548–83).

60. Michael Grant, "Crimes of the Future," *Screen* 39, 2 (1998): 183.

61. Fred Botting and Scott Wilson, "Automatic Lover," *Screen* 39, 2 (1998), 190.

62. See Butterfield: "Perhaps Ballard … is not ready for a world where even theory becomes fiction" ("Ethical Value and Negative Aesthetics," 76 n. 3).

63. Baudrillard, "Ballard's *Crash*," 311.

64. Barbara Creed, "The Crash Debate: Anal Wounds, Metallic Kisses," *Screen* 39, 2 (1998): 179.

65. The phrase was used in this context by Caryn James in her article "Clinton's Role of Lifetime Breaks Cinema's Rules," *New York Times*, Sept. 22, 1998.

66. While all three cable news networks—CNN, Fox News Channel, and MSNBC—decided to carry the entire testimony unedited as soon as they received it, some of the major networks deleted portions that were deemed too graphic.

67. See William Doyle, *Inside the Oval Office: The White House Tapes from FDR to Clinton* (New York: Kodansha International, 1999).

68. In addition, the Senate voted to include videotaped testimony by Monica Lewinsky (rather than to question her in person) in its deliberations about President Clinton's impeachment. Parts of her recorded deposition, as well as those of Clinton confidant Vernon Jordan and White House aide Sidney Blumenthal, were played at the nationally televised trial session on Feb. 6, 1999.

69. Families of victims shot at Columbine High School faced a similar situation when they succeeded in their efforts to gain access to surveillance video taken during the massacre only to learn that authorities also released the tapes to the public.

70. George F. Will, "Legalities, Tonalities," *Newsweek*, Sept. 28, 1998, 90.

71. Jeffrey Rosen, "Jurisprurience," *The New Yorker*, Sept. 28, 1998, 35, 37.

72. James, "Clinton's Role of Lifetime Breaks Cinema's Rules."

73. Michel Foucault, *The History of Sexuality, Volume I: An Introduction*, trans. Robert Hurley (New York: Vintage, 1980), 11.

74. Joe Klein, "No Exit," *The New Yorker*, Dec. 28, 1998–Jan. 4, 1999, 37.

75. Mary Leonard, "At Home, Timing of Move Appears Suspect to Some," *Boston Globe*, Aug. 21, 1998, A21.

76. Jay Carr, "Culture of Cynicism Makes Movie Comparisons Inevitable," *Boston Globe*, Aug. 21, 1998, A16.

77. Mark Alan Stamaty, "Monica in Medialand," *The New Yorker*, Sept. 7, 1998, 53.

78. Klein, "No Exit," 37.

79. Massachusetts Representative Martin T. Meehan, quoted in Leonard, "At Home, Timing of Move Appears Suspect to Some," A21.

80. It's curious in this regard that Reagan, the former movie star, was not featured in any major commercial film during his tenure as president, while Clinton was repeatedly depicted in pictures such as *The War Room, An American President, Dave*, and *Primary Colors*, as well as *Wag the Dog*.

Chapter seven: From Dream Work to DreamWorks

1. Janet Maslin, " 'The Truman Show': So, What's Wrong with This Picture?" *New York Times*, June 5, 1998.

2. Ibid.

3. Ada Louise Huxtable, *The Unreal America: Architecture and Illusion* (New York: New Press, 1997). See also the scene in Walker Percy's *Lancelot* where a film company shooting a movie near New Orleans needs "to use the hurricane machine even though a real hurricane is coming, not just because the real hurricane is not yet here, but because even if it were it wouldn't be as suitable for film purposes as an artificial hurricane" (1977; New York: Picador, 1999), 191.

4. A similar retrolook was adopted by automakers for the new millennium— e.g., Volkswagen's new Beetle and Chrysler's PT Cruiser.

5. "Photos that Lie—and Tell the Truth," *New York Times*, Mar. 16, 1997.

6. Timothy Egan, "Candymaker Wants to Use Town as Advertisement," *New York Times*, Oct. 6, 1997.

7. Kurt Andersen, "Pleasantville," *The New Yorker*, Sept. 6, 1999, 74.

8. Douglas Frantz, "Living in a Disney Town, with Big Brother at Bay," *New York Times*, Oct. 4, 1998.

9. Ibid.

10. Neal Gabler, *Life the Movie: How Entertainment Conquered Reality* (New York: Knopf, 1998), 213 n.

11. Andersen, "Pleasantville," 79.

12. Allan Sloan, "Pennies from Heaven," *Newsweek*, Apr. 3, 1995, 44–45. DreamWorks should not be confused with Dreamtime Holdings, Inc., the multimedia company based in Moffett Field, California. The company has been involved in many media projects with NASA and is currently trying to broker a new reality show with one of the major networks in which the winner of a group of contestants training at the Johnson Space Center in Houston would spend a week aboard the International Space Station.

13. Thus, in order to expedite the creation of Disney World, the Walt Disney Company had founded an independent governmental jurisdiction called the Reedy Creek Improvement District; two decades later, when the company developed Celebration, it removed its name from the title, turned matters of land use over to Osceola County, and turned the business of buying and selling the town's houses over to out-of-state companies.

14. Anthony Lane, "No Picnic," *The New Yorker*, Oct. 19, 1998, 94.

15. Edward Rothstein, "Heed the Arthropods; They May Have the Answers," *New York Times*, Nov. 23, 1998.

16. Gabler, *Life the Movie*, 58

17. Jack Kroll, "Cyberspies," *Newsweek*, Nov. 23, 1998, 83.
18. See Oliver Morton, "In Pursuit of Infinity," *The New Yorker*, May 17, 1999, 84–89. Morton argues, however, that the antitechnological thrust of Lucas's *Star Wars* films "is the antithesis of what Asimov believed. Asimov had an Enlightenment love of reason above all things; and he wanted a better future, not a stirring past" (88).
19. See Morton: "'Star Wars' treats technology as essentially malign, inhuman, and untrustworthy (except when producing special effects)" (ibid., 88).
20. K. C. Cole, "Unseen Dimensions Hold Theory Aloft," *Los Angeles Times*, Nov. 18, 1999, B2.
21. Dick Teresi, "The First Squillion Years," *New York Times Book Review*, Aug. 8, 1999, 6.
22. David A. Cook, *A History of Narrative Film*, 2nd ed. (New York: Norton, 1990), 14–16. As Cook reports, Méliès made his discovery when his camera jammed while filming a Parisian street scene in 1896, with the result that "in projection the omnibus seemed to change into a hearse" (15). Cook presents this fortuitous (and perhaps apocryphal) discovery as the inspiration that led Méliès and his successors "to *create* a narrative reality rather than simply *record* some real or staged event which occurred before its lens" (14).
23. Carolyn Geduld, "The Production: A Calendar," in Stephanie Schwam, ed., *The Making of 2001: A Space Odyssey* (New York: Modern Library, 2000), 3.
24. Tim Hunter, with Stephen Kaplan and Peter Jaszi, "A Film Review of Kubrick's *2001: A Space Odyssey*," reprinted in *The Making of 2001: A Space Odyssey*, 152.
25. *The Making of 2001: A Space Odyssey*, 142.
26. Quoted by Sharon Begley, "Barely Reaching Orbit," *Newsweek* Special Issue (Dec. 2000–Feb. 2001), 54.
27. Clarke reports feeling "that when the novel finally appeared it should be 'by Arthur Clarke and Stanley Kubrick; based on the screenplay by Stanley Kubrick and Arthur Clarke'—whereas the movie should have the credits reversed. This still seems the nearest approximation to the complicated truth" (*The Making of 2001: A Space Odyssey*, 33). So the film can be considered the visual and graphic correlative of the novel.
28. Arthur C. Clarke, *2001: A Space Odyssey* (New York: New American Library, 1968), 19.
29. *The Making of 2001: A Space Odyssey*, 62. Various techniques were tried to achieve a "blacker than black finish"; polished stone was tried and rejected since it looked "like useless chunks of rock"; eventually black paint mixed with pencil graphite rubbed endlessly on a block of ultra-smooth wood produced an "eerie blackness" with "a surface texture like nothing on Earth" (53–54).
30. Unlike *2001* and *Mission to Mars*, *Red Planet* is not concerned with any human encounter with alien beings; its chief "borrowing" from *2001* concerns the subplot of a renegade robotic computer. Instead of the masculine HAL in *2001*, the two principal computers in *Red Planet* are given women's names: Lucille and AMEE (Amy).
31. Flavius Philostratus, *The Life of Apollonius of Tyana*, vol. 2, bk. 6, ch. 19; trans. F. C. Conybeare (Cambridge, Mass.: Harvard University Press, 1912), 79, 81.
32. In this respect it's unfair of critic Stuart Klawans to say that "Ever since *2001: A Space Odyssey*, Earthlings in Outer Space have sought God, and found light shows." Klawans adds that "at least *Red Planet* [Hollywood's

other Mars film of 2000] spares us that final cliché—though it still makes us listen to a lot of spiritual blather" ("The Martian Chronicles," *The Nation* [Dec. 4, 2000], 42). While Kubrick may give us light shows, at least he doesn't give us spiritual blather. As he himself points out, "There are only 46 minutes of dialogue scenes in the film, and 113 of non-dialogue. There are certain areas of feeling and reality—or unreality or innermost yearning, whatever you want to call it—which are notably inaccessible to words" (interview with William Kloman, "In 2001, Will Love Be a Seven-Letter Word?," reprinted in *The Making of 2001: A Space Odyssey*, 162). As well as for not giving us "spiritual blather," moreover, Kubrick deserves credit for not giving us aliens.

33. Con Pederson, the special photographic effects supervisor on *2001*, reports that Kubrick considered portraying aliens in his film, and incorporating "a section of the book that would have explained a good deal of the film—the history of the extraterrestrials and ... their wonderful machines." But Kubrick ultimately abandoned the attempt, according to Pederson, because it was too difficult to produce a convincing illusion: "It is almost as hard to portray the alien world as the alien himself, because the audience is less prepared to accept it in a highly literal but non-story-oriented (a contradiction, really) form" (*The Making of 2001: A Space Odyssey*, 130–31). Another special photographic effects supervisor on the film, Douglas Trumbell, recalled that "repeated attempts to create a truly believable-looking extraterrestrial constantly ran into the Coefficient of Difficulty. We had to ask ourselves for a definition of what was possible to depict—it may well be there are many things that simply cannot be done to a certain standard.... If only we'd had a few more years" (ibid., 132–33).

34. *The Making of 2001: A Space Odyssey*, 31; Clarke's ellipsis. One objection raised by Kubrick to Clarke's novel was that the "literal description of these tests seems completely wrong to me. It takes away all the magic" (ibid., 66).

35. Noël Carroll, *The Philosophy of Horror, or Paradoxes of the Heart* (New York: Routledge, 1990), 162.

36. For that matter, the scene of Woody's sacrificial suicide in space is far more poignant and "real" than Hitchcock's sight gag in *North by Northwest* in which a close-up shot of Cary Grant dissolves into a shot of Mount Rushmore. Stanley Cavell has suggested that this cut from Grant's face to the presidential faces carved in stone raises a question "about what Grant is (made of), about what it means that he has become a national monument [in his own right], and hence what a monument is" (*Themes Out of School: Effects and Causes* [Chicago: University of Chicago Press, 1988], 163). But if Grant's larger-than-life chiseled features have become as iconic and monumental as the presidential faces on Mount Rushmore, De Palma has literalized and demystified Hitchcock's cut into an image of man reduced to a stone speck floating forever in space.

37. Siegfried Kracauer, *Theory of Film: The Redemption of Physical Reality* (Princeton: Princeton University Press, 1997), xlvii–xlviii.

38. Martin Scorsese, quoted by Bill Desowitz in "Michael Powell: Resurrecting a Cosmic Fantasy of Love and Death," *New York Times*, Oct. 31, 1999.

39. Sarah Boxer, "After a Freudian Century, There Are Good Dreams and Bad," *New York Times*, Dec. 3, 1999.

40. N'Gai Croal and Stephen Totilo, "Who's Got Game?" *Newsweek*, Sept. 6, 1999, 58.

41. Ibid., 59.

42. N'Gai Croal, "The Art of the Game," *Newsweek*, Mar. 6, 2000, 16.

43. Already in 2000 DreamWorks Interactive was bought by Electronic Arts as part of an effort to further develop Sony's PlayStation 2. Having failed in its multimedia ventures, DreamWorks has limited its operations to the relatively risky business of moviemaking, where it has been phenomenally successful: from 1997 to the fall of 2000 its twenty film releases averaged $78.7 million at the box office, 15 percent more than any other studio. Nevertheless, it would come as no surprise if the company was soon to merge or even be sold. See Geraldine Fabrikant and Rick Lyman, "DreamWorks Scales Back Its Once-Grand Vision," *New York Times*, Sept. 25, 2000.

44. Jonathan Schell, "Land of Dreams," *The Nation*, Jan. 11–18, 1999, 6–7.

45. Gabler, *Life the Movie*.

46. Nicholas Lemann, "Lost in Post-Reality," *The Atlantic Monthly*, Jan. 1999, 100–1.

47. Ibid., 101.

48. See Black, *The Aesthetics of Murder: A Study in Romantic Literature and Contemporary Culture* (Baltimore: The Johns Hopkins University Press, 1991), ch. 4.

49. Mark Seltzer, *Serial Killers: Death and Life in America's Wound Culture* (New York: Routledge, 1998), ch. 2.

Afterword on the Afterlife

1. Examples already discussed in this regard are *An Occurrence at Owl Creek Bridge* and *A Matter of Life and Death*. The male protagonists of two James Cain novels adapted to the screen—*The Postman Always Rings Twice* and *Double Indemnity*—tell their stories as confessions as they await execution.

2. David Denby, *The New Yorker*, May 17, 1999, 26.

3. David Denby, "Transcending the Suburbs," *The New Yorker*, Sept. 20, 1999, 134.

4. Miriam Bratu Hansen, introduction to Kracauer, *Theory of Film: The Redemption of Physical Reality* (Princeton: Princeton University Press, 1997), xxi.

5. Denby, "Transcending the Suburbs," 135.

6. Quoted by Kracauer as an example of film's unique ability to "record visible phenomena for their own sake" (*Theory of Film*, xlix–l).

7. I draw here on insights into Egoyan's films made by Austin Sarat in his presidential address to the Law and Society Association's annual meeting in Chicago, May 29, 1999.

8. Quoted by Gustav Niebuhr, "Hell Is Getting a Makeover from Catholics," *New York Times*, Sept. 18, 1999. The Pope's remarks were made a few days after the Jesuit journal *La Civiltà Cattolica* declared in an editorial that hell "is not a 'place' but a 'state,' a person's 'state of being,' in which a person suffers from the deprivation of God."

9. The Rev. R. Albert Mohler, Jr., president of Southern Baptist Theological Seminary in Louisville, Kentucky, in a response distributed by Religion News Service in August 1999; quoted in Niebuhr, "Hell is Getting a Makeover from Catholics."

10. Niebuhr, "Hell is Getting a Makeover from Catholics."

11. See Wendy Kaminer's recent survey of pop spiritualist and scientistic movements flourishing at the turn of the millennium, *"Sleeping With Extra-*

terrestrials": The Rise of Irrationalism and Perils of Piety (New York: Pantheon Books, 1999).

12. Biblical illustration provides an interesting parallel in this regard. In his recent illustrated edition of the Old and New Testaments, artist Barry Moser sought out scenes that emphasized the human drama. In this respect, his edition could not be more different from Gustave Doré's illustrated Bible of 1865 with its "cast-of-thousands pageantry, which could well have served as the model for many a Hollywood epic" (Miles Unger, "Illustrating the Bible: Putting New Pictures to Familiar Old Words," *New York Times*, Sept. 26, 1999. Actually, the epic films depicting events in the Bible drew on Doré's illustrations, while Moser's spare, human-centered illustrations were a reaction against this tradition of cinematic spectacle.

Name and Title Index

Subject Index